From Reconciliation to Revolution

Clergy and other marchers try to work out their differences, Montgomery, Alabama, March 16, 1965. Photo credit: Glen Pearcy Collection (AFC 2012/040), American Folklife Center, Library of Congress; afc2012040_047_27.

DAVID P. CLINE

From Reconciliation to Revolution

The Student Interracial Ministry,
Liberal Christianity, and the
Civil Rights Movement

The University of North Carolina Press *Chapel Hill*

Set in Arno Pro by Westchester Publishing Services
Manufactured in the United States of America

The University of North Carolina Press has been a member of the Green Press
Initiative since 2003.

Library of Congress Cataloging-in-Publication Data
Names: Cline, David P., 1969– author.
Title: From reconciliation to revolution : the Student Interracial Ministry,
    liberal Christianity, and the civil rights movement / David P. Cline.
Description: Chapel Hill : University of North Carolina Press, [2016] |
    Includes bibliographical references and index.
Identifiers: LCCN 2016012007| ISBN 9781469630427 (cloth : alk. paper) |
    ISBN 9781469630434 (pbk : alk. paper) | ISBN 9781469630441 (ebook)
Subjects: LCSH: Student Interracial Ministry. | African Americans—Civil rights—
    History—20th century. | Civil rights movements—United States—History—20th century. |
    United States—Race relations—History—20th century. | Civil rights—Religious
    aspects—Christianity—History—20th century. | Race relations—Religious aspects—
    Christianity—History—20th century.
Classification: LCC E185.61 .C627 2016 | DDC 323.1196/0730904—dc23
    LC record available at http://lccn.loc.gov/2016012007

Cover illustration: Sneering priest among Selma protestors ("Priest-Selma" by John F.
    Phillips, © 2016 Baldwin Street Gallery).

Contents

Preface

A Tale of Two Gatherings

It is only by living completely in this world that one learns to believe.
—Dietrich Bonhoeffer

Just after Christmas 1955 in Athens, Ohio, an organization called the Student Volunteer Movement for Christian Missions hosted a gathering of over three thousand students, representing sixty religious groups from eighty countries. Roman Catholic, Hindu, Muslim, and Buddhist groups attended, but the majority of students came from the mainline Protestant churches and collectively represented what was known as the Student Christian Movement (SCM). The title of the conference was "Revolution and Reconciliation."[1]

With its roots in the YMCA and YWCAs founded in the mid-1850s, the SCM was made up of those mainline Protestant campus ministries and organizations that were linked to one another and to their partners overseas through the World Student Christian Federation. It included within its ranks such venerable organizations as the Student Volunteer Movement for Foreign Missions, founded in 1886, and the Interseminary Movement, founded in 1880 to serve theological students.[2] Rooted in social Christianity but with an evangelical streak, the student groups thrived by offering a mixture of foreign service and domestic engagement. The SCM developed on a parallel path to the Social Gospel Movement, with which it shared many similarities, and it was not long before they met, incorporating into what had been a strictly evangelical Social Gospel Movement stated commitments, by 1905, to "social and economic justice." Race relations gradually emerged as an issue within the SCM, with the first integrated delegation attending a conference of the World Student Christian Federation in 1913. Engagement with social issues was further entrenched following World War I, as a new commitment to exploring social problems and working for global peace was developed within the context of Christian evangelicalism.[3] Through two world wars and into the Cold War, the Student Christian Movement "was where ecumenical awareness was cultivated and where the ecumenical vision challenged the churches in at least the first sixty years of this century. It held evangelical motivation and social involvement in creative tension. It was a vision of church renewal in mission, in and for the world."[4] Each year, thousands of students, often from around the world, would gather for conferences comprising several days of discussion, fellowship, and prayer. Although discussions often concerned the power of religious young people to address social ills, they were rarely focused toward a specific set of goals.

Then came 1955, the Montgomery bus boycott, and the "Revolution and Reconciliation" conference. In the humble surroundings of Athens, Ohio, amid the thousands of students from across the globe, the Student Christian Movement embraced the civil rights movement. During the course of discussions, the global gathering explored American anticommunism from global vantage points, highlighting American economic and cultural imperialism. Panelists asked how Americans could force their democratic ideals on the rest of the world when they weren't able to deliver on them themselves, and they charged the churches with leading a domestic change movement to bring about justice and equality at home.[5]

A similar conference, also in Athens, was held the following year and continued the discussions, with topics ranging from radical expressions of faith to the birth of postcolonial nations overseas to the necessity of missionaries to focus more on justice and less on conversion. An editorial in the conference newspaper declared, "Each of us must create for himself the bridge whereby his faith can lead to works."[6] Out of the Athens conferences grew a seminal mission project of the Student Christian Movement: the Frontier Intern program, a Christian precursor to the federal Peace Corps. The conference ended on January 1, 1960. Exactly one month later, four students from North Carolina A&T sat-in to protest segregation at a Woolworth's lunch counter in Greensboro, launching a wave of student sit-ins that swept through the South.

It was these sit-ins that inspired another important student gathering—this one held at Shaw University in Raleigh, North Carolina, over Easter weekend 1960—which brought together more than two hundred students representing some fifty-six colleges and high schools and thirteen activist and reform organizations. Called the Southwide Student Leadership Conference on Nonviolent Resistance to Segregation, it was organized by the Southern Christian Leadership Conference (SCLC) under the guidance of Martin Luther King Jr. and Ella Baker, SCLC's interim executive director, to discuss strategies for channeling the momentum generated by the sit-ins.

Ella Baker's invitation called on student leaders and supporters "TO SHARE experience gained in recent protest demonstrations and TO HELP chart future goals for effective action."[7] Union Theological Seminary in New York City was one of the few northern schools invited to send students. A leading ecumenical Protestant seminary, Union was located just around the corner from the Riverside Church, funded by Nelson Rockefeller, originally pastored by Harry Emerson Fosdick, and sometimes jokingly referred to as the "cathedral" of liberal Christianity. Union had seen a number of its students eagerly follow the sit-ins and stage sympathy pickets of New York Woolworth stores throughout the winter. A group of Union students had been considering venturing into the South to join the sit-ins directly, and when they heard about the Raleigh conference, they set their sights on that instead. As word of the journey south spread through the student body, the contingent grew from a group of four to twelve and finally to seventeen in a delegation that was both interracial and international in composition and that also included Union spouses and alumni.[8] While other seminarians and Christian students attended the conference at Shaw, including future movement leaders James Bevel and Bernard Lafayette from American Baptist Seminary and students from Gammon Seminary in Atlanta, the group from Union Theological Seminary—their journey partly funded by several of their professors—was by far the largest delegation from one seminary.[9]

The Union students who headed to North Carolina that Easter weekend also represented a trend among students involved in the Student Christian Movement; by 1960, many Christian students had already jumped to the other side of a generation gap forming between them and older ecumenical leaders. In the case of seminarians, that older generation included most of their theology professors, and students were running out of patience with the status quo. "It was a bust," recalled one prominent member of the older generation. "Students wanted to be inspired, but they were not interested in the wisdom their elders had gained from fighting other battles in other decades."[10] These students now had their own battle and were already imagining themselves as a potentially important cadre within the foot soldiers of the growing civil rights movement.

Ella Baker, who had grown up in the South but had cut her teeth in organizing in New York City and through a long association with the NAACP, was within a month of leaving the SCLC, to be replaced by Wyatt Tee Walker as director. She had chafed under the ministers' leadership, which she found imperious and often dictatorial, and was ready for both a change of scene and a change of leadership style. She relished the enthusiasm of the students, and especially the egalitarian, communitarian impulses of Reverend James Lawson and his student group from Nashville, which was rooted in a commitment to nonviolent protest and a belief in the so-called "beloved community."[11] Baker's position of responsibility within the SCLC and her willingness to challenge King, who had risen to national stature during the Montgomery bus boycott, came as a revelation to the students.[12] As the conference unfolded, Baker remained behind the scenes, convinced that the movement sparked by student initiative should continue to be student led.

During his opening remarks, Lawson claimed that students had long harbored strong beliefs about equality and justice but had been "simply waiting in suspension; waiting for that cause, that ideal, that event, that 'actualizing of their faith' which would catapult their right to speak powerfully to their nation and world."[13] Moreover, he characterized the sit-ins not as youthful acts of rebellion, nor even as challenges to unjust laws, but as conscious moral acts designed to showcase segregation as sinful. In other words, his approach revealed a greater evangelical purpose. He described the sit-ins and integration as a means, not an end—the end being racial reconciliation and redemption. As he put it, "The Christian favors the breaking down of racial barriers because the redeemed community of which he is already a citizen recognizes no barriers dividing humanity." In Lawson's belief system, the pursuit of racial justice was just one part of his Christian goal of realizing the "Kingdom of God" on earth. Defining nonviolence, Lawson described it as "Christian Love" and a "radically Christian method," as exemplified by Jesus Christ's suffering and the belief in his resurrection.[14] It soon became clear that others as well might suffer and die in pursuit of this vision in the South. Birmingham pastor Fred Shuttlesworth, when asked at the end of the meeting by Union Theological Seminary students what they in particular—as white students from the North—could do in the movement as it progressed, replied, "Sure we want your help, but it's our battle now. Sure we may be killed but somebody's always had to die for freedom, haven't they?"[15]

Throughout the weekend, James Lawson used religious rhetoric that was quite familiar to the Union students. He described the sit-ins as silent jeremiads meant to show that prejudice was a sin and that its manifestations in law and custom should be quickly dismantled. He described the nonviolence of the movement as testifying to "the reality of God's promise . . . non violence as Christian love exemplified in the voluntary suffering and forgiveness of the cross" and based on the hope of resurrection.[16]

Although the Raleigh conference was interracial, invoked Christianity, and was often guided by Lawson's description of the beloved community, his vision was not wholly embraced by all present, and the seeds of a different modus operandi for the freedom movement were also being planted.

John Lewis, the early Student Nonviolent Coordinating Committee leader who would go on to a career in the U.S. Congress, remembered that "some people opposed the idea of basing the movement on the Judeo-Christian heritage—a belief in love and nonviolence."[17] When the larger body at Shaw broke into small workshop sessions, one participant noted that the working group devoted to discussing the philosophy, goals, future, purpose, and structure for future action held such a diversity of ideas and strategies that he held out little hope that Lawson's vision for the movement would be sustained.[18] But when, on April 17, members of the Raleigh conference voted to form a temporary Student Nonviolent Coordinating Committee (SNCC), and when a smaller group convened in May to develop a statement of purpose and to formally establish the organization, Lawson's Christian language and ideas set the tone, at least for the time being.

It was a tone that resonated with the group from Union Seminary. One of them, a first year student named Jane Stembridge, wrote that day of "a mighty wind of change that would blow through the country." She wrote, "Down in Carolina there's a great Wind and it is not going to be stopped. It is the wind of the word of God. . . . People are always asking about God and always waiting for Him to act. Well now, it seems, He is. What a glorious, marvelous, unutterable April day."[19]

The seminarians from Union identified themselves as part of an interracial student movement to change society at large but also as individuals bound for ministerial or Christian education careers, or lives in some other way tied to the church. As such, they also felt called to act within the church itself. A movement for reconciliation and justice resonated with their understanding of the Gospel and seemed an opportunity for both action *and* service. Indeed, reconciliation as they understood it in the context of the original gathered church *was* revolution, or at least revolutionary. As one urban minister put it in an editorial a few years later, "The message and task of the church directs us to the place where God's love preceded us, wherever men are in darkness, or conflict or need. The church of Jesus Christ exists for the world, and not the world for the church." He went on to quote from Paul: "God was in Christ reconciling the world to Himself and entrusting to us the ministry of reconciliation."[20]

Jane Stembridge, who was a native of Virginia and the daughter of a Baptist minister, reflected that Lawson's message at the Shaw gathering was an "essentially spiritual [one], . . . that the purpose [went] beyond integration."[21] What other students may have interpreted as right or just, Christian students like Stembridge and her Union Seminary colleagues saw as providential.

They recognized the importance of student organizing and public demonstrations like the sit-ins, and they supported the creation of SNCC. But they also saw a need to bring the concerns of the movement into the church itself, to challenge congregations to live out the implications of their theology. The seminary students wondered if there was something they could do as seminarians that would differ from SNCC's approach and help foster racial reconciliation within and by the church.

The Easter weekend conference in Raleigh planted the seeds of two civil rights organizations. One, obviously, was SNCC, which would go on to play a major role in the civil rights struggle of the unfolding decade, although the influence of James Lawson and his Christian message about the beloved community peaked in Raleigh and had ever less influence in SNCC after the first two years.[22] The second and much less well-known organization that got its start at the Raleigh conference was the Student Interracial Ministry. This group carried the flame of Lawson's message far longer and brighter, although by design it flew largely under the radar. The Student Interracial Ministry, or SIM, was created by some of the Union Theological Seminary students and others of like mind in the months following the meeting at Shaw. By June 1960, two months after they had gathered in Raleigh, seven seminarians—four white and three black, six male and one female—were at work in the South as part of SIM's pilot summer.

This first group of seminarians would formally establish the Student Interracial Ministry in the fall of 1960 and would be followed, year by year through the spring of 1968, by more than 350 other seminary students attempting to become what Martin Luther King Jr. would later describe as "creative extremists for love."[23] These theological students—mostly from the mainline Protestant denominations but with a smattering of others, and hailing from every region of the United States and a handful of foreign countries—worked in churches, participated in marches, registered voters, and contributed to many other aspects of the civil rights movement. But they had other goals as well. These practitioners of progressive Christianity believed that the spirit of the church and its cultural role was changing, and that in order to remain relevant to a society in the process of being reshaped, the church as an institution must perforce change, too. As one seminarian put it, "The churches are in for a shocking century—at least that is my hope. It will be the century in which the churches died and the church was born again."[24] During the 1960s, the country was suffused with the turmoil and excitement surrounding racial change, but this was far from the only crisis. The mainline Protestant churches, battered by this tempest of social change, were also reeling and desperately trying to redefine themselves for the times. The Student Interracial Ministry addressed itself to both crises, and by exploring its story from its founding to its legacy, the pages that follow allow us to see how religion and race were intertwined during this period, a time that was moving rapidly from reconciliation toward revolution.

The civil rights movement—in both its "classic" phase, from the mid-1950s to the mid-1960s, and its longer iteration, stretching over most of the twentieth century—was imbued with religious faith and its expression. The movement was animated, in the words of Martin Luther King Jr., by "thousands of dedicated men and women with a noble sense of purpose . . . anonymous, relentless young people, black and white, who have temporarily left behind the towers of learning to storm the barricades of violence . . . ministers of the gospel, priests, rabbis, and nuns, who are willing to march for freedom, to go to jail for conscience's sake."[25] Even gatherings or organizations that were secular on their surface were still often supported by a skeletal structure based on religious ethics. The civil rights movement itself often took on the feeling of a religious movement and was pursued with similar fervor by its believers. John Lewis of the SNCC once described the mass meetings of the civil rights movement in this way: "[They] *were* church, and for some who had grown disillusioned with Christian otherworldliness, they were better than church."[26]

The simple but effective strategy of the Student Interracial Ministry, after its first pilot summer, was to place white seminarians in summer internships within black churches, and black seminarians in white congregations. Rather than asking blacks to continue to bear all the burden of crossing the color line, whites would cross it as well, working in black churches, living in black communities, and modeling peaceful interracialism for both blacks and whites. Such a strategy, benign as it may sound to later ears, placed those students who pursued it into grave personal risk. The Student Interracial Ministry organizers understood early and instinctively that racial reconciliation was not just a southern but a nationwide necessity, and they created pastoral exchanges in churches of all Protestant denominations across the country. Their quiet and decidedly local tactic assumed that as individual racial attitudes changed within a given community, the effects would ripple outward. With time, the group of seminarians grew to embrace other goals and strategies as well.

As the civil rights movement evolved during the middle years of the 1960s, so, too, did SIM. The summer internships extended into yearlong exchanges, and more and more students engaged in noncongregational fieldwork that encompassed community organizing, voter education, and economic project development. Beginning in 1964, inspired by a successful fieldwork experiment in its Southwest Georgia Project under the inimitable SNCC leader Charles Sherrod, the Student Interracial Ministry added a series of urban projects in such far-flung locations as Los Angeles, Baltimore, New York City, Minneapolis, Chicago, and St. Louis. SIM was not simply a civil rights organization, however; it was a coalition of seminary students, would-be and current ministers, congregations, and religious community organizations. As such, its mandate ran beyond the black freedom struggle to the efforts to reform church institutional structures and theological training in order to create what the seminary students perceived as a better and more just world. Project participants returned to their seminary campuses having experienced Dietrich Bonhoeffer's "church at work in the world" and were freshly motivated to reinvent the seminaries themselves, and especially how they trained ministers, to better reflect how the church should most successfully function in the modern world.

Over SIM's eight-year lifespan, its student ministers made up an important cadre of the civil rights movement's soldiers and participated in most of the movement's major battles, as well as in many unsung skirmishes. Seminarians from the project joined sympathy pickets of Woolworth's stores in the days immediately following the Greensboro sit-in in 1960, brought messages to Martin Luther King Jr. while he waited in the Birmingham jail in 1963, strode alongside the estimated 40,000 church people attending the March on Washington for Freedom and Jobs that same year, listened to Stokely Carmichael and others articulate a vision for a Black Power movement while trekking through Mississippi in 1966, helped start an international movement of divestment of funds from banks in apartheid-era South Africa, played key roles in the Columbia University Strike of 1968, and supported SNCC leader James Forman as he interrupted a worship service at Riverside Church in 1969 to issue the Black Manifesto, a demand for churches and synagogues to pay reparations to America's black citizens. SIM students worked with many well-known movement figures, including Ella Baker, Martin Luther King Jr., Martin Luther King Sr., Ralph Abernathy, James Lawson, Charles Sherrod, Julian Bond, Diane Nash, Jesse Jackson, and Andrew Young. They also studied and worked with many Protestant thinkers and leaders, including theologians Reinhold and H. Richard Niebuhr, Harvey Cox, and Paul Tillich; ecumenical leaders Eugene Carson Blake, Oscar Lee, Robert Spike, and others from the National and World Council

of Churches; and a range of influential and charismatic ministers and com-
munity organizers, from William Sloane Coffin in the Northeast to Will D.
Campbell in the South to Joe Matthews and Saul Alinsky in the Midwest.
They worked within and alongside numerous reform organizations, including the Mississippi Freedom Democratic Party, the Methodist Student
Movement, the YWCA and YMCA, the Student Nonviolent Coordinating
Committee, the Fellowship of Reconciliation, the Congress of Racial
Equality, the Delta Ministry, and the Council of Federated Organizations
during Mississippi Freedom Summer in 1964. They also worked with
dozens of groups, churches, and communities, and with many thousands of
people—ministers, laypeople, and grassroots organizers—whose names we
don't know but who contributed to the country's greatest mass democratic
movement. The Student Interracial Ministry was a unique effort in the
student-led civil rights movement—although born from the same ideas that
informed those two gatherings, the "Revolution and Reconciliation" religious student conference in 1955 and the Shaw University civil rights student conference in 1960—and it drew on a long tradition of religious social
concern and connected to a wide web of student and religious organizations
with whose paths it would occasionally intersect.

As the civil rights landscape rapidly changed through the 1960s, so, too,
did the church and theological landscape. SIM attempted to adapt, to remain relevant, to maintain a mission that was needed and wanted. By the
end of the 1960s, SIM was grappling with the post–civil rights legislation
landscape, the implications of the Black Power movement for its own projects, numerous calls for wholesale reform of theological education, reduced
funding options from "liberal" foundations, and increased demands for attention from the war in Vietnam and the students' rights movement. It was
also grappling with its own success, finding that it had grown too large too
quickly during 1967 and 1968 to sustain itself any longer. However, even as
the organization itself dissipated, its participants carried forward both the
ideas it had nurtured and many of its specific aims.

Just as the 1955 Student Volunteer Movement conference had presciently
acknowledged the need for both reconciliation and revolution in race relations in its very title, so, too, would the Student Interracial Ministry. Devoted from the start to reconciliation between God and humankind and
between whites and blacks, as the decade progressed and the civil rights terrain buckled and twisted and occasionally cracked, SIM moved more and
more toward a call for revolution, both socially and within the mainline
churches. The seminarians respected Shuttlesworth's admonition to support

a battle that needed to be fought by others willing to die for freedom, but they also challenged him by refusing to just help from the sidelines. Determined to achieve both reconciliation *and* eventual revolution, they, too, were willing to lay down their very bodies on the path to freedom. They found inspiration and comfort in each other, in their faith, and in the interracial beloved community they hoped to create. And sometimes they comforted or inspired themselves with scripture, such as these words from Chronicles: "And it shall be, when thou shalt hear a stirring in the tops of the mulberry trees, that then thou shalt go forth to battle, for God is gone forth before thee."[27] Even though it would not be easy and would often be frightening—very, very frightening—they were determined to join the battle. And so they went.

Abbreviations in the Text

BEDC   Black Economic Development Conference
COFO   Council of Federated Organizations
CORE   Congress of Racial Equality
ISM   Interseminary Movement
NCC   National Council of Churches
NSA   National Student Association
NSCF   National Student Christian Federation
SCLC   Southern Christian Leadership Conference
SCM   Student Christian Movement
SIM   Student Interracial Ministry
SNCC   Student Nonviolent Coordinating Committee
SSOC   Southern Student Organizing Committee
UCM   University Christian Movement
UTS   Union Theological Seminary

From Reconciliation to Revolution

CHAPTER ONE

So That None Shall Be Afraid

Establishing and Building the Student Interracial Ministry,
1960–1961

Only insofar as we lend our support and energies to a creative witness such as
this will we ever realize the promise of the Holy Scripture: ". . . And every man
will sit down under his own vine and fig tree and none shall be afraid."

—Reverend Martin Luther King Jr., March 29, 1961, offering to sponsor the
Student Interracial Ministry

The sun was just coming up on May 31, 1960, as John Collins, a gangly thirty-
one-year-old white seminary student and former naval officer from Chicago,
pulled his car to the side of the road outside Anniston, Alabama. Collins was
scared. He had been driving for several days from his parents' home in Illinois, bound for a summer of ministry among black "church folk." Four
months earlier, a series of nonviolent lunch counter sit-ins against segregation had rocked the South and much of the rest of the country. Collins was
studying to be a minister at Union Theological Seminary (UTS) in New
York City and wanted to take part in this potentially transformative social
movement, and so here he was, traveling for the first time into the Deep
South. He would be working hand-in-hand with a young black minister
named John Watts in Talladega, Alabama, under the auspices of an embry-
onic civil rights organization that would become known as the Student Interracial Ministry. The grand imperial dragon of the Ku Klux Klan was
reputed to reside in Talladega. For a Yankee like Collins, this was the belly of
the beast. And the racial situation was only getting hotter; Alabama had just
recently expelled student demonstrators from its state university and was
one of two southern states that reacted to the student-led sit-ins earlier that
year by passing new laws expressly prohibiting integrated dining facilities.[1]
He was suddenly conscious of the license plates on his car that proudly declared he had just arrived from "The Land of Lincoln."

Collins tried to calm himself by recalling the advice that Ella Baker had
given him a few weeks earlier, when he had admitted his fear over his im-
pending journey. Baker, the outgoing executive director of the Southern
Christian Leadership Conference and an adviser to both the Student

Interracial Ministry and the Student Nonviolent Coordinating Committee, told him, "Don't be afraid. You can go into a strange country. Abraham did."[2] Now, as he sat in his car parked in the dust by the side of a rural Alabama road, Collins cracked open the cover of his new journal and began to write: "I am not as frightened as I have been at times the past couple of days. I know that handling hostility will be my biggest problem and that if I can do that I can stick it out. Even with the apprehension, there is the thrill of being here and going into the midst of this situation. It is certainly being alive—I hope my fears will not blot out the vital sparks. I am determined to stay, not heroically, but just to stay. Grant unto me, O Lord, faith to know, when I need to know, that thy grace is sufficient."[3]

Collins had wanted to go south ever since February 1, 1960, when four students from all-black Agricultural and Technical College of North Carolina sat down at the segregated lunch counter of a Greensboro Woolworth's store and asked for service. That demonstration, while not the first of its kind in the South, garnered unprecedented publicity and launched a wave of nonviolent demonstrations throughout the region, one of the most visible and influential campaigns of the early 1960s' phase of the civil rights movement. Within six weeks, more than 935 black and white students had been arrested in nonviolent protests.[4] In the North, the Congress of Racial Equality (CORE), a nearly twenty-year-old interracial organization that promoted nonviolence and racial equality, organized "sympathy pickets" of a number of Woolworth's branches in New York City. Collins and some of his seminary colleagues, including Jane Stembridge, enthusiastically joined the picket lines to demonstrate solidarity with their southern brothers and sisters.

The CORE-led pickets connected the UTS students to the long lineage of their liberal Protestant predecessors. Many of these seminarians were questing for a real-world application of the Christian Gospel they were studying, and the pickets gave them an exhilarating taste of theology—whether it was known as Social Gospel or Christian Realism or some combination of these and other ideas—in practice in the world. In return, Collins, Stembridge, and some of their fellow students gradually integrated their religious beliefs and practices into the demonstrations, so that within several weeks, student-led "pre-picket worship services" had become an integral part of the New York Woolworth's protests.[5]

The racial crisis in the South sparked a movement of reexamination and self-reflection at both institutional and student levels at many mainline seminaries. It had special resonance for students studying a theology that stressed the importance of human beings' reconciliation to one another as well as to God and Jesus Christ. The sit-ins were cause for much self-reflection at Union, which was known for its liberal theology and its pioneering teaching on Christian ethics, and where, according to one student, "the whole seminary was faced with the realization that the church itself confronted a serious race problem within the fold."[6] For many students who had studied religion and philosophy only in the classroom, the southern situation brought biblical teachings to life and demanded an active response. "The sit-ins knocked us out of our arm chair theology," wrote another student in the seminary's newspaper. "Now we have to make a decision."[7]

On March 6, 1960, five southern veterans of those sit-ins presented a lecture at Union, regaling the seminarians with their firsthand accounts of lunch-counter demonstrations, arrests, and community reactions. What they described sounded to Collins and others like a true test of Christian faith. The final event that seems to have spurred the seminary students to take action, however, was an attack against one of their own. News reached Union that James Lawson, then a Vanderbilt Divinity School senior, had recently been expelled for his participation in the southern sit-ins, despite the fact that a majority of Vanderbilt's own faculty believed that Lawson had simply "endeavor[ed] to follow his Christian conscience."[8]

Many Union students and some faculty identified with Lawson—a fellow seminarian and a future minister—and rallied around his cause. Roger Shinn, Union's professor of Christian ethics, spoke to Lawson and to other students and faculty at the Vanderbilt Divinity School, reporting back that "they are greatly strengthened by the solidarity of Christians in theological seminaries and colleges across the country."[9] To be sure, Lawson was not a typical young seminarian engaging in theological consideration of the world around him for the first time. He was at that point already a committed pacifist and was fast becoming an established civil rights leader. He had spent fourteen months in prison as a conscientious objector in the early 1950s, after which he had served as a Methodist missionary in India, where he studied Gandhi's satyagraha techniques of nonviolent resistance. While attending the Graduate School of Theology at Oberlin College in Ohio, Lawson met Martin Luther King Jr., and they began a long association that had a strong influence on King's later adoption of nonviolence as a protest tactic. Lawson moved to Nashville toward the end of the decade to attend the Vanderbilt Divinity School and to work as the southern director of the Fellowship of Reconciliation. He developed a cadre of Nashville students who would become major civil rights leaders in their own right, including John Lewis, Marion Barry, Diane Nash, Bernard Lafayette, and James Bevel. With them, Lawson conducted some of the first test sit-ins at southern establishments in 1958 and 1959.[10] At the time of his dismissal from Vanderbilt, Lawson was three months shy of completing his bachelor of divinity, a degree now equivalent to the master's in divinity. Union's student cabinet sent a letter of protest to the Board of Trustees at Vanderbilt University, warning them that they were being watched by "fellow citizens, fellow members of the wider academic community, and Christians."[11]

The sit-ins and the Lawson incident created a division among some members of the Student Christian Movement. The National Student Christian Federation (NSCF), for example, celebrated the tide of reconciliation it felt was at work in the South, but it also urged respect for the rule of law. In a nationally circulated "Letter to Christian Students and Campus Christian Student Groups in the U.S.A.," the group's central committee wrote, "We, as Christian students, do not simply seek the realization of American democratic values; we witness to the fact that Christ died to reconcile all men to each other and to God." The southern situation was proof, they wrote, that a living Christ was hard at work, "healing and reconciling where our efforts have fallen short."[12] But rather than enjoin Christian students to join the sit-ins or similar demonstrations, they urged strict observance of the law, which they claimed had been divinely inspired "to preserve relative order and peace." They urged Christian students to embrace another kind of reconciliation—that between themselves and the demonstrators—so as to understand that black Americans' cause was just even if their methods were not.[13]

The national councils of the other leading national Christian student organizations, the YWCA and the YMCA, disagreed with the NSCF's position and took a more activist stance. While they urged students to inform themselves, they also cautioned against taking too long to act. In a nationally-distributed joint report, the YWCA and YMCA wrote, "Action apart from an attempt to keep informed is irresponsible. Yet to wait for the day when *all* the facts are in is to read history, not to participate in it significantly."[14] Among these student Christian groups can be seen the variety of liberal Protestant approaches to contemporary problems, from a social gospel faith in humankind's goodness and liberal progress to a Christian realism arguing for real-time action that met the world where it was.

At Union Theological Seminary, student reactions to the sit-ins varied widely, some agreeing with the National Student Christian Federation's cautious approach and others urging direct action and immediate change.

However, the entire campus community did take notice of the sit-ins and their religious implications. Many on campus went to listen to Martin Luther King Jr. speak at nearby Salem Methodist Church in Harlem on April 1, including Jane Stembridge. As she later recalled, King spoke about the growing protest movement in the South, "which was home," and thought to herself, "Why am I here, even though this is an incredibly fine and radical and free institution? . . . It was really on the cutting edge of biblical scholarship and on the cutting edge of social gospel, theology, and everything. . . . And I love it [but] . . . it was far, far away from the Bible Belt [and being at seminary] seemed so irrelevant, after I heard him. Then I wanted to go home and do something." She talked with King at a reception following his talk and asked him if she could help with the movement in some way. King invited her south and gave her the contact information for Ella Baker.[15]

Not all were as moved by King's talk and the student action in the South. Union's newspaper, the *Grain of Salt*, published an entire special edition on "the present racial crisis" under the headline "Report for Action."[16] At the same time, the student government's Social Action Committee called a special campus-wide meeting to discuss appropriate responses to the sit-ins and to Lawson's dismissal. Again responses varied. Some students vowed to travel south to join the sit-ins themselves, while others decried the public demonstrations as breaking the rule of law. Referring to those demonstrators who had been arrested for trespass, student Roger Nils Folsom claimed that they had broken good laws and violated the rights of others. "May we not recklessly destroy rights in the process of fighting for rights?" he asked. "At least may we consider what other rights we are destroying, and whether their destruction is really necessary."[17] Another student in the audience suggested a compromise: the seminarians, who regularly spent summers doing pastoral fieldwork, might involve themselves directly in the civil rights situation—and adhere to both civic law and their Christian consciences—by undertaking their assistant pastorates in southern communities.[18] This would soon become the plan of action pursued by what became the Student Interracial Ministry.

The students who urged caution and care for the rule of law and property typified the conservative, cautious, noninterventionist approach that characterized the mainline churches and most seminaries before World War II. Even in 1960, a liberal seminary like Union still harbored a number of faculty and students who thought the parish minister's duty was to attend quietly to the needs of his immediate flock or to convert heathens overseas, not to challenge American beliefs and social structures. As one Union student put it, "The seminary campus [at that time] was the last place one would have looked for an awakened social concern."[19] The Second World War, however, and the terror and cruelty it exposed, had shaken up a number of church folk, radicalizing them in their beliefs about the church's role in influencing social conditions. The traditionalists in churches and seminaries were thus joined through the 1950s by a swelling cohort of both faculty and students who urged the mainline churches to take a stand on social issues and actively involve themselves in contemporary affairs. Among this growing group of proto-activists were those who supported the ecumenical movement and found in it both common cause and strength in numbers. Chief among the supporters at Union, which was widely considered one of the most liberal of the mainline seminaries, were ethics professors Roger Shinn and Reinhold Niebuhr, one of the most influential theologians in the country at the time. At Union in 1960, the sit-ins, the local Woolworth's pickets, and the Lawson discussions eventually led directly to involvement in the southern civil rights movement. The student government established a new Special Committee on the Racial Crisis, whose first task was to organize a trip to the South during Union's spring break.[20] When Ella Baker's invitation to the Raleigh conference arrived, plans were modified, seventeen students and spouses eagerly signed up, Reinhold Niebuhr and several other professors donated travel funds, and the convoy of vehicles prepared to head South.[21]

When the cars caked in the dust of the new South rolled up in front of Union Theological Seminary again, Stembridge was the first out of her seat, eager to recruit others to the cause. Born in Georgia, she had been raised primarily in Kentucky, Tennessee, and North Carolina as the daughter of an often-moving Baptist minister. She had been the valedictorian of the class of 1954 at Cool Springs High School in Forest City, North Carolina, before attending Meredith College in Raleigh. She was at Meredith when the *Brown v. Board* decision was announced, remembering later that "the people that were around me ignored it. And I, consequently, wasn't terribly aware of it until I got involved in civil rights," which would come when she began her work at UTS just after graduation.[22] In addition to being a seminarian, Jane was a very good young poet who would go on to write a number of stirring poems about the developing movement. Taking flight on that "mighty wind of change" that she had described down South, she returned to New York City determined to keep alive the exciting vision she and her seminary classmates had encountered in North Carolina.[23]

They had some reason to be hopeful; not only had the gathering in Raleigh energized them with its emerging leaders and engaging religious rhetoric, but a civil rights bill, albeit a weak one, had survived a Senate filibuster and been signed into law on April 21, 1960. Inspired, Stembridge and the other returned Union students called an all-campus meeting to deliver a report on their trip to the South and to propose a resolution on the racial crisis for general discussion and possible approval by the student body. It read, in part: "As Christians, we seek the realization of the Kingdom of God and the reconciliation of man to man and man to God. Segregation is incompatible with this, God's plan for us by His love in Jesus Christ. Therefore we cannot remain silent in the face of recent events.... We thereby commit ourselves to the struggle against segregation and for full human dignity in our own churches and communities, wherever they may be."[24] In this modest way, the Union Theological Seminary committed itself to the civil rights movement. This commitment would play out in many surprising and impactful ways over the coming decade, as the seminarians navigated the waters of social and theological change that would eventually surge from the eddies of reconciliation they first found themselves in to the threatening—and exciting—cascades of revolution that would follow.

Jane Stembridge spoke of her experience in Raleigh before the Union student body and wrote of it in the student paper, the *Grain of Salt,* but she also regaled her friend John Collins with tales from the trip and her desire to return to her native South to join the struggle in some way. The two were working together in a storefront church on the Lower East Side and then picketed Woolworth's together after the Greensboro sit-ins in February. In some ways they were unlikely friends—Stembridge, just a first-year student and the young "pixie and poet" daughter of a southern minister, and Collins, a native midwesterner and a Navy veteran who had left behind a broken engagement and a relatively staid life as a lawyer in Chicago. But both had found themselves at the seminary in New York City: Stembridge as part of a spiritual search and possible ordination; Collins definitely on a career path to what he imagined would be a rather typical life in ministry.[25] But Collins, now in his second year, had been immediately entranced by both the city and the social engagement of many at Union. Union was located just north of the Columbia University campus and not far from Harlem, at 121st Street and Broadway in Manhattan's Morningside Heights neighborhood.[26] Even during his orientation week, the seminary's Social Action Committee had arranged for the incoming students in Collins's class to take a tour of the city and meet some of its progressive leaders. Their tour included a discussion with Brotherhood of Sleeping Car Porters' head A. Philip Randolph at his Harlem headquarters, and long visits with the pacifist activist Bayard Rustin and a leader of the International Ladies' Garment Workers' Union. The day concluded with a meeting with George William "Bill" Webber at the socially progressive East Harlem Protestant Parish, which Collins would later join as an affiliate after his ordination. Collins remembers thinking at the time, "Boy! This was where the action was, you know. This was on the very threshold of the sixties—there was no civil rights movement yet, other than the Montgomery bus boycott, but there was a stirring. And all of a sudden, I felt exciting things were happening."[27]

Others felt it as well, especially those of Collins's classmates who were attending seminary courtesy of the so-called Rockefeller grants. Created in 1952 by the Rockefeller Brothers Fund, these grants funded students interested in taking a trial year in seminary in order to consider a career in the church. The Rockefellers were particularly interested in keeping Protestantism "in the bloodstream of the country," and they used their foundations, including the Sealantic Fund and the Rockefeller Brothers Fund, to fund several efforts designed to replenish the stocks of Protestant pastors.[28] The trial-year grants had a different effect than intended, however, increasing the percentage of seminary students who were spiritually engaged and philosophically interested in religion but who often chose a nonministerial career over the church. The grantees tended to be bright students from the top liberal undergraduate institutions, and were more experimental in their thinking and social engagement than were more typically religious preministerial undergraduates who felt called to the church. Collins found the ideas and interests of these "Rockefeller types," as he called them, inspiring and engaging, and he soon fell in with them, joining in some of their social change efforts. But what Jane Stembridge was describing about the Raleigh conference and the possibility of going to the South to become personally and directly involved in challenging Jim Crow was at another level entirely and sounded intoxicating.

Stembridge soon had Collins convinced to join her by spending his summer ministry in service to a black church in the South. He in turn enticed two other Union students—Franklin "Chris" Gamwell, a northern Presbyterian from Bay Shore and Peekskill, New York, who was finishing his first year, and Charles Helms, a southern Presbyterian from rural northern Florida and southern Georgia, who was in his second (or middler) year—to undertake similar ministries. The four white seminarians—two Southerners and two Yankees, three men and one woman—hoped to use individual in-teraction to create understanding across racial, regional, and class lines at both the personal and the institutional level.

Not exactly sure how to proceed, Collins and Stembridge turned to J. Oscar Lee, the director of the National Council of Churches' Department of Racial and Cultural Relations and the only African American executive in that organization. The Federal Council of Churches, the National Council's pre-decessor, had established a Department of Christian Social Relations in 1908 and a Department of Race Relations in 1921. The Department of Race Relations had only a part-time director until 1934, however, when it named as executive secretary Dr. George Haynes, a black scholar and activist with a national reputation as one of the founders of both the Urban League and Fisk University's Department of Sociology. Haynes retired in 1947 and was replaced by his assistant, J. Oscar Lee, a native of Philadelphia who had been educated at both black and integrated institutions, including UTS in New York City and Union Seminary in Richmond, Virginia, from which he earned a PhD in 1946. Lee stayed on after his department became the De-partment of Racial and Cultural Relations under the new National Council of Churches in 1950. Under Lee, the Department of Racial and Cultural Re-lations steadily if slowly advanced its agenda, including hosting an annual "Interdenominational Institute on Racial and Cultural Relations" and pro-moting a national Race Relations Sunday among the Protestant churches, urging them to devote one yearly church service to questions of race and brotherhood. Taken together, the projects of the department were educa-tional in nature, with the occasional foray into interracial exchange and in-teraction. The somewhat isolated department seemed to focus on ideas rather than action and so didn't threaten the campaign of slow progress en-dorsed by the liberal white leaders of the council. However, by creating a network of supporters through the interdenominational institutes, by keep-ing lines of communication open with the black churches, and by developing interracial communication and cooperation, Lee and his department were quietly sowing the seeds from which change would grow.

Lee helped out the Union students by contacting Gammon Seminary, a black theological seminary in Atlanta. An announcement was posted at Gammon Seminary seeking black seminarians interested in experimenting with interracial ministries.[29] The Union students began to receive calls from Gammon seminarians, and soon they had formed three interracial pastoral teams: Charles Helms from Union would join Willis Goodwin at Wesley Chapel United Methodist Church in Greenville, South Carolina; Chris

Gamwell would work with Maurice King at Bethel United Methodist Church in Morristown, Tennessee; and John Collins would pastor alongside Gammon's John Watts in an African Methodist Episcopal Zion church in Talladega, Alabama, along with a small rural church in the nearby countryside. Jane Stembridge took a different approach, one that led her onto the front lines of the civil rights movement. In 1960, female seminarians did not have the parish ministry as a career option, although many sought church careers as music or education directors. Because joining a black seminarian in a team ministry was not an option for her, Stembridge contacted Ella Baker, whom she had talked with in Raleigh, hoping that the SCLC interim executive director could suggest another path of involvement. Baker was then in Atlanta, just getting the Student Nonviolent Coordinating Committee off the ground. She invited Stembridge "to come on down" and help her with SNCC.[30]

Baker had given SNCC a home by allowing it to use a section of the SCLC office in Atlanta, and Martin Luther King himself had given Jane a ream of typing paper, envelopes and stamps, and use of a secondhand typewriter.[31] Stembridge took control of this "SNCC corner," helping to coordinate monthly meetings, creating a newsletter called the *Student Voice*, and planning the second conference that would be held in Atlanta that coming October. "Things were happening," she later recalled, "sit-ins here, there, all over. And that was my job, that was SNCC's job, to help people get in touch with each other, and to help them with whatever they needed."[32] To provide these activists with financial support, Stembridge and SNCC established a fund-raising effort. Eleanor Roosevelt made the first donation—one hundred dollars—and Reverend Will Campbell of the National Council of Churches' Southern Project made the second, in honor of the recently deceased Patsy Cline.[33] Stembridge reached out to fellow students as well, giving a speech on behalf of the organization in front of a meeting of the National Student Association (NSA) in August 1960. The writer Lillian Smith, who provided early emotional and financial support, wrote of Stembridge: "The fact that she is white, and is southern, and is so beautifully reared and educated gives her real influence and breeds respect among the young whites."[34]

Stembridge and Baker became inseparable that summer, beginning what was to become a long friendship and working relationship. The duo was often joined by Constance "Connie" Curry, the director of the NSA's Southern Human Relations Project, who put Jane up in her apartment in Atlanta. Curry, though only a few years older than Stembridge and the other SNCC students, was, along with Baker, one of the so-called adult advisers to

SNCC. She remembers Stembridge then as "wide-eyed and full of Christian existentialism and faith in the movement."[35] In late summer, Stembridge and Baker hired Bob Moses, a New York City math teacher who had traveled to Atlanta to join the movement, and sent him to Mississippi as SNCC's first field organizer. But the three women, Baker, Curry, and Stembridge, were the true galvanizing force behind the organization's successful start. If it weren't for the team of Baker and Stembridge, SNCC might have remained nothing more than a clearinghouse for information on student protests rather than developing into an influential force in the black freedom struggle.[36]

When the summer of 1960 ended, Stembridge took a leave of absence from Union Theological Seminary and stayed on in Atlanta as SNCC's first white staff member in what she initially described as an "ex-officio" position. This developed into an on-again, off-again staff role managing the SNCC newsletter, trying to recruit white southern students, organizing in Mississippi and elsewhere, and in her words, "sort of free-lancing for the New South." In October 1960, she invited Bayard Rustin to give the keynote address for the second SNCC conference, to be held in Atlanta, only to have others in the organization balk because of his homosexuality. Stembridge, who was a lesbian but who was out to only a few of her SNCC colleagues, threatened that if she had to withdraw the invitation she would quit SNCC. Both came to pass, although she would return to SNCC again in 1961 and stay until 1964.[37] (She would return to seminary years later, earning a master's in divinity from Southeastern Baptist Theological Seminary in 1979.)[38] The work with SNCC was alternately "hard, depressing, utterly beautiful, painful, and full of great meaning." She was shaken somewhat by the hypocrisy she saw among leaders, especially in the church, and hoped that projects like SIM would challenge the church's tendency to "allow untruth to go unabated and even provide sanctuary for it." Her experience with SNCC in Atlanta and the difficulties the organization faced in the early years also challenged her faith that the beloved community could soon be realized. She foresaw that change might come in the form of civil rights legislation, but it would be essentially meaningless without a deeper spiritual change, without redemption. "Otherwise, we will only desegregate . . . we will never meet in understanding."[39] But even in 1960, with both SNCC and SIM just emerging, she could already see both these goals—legislative reform and spiritual awakening—as decidedly linked.

With Stembridge venturing down to Atlanta, the other seminarians in the burgeoning SIM organization headed out to their own postings. And so we rejoin John Collins on the side of the road at the Alabama border facing down his fears. He would find out that summer that these fears—of possible danger, of new experiences, even of the judgment of his fellow whites—could be almost overwhelming at times. Collins, who had never been south of Illinois, teamed up with the Reverend John E. Watts, an African Methodist Episcopal minister who was reared in Mobile, Alabama, and had never been north of Raleigh, North Carolina. Collins and Watts served two churches, the Star of Zion African Methodist Episcopal Zion Church in Talladega, Alabama, and a rural parish known as Wesley Chapel #2, about six miles out of town. They took turns preaching at each church, so that in one month, they would have each given two sermons to each congregation.

Collins met with the pastor of Talladega's white Episcopal Church later that June and learned that he was not alone in fearing for the consequences of upsetting the racial order. Although a self-described liberal Alabaman in his mid-thirties, and a graduate of General Theological Seminary in New York City, Reverend Franklin urged Collins not to introduce himself to whites as a pastor in a black church, and warned him that staying in the parsonage could make him the target of violence. Franklin confessed that he could not himself preach on the race issue in Talladega or he would be out of a job. "It's too bad you can't meet the whites and hear what they say," he told Collins, since doing so would be to invite danger. "There's plenty to learn and it's all bad." Collins did eventually meet with two other local white ministers, although they refused to meet with him in a public setting.[40]

Collins learned as well that middle-class blacks also feared upsetting the racial peace when a Talladega College faculty member implored him and Watts to conduct their activities only on the campus so as to avoid trouble in town. Collins confided to his journal that such an attitude impeded progress because the campus was relatively safe, and nothing would be accomplished by going the safe route. "But," he wrote, "it's not for me to push them—only to participate in whatever program is developed. Nor do I want to push them further that I am prepared to go."[41] However, pressure would soon come from above as well. A few days after Collins wrote these thoughts in his journal in June 1960, Democratic presidential candidate John F. Kennedy held his first meeting with Martin Luther King to talk about civil rights. It was a first step toward the tougher federal civil rights legislation of the 1960s that would overturn Jim Crow and guarantee black voting rights.

Collins found himself welcome in the black community and in the pulpit, although his presence caused one congregation to erect floodlights on the church grounds in the hopes of discouraging would-be bombers. The

church services themselves were a novelty to Collins, who was at first surprised by the active call and response of the congregation, whose noise and
spirit upset his midwestern Methodist sensibilities. However, he soon came
to see it "as a real dialogue [that was] extremely helpful to the preacher," and
he tried to get into the swing of delivering a real southern fire-and-brimstone
sermon. After one early attempt, John Watts congratulated him by saying,
"You *almost* preached!" and an elderly lady came up to him after the service
to say, "If you stay here long enough we're going to make a preacher out of
you!"[42]

Toward the end of the summer, Jane Stembridge telephoned to ask if
Watts and Collins could put up a fellow activist. " 'We've got a guy here from
New York,' " Collins recalled her saying. " 'He's a math teacher that wants to
work with us, and we're sending him over to Mississippi to kind of recon-
noiter. Could he stay with you guys at the parson's there on the way to Mississippi?' " The young math teacher was Bob Moses, SNCC's first field
worker, who would go on to do much of the key organizing in Mississippi
that would presage Freedom Summer. Collins and Watts found housing for
Moses although they had to arrange everything very secretly, since if word
got out that Moses was going to organize blacks, Collins said, it "could be
worth your life."[43] Collins later recalled introducing Moses to Billy Taylor,
one of Collins's hosts and a member of the church with which he worked.
Taylor, an Army veteran and former boxer, asked Moses, "So you're with
those nonviolent folks, eh?" The soft spoken Moses replied, "Yes, sir."
"Well," Mr. Taylor said, "I'm the enemy." Collins reflected that he learned an
important lesson that day about the divisions and multiple potential strategies within the black community and within the movement.[44] Eventually,
Watts and Collins did do some small-scale organizing of their own. They
took a church youth group outing to a supposedly segregated state park, and
when Reverend Fred Shuttlesworth's Birmingham church was bombed,
they brought the youth group to a support rally there. The only whites at
the rally, other than Collins, were sheriff's deputies.[45]

The second team of Gamwell and King set its sights on Morristown, Tennessee. Chris Gamwell, who had been born on Long Island in 1937, had already had a small taste of interracial exchange, having spent the previous
year working in the LaGuardia Houses public housing development on
Manhattan's Lower East Side. It had been a far cry from his own upbringing
in a conservative white neighborhood in Peekskill, New York, where his
only exposure to diversity was the few Italian and Jewish kids in his high
school. Gamwell attended Yale University and then, thinking about a career

in the ministry but unsure, decided to study religion at Union, which he described as having "a semi-religious nature [that] was appealing."[46] Reinhold Niebuhr was then at the end of his teaching career and had lost a lot of his dynamism following a stroke in 1952, but his neoorthodox theology still held strong at Union and immediately captivated Gamwell. Though most first-year students at Union were given fieldwork assignments in small parishes, Gamwell chose to work for the Henry Street Settlement, which at that time did community organizing in the LaGuardia Houses, home to a diverse mix of southern whites, blacks, Jews, and Latinos. There, he recalled, "though I was kind of wet behind the ears, I got educated in the problems of poverty and race in this country, somewhat at least, through the work at the Henry Street Project. So when the opportunity came to work with the Student Interracial Ministry, I leapt at it. That sounded like a great way to spend the summer."[47]

Gamwell was teamed with Maurice King to minister at Bethel Methodist Church in Morristown. Though also a young seminarian, King was already married and so spent most of his weekdays back in Atlanta with his family, staying in Morristown only during the weekends. Gamwell's closest association ended up being with Paul Edwards, the dean of students at Morristown College, a black institution that provided most of the members of the Bethel Methodist Church. Edwards served as Gamwell's local contact and hosted him in his house for several weeks. Gamwell later lived with several other members of the church and believed that the experience of living in the black community "helped to erase very real racial feelings within me," as well as contributed to the racial reconciliation of black community members to him.[48] In addition to working with Morristown's black community, Gamwell and King attempted to reach across racial lines to whites in town. They hosted a gathering of prominent white citizens at Bethel Methodist one Sunday evening, likely the first time whites in Morristown had set foot in a black church. Gamwell reported, "[The gathering] helped greatly to foster a certain, though far from complete, understanding of the attitudes of the white community and augmented my discussions with the Negroes in gaining somewhat of a picture of the racial situation in Morristown."[49]

The two ministers also worked with local teenagers who were interested in gaining access to the one movie theater and three drive-ins in town, all of which practiced segregation. Gamwell and King met with each of the three drive-in owners. The first two indicated that they were receptive to integrating if all three owners agreed, but the third was "about as rabid a racist as we'd met. We broached the idea with him and he just went into a tirade about what it meant for his snack bar and his restrooms." Gamwell recalled being impressed with the calm King displayed during the tumultuous interaction. "I was really impressed with Maurice himself, the control Maurice had. I would have become incensed."[50]

The drive-in campaign was a nonstarter, but Gamwell recalls that he and King were not really there to start any action but to listen and provide a presence—to in essence give witness just by being there. He also commented years later that the primary benefit of this summer for him, as for the many SIM students who would follow, was not to the community served but "to the people who participated in it. It educated us and we'd like to think it educated some of those in the congregations we were a part of, but that's not for me to say really."[51]

In Greenville, South Carolina, Charles Helms, a white Union student from Decatur, Georgia, partnered with a black ministerial student, Willis Goodwin, to pastor at two churches, the Wesley Chapel and the Minus Chapel. Helms had been born in New Smyrna, Florida, and raised in northern Georgia in a family with many generations of roots in the South and a strong commitment to segregation; race issues were not talked about in his family and certainly not in church. "There was no *need* to talk about it because there was nothing perceived wrong with the prevailing system. Questioning segregation was unthinkable."[52]

As an adolescent, he had a religious awakening while listening to a visiting missionary at his church and decided right then to join the ministry. He attended Davidson College beginning in 1954, with the goal of attending seminary afterwards. The *Brown v. Board* decision came down while he was at Davidson, which at least broached the taboo subject of race. Helms was among a small number of students who urged Davidson to desegregate and found himself numbered among the college's few progressives. He found an ally in his philosophy professor, a graduate of Union Theological Seminary in New York City who urged Helms to go there as well, which he did in 1958.

The theology he encountered at Union, in which the social and political aspects of the Gospel were highly emphasized, was distinctly different from that with which he had been raised. Most of his classmates had much more liberal backgrounds, and very few were also from the South. He recalls, however, that he readily accepted his upbringing as abnormal and embraced the tenets of the social gospel approach. He also embraced the living arrangements he experienced in his dorm, Hastings Hall, where he lived on the same floor with both African and African American students.[53]

During his first year at Union, Helms did his parish fieldwork in Hell's Kitchen in what had previously been a German Evangelical and Reformed Church but was now reaching out to the African Americans and Puerto Ricans who had recently moved into the neighborhood. Although the inequality was not legally enforced as in the South, Helms found it to be equally rigid, and he was taken aback by the high incidence of poverty and the few opportunities for advancement. He recalls that although he had not paid much attention to the Montgomery bus boycott, which had taken place when he was an undergraduate, while at Union he read on the front page of the *New York Times* about the first stirrings of the sit-in movement: "That was stunning to me because that was dangerous as hell, you could easily get killed doing something like that. Frightening but extremely moving and exciting." Inspired by the southern students' bravery and having already been working in a kind of interracial ministry among the poor in Harlem, he, like Gamwell, responded positively when their mutual friend John Collins proposed the summer program that would evolve into the Student Interracial Ministry.[54]

Willis T. Goodwin was from Charleston and had graduated from Burke High School there before attending Gammon Theological Seminary. His SIM work was just the beginning of a lifelong ministry to the poor. After seminary and SIM, he returned to South Carolina and ministered for some years to the Sea Islands, work that he'd begun even before the summer of 1960. He settled on Johns Island, where, in addition to church work, he helped organize a social service agency and a health-care corporation in the late 1960s and early 1970s. He later served churches throughout South Carolina before returning to Charleston, and was known for his commitment to justice and the eradication of poverty.[55]

During the summer of 1960, Helms and Goodwin lived together in the black community of Greenville and spent most of their time working with church youth, including working as advisers to an NAACP youth group. About a month into the experience, however, their summer took a sharp turn when the two preachers joined these students and a visiting Jesse Jackson—Helms later described him as "this tall, handsome, frowny-faced student from a college in North Carolina"—in a spontaneous protest at a Kress department store lunch counter in Greenville.[56] It was to be the first public demonstration of its kind in South Carolina, and the first known attempt to desegregate a lunch counter in the Deep South. As Helms exited the restaurant, he was attacked by "three big husky white guys," who cursed him and called him a Bolshevik, a Communist, and a "mulatto," who was "stirring up their blacks" and had "incited the niggers to riot," before proceeding to beat him up. Helms recalled that when "they started in, I remember I wasn't so much scared as I was remorseful—about all those teeth I was going to lose." Walking directly to the local police station, he received no assistance. Helms was vilified in the local press and spent the rest of his pastorate in Greenville shifting from house to house within the black community, afraid to stay too long in any one place for fear of further reprisals. Willis Goodwin was also feeling "uncomfortable and in danger," in part because he had been sharing the parish house with Helms, and blacks and whites living together just "wasn't done" in Greenville.[57]

While many of the resulting changes, at both the individual and the community level, were so subtle that they were barely noticeable to the young seminarians at the time, experiences like theirs in Greenville had such an impact that the Reverend William Crewes—the director of the Interseminary Movement, an influential ecumenical seminary program—claimed of the SIM projects that "in particular communities the whole pattern of social mores was destroyed and witness to peaceful reconciliation evolved."[58] Though this may have been an enthusiastic overstatement, it was becoming clear that personally demonstrating alternative racial relationships within the church, albeit a small step, could help to engender greater understanding and begin to break down patterns of segregation—and the mind-sets that supported them.

As the summer of 1960 ran toward its end, Maurice King, Willis Goodwin, and John Watts returned to their studies at Gammon Theological Seminary, and Jane Stembridge elected to stay on with SNCC in Atlanta. The other three Union students said good-bye to their co-pastors and their community hosts, but before heading their separate ways, they gathered at the Fellowship of Southern Churchmen retreat center in Swannanoa, in the mountains of rural eastern North Carolina. They reviewed their own summers as well as some of the events that had occurred in the growing movement, such as the integration of Nashville lunch counters in May; the desegregation of the Greensboro Woolworth's lunch counter in July, after spring sit-ins had sparked numerous others and led to the formation of SNCC; and changes in Martin Luther King Jr.'s SCLC, which included the resignations of Bayard Rustin and Ella Baker. Collins, Gamwell, and Helms stayed in Swannanoa for several days, swapping stories and aspirations, and on August 24, 1960, the three hammered out the text of what would become SIM's statement of purpose. "The Church," they claimed, "should be providing a witness to the true brotherhood of men in Christ and playing a role of leadership and conciliation in the struggle for social justice."

They framed the Student Interracial Ministry not as a civil rights organization per se but as a reform effort within the institutional church, one especially designed to use the means of church integration toward an end of achieving "reconciliation between the white and Negro races, and the redemption of segregated communities."[59] As one SIM participant noted, the sympathy sit-ins in Harlem in the winter and spring of 1960 had given those in the North a chance to participate in the movement, but they had not solved "a major problem for future ministers: How can the Church as an institution witness to the equality of all men under God?" The student also wondered if the conservative apparatus of the Christian church would even allow for such expression, or if students were better off joining "a secular organization such as the Congress of Racial Equality in order to really be Christian?"[60] The establishment of the Student Interracial Ministry was meant to answer these questions by creating an explicitly religious alternative to other, more secular civil rights participation *and* providing a unique opportunity for those planning to make careers of witness in the church.

John Collins and Chris Gamwell returned north to the Union Theological Seminary campus at the end of August 1960, but Charles Helms headed directly from the North Carolina mountains to an internship year as an associate campus minister with the Westminster Foundation's Presbyterian University Center in New Orleans, serving the campuses of Tulane University and its women's college, H. Sophia Newcomb Memorial College. Newly radicalized by his interracial SIM experience, Helms quickly ran afoul of the authorities when he helped establish an interracial study group and supported CORE protests in New Orleans, where CORE's Freedom Rides would travel to nine or so months later. He was dismissed from his campus ministry position by Christmas. Helms was given a new intern assignment at the University of Florida, in an area where there was less political activity and thus where, it was thought, he would get himself and the church into less trouble.[61]

Back at Union, Collins and Gamwell sought the support of their fellow students and some key adult advisers both at Union and across the street at the Interchurch Center, home of the National Council of Churches (NCC). Early that fall, they announced the official establishment of the Student Interracial Ministry project. With advisers from both Union and the NCC, they created a governing committee of fourteen students, which included the original seven, as well as five other Union students and a member each from Yale Divinity School and Drew University. The project would remain student-led throughout its existence. The governing committee issued the statement of purpose that had been crafted in North Carolina in August, declaring that "the Church should be providing a witness to the true brotherhood of men in Christ and playing a role of leadership and conciliation in the struggle for social justice."[62] The founders further enunciated five goals by which they hoped to turn their statement of purpose into a plan for action. The first was closely related to the common course of seminary study at the time: to provide student seminarians with a parish experience while aiding congregations through the addition of pastoral leadership. Most seminary programs required a practicum in parish ministry, and part of the genius of the Student Interracial Ministry was that it conducted the truly radical work of integrating church congregations through such a standard and comfortable structure. This enabled students to get academic approval and credit for work that otherwise may have been seen as too potentially volatile for a seminary to support.

The next two stated goals of the program also focused on the individual seminarians who would participate. These goals were to prepare white and black seminarians for future ministries by acquainting them with contemporary problems of human relations, and to aid in the development of an individual student's growth and personal maturity by placing him or her in a true intercultural and interracial exchange environment. The fourth goal—that students serve communities in which they were placed—returned to the congregational community setting and to relatively uncontroversial ground. The final goal, however, was "to increase communication and understanding between the races." The students stated this goal matter-of-factly, as if it were a simple task to undertake and to accomplish.[63] Nothing could have been further from the truth. In point of fact, they were taking on the number one social issue in the country, one that was at that point still building pressure that would take the nation nearly to the bursting point.

In addition to its five stated goals, SIM pursued an implicit sixth aim, one that it would increasingly strive to articulate as the decade progressed. This goal was to reform and renew the church itself, from the inside out. The students in SIM claimed that challenging the church and making its institutions both more accountable to the Gospel and more relevant to current social situations were integral parts of what they described as "Jesus Christ's work of reconciliation and redemption."[64]

Dr. Roger Shinn, professor of applied Christianity at Union, signed on as the project's academic adviser. Shinn had graduated from Union Theological Seminary with a BD in 1941 and a PhD in 1949. He returned to Union after ten years at Heidelberg College and Vanderbilt University. He had not been back at the seminary long when the student sit-in movement began. Shinn, an early supporter of the civil rights and ecumenical movements—he was arrested while participating in a Freedom Ride—eagerly supported the new organization. He felt that SIM could bring to the civil rights movement a focus on the development of interpersonal relationships and understanding at the local level, a point of contact "that is often neglected in the large, dramatic conflicts of our times."[65] In an era that became known for its mass protests and the creation of public policy to dismantle institutional racism, Shinn encouraged SIM's individual and personal approach, a hearts-and-minds conversion strategy steeped in the Christian Gospel. Shinn hosted the weekly SIM meetings over sandwiches in his campus apartment in Knox Hall. According to him, the students were so motivated and well organized that they didn't really need an adviser, but he recognized that a faculty connection would be helpful to them as they raised money and built the program.[66]

The students cannily sought the endorsement of a number of other religious leaders in addition to Shinn. J. Oscar Lee of the NCC; William Crewes, director of the ecumenical Interseminary Movement; and Will Campbell, director of the NCC's Southern Project, also became sponsors and advisers. Martin Luther King Jr. and the SCLC joined them a few months later. King endorsed the project as "a bold and creative venture in human relations." He mused that the white seminarians, by living and working within a black church community, would "know them intimately, sense their hopes and fears, their joys and sorrows," while the black seminarians would experience "the kind of exposure to a white community that they have never had and in the same will produce a broader and more sympathetic understanding to the very deep problems with which the white church has now to grapple in light of the South's severe social change." He predicted that by placing white seminarians in black congregations and black seminarians with whites, "the two church communities will be building significant bridges of mutuality which will better equip both for resolving the troublous times in which we live."[67]

These advisers helped to shape SIM's vision as interracial, interregional, and explicitly ecumenical. The program itself, from its first days, would be directed by and for seminary students. Crewes did not work as closely or as directly with the students as Shinn did, but his status as cosponsor ensured that the Student Interracial Ministry would be seen as an ecumenical project. The Interseminary Movement was the oldest continuing student Christian movement in the United States, begun as an alliance between thirty-two seminaries in 1880. In 1950, it became a founding agency of the newly created National Council of Churches.[68] In "adopting" SIM, the Interseminary Movement continued to develop its ecumenical, activist student ministry into the 1960s. Reverend Crewes, who spent most of each year traveling the country and meeting seminarians, agreed to handle the bulk of student recruiting for SIM, folding it into his other duties on the road.[69]

Will Campbell, assistant director of the NCC's Department of Racial and Cultural Relations, had more direct contact with the students, a role for which he was well suited. A native southerner, Campbell grew up in Mississippi in a racially tolerant family but within a church whose bibles were imprinted with KKK symbols.[70] He served in the army, then began serving as the campus chaplain of the University of Mississippi in Oxford in 1954. He was drummed out of Ole Miss after only two years for his attempts to racially integrate meetings and social activities on campus.[71] J. Oscar Lee hired him to lead the NCC's Department of Racial and Cultural Relations' new interest in pursuing more direct involvement in race relations in the South. Given the council's blessing and mission but little money and no staff, Campbell was a maverick churchman and a one-man movement, charged with traveling from his base in Nashville to wherever civil rights struggles broke out in order to provide moral witness and represent in person the support of the National Council of Churches. Campbell escorted young black students into the public schools in Little Rock, Arkansas; attended the Raleigh conference where the ideas for both SNCC and SIM were born; and was the only white person present at the founding of the Southern Christian Leadership Conference.[72]

Will Campbell volunteered to serve the Student Interracial Ministry "as a sort of clearing house for the placement of students" and to work with the SCLC to find suitable church congregations willing to host the seminarians. In addition, Campbell committed to convening an organizational conference at the start of each summer and to remaining in close contact with the students throughout their internships.[73] Campbell was enthusiastic about SIM and its promise for racial reconciliation in the South. "For a white minister to serve as assistant to a Negro pastor will break down the pattern in the South even before it is broken in other areas of the country. It will also break down the pattern in the South which is that it is acceptable for a white minister to go and preach to a Negro congregation as long as it is clear that he is there as a missionary to 'convert the heathen.'" Campbell predicted that student ministers could serve as bridges between southern black and white communities where the pastors themselves were too bound by tradition and fear to break social mores.[74]

Campbell also saw the SIM program as providing a valuable educational experience, especially for white southerners preparing for the parish ministry. "When they return to the South as full time pastors with churches of their own," he predicted, "they will be much better prepared to understand the complexities of the situation [and] will have a tie with the Negro community which will make it much harder for them to get caught up in their own problems, unaware that the Negro and his problems even exist."[75] In that way, Campbell and SIM's other supporters saw the project as educating pastors for what they hoped was to be a future of a more racially diverse and open Protestant church community.

Campbell's boss, J. Oscar Lee, quickly came to play a major support role for the budding student organization. Lee received NCC approval to sponsor SIM, and his Department of Racial and Cultural Relations became SIM's official administrator. Lee's office would be in charge of managing all funds and providing secretarial support in the form of his personal assistant, Doreen Graves, and office space in the Interchurch Center on Riverside Drive. Fondly called the "God Box" by students, the Interchurch Center housed both the NCC and the national headquarters of several of the Protestant denominations. It was just down the street from both Union Theological Seminary and Riverside Church, the three forming a triangle of Liberal Protestantism in upper Manhattan. While many grassroots organizations have complained about having to work out of a closet, SIM literally did. Lee had the boxes and old lamps moved out of the windowless storage room across from his office on the fifth floor and crammed in a couple of desks from which John Collins, Chris Gamwell, and a handful of other students created and ran the Student Interracial Ministry. By agreeing to sponsor SIM, Lee gave the group the benefits of being part of a tax-exempt organization through which the project could raise and administer funds.

The Student Interracial Ministry seemed on its surface to be a quiet, harmless initiative that would stay within the bounds of churchly good behavior. But in coming under the wings of J. Oscar Lee and Will Campbell, it had found perfect mentors for its vision of reconciliation leading to revolution, hardly heeding those bounds. Under Lee's guidance, the students pioneered a subversive platform of church integration under the guise of an educational training program. Under Campbell's influence, they were occasionally less than quiet as well, publicly and vocally bearing witness to the sin of segregation.

The SIM committee planned its second summer in the light of a growing number of recent civil rights events making news during the fall of 1960 and the spring of 1961. In October, Martin Luther King Jr. had been arrested—along with fifty-one others—protesting a segregated department store restaurant in Atlanta, sentenced to four months of hard labor, and then released on bond after nine days. In November, as courts ordered integration of schools in New Orleans, Ruby Sales became the first child to attend an all-white southern elementary school. In December, the U.S. Supreme Court ruled that segregated bus terminals violated the Interstate Commerce Act; taken in combination with earlier rulings, the effect was to outlaw segregated bus travel and terminals. The University of Georgia desegregated in January amid massive protests, and CORE members were arrested at a lunch counter protest in Rock Hill, South Carolina. CORE also began organizing a series of Freedom Rides, to commence that May, to test the interstate travel laws.

In planning its second summer, the SIM committee recruited white and black students and raised enough money to provide each with a $300 stipend, with room and board to come from the host churches. Campbell's office in Nashville was to serve as a base for the project coordinator. John Collins recalled that Campbell's commitment gave the project shape and really got it going: "Will encouraged us and supported us when we wondered if we were crazy idealists. There is no doubt in my mind now that he went out on a limb and that SIM is greatly in his debt."[76] Collins, with the help and suggestions of Campbell and Wyatt Tee Walker of the SCLC, contacted potential host churches, both black and white. Chris Gamwell recruited students and raised funds. From the start, the students were determined that SIM not be just a Union program, and so Gamwell set out on recruiting visits to Harvard and Drew Universities.

As the students recruited new volunteers, and applications arrived in New York, the CORE Freedom Rides began, leading to a series of dramatic events that highlighted the state of racial tension in the South. The first group of Freedom Riders left Washington D.C., bound for New Orleans, on May 4, but their bus was attacked and burned outside of Anniston, Alabama, on May 14, and the riders themselves were beaten when they arrived in Birmingham. They were then arrested in Jackson, Mississippi, and served forty to sixty days at Parchman penitentiary. On May 17, Nashville students, many associated with SNCC, picked up the Freedom Rides; and on May 21, the Freedom Riders, along with Martin Luther King Jr. and 1,500 parishioners, were surrounded by white segregationists inside Ralph Abernathy's Montgomery, Alabama, church until the following morning, when federal marshals intervened. That very church, along with a number of other sites across the country—sites now infamous but previously unknown—would soon become familiar to the students of the Student Interracial Ministry as they began their own journey of reconciliation.

In June, Union professor Robert McAfee Brown—who would go on to become an international leader of civil rights and social justice causes and a co-founder of the organization Clergy and Laymen Concerned About Vietnam—was arrested in Tallahassee, Florida. He was participating in a Freedom Ride with three black ministers, four other white ministers, and two rabbis. Refused service in the airport terminal restaurant, they determined to stay until they were served. After twenty-four hours, they were arrested, charged with unlawful assembly and incitement to riot, and found guilty.[77]

Writing in the Union Theological Seminary newspaper, Brown addressed his colleagues and students "en famille." He recounted the lessons he had learned during his Freedom Rides and the encounters along the way. He learned, he said, what it means to be a lonely minority, what it means to be misunderstood, and what it means to be hated. But he had one main lesson for the seminarians: that doing something once, like participating in a Freedom Ride or a boycott or a demonstration, was not enough, but had to be just one event in a life of commitment to struggle. "That I 'did something' for a few tumultuous days and nights does not give me the privilege of disengaging myself for the next few tumultuous months and years, even if in my weary moments I wish it did," he wrote. "We cannot, in other words, let past involvements go bail for contemporary responsibilities; the most we can do is draw on the past involvements as resources for meeting contemporary responsibilities a little more creatively."[78] It was a lesson about perseverance and the long haul that true change required—a lesson that would be repeatedly learned, relearned, and emphasized by a generation of SIM students and other seminarians through the remainder of the decade and beyond.

CHAPTER TWO

To Be Both Prophet and Pastor

Crossing Racial Lines in Pulpits and Public Spaces,
1961–1962

If the church has a mission of reconciliation and healing, can the Southern clergyman be both prophet and pastor?

—Bud Walker, Union Seminary Student, 1960

In their closet office in New York, the SIM students put together the necessary bureaucracy to help their project succeed. Relying on help from Dr. Lee and his assistant, the students raised money from denominations, congregations, foundations, and individuals.[1] By June, their kitty held $5,049, enough to pay stipends for twelve student pastors and a project coordinator. Constance Curry from the National Student Association and both Martin Luther King Jr. and Wyatt Tee Walker from the SCLC solicited interest from possible host ministers and congregations.[2] SIM placed eighteen students in Baptist, Southern Baptist, Presbyterian, Methodist, and Congregational churches in Maryland, Georgia, Tennessee, North Carolina, Texas, and Connecticut.

Before setting out for their postings, the students gathered for a June orientation at the same Fellowship of Southern Churchmen camp in Swannanoa, North Carolina, where SIM's founding statement had been hammered out nine months earlier. Located in the foothills of the Blue Ridge Mountains on a piece of river valley land, it was a historically fitting site to gather, having been purchased by an earlier generation of radical pastors in order to have a place where blacks and whites could freely gather in the South. Arriving students were required to have read Lillian Smith's *Strange Fruit*, Martin Luther King Jr.'s *Stride toward Freedom*, and Kyle Haselden's *The Racial Problem in Christian Perspective*. John Collins and Charles Helms helped organize the orientation, and Will Campbell, Vanderbilt professor Arthur Foster, and the National Student Association's Connie Curry led sessions. The opening discussion, "Facts and Presuppositions," looked at the "real and imagined differences, in worship and preaching, in theology, in culture," of blacks and whites. Other sessions focused on the role of the churches in race relations, the place of nonviolence, and how to react in stressful situations. A nonviolence role-playing exercise, modeled on the workshops James Lawson had led in Nashville, was meant to mimic the feeling of being harassed by white supremacists during a sit-in and prepare students should they find themselves under attack in such a situation.[3]

The SIM project was not the only organization offering reflection on race relations that summer. After the orientation, one student, Dennis Loo, went straight to the Institute for Race Relations, held at the historically black Fisk University and featuring James Lawson, Thurgood Marshall, and black historian C. Eric Lincoln. Joseph Carter, one of the three black SIM participants, attended a similar institute—this one run by the American Friends Service Committee, a Quaker social justice organization—before serving with a white church in Plattsburgh, New York.[4] Despite the pioneering efforts of J. Oscar Lee, the mainline churches and their ecumenical body, the National Council of Churches, had not yet committed to the race struggle in an organized way, but some black church leaders and the traditionally pacifist and activist Quakers were already substantively engaging with these issues. Others would follow in time.

Eighteen students participated in SIM that summer of 1961, including three black students and one Asian student. Of these eighteen, thirteen were male and five female. The majority of the students were from Union Theological Seminary, but there was one each from Candler School of Theology and Wesley Theological Seminary. Notable placements that summer were Gurdon Brewster with the Reverend Martin Luther King Sr. in Atlanta, Stephen Rose with the Reverend Kelly Miller Smith in Nashville, and J. Oscar McCloud with Reverend Collins Kilburn in Raleigh. Martin Luther King Jr. had originally offered to host a SIM student, writing in May that he was "happy to say we will be able to have one of the young men from the Student Interracial Ministry serve in our church this summer. We will comply with the usual requirements of providing room and board." But that summer found him often on the road, responding to what he termed the "numerous demands from the southern struggle," and so Gurdon Brewster instead spent his summer assisting King's father, Martin Luther "Daddy" King, at Ebenezer Baptist Church in Atlanta.[5] Among his duties was cooking Daddy King's breakfast each morning. But Brewster occasionally served the younger King as well, including running messages to him while he was in prison.[6] The next year, the Reverend Ralph Abernathy requested a SIM intern of his own, supposedly declaring, "Martin had one last year and I want one this year!"[7]

On his very first day in Atlanta with the senior King, after a long day driving down from North Carolina, Brewster was immediately invited to preach at Ebenezer. It was the first sermon he had ever given. A few days later, he had his first experience of a segregated lunch counter while downtown with six members of the youth group he had been assigned to lead. Separated from the black students at the restaurant, he smoldered with rage. "I began to wonder how, confronted with this indignity, I could ever be expected to contain my anger. For the first time in my life I knew I had enough violence in me to tear the world apart. My blood boiled over and I could feel in my bones the will to destroy anything and anyone who hurt these lovely people in my youth group."[8]

Brewster was not the only student to land an assignment with one of the better-known figures in the movement. Steve Rose, who had just graduated from Union Seminary, served with Rev. Kelly Miller Smith, the prominent leader of the Nashville Christian Leadership Council and a chief adviser to James Lawson and the Nashville movement. Rose served as Smith's assistant, preaching in his Baptist church and accompanying the minister to visit sick congregants in the hospital. He also participated in pickets against the employment practices of a local supermarket, H. G. Hill. Rose recalled that Jim Lawson visited to teach them nonviolence, and that SNCC stalwart Diane Nash got arrested in Nashville at some point that summer.[9]

Rose and his wife, Lois, and their daughter, Diana, had driven down from New York in a station wagon and lived in a small house east of Nashville, owned by one of the members of Smith's congregation, and they frequently socialized with Smith, his congregants, and his frequent visitors, many of whom were also movement leaders. The Roses grew particularly close that summer with C. T. Vivian, another leader in James Lawson's Nashville movement and a participant in the Freedom Rides of 1961. He recalled that a typical week might involve preaching, visiting hospital patients, "playing bridge on Sundays with all these black middle class families," and then having C. T. Vivian stop by his house to chat in the evening. "I had a high all the time," Rose recalled. "It's like saying, 'I want to meet all the people that are going to be famous in the civil rights movement and not get killed and have a fun time!'" Rose also began to develop a close friendship with Will Campbell, who as a representative of the National Council of Churches was at that point working throughout the South. At one point, Rose and Campbell wanted to go see a strung-out Johnny Cash perform at Nashville's Grand Ole Opry. When Rose asked Kelly Miller Smith if he had his permission to go, Smith responded, "If you must, but I'm not going, by any means!"[10]

Rose would remain involved in key ways as the church renewal movement grew into calls for church revolution; his story is emblematic of the journeys—theological and otherwise—taken by many seminarians during the sixties, although he would be more of a player in the movement and church circles than most. He would also continue to intersect with SIM throughout its years. Sometimes he acted as an ambassador for SIM, recruiting students on the road or writing profiles of its work; at other times he was almost a mirror, reflecting the organization back to itself, but also adding refractions of possible paths toward both reconciliation and revolution.

Rose was born in 1936 into a wealthy Manhattan family. His parents were, in Rose's words, "nominal Protestants," who belonged to the Brick Church on the Upper East Side of Manhattan but attended only occasionally. His father was a lawyer, who became one of Richard Nixon's legal partners. Rose was educated at Phillips Exeter, a private boarding school in New Hampshire, and at Williams College in Massachusetts. Even as a teenager, he had an interest in race relations; at Williams, Rose quit his fraternity when a West Indian student was denied acceptance based on his skin color.[11]

Looking for a place to live, Rose stayed for a time at the home of the college chaplain, William Sloane Coffin, and his wife, Eva Rubenstein. Had he been planning a life spent rattling the cages of the church establishment, Rose couldn't have picked better landlords. Coffin would go on to become chaplain at Yale University and later preside over Riverside Church in New York City. Coffin's liberal theology and social concern influenced the younger man. Rose also benefited from Coffin's predecessor at Williams College, William Graham Cole, whom Rose found pompous yet especially skilled at recognizing important thinkers and attracting them to campus. The theologian Paul Tillich was one such visitor, as was Don Benedict, a founder of the East Harlem Protestant Parish. Rose particularly fell under the spell of another visitor, James Robinson, the founder of Operation Crossroads Africa, and "became a convert to his idea of service and responsibility."[12] Operation Crossroads Africa—the "progenitor of the Peace Corps," in the words of President John F. Kennedy—began as a secular mission program that sent American youth to Africa to work within grassroots development efforts.[13] Inspired by Coffin's social concern and Robinson's idea of service but feeling that he needed a firm grounding in Protestant theology, Rose headed to Union Theological Seminary in the fall of 1958.[14]

Once there, however, Rose was disappointed by the coursework and unimpressed by the theological stars of the seminary, Reinhold Niebuhr and Paul Tillich. Rose saw Niebuhr at that time as "running a balancing act, a kind of stasis philosophy in which anything that you did that came from feeling was questionable." Rose was more impressed by Reinhold's brother, H. Richard Niebuhr, who was a visiting scholar from Yale during Rose's final year at Union, in 1961. Rose later recalled that Richard Niebuhr understood that theology was in flux during that time of uncertainty. "He gave a lecture in which he basically said, 'Liberalism is dead and neo-orthodoxy is dead, and I don't know what is coming after.' And he was right. That H. Richard was a smart one." He also recalled that he and other students bemoaned Union's stuffy curriculum, which failed to plumb deeper meanings and an intellectual environment in which "vital theological discussion seems to have stopped with . . . Tillich and [Reinhold] Niebuhr."[15] Faculty members were sympathetic, but as Rose wrote in an editorial in the seminary newspaper, they were as rattled by the rapid change as the students. "Perhaps," he wrote, "it is unfair to impose the burden of leadership on a generation which in many ways is as befuddled as we are."[16]

Not far from the triangle of Protestantism made up by Union, Riverside Church, and the God Box stood a legendary watering hole, the West End Bar, formerly a haunt of Beat Generation mavericks such as Jack Kerouac and Allen Ginsberg. Steve Rose and some other students began to hang out there, turning the triangle into a square with one more secular corner. The West End became a secondary seminary for them, a worldly yet still spiritual retreat for those seeking other paths. Rose, who was already formulating his own ideas about modern theology and the need for an activist church with greater relevance to the immediate concerns of its members, was then the editor of Union's newspaper, the *Grain of Salt.*[17] He contrasted the West End Bar to the seminary itself in an editorial on the crisis that he claimed Union had found itself in by that year (1960–61). According to Rose, worship attendance had fallen off, and the curriculum was no longer relevant to the ministry some of them faced, and both students and professors were questioning how to proceed. Rose wondered if the answer was to be found at the juncture of Union Theological Seminary and the West End Bar, where the seminarians crossed the threshold into a place that symbolized what were for them new philosophies and ways of seeking meaning.[18] For many, one path to discovering that deeper meaning was involvement in social issues. As Roger Shinn noted at the time, "For many of our students the time has come to break the prolonged mood of introspection [and] the fashionable reveling in anxiety."[19] Study and reflection had their place, but a time had come for action.

Rose graduated from Union in May 1961, and he and his family headed to Nashville. After spending that summer working with Kelly Miller Smith and

SIM, Rose and his family moved to Chicago, where Rose became the director of the Exploratory Program in Journalism of the Chicago City Missionary Society under the direction of Don Benedict, whom he'd seen speak at
Williams College. Ordination was a requirement for the job, though, so
Rose took a quick trip back to New York to be ordained at the Brick Church
by John Collins, his old friend and one of the founders of the Student Interracial Ministry. "The only other person to be ordained at the Brick Church
was Bill Coffin," Rose later recalled.[20] In much the same way that the South
had its genealogy of dissenting ministers, the progressive Protestants of the
North also had their lineage and networks, running not just through the
seminaries and churches but into the social service sector, government, and
elsewhere.[21]

In coming to work for the Chicago City Missionary Society and Benedict, Rose landed among progressive Christians working at the cutting edge
of change in American urban ministry. As a Union student and the editor of
the school paper, he had pondered about what future lay ahead for a church
that seemed so distant from the needs of society. Now he began writing
articles and books reflecting on the changing church, especially in the urban
context, and outlining where it might go. Under the aegis of the missionary
society's journalism program, Rose founded and became editor of *Renewal*,
a progressive Christian journal whose influential pages in the coming years
would feature timely commentary on the church and society by the likes of
Harvey Cox, William Stringfellow, William Sloane Coffin, Howard Moody,
Don Benedict, Malcolm Boyd, and Rose himself. And he began to write
books, first publishing a short study on religion and urbanization, *The Day
the Country Mouse Expired*, for the ecumenical National Student Christian
Federation. He followed this with a collection of *Renewal* pieces called
Who's Killing the Church?[22] In both his books and his essays and editorials,
Rose wondered what would replace the old ways of the church now that
they appeared to him no longer relevant, and was frustrated at what he described as a flood of recent books complaining about the wayward church
but offering no suggestions for righting its course. He would eventually take
on this task himself in a 1966 manifesto on church renewal.

Rose also wrote for a number of other theological publications, and in
March of 1962 he wrote about the Student Interracial Ministry for the *Christian Century*, a major periodical in the world of progressive Christianity. He
reflected on SIM as "a break in the wall" of southern race relations, and used
the occasion of the recently observed Race Relations Sunday to comment
that "the furtive once-a-year exchange of white and Negro ministers may

salve some consciences, but it actually demonstrates how far we are from achieving brotherhood."[23] J. Oscar Lee, it will be recalled, pioneered early reconciliation efforts by establishing Race Relations Sunday through the NCC. What had been path breaking in its day could now seem paltry at best and, at worst, like a dodge to avoid real action. Rose wrote that in order for churches to make the Gospel relevant, they needed to create concentrated efforts in racial reconciliation. He praised a group of Episcopal priests who had recently been arrested during a civil rights march in Mississippi, commented favorably on the establishment of a few interracial churches in the North, and put forth the Student Interracial Ministry as an example of a project trying to do more than embrace "a once-a-year approach to healing."[24] The Student Interracial Ministry, he wrote, was a northern seminary-born response to "the nascent nonviolent movement in the South. How, they asked, could northern seminary students participate in the struggle for rights which from the Christian point of view were self evident?"[25] As Rose pointed out, the seminary atmosphere had already changed in early 1961—from one of relative complacency to something new and as yet not totally defined.

If the form of change could not yet be named—or even imagined, for that matter—some of the reasons for it could. Seminarians in the early 1960s were more likely than those in previous generations to be either single or married but waiting to have families. The seminaries, which had previously been under pressure to get married students out into paid fieldwork positions as soon as possible, now had time to experiment with fieldwork education. The students were also younger, and they were coming to the seminaries in greater numbers. Thanks in part to programs like the Rockefeller Brothers Fund grants, and later to the Vietnam War and the draft, seminaries began to fill with students who were interested in theology and ethics but not necessarily in becoming parish ministers. Higher education had rapidly expanded over the previous decade, with the number of college teaching positions doubling, and it was now more common for students to continue on to graduate school directly from college.[26] In addition, students were now being trained by professors who were markedly more progressive than were those in previous generations.

Many of the theological schools had maintained hiring freezes from the Great Depression through World War II; as the freeze thawed, it created a boom market for young theological professors. These new professors were as likely to have been influenced by Christian existentialism as by the bible lessons they learned in Sunday school; they were also strongly impacted by an older generation of clergy radicalized by World War II. The religious historian and theologian Harvey Cox described them as "the 'New Breed' of socially activist clergy"—although as inheritors of the social gospel tradition, what they practiced was not entirely new—and called their emergence within both church leadership and social justice struggles "a nationwide phenomenon."[27] They played especially strong roles in some of the Protestant and ecumenical seminaries and in urban ministry programs. Notably, the new breed of ministers was also multiracial in its composition, including black preachers active in civil rights organizing and white ministers hoping to work toward the same goal. Chicago community organizer Saul Alinsky, who had worked since the 1930s with religious leaders, most from the Catholic Church, said he had never seen anything like the "pure flame of passion for justice you find in these young ministers today."[28]

Seminary students, too, had become more radical since the late 1950s, questioning the inherited wisdom of their elders amid a sense that what previous generations valued—jobs, family, progress—was shallow and not real, or not "authentic." Students of this generation were increasingly inspired by the quest for authenticity, a search that combined concern for society with acute self-examination and a desire to be true to oneself while partaking in "real" experiences. Fueling the search for authenticity was the growth of Christian existentialism, which, following the calamity of World War II, offered some way to understand the alienation, cruelty, and seeming meaninglessness of life that the war had highlighted. Students devoured the work of Bonhoeffer, Søren Kierkegaard, Rudolf Bultmann, and Paul Tillich. In particular, Bultmann's argument that Christianity's language and symbols needed to be modernized had obvious appeal for students searching for answers through faith. Bonhoeffer, too, called for "a new language, perhaps quite non-religious, but liberating and redeeming—as was Jesus' language; it will be a new language of righteousness and truth."[29]

Students living in a time of great anxiety found that the existential Christian faith of these writers and thinkers offered one path to authenticity, a term that was popularized by the Student Christian Movement and, through it, would find its way into *The Port Huron Statement*, the defining statement of the sixties' "secular" student movement.[30] Released by the Students for a Democratic Society (SDS) in 1962, *The Port Huron Statement* declared the necessity for finding "a meaning of life that is personally authentic," and indeed several key SDS leaders, including chief author Tom Hayden, were deeply rooted in the Student Christian Movement. Dick Flacks, an SDS activist, defined *authenticity* as "acute sensitivity to hypocrisy, a wish for self-knowledge and understanding, concern that one's own personal poten-tialities—as well as those of others—be realized, rejection of imposed stan-dards of behavior, and acceptance of situational ethics."[31] In general terms, it meant that something must be pure, "feel right," and resonate with one's ethics and morals. In a sense, authenticity was the antithesis of alienation, if by the latter one meant, as Lionel Trilling wrote in 1970, "the sense of some-thing intervening between man [and] his own organic endowment."[32] Find-ing authenticity, it was thought, would restore one's wholeness.

Authenticity also equated truth and justice with democracy on the one hand and personal fulfillment on the other, both of which were attractive goals to young people coming of age in the 1960s. If the 1950s had been cloaked in a sort of suburban dream, a non-reality of white faces and picket fences and meals waiting on the table, the search for authenticity in the 1960s rejected that falsehood and sought to replace it with honesty and im-mersion in the world as it really was. To such young men and women, the Student Interracial Ministry program offered what they considered an au-thentic experience—real-world parish training in an interracial setting with the possibility of nitty-gritty civil rights work.

One placement in particular that summer of 1961 would help lay the groundwork for further development of the SIM project. J. Oscar McCloud, a black Union Theological Seminary student from Georgia, and his new wife, Robbie, joined the United Church in Raleigh, where McCloud as-sisted white pastor Collins Kilburn, a bona fide member of the network of local ministers who dissented from adherence to the racial status quo. McCloud reported that the all-white church was attended by a number of North Carolina State University faculty members and had a reputation as a "radical institution" in downtown Raleigh. The first Sunday he was there, the church initiated selective buying campaigns at two local supermarkets, demonstrating that it could use its economic purchasing power to pressure local businesses to do away with discriminatory hiring practices. McCloud also built a close relationship with a white SIM student, Tom Frazier, who was working with a black church, Oberlin Baptist, also in Raleigh. Since each was responsible for his church's youth group, they held joint, integrated meetings. Through this interracial work in Raleigh, J. Oscar McCloud got to know some of the members of Davie Street Presbyterian Church, a black congregation downtown, which invited him to apply to be their minister. The Davie Street church elected McCloud as its new pastor directly after his

SIM summer, and he continued to collaborate with Collins Kilburn, his former host pastor. The two ministers and congregations hosted numerous SIM students over several years.

As in the pilot summer of 1960, with the leading participation of Jane Stembridge, SIM continued to attract female students, even though most denominations did not yet ordain women as ministers. Nevertheless, female students were highly involved in the Student Christian Movement and attended seminaries, although at a rate below 10 percent. Some would go on to careers as music directors or in other areas of the church. The civil rights movement opened up another rich path of involvement for many religious young women.[33] Alma Wolber, one of the three female students in 1961, made SIM's first steps into urban ministry while working in Baltimore, Maryland. She served a middle-class black church located in a low-income and racially diverse neighborhood and devised a weeklong summer camp program for the "unchurched" local kids.[34]

During the final days of August, nearly all the students and a few of the ministers convened for an evaluation conference in Nashville, Tennessee. In discussing what had most surprised them during their work, the students largely agreed that whereas they had previously thought of specific problems as racially coded, some being white problems and some being black, the interracial experience showed them a common humanity that seemed to prove such problems universal. They reported that for the most part, personal relations had been "surprisingly smooth." The black students were pleased to discover that allegedly superior white churches suffered the same financial difficulties and internal squabbles that beset black churches.[35] One black student felt that the program had prepared him to work in any congregation in the country. Some of the white students saw SIM as a "theological laboratory" and believed that their studies gave them insight into the theology of the black church, which they concluded mixed both fundamentalist and liberal theologies. Based on the black churches they served that summer, some of the white students concluded that, unlike the white churches that they well knew, the black churches and ministers were as concerned with civil rights and social action as they were about individual souls.[36] The ministers they served, however, were a unique group, both select and self-selected, who were already dedicated to, and in many cases leading, local or national civil rights efforts. However, not all black ministers were similarly devoted to civil rights; many were more motivated by self-interest and preservation of the status quo than they were interested in promoting voter education, school integration, or other efforts at achieving greater rights for blacks.[37]

The students found less agreement on the question of the proper role of the churches in reconciling the races. Some questioned whether the church as an institution should be engaged directly in social action or whether it should serve more as "a 'sustaining colony' out fighting the battle through the NAACP, CORE, etc." Other students wanted to define the relationship between organizations like CORE and the church, wondering if in some ways CORE *was* the church, or, in other words, if involvement in social actions could be described as a form of ministry. King's SCLC had begun offering citizenship classes that July under the directorship of Andrew Young; perhaps that could be another form of outreach? One student insisted, "We must find radical new forms for the Gospel outside the institutional church." Others felt that ministers need not necessarily be out in the streets but should be teachers impelling their congregants outward.[38] Clearly, a number of concerns and ideas were at play, and answers were far from clear.

The students agreed that their primary task in SIM was to create deep relationships across the boundaries of race and thus to witness to the Christian concern for racial reconciliation. They felt that white SIM ministers should particularly reach out to other white ministers in the South, and also pointed out that while the presence of whites in black churches was by no means new—whites had often visited black churches as guest preachers, evangelists to the "heathens," and paternalistic "older brothers" lending a hand—what was new with SIM was the kind of relationship involved. Kelly Miller Smith said of the project, "There's a big difference between lending a helping hand and extending a brotherly hand."[39]

The students also reflected on their personal transformations. As the project required a commitment of three months of full immersion, it tended not to attract those students looking for a quick fling in the movement or a "contact high" with revolution. Doug "Buddy" Renick—a white seminarian from Texas, who worked in a black church in North Carolina—reflected on the early years: "To picket, sit-in or engage in a 'freedom ride' requires a certain amount of courage, but to live in the Negro community for three months—more especially, in the home of a Negro family—requires more than courage. It requires . . . the ability to face oneself honestly with all the masks removed." The process of facing oneself and one's own bigotry and limitations made Renick and others understand unity and brotherhood not as theological abstractions but as realities. And while such insight could certainly be achieved in a secular setting, the seminarians and SIM operated in a different way. Renick and others experienced the process of greater understanding—taking place within the context of the church and according to religious rhetoric—as no less than a conversion experience. "This is not theory," Renick insisted. "It has happened to me and to many others who have participated in SIM."[40]

Returning SIM students described learning several lessons from their experiences in living and working across the color line. These included new sensitivity to social and racial prejudice and to daily injustices perpetrated and endured, and greater empathy for others. The founders of the Student Interracial Ministry proclaimed, "We are convinced that this project will have a significant impact upon the life of the communities involved. Our need today is for understanding between individuals." Prophetically, they declared, "Legislation alone will not bring understanding. New channels of communication between negro and white communities must be found if we are to move, on the deepest levels, toward a genuinely integrated society."[41] Roger Shinn described the project as "cultivat[ing] human understanding through shared experiences. The aim has been development of person-to-person relationships and understanding, especially within the Christian church." Shinn further wrote, "Theological education in these times is greatly concerned with the relationship between its scholarly aims and the functional life of the church. Among the many experiments in field work, internships, clinical years, etc., this summer student interracial ministry is one of the most imaginative."[42]

SIM alumni also noted that the project taught them a new appreciation for the impact of the church on a given community and its struggles to maintain relevance and membership. Often, this appreciation for the church came through firsthand involvement with daily congregational activities, both humdrum and exhilarating. For nearly all the SIM students, this was their first practical ministerial experience outside classroom training exercises. Having studied the finer points of theology, they now ran vacation bible schools, visited the sick in hospitals, organized playgrounds and baseball games, ran bible study, cut stencils for songbooks, preached Sunday sermons, bought supplies for the parsonage, facilitated or created youth groups, gave Communion, sat in finance committees, and did office work. And they did all of this within a community of another race.[43]

The evaluation conference also included discussions of practical matters for continuing the program and enhancing its effectiveness. It was suggested at this early date that yearlong internships be considered, since the summer was so brief and was not entirely representative of the life of a given congregation in that many members were often absent during that period. Clusters of SIM students in the same cities were suggested as a way for students to interact, reflect, study together, and support one another during the program. This had been modeled in Nashville, where Dennis Loo, Steve Rose, Alistair Raynham, and Marion Cox met weekly with Vanderbilt professor Arthur Foster to interpret their experiences of interracial ministry through their theological studies. A discussion also ensued as to whether SIM should remain independent and student run or whether it should seek to affiliate with another institution, such as the NCC or the Interseminary Movement. One minister pointed out the potential impact of certain alliances, such as with the SCLC, on fund-raising. Another minister hoped that the program would retain its ecumenical nature and continue to send students across not just racial lines but denominational lines as well.[44] The group also pointed to the successful ministry of the black students in white northern churches and of J. Oscar McCloud in Raleigh, and urged that more southern white churches be enlisted as hosts for black SIM students.

Summing up the first two years of the project, John Collins reflected that the student leaders should continue to refine and reflect on their goals and to pray for inspiration. "Without this kind of continuing analysis," he wrote, "and without consciously submitting to the leading of the Holy Spirit, the program will become stagnant, uncreative, dull and very successful. That is the time to turn it over to a stagnant, dull, uncreative, and very successful institution to administer."[45] Barring that, the students would continue to lead and experiment with additional forms of interracial ministry.

The second group of SIM participants returned in the fall of 1961 to a seminary campus that had changed palpably since the previous fall. Many more students had been stirred to action, were restless with the pace of change in the country on race issues, and were dissatisfied with their institutions' response to the racial crisis and to a theological curriculum that seemed suddenly out of step with the times. Some called for change in the seminary, but there was also the first glimmer of a countertrend. Rather than working to create change from within their institutions, some seminary students in what the *New York Times* termed "the post-Protestant era" were either jumping ship from the seminaries or not coming aboard in the first place. Some who left were seeking immediate authentic action in the world; at least twelve members of Union's junior class dropped out at the end of 1961 to join the newly minted Peace Corps to work overseas.[46] Seeking to serve others in a meaningful way, they preferred to leave the seminary and join a federally sponsored secular program rather than continue on into parish ministry careers for a church that seemed unclear about who it was to serve—and how.

While the search for a coherent way to practice the Gospel in service to others drove some seminarians away, others of the type John Collins had referred to as "seekers" found themselves drawn more deeply inward to questions of meaning and faith. Religious structures and ideas that they had long assumed steadfast now seemed fragile. Just as the stirring in the mulberry trees was said in Chronicles to indicate the presence of God about to act in the world, so, too, was there a palpable stirring on racial matters on and off the seminary campus. The federal government put more and more pressure on the South to desegregate its transportation, culminating in September with the Interstate Commerce Commission finally ending discrimination in interstate travel and the Supreme Court in February ruling that segregated transportation facilities—local as well as interstate—were unconstitutional. In southwest Georgia, two young SNCC activists—Charles Sherrod and Cordell Reagon—began working with what would become the Albany Movement, testing waiting rooms, attempting to register voters, and pushing for open accommodations. By December, after arrests of some activists led to mass protests and arrests in Albany, local leaders invited Martin Luther King Jr. to join their efforts. King was arrested soon after, and he left town after someone paid his bail, but he would return on and off; meanwhile, the young SNCC workers continued on in a community determined to create change.

Throughout the academic year 1961–62, the students on the SIM committee again recruited students and host churches and raised money for the next summer's project, which would eventually number fifteen students: thirteen white and two black. Of the thirteen men and two women, four hailed from Union Theological Seminary, along with one each from Bethany, Drew, Southeastern Baptist, Duke, Garrett, and McCormick seminaries; the University of Pittsburgh; Chicago Seminary; Harvard Divinity School; Eden Seminary; and Atlanta's Interdenominational Theological Center, which had previously been Gammon. Word had certainly spread about the SIM program. The students served churches in North Carolina, Texas, Tennessee, Georgia, Washington D.C., Alabama, Mississippi, New Jersey, and Florida. Once again, the project emphasized improving race relations through interracial witness at the congregation and community levels. The program raised nearly $7,700 from individuals, congregations, seminaries, foundations, and denominational boards, with the bulk of the expenditures going toward $300 stipends and insurance policies for each of the summer students.[47]

The summer program of 1962 again began with an orientation at the Fellowship of Southern Churchmen camp at Swannanoa, North Carolina. Participants were instructed to bring sleeping bags, bathing suits, and bibles to the three-day meeting. From there, the fifteen students headed out to their assignments. Students were again assigned to work with Kelly Miller Smith in Nashville, Martin Luther King Jr. in Atlanta, and Collins Kilburn in Raleigh. In addition, J. Oscar McCloud, who had participated in SIM the year before and then been called to a black church in Raleigh, and Joseph Ellwanger, the well-known Lutheran pastor who was to be Martin Luther King Jr.'s key white clergy ally in Birmingham, each hosted a student for the first time.

The students in general were welcomed into their host churches with a minimum of complaint, although the same could not be said for their reception in the communities at large. In Macon, Georgia, Ralph Luker's plans to stay with another white student with whom he had attended Duke University ended when his friend's parents objected to Luker's interracial summer plans. Suddenly lacking a place to live, Luker rented a room at the YMCA in Macon, only to be turned out for the same reason. He recalled that the director of the Y told him, " 'You have spent the last night you're going to spend at the Y, and if you know what's good for you, you will pack your bags and get out of town.' " He eventually secured an apartment with another SIM student, but even then, their landlady forbade them from having black visitors.[48] Later that summer, Luker traveled to Albany, Georgia, where SIM would develop a major presence in future years. Luker recalled meeting Martin Luther King Jr. in the living room of Albany Movement leader William Anderson as well as Clarence Jordan at his Koinonia Farm in Americus, Georgia.[49]

Luker also visited with Hank Elkins, who was in Atlanta working with Martin Luther King Jr. and his father, Daddy King, at Ebenezer Baptist Church. Hank Elkins was another southerner, raised in Winston-Salem, North Carolina, where he attended R.J. Reynolds High School before heading off to college at Yale. Like Steve Rose, he got to know Bill Coffin at Yale, and was also mentored by Kenneth Scott Latourette, a noted historian of world Christianity. After graduating with a history degree in 1959 but seeking a career as a Baptist minister, he enrolled at Southeastern Baptist, where in his senior year a professor was seeking students interested in joining the Student Interracial Ministry. Elkins applied, requesting "an urban

Baptist church in the South"; in reply, he got posted to *the* urban Baptist church in the South when a letter arrived from Martin Luther King Jr. inviting him to Atlanta.[50]

Elkins spent the majority of that summer living with Martin Luther King Jr. and his family, working with the Ebenezer youth group, and getting to know the Kings. He even made it into the pages of *Jet* magazine, in a picture with Martin Luther King Jr. and Alberta "Mother" King.[51] In his last couple of weeks, with King Jr. on the road and in and out of jail, Hank lived with the elder Kings. Hoping to create interracial youth group meetings with white churches, Elkins ran into resistance in Atlanta, finally partnering with a Quaker meeting and, for a couple of times, with a Unitarian Universalist congregation. He did get a chance to preach at Ebenezer, as well as at some other black churches in Atlanta, and of course to experience firsthand the preaching of both Kings. He later recalled, "The experience to me, having grown up in a white segregated Baptist church, made me very appreciative of the prophetic mode that Martin and his father contributed at Ebenezer. And I think one aspect that many do not fully appreciate was how much Martin was really a direct descendent of the prophetic note that his father so eloquently sounded." At one point, Hank served as chauffer for Daddy King—even stopping in at a segregated restaurant to bring food out for them both—on his way to a preaching engagement in Macon, a night on which "he was absolutely eloquent. Daddy King's own convictions in regard to race and civil rights certainly were the foundations, I'm convinced, for Martin's and for Martin's life. The acorn certainly did not fall far from the tree in that sense."[52]

One of the highlights of that summer, Elkins recalled later, was a retreat to Koinonia, capped by a Sunday service led by Clarence Jordan. Elkins also made at least two visits to nearby Albany that summer, where King and the Albany Movement were currently being frustrated by the delaying tactics of police chief Laurie Pritchett. Elkins in fact made visits to King and Ralph Abernathy in the Albany jail in late July to deliver books, papers, clean towels, and soap. During one visit, he was surprised to find a member of his boy scout troop from back in Winston-Salem now working in the Albany jail and clearly not supportive of the movement. "Elton just got up and walked away," Elkins recalled years later, "an indication of a kind of tension, a polarization, that prevailed in those days."[53] After King's release from jail, Elkins and the lawyer Bill Kunstler formed a doubles tennis team to play against two African American players in the public Tift Park. At the same time, some of their colleagues, also an interracial group, went to use the adjacent swimming pool, both groups testing the local segregation laws. Within about ten minutes, police chief Laurie Pritchett arrived at the tennis court to "order the nets taken down [and announce] the park was closed."[54] In a nearly trembling voice, Pritchett blamed the park closing on "outsiders coming in here and trying to change our way of life." That August, *Jet* magazine ran a photo of a black civic worker cutting down the tennis nets while Rev. D. J. Smith, Bill Kunstler, and Hank Elkins looked on.[55]

Despite numerous such run-ins, the students' summer reports for 1962 repeatedly attested to their conversion experiences as the seminarians described discovering, as if for the first time, a joint humanity and faith not bound by race. For many of the SIM students, like their forerunners in the YWCA and other interracial organizations decades earlier, this discovery challenged notions of racial superiority and inferiority that remained at the bedrock of both their educational and their social formation. They rethought how they understood basic human equality beyond the abstraction of theological study. Students who had been so "converted" then proselytized to others and drew them into the fold. Buddy Renick testified that it was the "enthusiasm and sincerity" of former participants that attracted him to the project. "All the facts and figures about SIM's work meant little to me, but the people who had been in the work were alive with new insights into themselves and the nature of the church. This 'aliveness' was catching."[56]

For most of the students, the major learning opportunities came in two ways: through hands-on involvement with the functions of a church, and through personal interactions across the lines of race. In many cases, the two were intertwined. All seminarians did fieldwork within congregations as part of their training, but the SIM experience, set within the context of an experiment in racial exchange, forced students to interact with the experience at a more profound level. As J. Oscar McCloud, the black Union seminarian who served as both student and host pastor, recalled in 1962, whatever a student's race, "you earn your acceptance and understanding . . . because [you] are able to minister in some meaningful way to these people."[57] Both black and white students reported that the project gave them their first intimate interactions with the other race, and most drew the same two conclusions: that they were indeed prejudiced, and that the members of the other race, once they got to know them, were not so different from themselves. White seminarians, who lived in the neighborhoods in which they worshipped, were often the first and only white people many black congregants came to know personally. The same held for many black seminarians who lived among white congregants. Students reported this personal transformation in terms varying from how they had learned the true meaning of love to how they had been unaware of what it meant to be in the minority until they had personally experienced it.[58]

Martin Luther King Jr., who had hailed the interracial approach in his endorsement of the SIM program, had had a similar experience while an undergraduate at Morehouse and had reached much the same conclusions. During that time, he had participated in Atlanta's interracial Intercollegiate Council, which he said convinced him that there were indeed allies to be had among whites, especially younger whites. Through knowing and working with white individuals, his "resentment was softened, and a spirit of cooperation took its place."[59] Students in SIM were able to delve more deeply into race relations precisely because they were able, by virtue of a relatively short but concentrated stay of three months, to become deeply involved in the personal lives of their hosts. In the words of one of the student founders, the project was "attempt[ing] to . . . bring confrontation in depth. Just as each group has its own role to play, so SIM is concerned with grace, with reconciliation, with opening lines of communication where none have existed, and with reopening those which have been temporarily cut off."[60]

Students came to know people within their congregations not just as people of another race whose cause they supported but as individuals, whose personal stories they carried with them. At the same time, they witnessed the ramifications of the racial divide in America much more thoroughly than they would have at a one-day protest or through "regular" ministerial fieldwork. It was a demanding experience. One southern college chaplain, when asked why his students joined public demonstrations yet were not willing to sacrifice a summer to serve with SIM, replied, "Well, you know, it's relatively easy to go out and walk a picket line for a couple of hours—you can do it without giving much of yourself; but to deeply involve yourself in people's lives for three months—that is a different matter."[61]

As for the congregations, Roger Shinn—the professor of applied Christianity at Union—felt that many of them were roused by the presence among them of a young person of faith, whose work in their churches was a kind of Christian witness that "jarred their complacent assumptions."[62] Presence alone, however, was no simple matter. To just be in these churches and communities was to confront a long history and to take on the baggage that came with it. J. Oscar McCloud pointed out that whites serving in black churches was nothing new, but that in the past, such relationships had usually been in some manner exploitative, and that blacks had learned "to suspect the 'outgoing' white who was traditionally the 'bait' or instrument of the segregationist." Consequently, the white SIM student had to confront this legacy while establishing his or her own personal relationships. Mc-Cloud also cautioned that white SIM students would encounter black church folk who would make no effort to get to know or understand them, "because they feel that they are the only ones who need to be or should be understood."[63] Also, having chosen to serve a black church, the SIM student was not likely to be accepted by the majority white community in the area, compounding the possibility for rejection but also sending the student deeper into the arms of the host community. Additionally, as one black pastor warned incoming seminarians, the host congregations were being asked to challenge their own racial prejudices and convictions, and a student should not assume that all within a congregation, simply because it had extended the invitation, would be especially welcoming. "It should always be remembered that interracial confrontation is not the customary way in which the people express their Christianity. . . . [They] are not accustomed to the type of relationship which is now placed before them. Negroes as well as whites have to learn how to like another person and accept him."[64]

Collins Kilburn also attested to the value that personal interactions with the student minister had for members of his Raleigh congregation. He wrote that through daily interaction, sharing meals, and visiting with one another, "the students get to know us as people," and the congregants, "in turn, come to know the student not just . . . as a representative of another group, but as a person with needs and sins not so different from our own. Dialogue on the personal level breaks down stereotypes on both sides, and real human contact is achieved. Often hidden hostility and fear emerge. But when this happens in the community of faith, it is the opportunity for deeper reconciliation."[65]

The placement of James Forbes with the Olin T. Binkley Memorial Baptist Church in Chapel Hill, North Carolina, led to just such reconciliation, and deeply and permanently affected not only the congregation but the future work of both the white and black pastors involved—work that would have significant impact both locally and, eventually, nationally. Binkley Memorial Baptist Church was only four years old in 1962, hardly much of a pedigree for a southern church. The church was formed by a group of about forty parishioners who had left the all-white Baptist Church at Chapel Hill to offer an alternative, racially inclusive worship option to local Baptists. In some ways, it was a typically southern story. Although the vast majority of white southern congregations supported—often adamantly—the racial status quo, the church community was expansive enough to accommodate rogue outliers, inventive experiments, and the possibility for change. Indeed, many southerners seemed to pride themselves on their potential for nonconformity. The "bootleg preacher" from either end of the theological or political spectrum was sometimes tolerated, even celebrated—SIM's adviser Will Campbell being one notable example.

The new congregation named itself in honor of Olin Trivette Binkley, a North Carolina native and a Wake Forest University theology professor. Binkley had once been the minister of Chapel Hill Baptist Church and had moved on to Southeastern Baptist Theological Seminary, where he served as president from 1963 to 1975. He was part of that small group of southern progressives, many of them Baptists, who formed a "genealogy of dissent," influencing and encouraging one another, often in transgressions of the formidable boundaries of Jim Crow.[66] This lineage was especially strong in North Carolina, where a network of shared ideas, training, and experience united ministers like Binkley, Carlyle Marney in Charlotte, Collins Kilburn and William Finlator in Raleigh, and Charles Jones in Chapel Hill.[67]

Many of the southern ministers who formed the small community of dissenters were educated in northern institutions, where their southern identity merged with the liberal modern theology more typical of the North. These southerners—including James Lawson, who inspired the first nonviolent sit-ins in Nashville; Myles Horton and James Dombrowski of the Highlander Center; Howard Kester of the Southern Tenant Farmers' Union; Martin England of Koinonia Farm; and Sherwood Eddy of Delta Cooperative Farm—patched together their own theology, agenda, and methods based in part on the Social Gospel Movement but also taking equally from the jeremiads of the Old Testament prophets, the neoorthodoxy of Reinhold Niebuhr, the existentialism of Karl Barth, and even the evangelicalism of the black church. Many of the students who participated in the Student Interracial Ministry, and particularly those who created and helped to shape it, were northern-educated southerners made in this same mold.

By naming their congregation after Binkley, the founders of the new church in Chapel Hill clearly signaled their intention to pursue a more radical approach to Christian social concerns. The congregation set out to find a minister who was at least as progressive as Binkley, and in the summer of 1958, a search committee called on Dr. Robert Seymour, a natural inheritor of the genealogy of dissent and a man committed to racial and social justice principles. The new congregation of the Olin T. Binkley Memorial Baptist Church offered him a rare chance to focus his ministry on such principles.

Seymour had been born and raised in Greenwood, South Carolina, and educated first at the Citadel, then Newberry College, and finally at Duke University, courtesy of the Navy's V-12 pre-chaplaincy program. These segregated institutions did little to challenge the racial norms with which he had grown up; attending Yale Divinity School, however, turned his sense of proper relations between the races upside down. "Like explosives with delayed timing devices," he wrote later, "the biblical message eventually jolted my life and made it imperative for me to challenge the culture that had cradled me."[68]

At Yale, Seymour found himself in a dormitory where black seminary students lived in adjacent rooms, and white folks cleaned the buildings and cooked the food. Raised a fundamentalist Southern Baptist, he now studied Christian ethics with H. Richard Niebuhr, and studied the social gospel with Liston Pope, who taught it as the enactment in everyday life of the commandment to love God and to love thy neighbor as thyself. "It all seems so obvious now," Seymour later wrote about learning the lessons of the social gospel. "These are not two commandments; they are one. Personal gospel and Social Gospel go hand in hand. Not until Yale did the full impact of this insight begin to inspire the direction of my life and become the mainspring of my later ministry in the South."[69]

Seymour pastored churches in Warrenton and Mars Hill, North Carolina, gaining a reputation as an early progressive on racial issues. By 1953, Seymour sensed that his time in Warrenton had come to an end—his petition to the town to hire a black policeman was the final straw—and he counted himself lucky to have survived three years and to have risen to the "challenge to confront persons in that kind of setting [with] what the Gospel demanded of them."[70] Upon Seymour's departure, Bignall Jones, the editor of the *Warren Record* and one of Seymour's few allies in town, wrote in the paper, "For three years Bob Seymour has served the members of his congregation well, through precept and example, preaching the brotherhood of God, building and strengthening his church. Because of his sincerity [and] a liberality of views which at times has seemed shocking to his congregation . . . he has been tolerated by those to whom such views are anathema and even, happily, some of those views have become accepted."[71]

Seymour completed a PhD in Scotland at the University of Edinburgh before returning to North Carolina to pastor Mars Hill Baptist Church, where he again delivered sermons on racial justice and integration. He preached one such sermon in the spring of 1957 on what he called a coming revolution in race relations in a sermon titled "Trumpets of Uncertain Sound." He borrowed from Corinthians the metaphor of a weak trumpet call to describe the anemic message that the southern churches had been sending out about racial equality. Seymour said that in the midst of a social revolution, "the Church seems to have closed her eyes and gives every appearance of sleeping comfortably in the midst of the tumult . . . now the time has come for action. The trumpet of Christian truth has not been loud enough to protect us from following the Pied Pipers of expedient compromise."[72]

When Seymour arrived to take up the reins at Binkley, the small congregation was just nine months old and had already welcomed its first black member, George Grigsby, a student at the University of North Carolina at Chapel Hill. Grigsby was reported to be only the second black person to cross the race barrier as a member (as opposed to a nonmember worshipper) in a North Carolina church.[73] The new integrated church remained mostly below the radar until Seymour offered the apartments in the parish house to Grigsby and some fellow students in exchange for upkeep of the building. This interracial living situation in the heart of Chapel Hill displeased neighbors and brought Binkley Church to the attention of the *Durham Morning Herald*, which announced Grigsby's church membership under the headline "Negro Joins White Church." Subsequently, letters of both praise and damnation came from throughout the region. One writer told Seymour, "[I was] shocked and grieved when I saw that one who professed to be a Christian . . . had committed such a sinful thing as to take a Negro in your church. I'm a Baptist and believe the teachings of God, and He taught segregation from cover to cover."[74] Such was often the lay of the land in the "Christian" South of 1958.

Seymour was not the only progressive minister in the area—a number of other "dissenters" pastored nearby—and when the sit-ins in nearby Greensboro began in February 1960, the members of the Chapel Hill Ministerial Association publicly supported pickets and demonstrations. On March 24, 1960, Seymour was one of twenty-seven Chapel Hill ministers to sign a "Statement of Convictions," which ran as a full-page advertisement in the *Chapel Hill Weekly* "confess[ing] our own responsibility for the existence and toleration of such attitudes and practices as make this request necessary."[75]

And so it was to this pastor and congregation that SIM's James Forbes was assigned in the summer of 1962. Binkley's deacons' recommendation to invite a black SIM student was approved by the congregation, with one negative vote and several abstentions.[76] Even given the founding notion of the congregation, Forbes's visit marked a fundamental turning point in the life of the church, as Seymour later recalled. "Our people were intellectually committed to an inclusive church, but having this black pastor with us for the summer helped them work through some of the emotional vestiges of feelings that were still there."[77]

James Forbes was also a North Carolina native, born in 1935 as the second oldest of eight children. His father was the pastor of Raleigh's Pentecostal Providence Holy Church on the weekends and a candy salesman during the week, and would go on to become a Pentecostal bishop. His mother worked as a domestic servant for a white family. Forbes, too, had gone north for college, earning a degree in science at Howard University. He had intended to pursue a career in medicine before being called to the ministry in his junior year. After graduation from Howard, he enrolled at Union Theological Seminary, having been rebuffed by Duke University, which did not welcome black students into its divinity school until March 1961, despite continuous demands from students and faculty dating back to 1948.[78] Forbes entered the seminary in New York City still considering himself to be a doctor of sorts—"God called me to be a healer, but a healer of souls and culture."[79]

Forbes received his master of divinity from Union Theological Seminary in May 1962, and in the absence of an immediate call to a congregation, he accepted the summer internship in Chapel Hill that SIM offered him. This was not his first experience with an interracial project. While in college, he had participated in the Panel of Americans, an organization devoted to interracial understanding, which had formed on college campuses in California in response to anti-Japanese sentiment during World War II. The project sent white, black, Puerto Rican, Christian, and Jewish representatives to high school and college campuses to discuss bigotry and understanding.[80] He entered into the SIM experience looking forward to seeing a white church from the inside and hoping to learn "what causes some white folks to run away from others who are different and what causes others to be open to actually help to build the beloved community. As Dr. King used to say when he'd roll past these white churches, 'What kind of people are in there? What kinds of gods do they serve, and what kind of values do they hold?' "[81] He was soon to find out.

As the summer-long associate pastor of the Binkley church, Forbes ran the interracial vacation bible school, led a bible class and a supper seminar for university students, and served as the church's liaison to the Baptist Student Union. In August, he gave his own sermon at the Binkley church and led a retreat to the beach. While in Chapel Hill, he lived in the parish house and took most of his evening meals with church families. For many parishioners, his presence marked the first black visitor to their homes. Forbes reported at the time that the church work itself was no different from what he would have been doing in a black church, "but because most of the members of this church are white I have had an opportunity to approach my work from a slightly different perspective. I have attempted to understand more fully some of the problems of the white community during this period of social change. One thing has become increasingly clear and it is that real understanding requires genuine confrontation. Mere contact has not been productive of deepened understanding."[82] Forbes regarded his serving a leadership role in the church as providing a "vital Christian witness to the larger Chapel Hill community."[83]

Forbes also found personal fulfillment through the experience. Recalling a time when Reverend Seymour was out of town and parishioners sought him out during the birth of a baby and during a medical crisis, he wrote to Seymour, "I could have wished for you, but I would take nothing for their looking to me; I have never felt so completely a person!"[84] He later reflected that the experience had surprised him with how it broke up his preconceptions of southern whites. "All my life I have heard white people say, 'we know our colored folks'; until this summer I thought I knew our white folks."[85]

In a few cases, however, his prejudgment of the situation that he thought he would encounter at Binkley turned out to be unfortunately accurate. As had happened with George Grigsby's membership in 1958, hate mail once again came pouring in from outside the community in response to news reports of Forbes's ministry, but there was plenty of positive attention as well. The *London Illustrated Times* sent a photographer all the way from England to create a photo essay depicting the integrated congregation. And in 1963, the *Southern Patriot*—the newspaper of the Southern Conference Educational Fund, a progressive project founded in 1946 to address segregation in southern schools—wrote of SIM and Forbes's ministry at Binkley, "It is one of the most promising of a number of projects which concerned people are carrying on quietly in an effort to move beyond the stage of desegregation to a glimpse of real integration."[86]

From his perspective, Forbes was both welcomed into the Binkley community and protected by them. "They received me with absolute open arms," he recalls, "and granted me all the rights and privileges of inclusion in their community. Of course, the [outside] culture itself had not yet turned the corner." This meant that service at restaurants would be inordinately slow for him and that at a town softball game, the opponents peppered him with racial epithets. But the Binkley congregation rallied around him at the softball game and at other times, making him feel that he was, "in a sense, within that community, . . . in a protective relationship that was totally committed to full inclusion . . . [and] accepted beyond the consideration of race."[87]

Ordained in both the American Baptist and the Original United Holy Church of America, Forbes went on to pastor his father's church in Roxboro, North Carolina, and the Holy Trinity Church, a large black Presbyterian church in Wilmington, North Carolina. It was at this church that Robert Seymour officiated Forbes's wedding to Bettye Franks. (Seymour also presided over the wedding of another former SIM student, Hank Elkins, who after his summer working with Martin Luther King Jr. and Sr., had become a campus minister at the black North Carolina College, now North Carolina Central.)[88] Forbes pastored in Wilmington from 1960 to 1965, then moved on to St. John's United Holy Church of America in Richmond, Virginia, where he stayed until 1973. In 1976, he was invited back to Union Theological Seminary as a professor of homiletics, the art of preaching. In June 1989, he became the senior minister at Riverside Church, the historic congregation of Harry Emerson Fosdick and one of the few nationally known churches that proved the exception to Martin Luther King Jr.'s statement that "at 11:00 on Sunday morning when we stand and sing and Christ has no east or west, we stand at the most segregated hour in this nation."[89] Not so at Riverside Church, which was 60 percent white and 40 percent black when Forbes arrived. He served as senior minister there until June 2007.

Forbes's eighteen years at the helm of Riverside Church were not without controversy, but he nevertheless established himself not only as a force in New York City but as one of the world's great practicing preachers. During his tenure, the racial composition of the congregation changed to about 70 percent black. Forbes's "Southern," Pentecostal-inspired preaching style did not sit well with some members, nor did his altar calls, occasionally authoritarian leadership style, AIDS ministry, or acceptance of gay and lesbian members. Like Robert Seymour, his mentor at Binkley, Forbes was not afraid to rattle cages by taking unpopular stands that he considered just. And he did so with such style that a 1996 Baylor University worldwide survey, reported in *Newsweek*, recognized him as one of the twelve "most effective" preachers in the English-speaking world. Additionally, *Ebony* twice recognized him as one of the country's greatest black preachers. He continued in retirement to speak and preach nationally, founded the Healing the Nations Foundation of New York City, and hosted a radio show, *The Time Is Now*, on the Air America network in 2006 and 2007.[90]

Forbes later looked back on his experience as an assistant pastor through the SIM project as a formative part of his ministerial training and "almost a forecasting of the fact that my work would be across boundaries. It opened up the world of interracial activity, making it a norm. For me, my world became not an isolated black existence but a world in which black and white had commerce together on many different levels . . . so that living in a subset was no longer a natural way to be. Binkley was a boot camp for the extended interracial ministry that I would experience."[91]

For his part, Robert Seymour continued on, even more determined after his work with young Forbes to use the pulpit for social justice. In May 1963, Seymour attended the Southern Baptist Convention in Kansas City and proposed a resolution against prejudice in the church and in support of the protesters, including Rev. Martin Luther King Jr., who at the time was in jail for marching against discrimination in Birmingham, Alabama. The convention would not even hear the mild words of Seymour's resolution; it was shouted down and then buried in committee. It did, however, get written up in the newspapers, and in the weeks that followed, the hate mail again flowed into Dr. Seymour's church. One woman from Texas invoked the supposed biblical curse of Ham, while another writer from Alabama wrote, "Us Baptists in Birmingham know you're a communist listed with J. Edgar Hoover in Washington—you're red. Hoping you're git your ears trimmed at convention in future."[92] Seymour recalled later, "I think it fair to say that I was pretty well labeled during those years as a person who was concerned with this issue [of racial equality] and almost nothing else. I have been virtually ignored and isolated by North Carolina Baptist churches since the Sixties."[93]

Seymour had a strong influence not just on Forbes but on others as well. Dean Smith, the soon-to-be-legendary head basketball coach for the University of North Carolina Tar Heels, joined Binkley Baptist Church with his wife, Ann, in 1959, when he was still an assistant coach. Seymour immediately asked him to serve as the chair of the church's Student Affairs Committee and influenced him in the recruitment of black athletes. Smith also joined Seymour and a black colleague for a meal that effectively integrated the Pines, a venerable Chapel Hill restaurant that served as the site for the basketball team's press conferences and for their pregame meals. The three-some was served promptly and without comment. Seymour recalled that this incident took place around 1964, but author Art Chansky locates it in 1959, just after Seymour arrived at Binkley.[94] In either case, the incident became part of the Dean Smith legend, and in a 1982 *Sports Illustrated* article, it was again recounted, alongside a picture of Robert Seymour and Coach Smith.[95] Smith also recalled, "My pastor, Dr. Robert Seymour, said my first job was to get a black athlete. Of course, I was well aware of that and wanted to."[96] The first two black players Smith recruited were unable to join the team because of academic reasons, so it was not until 1966 that Smith succeeded by bringing Charlie Scott to the team, UNC's first black scholarship athlete. Smith was eager to make Scott feel welcome, and he reached out to black Binkley congregants Howard and Lillian Lee, who would serve as Scott's Chapel Hill "parents" throughout his time as a Tar Heel. Howard Lee himself, with Seymour's help, would in 1969 be elected mayor of Chapel Hill, the first North Carolina black mayor elected by a majority white electorate since Reconstruction.[97] Recalling his pastor's influence, Dean Smith later wrote, "Through the years, I have publicly taken 'controversial' stands on issues beyond race, such as supporting a verifiable freeze on nuclear weapons, ending the death penalty, and promoting tolerance for gays and lesbians. While I'd like to think that I would have taken these stands on my own, there is no doubt that the support of Bob Seymour and the faith community that he helped to create and foster encouraged me to speak out sooner and made it easier to do than would have been the case without him."[98]

S. Collins Kilburn, the white minister at the United Church in Raleigh, not far from Binkley Baptist, also hosted black SIM students. Of SIM and the changing church, he quoted the Jewish scholar Abraham Joshua Heschel, saying that religion in America had waned not because of its defeat by science but because it had become predictable and dull, bureaucratized, suburbanized, and out of touch with society. "The sins of the modern church are its isolation from life, its tired blood and its attachment to boredom. In contrast, the Student Interracial Ministry is exciting. It has to do with reality. It is a pioneering venture. It ploughs open some of the dry, parched ground and brings fresh soil to the surface."[99]

The project indeed produced exciting results in Chapel Hill. Binkley Baptist was but one church of many that participated in the SIM program over the subsequent years, but its story illustrates how the project tapped into existing forces for racial change in the South and how its own efforts could forward them in major ways through seemingly quiet interpersonal interaction. Robert Seymour was not as radical in his views or his approach as better-known Christian progressives like Howard Kester or Carlyle Marney. He was more classically liberal in his approach, and yet his theology of Christian humanism and the impact he had in his community were revolutionary for the times. He is proof of the varieties of resistance to southern racial mores and to the power of an individual to change them.

James Forbes's story shows that racial reconciliation took place at the individual level but in such a way as to continue to replicate itself to the point of creating great impact within the larger community and sometimes even farther away. As Seymour pointed out, racial inclusiveness was an ideal until Forbes stepped to the pulpit and gave form to the abstract. Like the proverbial pebble in the lake, his short stay in Chapel Hill caused a series of ripples of change that continued for years. He, too, absorbed the experience and carried it with him through his career and into the Riverside Church. Forbes's work in Chapel Hill and the ministry he did subsequently resulted directly from the Student Interracial Ministry's approach to Christian racial reconciliation. It was one of SIM's clear success stories. However, as the 1960s proceeded and the war for equal rights grew bloodier, new tactics were required.

CHAPTER THREE

These Walls Will Shake

New Forms of Ministry for Changing Times, 1962–1965

If by the church we mean the fellowship, both visible and invisible, of
those committed "in Christ," to each other and to the world, then the problems of the people . . . are the problems of the Church. Such problems include
urbanization, the population explosion, new interpretations of ministry, laity,
work, leisure, and the "holy." The churches are in for a shocking century. It will
be the century when the "churches" died and the Church was born again.
At least that is my hope!

—Ed Feaver, Student Interracial Ministry, 1966[1]

Following its successful summer of 1962, an energized SIM executive committee convened in the early fall. Responding to the fact that increased participation in the program and successful fund-raising brought with it new
institutional complexities, SIM administrators voted to create the organization's first paid staff position, a student coordinator who would start in
the late spring of 1963 and be underwritten by the Field Work Department
at Union Theological Seminary.[2] A second volunteer-staffed office was established in Chicago. The students also decided, after briefly considering
closer alliances with the Interseminary Movement and the National Council of Churches, to keep SIM independent and student-run. The project
shored up its financial footing as it grew, raising $13,500 during the year from
individuals, churches, denominational boards, and private foundations.
The Field Foundation and the William C. Whitney Foundation, known for
supporting social justice causes, each gave substantial support.[3]

As the SIM students began organizing that fall for the next summer, they
did so in the context of a number of nationally significant events that clearly
signaled the momentum of the civil rights movement. In September, two
Georgia churches that SNCC had used as voter registration sites were
burned, and in Mississippi, James Meredith was barred from entering the
University of Mississippi. When the U.S. Supreme Court intervened on
his behalf, riots engulfed the area, leading to two deaths. In November,
President John F. Kennedy eliminated segregation in federal housing by
executive order. And in Chicago in January 1963, the country's religious

establishment acknowledged its concern over racial issues at the National Conference on Religion and Race, the first national ecumenical meeting devoted solely to the topic of race. The conference brought together several hundred Protestant, Catholic, and Jewish clergy and laypeople, and featured a number of prominent speakers, including Martin Luther King Jr.; Jewish theologian Rabbi Abraham Joshua Heschel, a prominent white King ally; and Will Campbell, director of the National Council of Churches' Southern Project and one of SIM's advisers. Stephen Rose, who had participated in SIM in 1961 and now lived in Chicago, where he edited the magazine *Renewal,* also attended the conference. He was there both as a writer-editor for the magazine *Christianity and Crisis* and as a good friend of Will Campbell, whom he had first met and befriended while participating in SIM.

The conference included a number of breakout sessions designed to formulate specific proposals for action. Among the suggested plans was one for blacks to take memberships in predominantly white churches, and vice versa—a proposal that bore more than a passing resemblance to the SIM strategy. Other proposals suggested sponsoring voter education drives, forming small activist cells of laypeople within churches, and eliminating racial discrimination in church hiring practices.[4] Will Campbell, however, saw the gathering as too little too late, and used the occasion to chide church leaders for being too self-congratulatory about the little progress they had achieved on civil rights. Campbell, however, offered not just criticism but solutions, and he urged the churches and seminaries to widely adopt the Student Interracial Ministry project. He also argued that they embrace full integration of housing and promote scholarships for minorities to attend majority white colleges and universities.[5] It was to be one of the last times Campbell addressed the NCC, which had grown unwilling to support this rogue minister who spoke his mind. Before the year was out, Campbell had quit the Southern Project and retreated to the mountains of Tennessee, where he continued to play an important role in progressive Christian thinking, although more often as a writer in semi-seclusion than as a front-line leader. Martin Luther King Jr., another of SIM's advisers, also addressed the national gathering, hailing it as "the most significant and historic ever held for attacking racial injustice," despite the fact that he was the only black person to give one of the eleven major speeches. His public assessment of the conference, however, belied his declining faith in the white church as an ally in the black freedom struggle. He, too, was growing frustrated, and he did not hold back for long from addressing these shortcomings directly and in devastating fashion.[6]

A few days after King addressed the gathering in Chicago, George Wallace was inaugurated as governor of the state of Alabama, calling for "segregation now, segregation tomorrow, segregation forever."[7] King and the SCLC joined with the Alabama Christian Movement for Human Rights to launch the Birmingham campaign against segregation in early April. King was arrested and incarcerated in Birmingham while leading marches to desegregate the city. From his cell, King wrote what became known as "Letter from a Birmingham Jail," in which he excoriated white clergy for their lack of understanding and support of the black struggle. Incensed at having been termed an extremist by a group of Birmingham clergy, King responded that extremism, especially for those involved in the ministry, was necessitated by the times, but that the true question was about what kind of extremism was required: "Will we be extremists for hate or for love? Perhaps the South, the nation and the world are in dire need of creative extremists."[8]

Students back at Union Theological Seminary responded to King's letter by proposing an immediate and local plan of action. Val Frakes and Lefty Schultz asked their fellows students to address King's critiques within the churches that they were serving in New York. "We suggest," they wrote in the school paper, "that you go to your fieldwork churches this weekend and lay before them our responsibility as Christians to work and pray for equality and freedom for the Negro community—in the North as well as in the South."[9] Union students also held a fund-raiser to support a student to work directly with the Alabama Council on Human Relations for the summer and report to SIM directly from Birmingham.

In North Carolina, another member of the SIM network—Robert Seymour, who had so recently hosted black seminarian James Forbes at the Binkley Baptist Church in Chapel Hill—responded to King's jailing in Alabama. Seymour submitted a resolution on May 8, 1963, to the Southern Baptist Convention that he was attending in Kansas City. Seymour expressed solidarity with those fighting against segregation and called for the denomination to commit itself to eradicating discriminatory customs of all kinds, which he described as a violation of Christian witness. Seymour closed the resolution by asking that a message be sent to those jailed in Birmingham: "You who are free in there, pray for us who are in prison out here."[10] Lamar Jackson, a Birmingham minister, opposed Seymour's resolution, after which it was buried in committee and never revived. The *Christian Century* reported several weeks later that the convention had "ignored completely the oppressed Negro and the racial strife in that part of the nation where Southern Baptists are the predominant Christian body."[11] Despite Seymour's attempt to raise the subject, his denomination remained tight-lipped on racial change. Not all the churches were so mute, however. On May 20, 1963, the United Presbyterian Church (USA) established a commission on religion and race and provided $150,000 in support for the remainder of the year. The NCC followed in early June by establishing a new Commission on Religion and Race and backing it with $450,000 through the end of 1964.[12] And so it was in fits and starts that the national denominational and ecumenical bodies were at last moving forward on race.

This was the climate within which the Student Interracial Ministry convened its 1963 summer orientation weekend in Raleigh, North Carolina. A record twenty-eight student participants were off to work at placements in North Carolina, South Carolina, Tennessee, Georgia, Colorado, Washington D.C., Alabama, Missouri, Virginia, Texas, New York, and New Jersey. Of these, twenty-three were white and five black, with twenty-three men and five women; there were three married couples. And they came from fourteen different seminaries, universities, or colleges: there were ten students from Union Theological Seminary; four from the Interdenominational Theological Center (formerly Gammon) in Atlanta; two each from Bethany and Drew; and one each from Andover-Newton, Boston Theological, Hamma Divinity School, McCormick, Emory, Vanderbilt, Nazarene Theological, Biblical Theological, Wesleyan, and Western Theological. The program had certainly extended its reach and found willing participants across the nation.

J. Oscar McCloud, Collins Kilburn, and Robert Seymour—North Carolina ministers who had participated in SIM the previous summer—kicked off the orientation program on Monday, June 3, 1963. They were joined by a panel of lay members from the Raleigh churches that had previously hosted SIM students and by James Forbes, who had worked with Binkley Baptist Church in Chapel Hill and was now representing his new church in Wilmington, North Carolina. Much of the orientation was spent in group sessions, such as one that closely examined stereotypes held between the races and by some of the students brave enough to admit them, and the students and ministers role-played several scenarios, including a typical encounter on a segregated bus and a SIM student's first meeting with a host pastor.[13]

The summer of 1963 also featured two firsts for the SIM program: two of the students would stay on for yearlong internships following their summer placements, and a noncongregational placement was made, that of George McClain with the Alabama Council on Human Relations in Birmingham. Working with the Reverend Norman Jimerson, McClain would be right in the heat of the battle that was Birmingham that summer. In fact, SIM itself could be said to be at the heart of the southern civil rights movement in the summer of 1963, as students worked with a number of the movement's national leaders. Bob Carey of Union Theological Seminary worked in Atlanta with Revs. Martin Luther King Jr. and his father, Robert Sullivan of Nazarene Theological Seminary worked in Nashville with Rev. Kelly Miller Smith, Ronald Young of Wesleyan University worked in Memphis with Rev. James Lawson, and Bud Walker of Union worked in Atlanta with Rev. Ralph Abernathy, who had learned of the program through Martin Luther King Jr.

George McClain, whose work with the Alabama Council on Human Relations had been supported by a UTS fund-raiser, arrived in Birmingham soon after the notorious police chief Bull Connor was removed from office. City officials had just reached an agreement with demonstrators and consented to integrate public accommodations later that summer. Nevertheless, McClain found the city "still very much divided and rent by fear," with a "corresponding gulf" between blacks and whites and a great deal of apprehension on all parts around the coming desegregation plan.[14] Whites, he reported, felt the demonstrations unnecessary given that progress was being made, while black leaders said they had no reason to believe anything would be achieved without applying pressure. Nevertheless, McClain found a certain amount of exhilaration in the middle of the fray, both of the southern civil rights movement and of the churches' attempt to work relevantly in this context. Writing before the planned desegregation deadline of July 23, 1963, he reported that at the very least, the demonstrations had "given the traditionally passive Negro community genuine hope for a change." That "newly found courage and enthusiasm" was being used to bolster a voter registration drive, and McClain couldn't help but feel "the excitement of helping to create a new church and a new world—you knew what you were working against."[15] However, he also predicted that if the courts required school desegregation in September, the biggest furor would come from George Wallace and "local extremists." He was painfully prescient. On September 15, 1963, less than a month after McClain returned to Union, members of the Alabama Ku Klux Klan bombed the 16th Street Baptist Church in Birmingham, killing four African American schoolgirls.

Bob Carey, a white Methodist from Connecticut, had graduated from Wesleyan University before attending Union Theological Seminary as a Rockefeller fellow. While still an undergraduate, he and some friends had organized demonstrations at a Woolworth's store in downtown Middletown,

Connecticut, in sympathy with the sit-ins in North Carolina. Carey was also a veteran of Operations Crossroads Africa, the same mission-oriented project that had inspired Steve Rose to come to Union, and had served in Dahomey, in what is now Benin. At Union, where he was uncertain whether or not he would go into the parish ministry, he met John Collins and became interested in SIM and the civil rights movement, "an issue that was very much in the air."[16] Carey recommended that SIM adopt an intern-year program as well, since "the summer is too short. One needs to get 'integration' out of his system so that he can encounter and be encountered as he is himself, not an abstraction."[17] It took time to get beyond the novelty of the interracial experience to a place where, it was hoped, racial reconciliation might be possible. Carey was selected, "by the luck of the draw," to spend his yearlong internship with Daddy King at Ebenezer Church in Atlanta. He had enough of a sense of the momentousness of such a posting, though, to travel south by train rather than flying. "I thought I'd be very historic," he later joked, "and go by train." He initially lived with "Daddy and Mother King," as he was to call them, in their own home, before getting lodging at the nearby Mennonite House, run by the Mennonite Central Committee under the direction of historian, activist, and Martin Luther King Jr. associate Vincent Harding. At Ebenezer, Carey worked with the youth group, did hospital calls, and attended to other parish business, getting to "know the texture and the daily life of the parish and the importance of it." He recalled later sitting in the Ebenezer offices with Daddy King listening to the radio coverage of the assassination of President Kennedy. "Johnson will be all right," King commented.[18]

At one point, Carey took kids from the Ebenezer youth group on a picnic to a state park northwest of Atlanta. He was driving the church car, a mid-fifties Ford station wagon in a high state of disrepair. "As luck would have it," Carey recalled, "the whole tailpipe fell off and it was really just clatteringly loud. And we came over a rise and down at the foot of this hill were Georgia state troopers. And needless to say we were pulled over." Carey was arrested and placed in jail by an "icy cold" judge in Decatur until bail could be raised, introducing him to "the swift realities of the power that people with guns have." He said later that this gave him insight into "how people got disappeared. That burned itself into my mind, always just beneath the surface of that 'y'all' is the capacity for sudden and brutal violence. You never forget that, and you live with that. That was the deeply sad part—that you realized that this is very, very close to the surface in American life."[19] The following year, when three civil rights workers went missing in Mississippi in the opening days of Freedom Summer, the rest of the nation would realize it too.

Carey also spent time working on the SCLC's local initiatives, including the early Operation Breadbasket project, targeting local employment practices among other efforts. He also got to know Georgia state representative Ben Brown and a number of the SNCC workers based in Atlanta, including Julian Bond; at one point, he drove to the Georgia sea islands with Dorothy Cotton to attend a SNCC training session.[20] After Carey's internship year officially ended, he stayed on for a second year in Atlanta, working on after-school programs and a few other projects at Ebenezer but primarily working with the Greater Atlanta Council on Human Relations as acting director, while Eliza Paschall took a sabbatical leave. His office was on the same floor of a building with Les Dunbar, Vernon Jordan, and the Southern Regional Council.[21]

Carey knew interracial experiences rather personally, having several years earlier begun dating Pat, a black woman from Chicago and a fellow Operation Crossroads volunteer. Bob and Pat's relationship had continued after he entered Union Theological Seminary and Pat went to Michigan State to study for a master's degree in psychology. After Bob's second year in Atlanta, he married Pat in Chicago, interracial marriage still being illegal in Georgia. He recalled that they went into an Atlanta jewelry store on separate days to pick out their rings, lest they alert locals to their intent. Even in the civil rights environment of Ebenezer Church and in the Mennonite commune in which they lived, Bob and Pat's relationship was unique and sometimes a challenge. "The first time I attended the church service," Pat later recalled, "Daddy King was trying to introduce me . . . and he could not . . . he didn't know how to introduce me. Because it was so startling to him. . . . I don't think he knew [before he met me that] I was black. He says, 'Well, Bob Carey . . . I want to introduce Bob Carey's . . . well, Bob has a friend . . . well, uh . . . well, Pat, just stand up."[22] Carey was one of two white SIM students that summer who were in interracial long-term relationships; Robert Sullivan reported from Nashville that his mixed marriage had not garnered much attention from the locals, who he thought regarded it as "a matter of course." Exactly which locals he meant, white or black, he didn't specify.[23] As for Bob and Pat, after his arrest in Decatur, Carey was more on guard about possible reactions. He remembered that one night, coming home late from a party and driving through the backstreets of Atlanta, he had Pat lie down in the back of the car lest they be spotted as an interracial couple and get pulled over by the police again. "I didn't want any trouble, didn't want to invite it [because] I knew they were out there lurking."[24]

Bob and later Pat, by virtue of his work and their residence at Mennonite House, were often right in the middle of the civil rights movement during those two years. Mennonite House especially, in ways similar to Highlander Center in Tennessee, "was something of a catbird seat in terms of the people coming and going from South[west] Georgia and the Mississippi [Freedom] Summer and all of that." The Mennonite Church has a strong tradition of community service, and Mennonite House served as a place where Mennonites, mostly from the Midwest, came to do two years or so of service, working with schools in Atlanta or in the social service sector. But during this period of increased civil rights activity, a number of others stayed at the house for varying amounts of time, among them Septima Clark—"she had a little room to herself off the landing, a totally awesome woman," Carey later recalled. So many folks were "backing and forthing" that a second house on Houston Street was added to the Mennonite complex before Bob and Pat left for Chicago in the summer of 1965. During Freedom Summer especially, Mennonite House was full of people coming and going to various movement campaigns and locations.[25]

Rinaldo Walker, who went by the nickname Bud, landed another of the high-profile SIM postings, working with Ralph Abernathy at West Hunter Street Baptist Church in Atlanta. Born in Missouri and raised mostly in Clinton, Mississippi, Walker had attended Mississippi College, a segregated Southern Baptist school, where he had been elected both class president and "Mr. Mississippi." As class president, Walker normally presided over Sunday chapel, but one morning the college's guest was future Mississippi governor Ross Barnett, who proceeded to deliver "a forty-five minute segregationist harangue and defamation of Gunnar Myrdal."[26] When Barnett concluded, Walker took the podium to close the service with a prayer, saying, "Oh God, in this institution of truth and virtue [the college's motto], help us to see all of your truth." A faculty member later congratulated him for delivering the shortest ever rebuttal.[27] After college, Walker spent two years in the Marines and one year in an English master's program at the University of North Carolina before accepting a Rockefeller grant to Union Theological Seminary. As it had done for other southerners before him, Union introduced Walker to brand-new ways of looking at the world. One notable experience was listening to and meeting Bayard Rustin at a seminar talk in 1959. Walker noted at the time, "To hear him talk, I felt a sense of calling. . . . He was in a word clearly prophetic."[28]

Along with Jane Stembridge, Walker had been the other future SIM participant to attend the conference in Raleigh over Easter weekend back in 1960, the gathering at which both SNCC and SIM were created. At Union, he had spent two years doing fieldwork at the East Harlem Protestant Parish. Now, three years later, Walker was deeply moved by his personal experience of Abernathy, who was navigating a congregation in which two generations had different expectations for change while also playing a leading role in the national movement through the SCLC. "His Christ-like spirit and huge capacity for work," Walker wrote of Abernathy, "are at the same time inspiring and staggering. One feels immediately the tension between love and justice—the prophetic and the pastoral. The problems are thorny and complex: there are no easy solutions. Perhaps this is the best possible introduction that I could have to beginning a ministry in the South." Walker, however, saw that such a ministry, one that combined love and faith in God with a desire to create meaningful change in the immediate present, would not be easy. "I find myself continually caught [between] a desire to see social, economic, and political justice achieved and . . . the command to preach and teach the gospel of God's reconciling love and ministry of compassion."[29] This commonly experienced tension had only recently been eloquently—and adamantly—addressed by Martin Luther King Jr. in his "Letter from Birmingham Jail," which had been published under the title "Why We Cannot Wait." It was also a common theme upon which numerous SIM students, reconciling their faith with the world and trying to find appropriate roles for themselves, mused in great detail.

Walker lived with Ralph and Juanita Abernathy at their home, and spent most of the summer working with the church's youth group. A month after his sojourn with Abernathy had ended, Walker took careful note of the bomb that took four little girls' lives at a church in Birmingham. Although his seminary study, work in East Harlem, and SIM placement with Abernathy had been important steps in his personal journey of reconciliation, the bombing was a turning point for him. He and a number of other Union students, he recalled, " 'made a pledge that racial justice and reconciliation would be an important part of our ministry for the rest of our lives.' "[30]

Other students served with less famous but equally adventurous clergy members in Winston-Salem, North Carolina; Macon, Georgia; and

Portsmouth, Virginia, among other places. Although the students' primary duties were as assistant pastors tending to church business, they also immersed themselves in the lives of each congregation, participating as members of the community. The students were expected both to lead and to follow their new flocks, wherever they went, and the seminarians at times found themselves engaged beyond the confines of the local church. They accompanied congregants not only to picnics, beach outings, and basketball games, but also to newly formed interracial ministerial association meetings, biracial community negotiations, voter registration drives, and picket lines outside segregated businesses. The reports students sent back from their assignments, however, reflected the fact that the civil rights movement in 1963 was far from cohesive and that in different locations, it had proceeded in different directions and at different paces. While some students found that little headway had been made in achieving even basic integration of public facilities, others worked in areas with a high degree of integration and that seemed to be proceeding relatively quietly and peacefully. In some areas, it seemed that the civil rights movement hardly existed. In others, change was coming at breakneck speed.

No matter their situation, the students kept abreast of each other's activities as well as of other events throughout the South during that turbulent summer, which saw the beatings and deaths of black leaders, the registration of numerous black Mississippi voters, and the beginning of federal civil rights legislation. Events unfolded quickly. On June 9, 1963, just days after the students arrived at their postings fresh from the orientation in Raleigh, Fannie Lou Hamer and other SNCC workers were arrested in Winona, Mississippi, and badly beaten by police.[31] Two days later, Alabama governor George Wallace made "the stand in the schoolhouse door," trying to prevent the enrollment of two black students at the University of Alabama. The same day, President John F. Kennedy addressed the nation via television and radio to deliver what became known as the Civil Rights Address, in which he proposed the Civil Rights Act of 1964 and described the achievement of civil rights not as a legal act but as a moral imperative.[32] The next day, June 12, 1963, NAACP activist and community leader Medgar Evers was murdered in Jackson, Mississippi. One week later, on June 19, President Kennedy sent the Civil Rights Act to Congress. The hectic summer of civil rights would reach its crescendo in late August with the March on Washington for Jobs and Freedom, with a number of SIM students, clergy, and congregation members in the audience, and with one SIM host pastor, Martin Luther King Jr. himself, standing at the rostrum.

But as the summer began, not all was excitement for every student. Donald Black, who served with Orval Black at a Presbyterian church in Nashville, was disappointed by the staid atmosphere at his small middle-class black church and by the relative lack of civil rights activity in Nashville. Black complained, "Many people have begun to feel that the battle is over, not just starting."[33] This peace could be attributed to Nashville's early and particularly enthusiastic complement of young civil rights leaders, as well as a function of several years of successful efforts and the cooperation of the mayor and his Human Rights Committee. But Nashville was the exception rather than the rule. In Raleigh, North Carolina, white seminarian Charles Boyer worked in a black church, and he and his wife boarded with an African American widow in a black neighborhood, where their presence roused the ire of segregationists. The Boyers and their host were awakened one night by the sight of a crude cross, wrapped in paper towels soaked with motor oil, burning on the front lawn. At another point during the summer, Boyer was excited to hear that North Carolina governor Terry Sanford had called a meeting of black leaders in Raleigh, where a series of pickets of segregated businesses was underway. Expecting an important announcement from the governor and an equally strong response from the black community, Boyer was frustrated to hear Sanford instead order that civil rights protests in the capital city cease immediately. Boyer was equally dismayed by the fumbling response from black leaders, whom he characterized as disunited and disorganized. "I don't know with whom I was more disgusted," he commented, "the whites or the Negroes."[34]

Whereas Black worried that he had missed the main thrust of the civil rights campaign in Nashville and Boyer found himself in the confusing middle stage of the Raleigh fight, Douglas Parks managed to alight in Charleston, South Carolina, on the same day that the NAACP's national leadership arrived to begin a major statewide campaign to integrate public facilities. The NAACP worked through a network of local churches that turned out crowds as large as two thousand people for twice-daily mass meetings, prompting Parks to write, "This is the church in the street, this is the church at work!"[35]

The students also experienced a range of personal responses, from a sense of having gained a greater understanding of the black situation to experiencing guilt and shame at white contributions to black degradation, arguing that racial reconciliation could be achieved through personal interaction, and believing that God was working through them and the people of the church to heal racial tensions. Thomas Hoyt, a black seminarian from the

Interdenominational Theological Center in Atlanta, who had been born in Alabama and raised in Indiana, wrote from a white church in Colorado Springs, Colorado: "It is my opinion that via this method of reconciliation to God through Jesus, we shall break down the walls of segregation, fear, prejudice, mistrust, hatred and guilt. Laws cannot do what a changed heart, mind or attitude can do." He went on to say that civil rights laws could regulate behavior and mandate desegregation of certain parts of society, but that it was up to the church and programs like SIM to change people's hearts. "Through SIM," he wrote, "I can see the hand of God moving."[36]

George McClain, back in Birmingham, agreed. "In the midst of a society wrent [sic] asunder," he wrote, "a kind of eschatological vision compels certain people to work courageously even in the darkest hours for its transformation and healing . . . a genuinely Christian vision of an open society ruled by love."[37]

Another student, Daniel Klement, who worked in a black church in northeastern Washington D.C., had to keep reminding himself that his work and his daily interaction with black folks was based in an attempt to "live out the faith." Inherent, but unexplored, in his reports back to SIM headquarters was the frustrated conclusion that activities like community organizing or running teen recreation programs could easily be considered secular and, but for his constant effort to remain grounded in faith, would have little effect on the church as an institution or on himself as a minister.[38]

Ronald Young, who served with the Reverend James Lawson in Memphis, had some similarly frustrating experiences—at one point while leading three church baseball teams, he feared he had become more coach than pastor—but the overall experience "allowed [him] to have challenging glimpses of the true nature of the Christian church." Young, whose SIM summer was part of a full year spent at Lawson's Centenary Methodist Church, returned to college at Wesleyan "quite a different person," having gained "a heightened awareness of the tragedy of racial discrimination, but also a very strong sense of the redemptive possibilities of genuine reconciliation upon individuals, both Negro and white, and upon the nation as a whole."[39] He also recounted a story to illustrate the personal nature of change as the members of the church began to see him "now most fundamentally a person instead of a 'white man.' Just the other day, Mrs. Lawson, in trying to convince our choir director that a certain meeting downtown was open to Negroes, said, 'Yes, I am sure [it] was open, Ron went.' Mr. Bond laughed and answered, 'Yes, but Ron is white.' 'Oh, I had forgotten,' replied Mrs. Lawson."[40] Again and again, white SIM students' reports demonstrated delight at being "mistaken" for black, taken by them as a true sign of acceptance.

Students who engaged in urban ministry that summer learned that it could differ greatly from scholarly portrayals of the inner-city church. Most discussions of urban church flight and suburban church captivity assumed that those few white churches that stayed in urban areas adapted to a non-white congregation and that black churches that remained had no problem attracting black congregants.[41] Robert Lynn's experience at the black Liberty Baptist Church in Atlanta challenged this easy understanding. Much of the housing in the urban landscape around the church building had been cleared as part of urban renewal, and nearby neighbors—the church's traditional attendees—had relocated to other parts of town. The church had literally been stranded, a lone edifice in a now largely vacant neighborhood; and without adequate private or public transportation, traveling downtown to attend the church became a burden for its poor and working-class members. To help, the church created a transportation committee and carpool and worked to raise funds for a communal church vehicle.[42]

Warren Moore served his internship with the Northside Community Church in Kansas City, Missouri, where he was one of sixteen members of a summer project called the Service Corps of the Christian Inner-City Council of Kansas City. One of the few black students in the program, he lived and worked communally with the other corps members, most of whom were undergraduate college students, in an urban environment he described as "a crisis situation."[43] He spent much of his summer trying to help negotiate an agreement between the city's housing officials and the tenants of a housing project who were trying to establish a new community playground. Because of his willingness to listen to their needs and to appeal to city officials on their behalf, he gradually won the tenants' acceptance, but he stressed, "I was given no quarters due to my black skin."

The Northside Community Church was a pilot inner-city mission project of an all-white Presbyterian Church. Large parts of the congregation had not bought in to the new mission, nor did they endorse Moore's presence among them, and some tried to pit Moore and the senior pastor against each other in arguments over these issues. This caused Moore to wonder if his presence in Northside would result in sustained interracial contact and greater understanding, or if it would have a net negative effect. By the time he left Kansas City, the answer was still not clear. Nevertheless, Moore found the experience a profoundly enriching—and religious—one. The language with which he described the interracial ministry testified to the intensity of his conversion experience. "I can only submit," Moore wrote," that the experience is a genuine opportunity for any sincere seeker to do significant work, while finding himself. He may come to know the will of God through a concerted effort to implement the proclamation of the Gospel."[44]

Students like Moore understood their acts as a radical Christian witness to God's intended plan for brotherhood and equality on earth. A personal witness, seemingly a quiet, individual act, could shock the sensibilities of a community and often resulted in strong reactions. Of all the summer placements in 1963, that of David W. Jones, who was assigned to work with a church in Wilmington, North Carolina, best illustrates the clash that could result from taking one's ministry into the street, even in such a seemingly personal and earnest way as praying and singing on the steps of a courthouse. What began as a simple and peaceful ecclesiastic protest eventually led to harangues by Jesse Helms and attacks on the National Council of Churches itself.

Wilmington, the site of an 1898 race riot that resulted in the deaths of at least twenty-two African Americans, was a city not historically noted for its progressive race relations.[45] Jones, a young white Presbyterian from St. Louis, Missouri, and a student at McCormick Seminary, came to serve in the Gregory United Church of Christ, a middle-class, black Congregational church. According to the pastor, George Gay, Gregory United's congregants were an unlikely group to challenge the racial status quo; rather, they primarily "worshipped the great god suburbia" and seemed unlikely to do anything that might endanger their upper-middle-class standing. As associate pastor, Jones participated in all sorts of traditional church activities, and when Reverend Gay left for the month of July, Jones filled in by preaching Sunday sermons and recording a series of five meditations for broadcast on local radio. He supervised the vacation bible school, was guest preacher at an African Methodist Episcopal Church, and led a church study group.

Jones found that Gregory United's parishioners were a relatively exclusive group, with little interest in social protest. However, he sensed this might be changing as a result of the willingness of a local NAACP youth group to take a leading role in demanding social change. Soon after his arrival in town, the NAACP youth group began planning demonstrations against segregated restaurants, and Jones "was fortunate enough to get in on the ground floor of these meetings and be generally accepted as one of the student demonstrators." Jones joined about fifty students in an attempt to integrate Wilmington's leading cafeteria on June 12 and was arrested along with everyone else. Two days later, a larger group of students staged a second round of demonstrations, and they were also arrested. When it was over, 131 black demonstrators and one white demonstrator, Jones, had been arrested for trespass and one white cafeteria owner had been arrested on two charges of assault. All of the arrested demonstrators stayed a night in the Wilmington jail before being released. Jones, being white, was held in a separate cell, where he "received a slight beating by the inmates."[46]

After these arrests, members of a newly formed biracial civic committee agreed to suspend demonstrations in favor of negotiating with the city government for the desegregation of all public facilities by July 8. Jones wrote from Wilmington to SIM headquarters in New York at the beginning of July to report that the negotiations had failed and demonstrations were due to resume on July 9. The youth group members planned to seek service at a number of restaurants, while the members of the black Ministerial Alliance, with Jones among them, led a silent march to city hall.[47]

The demonstrations began as planned on July 9, but when the ministers reached city hall, they found the area outside blocked by construction, so they moved across the street to the steps of the county courthouse. There the ministers talked, led prayers, and sang freedom songs. Events then took a dramatic turn. Judge H. Winfield Smith, the same judge who was scheduled to hear the case of the June arrests in a matter of days, was at the time holding a session of the recorder's court inside the building. The judge became enraged at the singing and praying, which he claimed "broke up" his court so that it could not function.[48]

Judge Smith ordered all ninety-seven demonstrators, including nine black ministers, arrested on the spot and marched directly into his courtroom, where he subjected them to an angry lecture that the local paper described as "one of the stiffest tongue-lashings ever heard in a local court." When he at last finished yelling, he sentenced all present to thirty days for contempt of court. The next day, Judge Smith dismissed the charges against all the demonstrators except Jones. He called Jones forward to the bench, asked why he had lied about being assaulted while in jail in June, and finally accused him of coming down South for the purpose of riling up the local black population. "People like you are causing all of this. You are trying to intimidate whites. They have some rights, too, and this has got to stop." As he sentenced Jones to thirty days in prison, Judge Smith scolded him, "You are just as sorry as you can be." Smith added that Jones and any other future demonstrators could "sing all they want to" in jail, "and if they bothered people there, we'll move them out to the county farm where they won't bother anybody."[49]

In charging Jones alone with being responsible and painting him as an outside agitator who had caused Wilmington's blacks to rise up in protest, Judge Smith invoked what was by then classic segregationist rhetoric: the assumption that the only way local blacks could have been inspired to protest a perfectly good system was if they had been stirred up by foreign provocateurs, usually from the North. "The NAACP," Judge Smith proclaimed from the bench, "is just as bad as the Ku Klux Klan."[50]

After Jones's arrest, the local black community rallied to his aid, passing food to him and singing freedom songs with him, forging an even closer bond through the bars of his jail cell. Jones himself came to believe that his incarceration became the bedrock of the work of reconciliation he was attempting that summer. He believed that many blacks in Wilmington "came to view their strife for freedom no longer as black against white, but as members of both races proclaiming the truth about all men as children of God against the old myths of racism." Before his arrest, he wrote that the acknowledgment of the real nature of the struggle was largely academic; afterwards, it "became for a large number of Wilmington people a living conviction because they finally actually saw 'black and white together now.' "[51]

Jones later reflected that he could understand how some might believe that in joining a public protest he had veered beyond an assistant pastor's appropriate expression of concern about racial issues. He said he would leave that discussion to the Christian ethicists, but he held out little hope that they would understand. "There was growing in me the feeling that the Christian witness I hoped to establish by my identification with the Negro community could not realistically be contained strictly within the life of the church." By taking his witness into the streets, Jones reported that he understood himself to be part of the prophetic tradition of Amos and Isaiah.[52] Martin Luther King Jr. was also particularly fond of the prophets and invoked their example in relation to his own public campaigns.

At least one man, interviewed by the local black newspaper, agreed that the young seminarian had made a step in the direction of racial reconciliation and had, to his mind, redeemed a suspect church. "I have changed my mind on religion. The Rev. Mr. Jones, a white man, has shown us Christianity in action. The people who profess to follow Christ and treat the Negro so badly are not Christians. But, the Rev. Mr. Jones has demonstrated what Christ preached. Here is a man ready to lay down his life for a friend, be he a black one."[53] Jones's witness, it would seem, had indeed been effective.

The arrest of David Jones caused a ripple effect that emanated from Wilmington to the state capital at Raleigh, where, in the hands of conservative television journalist and future senator Jesse Helms, it turned into a smear campaign against the National Council of Churches. Among the items in Jones's pockets at the time of his July arrest was his paycheck from SIM, drawn on an NCC bank account, with the memo: "Grant for participating in Student Interracial Ministry program." Facsimiles of the check mysteriously found their way from the police station to the media and into the hands of segregationists. Pictures of the check were used in newspaper advertisements deriding the support of the NCC. In an evening WRAL-TV news editorial on Jones's arrest, Helms reported that the NCC was underwriting outsiders to come down and "meddle" in North Carolina's business.[54] These inflammatory remarks spread throughout the South and generated negative letters and complaints from NCC members from as far away as Virginia, Alabama, and Florida. In a typical letter, a minister from Monroe, North Carolina—in the central part of the state—castigated the NCC for supporting "young Jones, [who] had precious little time for preaching, [but] instead . . . spent his time leading masses of young Negroes through the downtown section of Wilmington."[55]

Jones's arrest and the ensuing media hullabaloo caught the NCC at a vulnerable time on the race issue. Throughout the 1950s and into the early 1960s, the NCC had taken only cautious steps in calling for an end to segregation or committing itself to the civil rights movement.[56] As a consequence, it was left on the sidelines of a movement that many, both within and outside the church, felt it should be leading. The council thus reacted to the Jones affair in its usual conservative fashion when it came to issues of race. However, contained within that response could be seen the glimmer of a changing attitude. Indeed, less than a month after Jones's July arrest, former NCC president Eugene Carson Blake addressed the crowd at the March on Washington, admitting that the churches had come to the cause too late.

But others at the NCC did not deal with the Jones situation in a similar tenor. NCC administrators could have used the opportunity to make their own Christian witness, to stand behind one of the student members of a project it had been sponsoring for several years. Instead, the council panicked in the face of negative press coverage and went to some lengths to distance itself from Jones and SIM. Fletcher Coates, executive director of the NCC's Department of Information, fired off a memo to J. Oscar Lee complaining that the NCC now had another public relations mess on its hands. Coates chastised Jones for letting the police copy his check, and requested that SIM find another fiscal agent to handle its payroll. Coates wrote, "There is, as I see it, no moral or ethical issue involved in this suggestion, just simple common sense."[57]

Roger Shinn traveled down from Union Theological Seminary to Wilmington to plead Jones's case in person while Lee defended Jones to the National Council of Churches, pointing out that the NCC was much more to the Student Interracial Ministry than a fiscal agent. Since March 1961, the Student Interracial Ministry had been in effect a cooperative effort between the SIM committee at Union and the NCC, Lee argued. "It would be poor judgment of the Department to consider transferring or repudiating a program that it has had an integral part in developing, merely because irresponsible sources are misinterpreting it for their own purposes."[58] The NCC ignored Lee's pleas and continued to portray SIM as a distantly related and "informally organized group . . . of theological students," not as a project that the council had directly sponsored for the past three years. The council's response to the Jones case in fact indicates just how conflicted the NCC was about when and in what way to join the racial struggle. As late as 1963, it was reacting to the Jones situation with confusion and a seeming unwillingness to defend its own program according to its own stated beliefs.

Another sign of the confusion was that at the same time as it was distancing itself from Lee and the Student Interracial Ministry, the NCC was in fact quietly making some of its largest forward steps on race issues. It is even possible that the Jones situation in some way ruined the council's plans to announce its new efforts to engage with the southern situation. A group of black cultural and intellectual leaders—including writer James Baldwin, sociologist Kenneth Clark, playwright Lorraine Hansberry, and singers Harry Belafonte and Lena Horne—had approached the NCC in May, calling for its greater involvement in the racial crisis. The General Board of the Council responded to this request and other pressure from its member denominations by creating the Commission on Religion and Race on June 7, 1963. The board chose to directly supervise the new commission itself as a way of bypassing bureaucracy and guaranteeing that money would flow quickly to its projects. However, by creating the Commission on Religion and Race in this way, the General Board effectively sidelined J. Oscar Lee and the Department of Racial and Cultural Relations, cutting them out of the NCC's racial justice efforts. The Department of Racial and Cultural Relations had been working toward this end since 1903, and now Lee and his office were shunted to one side in favor of a young white minister, Robert Spike, who was named the director of the new commission and granted nearly unprecedented autonomy and a sizable budget.[59]

In passing over an experienced black leader for a young white pastor to direct the commission, the NCC dismissed Lee and his office as a Negro toiling at Negro matters. Announcing the formation of the new commission, a spokesman for the council even seemed to implicate Lee in the NCC's formerly slow progress on race issues, claiming that the days of gradualism had passed. "Up to now," he said, "modest tokens of progress in racial justice were accepted as the best we could do. . . . This summer may be a decisive period in American history for beginning to deal with this haunting sin. The world watches to see how we will act—whether with courage or with fumbling expediency."[60] However, in trying to paint its new effort as a radical involvement in racial justice, the council downplayed and dismissed its previous efforts, hardly acknowledging Will Campbell's Southern Project, J. Oscar Lee and the sixty-year track record of the Department of Racial and Cultural Relations, or the Student Interracial Ministry project. Perhaps NCC leaders ignored these continuing efforts largely because they saw them as outside of their direct control, and the flap over David Jones's work in Wilmington was just further irritation.

At one point in the drama over the Jones arrest, an NCC executive did acknowledge the work of the Student Interracial Ministry, saying that it would "hopefully lead to the broad kind of fellowship within the church which Christ clearly asked his followers to establish."[61] But a closer relationship between SIM and the council's new commission was not to be. SIM was closely tied with J. Oscar Lee and the Department of Racial and Cultural Relations, and that department was now old hat. In fact, the council's Southern Project, which had only ever had about one-tenth of the budget granted the new commission, was shuttered for good, and Will Campbell left the council at the end of the year. Had the NCC addressed its new efforts on race through its established programs, Lee and the Student Interracial Ministry might have taken a much larger and more public role than they did. Instead, they were both left to continue their work with little institutional support.

The NCC, though, did finally begin to take very public stands, embracing the kind of prophetic witness that the Student Interracial Ministry had long employed. The new Commission on Religion and Race, with the encouragement of Jewish and Roman Catholic leaders, prioritized the passage of a federal civil rights act. Religious leaders met with President Kennedy on June 17, 1963, in a meeting led by NCC president J. Irwin Miller. Kennedy's suggestion that Miller chair the meeting and lead follow-up efforts points to the close ties between the liberal establishment church and the presidency, and also signals the turn that both had just made toward seriously addressing the racial crisis.[62]

Attempting to make up for lost time, the NCC hurried to make sure it was well represented at the March on Washington for Freedom and Jobs on August 28, 1963. The Commission on Religion and Race led that effort, coordinated by a new black staffer, Dr. Anna Hedgeman, a long-time organizer within another large religious body, Church Women United. About 40,000 church people joined the March on Washington, a significant percentage of the estimated 250,000 who attended.[63] Student Interracial Ministry students and host pastors were among the marchers that day, including Bob Hare from Richmond, Virginia, who would host some of SIM's first experiments in urban ministry. Hare, though white, was pastor at a black church in Richmond and brought a group of his parishioners to the march, where they stood right at the front of the crowd, within easy view of the speakers.[64] Bud Walker, who had interned with Ralph Abernathy and was now serving as the director of religious activities at Meredith College in Raleigh, North Carolina, was also in attendance with a small group of female students.[65] On the return trip, Walker's bus was stopped by police and detained for an hour in a police department parking lot.[66] George McClain, who had spent his SIM assignment with the Alabama Council on Human Relations, was also in Washington, one of two whites on the six buses of movement folk who had ridden up from Birmingham.[67]

The National Council of Churches was represented both on the podium and behind the scenes, where council volunteers put together some 80,000 box lunches—composed of a cheese sandwich, an apple, and a slice of pound cake—available to marchers for fifty cents each.[68] The council was also represented within the crowd of marchers by a delegation of some one hundred clergy council members, many in religious regalia. Robert Spike described the appearance of this delegation as "an act so full of symbolism that no one could escape it." Spike felt "the satisfaction that we were no longer token representatives. The power of Protestantism was marching with us, and we had a right to be there at long last."[69]

Eugene Carson Blake, stated clerk of the Presbyterian General Assembly, former president of the NCC vice chairman of its new Commission on Religion and Race, and a cosponsor of the march, struck a less triumphant tone. He represented the NCC on the podium and gave the day's fourth speech, directly following A. Philip Randolph and just before Daisy Bates and Rosa Parks were honored. Although Martin Luther King's "I Have a Dream" speech would be the day's iconic oratory, Blake's speech, which was also broadcast across the country and throughout the world, was notable for the position he took on white church involvement in the racial struggle, humbling himself and the mainline churches before the crowd.

The churches, Blake admitted, had not done enough to address racial and economic inequalities. Earlier in the year, at the National Conference on Religion and Race in Chicago, Martin Luther King and Will Campbell had called out the churches in the manner of biblical prophets. Now here was one of the churches' actual and symbolic leaders stepping forward to accept a portion of blame and, in this very public way, to use his power to urge the churches deeper into the struggle. Blake organized his speech around the refrain "late, late we come," a reference to the tardiness with which he felt the white churches and the NCC had brought their support to the black freedom struggle. Blake admitted that although the NCC and its constituent bodies "have said all the right things about race," they had failed to accompany their rhetoric with action. He pointed especially to the functional segregation of most churches. "It is partly because the churches of America have failed to put their own houses in order," Blake said, "that . . . the United States of America still faces a racial crisis."[70] Blake did have hope, he said, now that "there is a new spirit abroad in the Churches. We have come to know that we can no longer let the burden of the day be borne alone by those who suffer the discrimination we contest. We who are white have been at best followers, certainly not the leaders."[71]

Blake's act on behalf of the National Council of Churches was significant in two ways: first, it applied public and prominent pressure on the Kennedy administration to get civil rights legislation enacted; and second, it provided a directive to its member churches to actively address the racial crisis. Most of the Protestant denominations had already begun to take steps at this point, but the NCC's position put direct pressure on individual member congregations as well. Thus, by mid-1963, the council's top brass committed the organization and its churches to a public role in the civil rights struggle, albeit belatedly—and at least some were listening. If Blake's point was to get other white Christians to ask the same question, to understand the racial struggle as a moral cause, than his speech succeeded. Bill Troy, who was preparing to travel from his home in Marston, Tennessee, to New York City to begin his first year at Union Theological Seminary, recalled watching the march on television with his parents. "I remember thinking to myself at the time, What am I doing here? But I had had no exposure . . . to anything having to do with civil rights, except I knew it was all going on. But we were very secluded here. It's a predominately white area, and I never went to school, until I got to seminary, with a black person." Troy would join SIM while at Union and, completing the circle, spend the summer of 1966 working in Mississippi with the National Council of Churches' Delta Ministry project.[72]

The NCC's stance on race, however, did not necessarily mean that congregations would follow suit; at the local level, churches and especially individual churchgoers were not of one voice when it came to racial issues. For those who disagreed with the new efforts, the council was considered elitist and out of touch with congregational realities. What this meant for SIM going forward was that its students were increasingly undertaking their missions within a fractured church climate and in a society where the racial crisis was no longer seen as a strictly southern phenomenon but one with which congregations from Minneapolis to Seattle were now struggling.

In the fall of 1963, with the speeches from the March on Washington still ringing in members' ears, the SIM committee met at Union Theological Seminary to review its accomplishments and plan its goals for the coming year. Committee members combined practical tasks—an overview of budgets, numbers of students, and the need for a larger and more advanced administrative structure—with the philosophical. In 1960, SIM's founders had proclaimed that the initial goal of the project was "to witness to the concern of the church for the problem of human relations in the South and to further the work of reconciliation between the white and Negro races in the South and the redemption of segregated communities."[73] In reworking the project's statement of purpose in 1963, the second generation of SIM leaders left it unchanged except for the notable removal, twice, of the phrase "in the South."[74] The new statement reflected SIM's growing understanding of the widespread problems of racism and inequality to which the church had historically been a partner. By removing the words "in the South," the students indicated their understanding that the problems of human relations knew no regional bounds, nor would the project confine itself in addressing them.

The students were staggered in November by the assassination of President Kennedy, and reenergized to push for change in civil rights. Others saw the tragedy as signaling a providential moment for calling for renewal within the Protestant churches—for a relevance to the here and now that many found lacking. The cover of Steve Rose's *Renewal* magazine the next month featured a drawing by Bill Mauldin of the Lincoln Memorial, except that Lincoln had his head in his hands, weeping.[75] The inside of the magazine featured that very call for renewal, a message that Rose had been building toward and now carefully crafted in the pages of his magazine. "It became clear, amid the pressure of national calamity," he wrote, "that the time had come to begin in some small way the task of drastically reevaluating the place and function of the Protestant church in American society." *Renewal* would use its pages to host a debate on why and how to renew the church. Not only were King's words from the March on Washington still echoing in the nation's ears, but perhaps Blake's were, too—and the death of the president had only magnified the sound. "It is hoped that the spirit of self-searching begun with a bullet's fateful journey in Dallas and continued in the silent moments of Christmas contemplation may provide an instant where the Divine Spirit might speak with conviction and force," wrote Rose.[76] Some within the churches, of course, had for some time been already moving in the same direction as the civil rights movement, some in lockstep, but that long march now seemed to be gaining momentum.

That sense that the church and church people needed to be part of the struggle, coupled with the March on Washington and the subsequent lobbying effort of the National Council of Churches for passage of the Civil Rights Act, may have had something to do with SIM's newly stated national objectives. In any case, like the clergy leaders in the NCC, seminarians were becoming aware that their battle was not just in the South but also in the halls of Congress. Kennedy's civil rights bill introduced the previous spring had by April 1964 made it as far as the Senate floor but was being held up by Republican filibuster. In response, seminarians organized a silent vigil, known variously as the Theological Students Vigil for Civil Rights and the Interfaith Vigil for Civil Rights. Standing outside the Lincoln Memorial twenty-four hours a day, groups of three and four students on three-hour rotations bore public witness to what they saw as the travesty taking place on Capitol Hill. Beside them stood a hand-lettered sign that read: "Theological Students Civil Rights Vigil. Protestant-Catholic-Jewish. Civil Rights is Basically a Moral Issue. We Are Here to Speak to the Conscience of Every Man. We Are All Brothers Before God."[77]

The seminarians began their vigil on April 19, 1964, and in short order, the students had two hundred people signed up each week, with the schedule filled all the way through June. While many of the Catholic theology students who participated came from seminaries in the greater Washington, D.C., area, most of the Protestant and Jewish students, including those from Union Theological Seminary and Jewish Theological Seminary next door, drove down from New York City. Every day, a rental car left the Lincoln Memorial for New York at 9:30 p.m. carrying the previous night's participants, and every afternoon it left the corner of Broadway and 122nd again, heading to Washington with two Jewish and two Protestant students on board. John Bennett, president of Union Theological Seminary, briefly joined the vigil for a shift on May 1, 1964, accompanied by the provost of Jewish Theological Seminary and the assistant to the president of Georgetown University.[78] One Union student recalled that in addition to the regular cars ferrying demonstrators to their shifts at the Lincoln Memorial, "at the seminary we had a room set up as a letter-writing campaign headquarters. It was a really big deal at Union. [It made the] front page of the *New York Times* and five minutes on 'Huntley-Brinkley,' and a number of students became so involved they took incompletes for the semester."[79] When they were not on duty, up to eight students at a time would sleep in the basement of the Holy Comforter Roman Catholic Church at Capital and Fourteenth Streets, where local women's organizations provided them with hot meals.[80] By the time the Civil Rights Act of 1964 was actually passed on July 2, the theological students had been on duty for approximately 1,536 hours over sixty-four straight days.[81]

The origins of the vigil in Washington are slightly contested. Religious historian and former Union Theological Seminary professor Robert Handy maintains that the vigil was first suggested by Jack Pratt, a staff member of the NCC's Commission on Religion and Race, and then organized by Union Theological Seminary student Tom Leatherwood, who, two years later, would serve with the Student Interracial Ministry in Kingstree, South Carolina. A contemporary Catholic weekly magazine, however, credited Leatherwood with the idea and claimed that he and Jewish Theological Seminary student Jonathan Levine then met with Archbishop Patrick O'Boyle of Washington D.C., who pledged the involvement of 1,500 Catholic students and the provision of the basement quarters at Holy Comforter.[82] Virginia Wadsley, however, another volunteer in both the vigil work and SIM, credits the vigil to yet a third source: none other than John Collins, one of the founding students of the SIM project. She recalls that Collins approached Union's Social Action Group about the possibility of members of his New York City church standing witness with Union students at the Lincoln Memorial, although Collins does not share this memory.[83] Whatever the particulars, participants in both SIM and the vigil recall that the two projects fed and inspired each other. Tom Boomershine, who worked on both projects, was excited to "tap a lot of the energy that was shown in the Vigil and channel it into SIM."[84] Wadsley, who later served a black Presbyterian church in Charleston, South Carolina, for almost fifteen months, noted,

"From my perspective, SIM blossomed after the Theological Students Vigil for Civil Rights. When we came back to school in the fall of 1964 after the bill had passed, we raised the question of where to go from there and SIM seemed the logical step."[85]

This momentum helped the Student Interracial Ministry grow even larger. From 1960, when seven students worked together in the South, the project had evolved by the summer of 1963 to twenty-eight students working in eight southern states and in Washington D.C., upstate New York, New Jersey, and suburban Colorado. For the upcoming summer of 1964, thirty seminarians—twenty-four white, five black, and one Burmese—from fifteen seminaries, joined the project. The twenty-seven male and three female students came from Union Theological Seminary (10); the Interdenominational Theological Center (2); Boston (2); Bethany (2); Yale (2); Andover-Newton (2); and one each from Luther, Emory, Mennonite Biblical, Colgate Rochester, Vanderbilt, Drew, Williams, Duke, Wesleyan, and Southeastern. These students were bound for placements in North Carolina, South Carolina, Tennessee, Virginia, Alabama, Mississippi, Louisiana, Georgia, Ohio, Michigan, Washington, New Jersey, and Connecticut. They represented thirteen different denominations: Atlantic United Baptist, American Baptist, Church of the Brethren, Christian Methodist Episcopal, Community Church Movement, Disciples of Christ, the Lutheran Church of America, the Mennonite Church, the Methodist Church, the Netherland Reformed Church, Southern Baptist, the United Church of Christ, and the United Presbyterian Church (USA). In total, ninety-eight students had participated in the Student Interracial Ministry since the project's inception.[86] The SIM budget had grown, too, to just under $12,000, with the majority being used to cover the students' modest $300 stipends. This money was raised from seminaries, denominations, individuals, foundations, and individual congregations. The William C. Whitney Foundation and the Field Foundation, both regular funders of progressive social causes, together contributed $4,000.

The SIM students were, for a change, far from alone in their decision to head South in the summer of 1964 to work for the movement. In 1962, representatives of SNCC, CORE, and the NAACP had formed the Council of Federated Organizations, or COFO, to consolidate civil rights work in the South. For 1964, along with the SCLC, they organized the Mississippi Summer Project, soon to be known as Freedom Summer, as a massive voter registration drive throughout the state, which had the lowest percentage of registered black voters by population in the country. Over one thousand out-of-state volunteers, 90 percent of them white, came to Mississippi to work alongside thousands of local black workers.

The first workers began training in Ohio on June 14, 1964; on the night of June 20–21, three young volunteers—two white, one black—who had left the training early to investigate a church burning disappeared outside Philadelphia, Mississippi, and their bodies were not discovered for six weeks. Jane Stembridge, one of the first seven SIM students and now a SNCC worker in Mississippi, wrote an "Open Letter to America" on June 31, stating, "America, we paid a high price for your attention," and noting that it took two missing white students to focus the nation's thoughts on black folks in Mississippi. "We are in Mississippi this morning because we believed what we learned in the schools of this country—freedom and justice for all, but we did not see freedom and justice. We are here because we believed in this nation. . . . We are your children, living what you taught us as Truth."[87] A high price had indeed been paid; by October, thirty-seven Mississippi churches had been bombed or burned, fifteen people had been murdered, and over one thousand people had been arrested.[88]

Church folk played a number of visible roles throughout Freedom Summer. The NCC's Commission on Religion and Race supported clergy members and seminary students involved in the project. One SIM student, Maryka Matthews—a Baptist seminarian from Union—worked directly with COFO in Jackson, Mississippi, where she saw Freedom Summer as a kind of religious rebirth. "Many of the freedom workers," she wrote, "are people who have renounced the trappings of the old world—money, fashion, acceptability—and taken on the new, where the premium is set on commitment and leadership is judged on how many times you've been beaten or jailed . . . . The elements of the Christian faith are present and in fact one can see the ritual functions being implemented without being defined. . . . The singing is wholly and completely involving and fortifying in a unique way. . . . The sermon is about love and non-violence and the requirement is a stiff one, for these people know it's not easy to love."[89] Matthews also worked with members of the White Folks Project, a short-lived project-within-the-project of Freedom Summer, the goal of which was to target more liberal white citizens and create a white counterweight to the White Citizens' Councils and the Klan.[90]

Unlike in the previous year, only one of the high-profile civil rights ministers hosted a SIM student in the summer of 1964, possibly because the fall of 1963 and the spring of 1964 had been so rife with events, and possibly because the Mississippi Summer Project and its demands had taken precedence. In any case, only the Reverend Ralph Abernathy in Atlanta hosted a student, Jim Russ of Union Theological Seminary. Russ, like his SIM predecessor in the posting, was effusive in his praise of Abernathy, whom he described as "the personification of love and compassion," and who modeled pastoring and preaching at the highest levels.[91] Russ also concluded that his summer ministry wasn't so much interracial as it was interpersonal, involving one-on-one understanding that broke down stereotypes and resulted in mutual understanding.

This was true as well for many of the other students during the summer of 1964. For Ruth Brandon, who was serving a church in Raleigh, North Carolina, and would soon marry fellow SIM student Bill Minter, this meant something as simple as recognizing that race itself was constructed and essentially meaningless. "I look out into the congregation on Sunday morning and think we have several white visitors," she wrote. "If placed alone in Vermont, they'd be found lighter than many Italians or French Canadians, and nobody would think of the possibility that in the South they would be claimed to be Negros."[92] Another student recounted how a neighbor was convinced that he, though white, *had* to be a light-skinned black man, otherwise why would he be there?[93] In High Point, North Carolina, a white student named Ken Rupp from Mennonite Biblical Seminary enthused that through living with a black layman in a black neighborhood he had "learned much about the South and about the racial problem which exists here."[94] Another white student, Robert Blair, worked at Presbyterian Church in Martinsville, Virginia, and was occupied mostly with routine church business. Likewise, most of the other volunteers spent their time running youth groups, teaching vacation bible school and Sunday school, visiting parishioners, and offering the occasional sermon. Blair seemed to lament that his summer was "uneventful in terms of revolutionary civil rights action."[95] With the March on Washington, the passage of the Civil Rights Act at midsummer, and the events of Freedom Summer, some students' expectations had changed from reconciliation through "mere" interracial understanding— remember how extraordinary that was for John Collins just a few short years earlier—to "revolutionary" action.

A few students got a bit more of what they were expecting in terms of direct action. Keith Churchill and Beryl Ramsey joined the forces of their respective youth groups to test a segregated swimming pool in Norfolk. Ramsey also attended SCLC meetings in Norfolk led by C. T. Vivian. With the Civil Rights Act of 1964 signed into law on July 2, a number of students participated in testing various establishments for integration. William Whit, a white student from Andover-Newton seminary, worked with the First Baptist Church in Winston-Salem, North Carolina, but at the beginning of the summer was also elected chairman of the local chapter of CORE. He reported that after some initial testing of the Civil Rights Act, his chapter was left wondering what it should do, or if it should even continue. The chapter decided to move forward by focusing on voter registration and outreach to whites.[96] This was to become a not uncommon tactic for whites in the movement over the next few years, with the blueprint in some ways having been created by the White Folks Project of Freedom Summer as well as by an organization that had formed in Nashville a few months earlier, over Easter weekend 1964, called the Southern Student Organizing Committee, or SSOC. Connie Curry, who it will be remembered was one of SNCC's original advisers and Jane Stembridge's Atlanta housemate, had extended invitations to the founding SSOC conference in her capacity as director of the National Student Association by saying, "There is a feeling that a need exists for white Southern students who are involved in the Civil Rights movement to come together and exchange ideas about things which are most relevant to their situation."[97] Many of the founders of SSOC were also rooted in a Christian progressive tradition, and although they decided to experiment with breaking from interracialism, they nevertheless shared with SIM many of the same goals, including eventual racial reconciliation.

Another student placed in North Carolina, Russ Richey in Rocky Mount, had a decidedly different experience of the Tar Heel State when a contingent of local Klan members showed up to challenge an interracial work camp painting the home of a black church parishioner. With two hundred Klansman standing outside the home, Robert Jones, the grand dragon himself, delivered the message that the youth group had until noon the following day to disperse. The ministers and Richey decided to retreat with the youth rather than face possible bloodshed and to return with an older group and more ministers to finish the job another day; the governor of North Carolina promised protection for this second group amid continued threats from the Klan. Some despaired handing the Klan a "victory," but Richey found some solace in the fact that "the klan's act of intimidation frustrating the witness of the church has given us food for much reflection. It has aroused Rocky Mount and [the] surrounding area. As the church here prepares to feed and house the second group, it recalls what it means for the Church to witness to Christian brotherhood in an unreceptive world."[98] As it turned out, among those in the second group of painters was George Walters, a SIM student from Southeastern Baptist Seminary who had been working with J. Oscar McCloud at his Presbyterian church in Raleigh, and was filling in as supply pastor for McCloud since the latter had recently departed for a new church assignment in Atlanta. Acting on orders from the synod, Walters and other ministers from across the state finished the painting and provided their own witness in front of the Klan.[99]

Witness was a common theme in the students' writings that summer, but what it meant could be interpreted in a number of ways. The seminarians who participated in the program came from a multitude of religious backgrounds, and some participated out of a commitment to social justice, while others regarded the work as part of an evangelical expression. Many of these latter students interpreted the civil rights struggle through the lens of Christian conversion and a belief in Jesus Christ having died for mankind's sins. A seminarian from Germany who was working with SIM in Greensboro, North Carolina, thus understood SIM's work as spreading to southern whites the good news that their sins of segregation had already been forgiven by Jesus Christ. Russ Richey, himself a white southerner, argued that while one must still work at race relations, it must be remembered that "the victory is already won; it was won upon a cross in Galilee," or, in other words, that mankind has already been redeemed by the death and rebirth of Jesus.[100] However, most students in the project, even those who believed similarly, also understood that a long period of racial interaction—certainly more than a summer—might be required to bring about true racial reconciliation.

This was the thinking behind SIM's experiment with adding yearlong ministerial placements to the usual summer program. Two of the 1963 summer students, Bob Carey and Ralph Ross, the latter a black Baptist Interdenominational Theological Center seminarian from Miami, stayed on in their summer placements for their seminary fieldwork intern year through the spring of 1964. (All seminarians in a four-year degree program spent their third year in a fieldwork placement, then returned to school for their senior year. The sophomore year, which was technically the second of three years on campus, was called the middler year.)

For the present, SIM decided to adhere to its practice of working within churches, but the question of tactics had now been raised and would be tested during the coming year. Interracial ministry, however, required integration in both directions, and the student co-coordinators were frustrated at their inability to attract more black seminarians to participate. One of the obstacles was apparently the relatively low stipend. Many seminary students used summer work, church or secular, to make enough money to get them through the coming year of school, and the SIM stipend was not competitive with what a student could otherwise save. Another obstacle was simply demographic; there were relatively few black seminarians and only a handful of accredited black seminaries. One of the SIM student coordinators, Tom Boomershine, worried that if he tried to recruit black students from other institutions, "there may be a danger in trying to attract fellows that may not be too talented."[101] Nevertheless, the student leaders worried that their interracial ministry program was becoming a one-way conversation; they were determined to involve more black students in the program.[102] In an attempt to make sure that black churches remained involved, the project tried to create a sister church program, whereby a white church that "wasn't ready" to host its own black seminarian could become a sister church partner to a black church, providing the $300 stipend for it to host a white student.[103]

At the end of the summer of 1964, as the Mississippi Freedom Democratic Party was fighting to be seated at the National Democratic Convention, SIM again held an evaluation conference. The organizers posed a series of questions to the students, including whether the SIM experience had changed their vocational plans, how the experience had changed their "image of the ministry," and how the problems of their host congregations compared to the problems of the church in which they were raised.[104] The students concluded that most seminaries, which did not provide interracial ministerial experience or directly address racial relations, perpetuated prejudice or at best ignorance of other races. They hoped to combat this in part by increasing the size of the SIM project through recruiting about one hundred summer students for the following summer.[105]

As SIM students returned to their seminaries or headed on to new churches or adventures that fall, and as SIM administrators began planning for another year, the ministry's work was flattered by the imitation of the National Council of Churches' new program in Mississippi. The council, which had supported SIM but distanced itself during the David Jones "scandal" and had been relatively slow to take direct action on race, finally followed SIM's example when it launched the Delta Ministry field project in September 1964 as a follow-up to the work of the Freedom Summer volunteers. Maryka Matthews's work with COFO had in part been to lay the groundwork for the NCC's new project. (She was also credited as an early worker for SSOC.)[106] The Delta Ministry's primary goals were to deploy church folk to continue COFO's voter registration drives but also to develop programs to provide economic relief and development, advance literacy, and organize communities in the Mississippi Delta. One SIM student, Mark Lundeen, would head to work with the Delta Ministry the following summer of 1965 and end up staying two years.

While the summer of 1964 had been successful, the relatively larger number of participants stressed the all-volunteer staff and prompted the organization to restructure into two regional committees and to hire an administrative staff. The expansion consisted of an Executive Committee based in SIM's regular office at the God Box in New York City, chaired by returned Union student Doug Renick and in charge of administering the program. The second group was the National Committee, made up of representatives of seminaries across the country. These representatives created satellite offices of SIM in five regions—Northeast, Midwest, West, South, and Southwest—and took on much of the responsibility of recruiting students and host churches.

With SIM moving from focusing primarily on pastoral exchanges to team ministries and yearlong internships, it necessarily expanded and revised its organizational structure as well. Preparing for the summer of 1965, when it would send its first group to Southwest Georgia and follow it with its first roster of yearlong interns, SIM hired its first full-time staff member. M. George Walters, recently graduated from Southeastern Baptist Seminary in Wake Forest, North Carolina, had been a SIM student in Raleigh, working with J. Oscar McCloud at Davie Street United Presbyterian Church during the summer of 1964. Walters moved to New York City to serve as SIM's intern coordinator and field representative, as well as chair of the National Committee, traveling the seminary circuit, recruiting students, and starting the beginnings of regional SIM offices. Another former intern, Doug Renick, served as student coordinator; and Walters's wife, Carol Walters, served as a part-time secretary. Union Theological Seminary and the National Council of Churches' Division of Christian Life and Mission, to which J. Oscar Lee had been moved, remained the program's chief sponsors.

In previous years, Will Campbell of the NCC and William Crewes of the Interseminary movement had recruited potential participants to the summer program during their cross-country travels. Now, with Campbell having left the NCC and the Interseminary Movement in a quiescent phase, SIM took it upon itself to find interested students and congregations. George Walters and the National Committee members worked through a network of contacts—within the seminaries and in the civil rights movement—to recruit host churches to the program and to entice interested students. In Arkansas in 1965, for example, Walters collaborated with members of SNCC's Arkansas Project to recruit two likely host ministers. He also crisscrossed the country, visiting over seventy college and seminary campuses by the end of March 1965. The result of this ambitious effort was the much-expanded project for the summer of 1965 and a budget in excess of $29,000.

Thirty-five summer students and five yearlong interns served with SIM in 1965. Recruitment of black seminarians had been more successful, and they now made up eleven of the thirty-five, along with two Japanese and twenty-two white students. Seven women were among the forty total students that served in either the summer or year-long placements in sixteen states: North Carolina, South Carolina, Virginia, Alabama, Georgia, Tennessee, Mississippi, Maryland, New York, Wisconsin, Minnesota, Ohio, Missouri, Illinois, Colorado, and Washington. Twelve came from Union Theological Seminary; four from Duke; three from Andover-Newton; two each from Yale, Lutheran at Maywood, Perkins, Wartburg, ITC, and Johnson C. Smith University; and one each from Biblical Theological, Stillman, Pittsburg, Virginia Union, Pacific, Luther, Bethany, Harvard, and Southeastern.

Students in the summer of 1965 again worked with Ralph Abernathy in Atlanta and Joseph Ellwanger in Birmingham, but they also worked in a Baptist church in a highly segregated black neighborhood in East Harlem; in a Methodist parish in the poor, mixed-ethnic neighborhood of Fells Point, in Baltimore, Maryland; and back at some similar SIM sites throughout the South. One of these was Davie Street United Presbyterian Church in Raleigh, which had just welcomed a new pastor to replace J. Oscar McCloud. This was significant because the Reverend Frank Hutchinson was white, and not only was his call to lead the black church controversial among the membership but his successful appointment had been credited in large part to the influence of the SIM program on the church over the past four years.[107] The student placed there—Cheryl Ogawa, a Japanese American from Hawai'i—was struck by the class discrepancies and lack of cooperation within what she had imagined was a cohesive African American community. Her realization of these divisions—which she described in terms of a warning "that we will not have eradicated all enmities if and when we overcome the enmity between the races"—revealed a growing sophistication on the part of the SIM students as to the realities of their reconciliation project.[108]

The Student Interracial Ministry launched two new efforts during the summer of 1965, both of which not only changed the path of the organ-

ization but also reflected the changing nature of both the civil rights movement and the church in America at mid-decade. The first of these was the
deployment of the interracial team of Keith Davis and Carol Lucas to work
together at an inner-city church in Richmond, Virginia. The second was the
launching of the Southwest Georgia Project under the leadership of Charles
Sherrod, an important SNCC leader and instigator of the Albany Movement, who had become a Union Theological Seminary student in the fall of
1964. Sherrod's impact on SIM and SIM's impact on the Southwest Georgia
Project are detailed in chapter 4.

The Richmond project, however, was notable because it represented
SIM's first experiment with a team ministry, its first experiment with an interracial team, and its first serious foray into urban ministry. Carol Lucas, a
black Presbyterian who had just graduated from Johnson C. Smith University in Charlotte, North Carolina, teamed up with Keith Davis Jr., a white
Lutheran from Nebraska and a student at Lutheran Seminary at Maywood.
The two worked with Robert Hare, the white minister of an all-black, inner-
city church, First United Presbyterian. Hare, who had hosted Douglas
Cruger from SIM the previous summer, was the same minister who had
participated in efforts to desegregate public facilities in Raleigh while an associate chaplain at North Carolina State University in early 1963 and had
aroused the ire of Jesse Helms. The ultra-conservative pundit and future
politician used his television position to help run Hare out of town. Black
ministers in Raleigh who had come to know Hare through the civil rights
movement helped connect him with the church in Richmond, where he became the first white minister freely elected by the members of a black Southern church.[109]

Most travelers to Richmond at that time snaked through the city on the
shiny new Richmond–Petersburg Turnpike, unaware of the urban chaos
that lay just off the exit ramps in the city's Jackson Ward. This was First
United Presbyterian's neighborhood, and it was choked with crowded
streets and crumbling houses, many of them without water or electricity.
The congregation was in fact an original mission church, founded by the
Presbyterian Church (USA) in 1890, and the proud brick and stone structure at the corner of Monroe and Catherine Streets was completed three
years later, becoming the cornerstone of a busy metropolitan neighborhood.
In 1963, however, the neighborhood had retreated into severe decline; a
bootlegger now sold illegal liquor two doors down from the church, and a
brothel operated with impunity farther down the block. A few of First
United Presbyterian's members still came from the neighborhood, but a

large portion of them had moved out and now commuted to the church from the more affluent working-class neighborhoods that ringed Jackson Ward. The congregation had even purchased its minister a home in one of these outlying neighborhoods, not wishing to subject him to the immediate area.[110] However, the neighborhood problem that was perhaps most obvious in the early summer of 1965, when the seminarians first arrived, was the hundreds of children of all ages running wild in the streets and alleys, with no camps or schools or other programs to occupy them.[111]

Carol Lucas recalled that the local boys complained that "'there isn't nothin' to do around here, nothin' to do at all, man. Nowhere to go but the streets, man!'" According to Lucas, most of these boys and young men had unhappy home lives, had dropped out of school by the tenth grade, and had spent much of their time in the streets. Frequently in trouble with the police, they were "generally distrusted and feared by the entire community."[112] On his first evening in the neighborhood, Davis was chased down and accosted by a group of teenage boys, who released him only when he calmly introduced himself by saying, "Hello, I'm Pastor Keith. Is there anything I can do for you?" Davis always wore a clerical collar after that, with the hope that this outward sign of his religious affiliation would protect him.[113]

Hare gave Davis and Lucas the task of bringing the wayward boys back into the fold of the community. The two interns applied for and received funds from the United Presbyterian Church (USA) to institute summer recreational programs. Absent "a public blade of grass for probably 20 or more blocks," they used an asphalt school playground and the streets themselves.[114] One day, while seeking some help with setting up for an arts and crafts session, Carol Lucas struck up a conversation with a few of the young men who regularly loitered near the church. This casual conversation led the young ministers into an informal outreach program to the local street gang, the Chandeliers. Soon the gang members were stopping by the church, which most had not been inside of in at least a decade, to play chess and checkers and drink Kool-Aid. This relationship culminated in the ministers and the gang members collaborating to refurbish the church basement as a recreation room. A church member taught the boys how to level the old foundation, put up studding and drywall, and paint the new walls.[115]

The basement project went so well that Lucas and Davis asked the boys to help them turn an abandoned barbershop near the church into a community recreation center. The gang members cleaned and painted the space, negotiated for a jukebox, and built a Ping-Pong table. (Davis noted wryly that the men who sold him a suspiciously discounted pool table were

Lutherans.)[116] The boys themselves established the center's rules, which included a ban on using profanity, and created a cleaning schedule. Of their own volition, they built a cross and put it prominently in the window. Not all ran perfectly smoothly, however. One morning, after he and the gang had spent the day before putting up walls in the new clubhouse, Davis was awoken from his bed by the leader of the Chandeliers who admitted that all the drywall they had just hung the day before had not been donated but rather had been stolen. Davis helped him take it down again and return it to its rightful owner.[117]

Despite the hurdles, the biracial team of Davis and Lucas felt that they had begun to find their mission through service to a previously abandoned constituency, a group that was reachable simply by plugging in a jukebox and offering some basic respect. They called their project Shepherd of the Streets, though this necessitated explaining to the boys what a shepherd was. The boys accepted the name but mostly referred to the place simply as "the Center." The Center served a mostly secular purpose in the community, and Davis noted, "We only casually mention the church and preaching. We share Christ, we don't dispense him."[118] Instead of taking a heavy-handed mission approach, the students elected to just make the Center a place where kids would want to hang out, and if religious folks were there as well, then perhaps that example would rub off.

Carol Lucas had grown up in Laurinburg, North Carolina, where she had been active in her Presbyterian church and in the United Presbyterian Youth. She and Davis made an effective, if unlikely, team, although they often fell into traditional gender roles, Davis playing football and pool with the boys in the gang while Lucas played house with and tended to the needs of the girls. In one instance, when one of the girls from the Center was arrested, Lucas acted as pastor, parent, and counselor all in one. The girl refused to give the police officers her name or address; instead, she would give them only the address of the church and Davis, Lucas, and Reverend Hare's names. Davis and Lucas decided together that Lucas would go down to the station, after which the girl was released into her custody. Lucas's explanation was that "the church was the only place the girl was assured of help," but it seems obvious that she and Davis had also succeeded in establishing trust with the kids in Jackson Ward.[119]

Davis remarked at the time that the recreation center "is almost like their church—a place of freedom, joy, and fellowship," although he added, "The Center can never and will never be a substitute for the church, but it is an effective and relevant means of spreading the Gospel of Christ. The youth know that we care. Now we've got to help them understand that God cares, and that Christ died on that cross they put in the window."[120] For Davis, the SIM program was his missionary work, and the Jackson Ward, his mission.

Lucas would stay on as an intern throughout that academic year, to be joined again the following summer by Davis and four additional SIM interns, two from Union Theological Seminary and one each from the Presbyterian School of Christian Education in Richmond and the American Baptist Theological Seminary in Nashville. Davis remarked in a 1966 magazine article that "by the end of my two summers there, I was being introduced by the members of a Negro gang as their 'brother.' The fact that I came back a second summer was significant to them."[121] The students continued to develop Shepherd of the Streets, although by that time the original pool table had worn out and the gang members had purchased a replacement. The students also added a playground, a tutoring program, and a street ministry project.[122]

The Student Interracial Ministry had grown in size each year during the first half of the 1960s, placing students in congregations of a different race from New York to Georgia and from Washington, D.C., to Washington State, while moving toward yearlong placements, direct action civil rights work, and urban ministry. SIM's initial phase, from its pilot summer of 1960 through the summer of 1963, when twenty-eight students participated, can be characterized as being devoted to the goal of achieving racial reconciliation. By 1964, however, the thirty students' reports contained fewer references to reconciliation and more calls for revolution. Revolution was often ill defined; it could mean throwing out racially constricted legal and cultural structures, reimagining the church mission, or, for some, reinventing the church itself. Often, the students did not know what specific change they sought, only that they wanted the present to be different from the past. During this period, they tried on a series of new ideas pertaining to activist ministry, especially in regard to race issues, and their calls for revolution grew louder and more strident.

As they embraced the changed civil rights and social change landscape at mid-decade, the students began to refer to the churches as "the establishment" and looked back on the first years of the Student Interracial Ministry as being part of "propping up this establishment." As one student put it a few years later, if the founding approach and strategies of SIM were to be given "a temporary label, it should read: *idealism seeking experience.* The idealists got their experience but they probably didn't change very much of the establishment." He went on to say that SIM, as a "child of the establishment," reflected both the establishment's concerns with its own structures—that is, even though reform was sought, it was conventional reform of existing systems, not radical rethinking—and the establishment's ruling white ethos. Calling the program "a white man's movement with marginal participation by Negroes," he excoriated SIM's past leaders for not including an equal number of blacks in its administration and not involving the all-black denominations in recruiting host churches. He went on, however, to note that there had been a change in the "mood" of SIM participants, who were no longer motivated by personal guilt to "passionately, righteously," reform the church, as their predecessors had been, but had been freed by secular influences to think outside the rigid vocational patterns of seminary training, parish ministry, and denominational leadership. Students participating in SIM at the time "may not actually give a damn about the church as it now is" and were open to more radical rethinking of the concepts of worship, congregation, and community. The implication was that there were not only many students in seminary at the time who were not seeking vocational training for a life in the ministry but also many who were not even believers. These were students who were prompted to study Christian theology in their quest for authenticity or who were, in some cases, merely pursuing a higher degree to receive shelter from the selective service draft. The SIM program could serve "as a tool for revolutionary change," one part of SIM's "attack upon the target" of the seminaries, which needed, one student wrote, to be shaken up so that they in turn could reform the church.[123]

The Student Interracial Ministry had reached a critical juncture and needed to declare its allegiances in order to select its future path. The organization could go in one of three directions: it could become absorbed by the establishment, continue consciously to try to revolutionize the establishment, or simply fade away. For some within the organization, its work in southwest Georgia would hold the answer.

CHAPTER FOUR

Into the Heart of the Beast

Ministry in the Fields and Towns of Southwest Georgia, 1965–1968

I don't know that there were any more powerful and beautiful people. Albany was one of those areas where blacks seemed to be still intact culturally. The singing, the folklore, had a kind of indigenous power to it that meant you couldn't walk away from Albany, Georgia.

—Andrew Young

Charles Sherrod—slight and reedy, with a medium-brown complexion and horn-rimmed glasses—arrived at Union Theological Seminary in the fall of 1964 with more baggage than the usual student. Along with his suitcase, he brought along the scars and joys and fatigue and commitment he had gained while working on the front lines of the civil rights movement. After three years in southwest Georgia as the first field secretary for SNCC, and having been very nearly beaten to death by whites in Newton, Georgia, several months before his arrival in New York, Sherrod had taken a leave of absence from the movement to focus on his theological training. He had temporarily left the movement; however, the movement would not leave Sherrod.

At Union, the Student Interracial Ministry was preparing for its fifth year pursuing its own form of civil rights work. With its program of interracial church work, the students had hoped to make change one person at a time, one church at a time. But the pace of such change was glacially slow compared to other events in the movement: the March on Washington, the achievement of federal civil rights legislation, the Selma-to-Montgomery march, Freedom Summer, and the list went on. For some active church people, there was a sense that the main civil rights movement was moving on without them. SIM was ready for something new, and Charles Sherrod, standing on the steps of Union Theological Seminary, had something to offer. He needed willing workers—white students if possible—for the project he had created several years earlier in the heart of the Deep South: the Southwest Georgia Project in Albany, Georgia.

SIM began sending students to the region with Sherrod in the summer of 1965, and SIM's partnership allowed the Southwest Georgia Project to continue its political and economic development work in the region even as its other stakeholders, the SCLC and SNCC, discontinued their involvement. And even though SIM as an organization didn't exist after 1968, some of the former SIM interns stayed on in Southwest Georgia, working with Sherrod for up to a decade.

Albany, the largest city in the region, came to national attention when Martin Luther King Jr. led mass demonstrations there during the winter of 1962 and was jailed along with hundreds of ordinary black citizens. King's efforts in Albany highlighted civil rights issues in the South but failed to win any immediate concessions from white civic leaders. King left Albany behind and went on to other more successful marches and campaigns. Most accounts of the civil rights movement describe Albany as King's major failure and pay no more attention to it after he left in defeat. But the struggle to achieve civil rights and economic justice for blacks in Southwest Georgia, led by Charles Sherrod and Cordell Reagon and a host of brave locals, continued apace long after King's supposed defeat. And during a key period from 1965 to 1968, the Southwest Georgia Project received a tremendous boost in energy and manpower from the Student Interracial Ministry. The involvement of the SIM volunteers allowed the project to continue to expand long after its supposed demise. Under Sherrod and with SIM's help, the Albany Movement segued into the Southwest Georgia Project, an ongoing, persistent attempt to realize the beloved community through interracial cooperation and a combined program of economic and political action and, importantly, religious faith.

The Southwest Georgia Project also gave the seminarians of SIM another opportunity to leave the walls of the institutional church and to join in local struggles in a longer and more meaningful way than, for example, those who had gone into Mississippi as part of Freedom Summer. And the tenor of the movement had changed; the passage of national civil rights legislation had failed in many ways to change the racial inequities that existed in the South— and certainly so in Southwest Georgia—and those who demanded equality were now both more impatient and more sophisticated in their understanding of the deeper structures of racial and economic inequities. The Student Interracial Ministry embraced the opportunities that Sherrod's project offered for seminarians to involve themselves in voter registration, political campaigns, business projects, and other ventures that aimed at racial reconciliation but did so outside the walls of the conventional church.

Albany lies two hundred miles west of the Atlantic Ocean and two hundred miles south of Atlanta. A one-time slave-trading center and home to

King Cotton, it had over the years earned a number of nicknames, including "the buckle on the Black Belt" and "Egypt of the Confederacy," overflowing with goods and profits. W. E. B. DuBois, referring to Albany's role as a major slave market and distribution point, described the city as the domestic birthplace of the country's "Negro problem—the centre of those nine million men who are America's dark heritage from slavery and the slave-trade."[1]

One hundred years after the Civil War, the impoverished rural peanut-, cotton-, and corn-producing counties of southern Georgia provided a sharp contrast to thriving urban Atlanta and Savannah. The black and white populations of Albany were roughly equal, and although blacks had achieved some level of mercantile independence in the city itself, the vast majority in the surrounding counties remained outside the political system, disenfranchised, exploited, and very, very afraid. It is difficult to overemphasize how much terror had played out in that part of the world, seeming to have permanently dissuaded most African Americans from even attempting to register to vote. The entrenched poverty and control of local whites was further exacerbated by the region's economic and political isolation from the state's centers of wealth and power. While the rest of the state's population grew during the 1950s and 1960s, it declined in Southwest Georgia. Only five of the region's counties had populations over five thousand. The median income for a farm family in those decades was under $1,170 per year, roughly half that of the state average.[2]

Distanced from state government and funding, local white authorities ruled with an iron hand, propping up a system of white supremacy that had been somewhat tempered elsewhere in the state. Southwest Georgia, according to a SNCC volunteer, was "a tragic area, the stepchild of the New South."[3] County sheriffs ruled as if over personal fiefdoms, and if they didn't perform all acts of racial violence themselves, they certainly endorsed them. Elijah Poole, later known as Elijah Muhammad and the founder of the Nation of Islam, was in Cordele, in Crisp County, where he witnessed the lynching of his best friend.[4] The region's deadliness gained national attention in June 1958, when during the course of a single week, numerous blacks were beaten by whites, and three black men were shot dead by white police officers. The *Washington Post* ran a cover story under the headline "The Negroes of This South Georgia Town Are Scared."[5]

Charles Sherrod and another young SNCC worker, eighteen-year-old Cordell Reagon, were dispatched to Albany—which the locals pronounced "Al-Benny"—in the middle of the summer of 1961, not only because the area was representative of the racial and economic problems of the Deep South but also because it had recently been the site of the first federal action against unfair voting practices under the Civil Rights Act of 1957. Terrell County, Georgia, had been singled out by the U.S. Department of Justice as having a voter registration record that exemplified the practice of black disenfranchisement at the whim of local white authorities. In 1958, only forty-eight black voters were registered in the county, where they made up 64 percent of the population.[6] Voting registrars held whites and blacks to different standards of literacy and competency, and local officials routinely rejected even those applicants who managed to pass the rigged tests. The Justice Department brought suit in 1959, demanding an injunction against Terrell County's discriminatory practices. Even though the Justice Department won its case, a year later only five more black voters had been added to the county roles.[7] The students in SNCC saw the injunction as a crack in the edifice of white power, and Sherrod and Reagon ventured to Georgia to push and prod and to perhaps cause the whole structure to collapse.[8]

Sherrod was just twenty-one years old when he first went to Albany. He had grown up poor, the oldest of eight children in Petersburg, Virginia, and had worked in the school cafeteria to put himself through Virginia Union University, where he earned both a BA and a BD in theology, the latter the equivalent of today's master of divinity. Described years later as "a Christian mystic" by journalist Taylor Branch, Sherrod held deep religious beliefs and even at that young age was intensely committed to the ideal of the beloved community, the Old Testament–based concept that had anchored the thinking of James Lawson and some of the other religious SNCC founders.[9] Put simply, the beloved community envisioned the embodied expression of Christian faith as an integrated society based in brotherhood and built on love and justice. Racism could be escaped, Sherrod expressed in an oft-quoted statement, if only one could "free men's minds."[10] Sherrod, in describing this utopian goal, was given to high-flown language, "always making allegories and imageries," using turns of phrase he himself referred to as "Sherrodian."[11] SNCC executive secretary James Forman called Sherrod's field reports "Proustian," and Julian Bond remarked that Sherrod wrote "like a drunk Jack Kerouac and [that the other field workers] write like drunk Sherrods."[12] Although religious faith lay at the foundation of SNCC, the organization was not in 1961 an explicitly religious project and over time became more distanced from the theology and biblical language of Sherrod and Lawson. But Sherrod's religious upbringing, deep faith, and theological studies guided and sustained his activism, and they became a hallmark of the movement in Southwest Georgia.

The local black citizens—especially eager high school students and college students at Albany State College—were fed up with the system of white domination. By the time of SNCC's arrival, locals were ready to strike and waiting only for the motivation of good organizers. Sherrod and Reagon worked directly with students but also helped encourage local leaders to form the Albany Movement, a coalition of six middle-class black organizations, which elected a young black doctor—William Anderson, a relative newcomer to town—as its president. During 1961, the Albany Movement organized a series of very large, nonviolent marches to put pressure on white leaders to desegregate Albany's businesses.[13]

Sherrod, himself an ordained minister, and Charles Jones, a seminarian at Johnson C. Smith University who had arrived in Albany soon after Sherrod and Reagon, met with local church leaders.[14] They encountered some resistance but managed to convince most ministers in the city of Albany to open their doors for the mass meetings. Allowing their churches to be used as staging areas for mass resistance was, Sherrod said, the ministers' "gift to the movement."[15] Sherrod and his colleagues also reached out beyond the pastors themselves directly to the congregants, crafting their civil rights rhetoric in the familiar prose of a revival meeting. However, Sherrod also consciously employed a rhetoric of interracial cooperation and invoked the beloved community. In the flyer he posted announcing Albany's first mass meeting on November 9, 1961, Sherrod beseeched locals to "COME, LISTEN, LEARN AND LOVE!" and proclaimed: "If we are of one blood, children of one common Father, brothers in the household of God, then we must be of equal worth in His family, entitled to equal opportunity in the society of men. . . . We are called upon, therefore, to love our fellow man, all of them, with all the risks that implies and all the privileges that it promises."[16] Sherrod knew the power of his prophetic stance and to whom he was preaching—the black churches and their congregants were at the center of community life and would form the linchpins of the Albany Movement— but he likely hoped that his handbill would happen to fall into the hands of white church folk and challenge them as well.

The familiar culture of the black church nourished and sustained the movement, and music was at the center, particularly the black spirituals that were molded into freedom songs. From Albany came the adaptations of "Eyes on the Prize" and "We Shall Overcome," as well as locally specific songs, including "Oh Pritchett, Open Them Cells." Song had the unique ability to reach across boundaries and unite diverse peoples, recalled Bernice Johnson Reagon, a member of Albany's Freedom Singers. "After the song, the differences among us would not be as great. Somehow, making a song required an expression of that which was common to us all." The song itself was a weapon in the battle for freedom, "like an instrument, like holding a tool in your hand."[17] Civil rights activists in other regions knew of Albany as "the singing movement," and the songs first sung in Albany were heard throughout the movement and across the country.[18]

But Albany could just as well have been called "the praying movement," distinguished by hours-long mass meetings in its churches and by large groups of demonstrators bowing in silent prayer on the steps of municipal buildings. Sherrod felt that prayer united Albany's blacks across class lines that had previously been nearly impassable. "There were people from all walks of life," he described in 1962. "The professional man, the preacher and the man on the street, the nurse, the housewife, the busboy, the shoeshine boy—they stood in front of the courthouse praying to almighty God that justice would come to Albany, Georgia."[19] Prayer and song often went together and could be especially powerful, as one Albany woman remembered: "Two things we knew held us together: prayer of something good to come and song that tells from the depth of the heart how we feel about our fellow man."[20]

By December 1961, Albany had developed into the largest mass movement in the South, aimed at increasing voter registration and achieving desegregation of all manner of public accommodations and facilities. Several hundred people had been arrested, and many were still in the county jails. Business in downtown Albany dried up as shoppers stayed away for fear of getting involved in another demonstration or possible violence. The white leaders eventually agreed to unofficial talks on December 15, 1961, meant to end the impasse, but the talks collapsed without effect. One result was that William Anderson, on behalf of the Albany Movement and without consulting SNCC, contacted Martin Luther King Jr. for help. King arrived later that same day and assumed a leadership role that effectively sidelined the young SNCC organizers. Wherever King went, the media followed, and the Albany Movement's decision to involve him significantly raised Albany's public profile and would, it was hoped, bring pressure on whites to reform.

But police chief Laurie Pritchett and the white Albany elites ultimately out-maneuvered King. Between December 1961 and July 1962, seven hundred blacks were arrested and imprisoned, and King personally went in and out of jail three times, each time believing he had won concessions. The final time he even broke the Albany Movement's unofficial "jail not bail" rule when he agreed to be bailed out by a lawyer who was probably financed by a nervous Kennedy administration. He left Albany for good that July, humbled by his first major defeat.[21]

According to some historians, after King left Albany, "the emotion and sense of hope were never recaptured."[22] In their version of the Albany story, the black citizens of Southwest Georgia, left with nothing to show for their months in jail, gave up the fight for civil rights and returned to their lives, where little had changed. However, by switching the focus from King to Charles Sherrod and the citizens of Southwest Georgia, one can see that the movement not only survived but achieved many of its goals, although over a longer period than had been originally sought. After King and the accompanying caravan of journalists left Albany, Sherrod stepped back in to lead the local effort, building a network of county-based volunteers who registered voters, started new business ventures, and even ran political candidates. This story of the perseverance of the Albany Movement after King directly challenges the assessment that the movement there collapsed after 1962. "Where's the failure?" Sherrod demanded a few years later. "Are we not integrated in every facet? Did we stop at any time? What stopped us? Did any white man stop us? Did any black man stop us? Nothing stopped us in Albany, Georgia. Now, I can't help how Dr. King might have felt, or . . . any of the rest of them in SCLC, NAACP, CORE, any of the groups, but as far as we were concerned, things moved on. We didn't skip one beat. We showed the world."[23] Social movements inevitably experience defeats along the way, but their success can be judged in the eventual erosion of the old order, even if this occurs over a significant amount of time. SNCC's own standard held that when members withdrew from a community in which they had organized, that they left behind "a movement with local leadership, not a new branch of SNCC."[24] Judged by this criterion, the civil rights movement in Southwest Georgia was indeed an eventual success.

Sherrod and a few other volunteers carried on what became known as SNCC's Southwest Georgia Project, bringing the kinds of activism and demands used in the city of Albany to the other rural counties of the region. Due to the oppressive rule of their white authorities—primarily county sheriffs—local blacks had developed a number of nicknames for these counties: "Terrible Terrell," "Unworthy Worth," "Bad Baker," and others. It was into these uncharted, and potentially fatal, waters that Sherrod and his colleagues now waded, and by 1963, the Southwest Georgia Project had developed a multifront approach to political and economic issues in all twenty counties of the region. But success did not come easily.

One problem was ongoing tensions within SNCC. Sherrod bridled under the supervision of the SNCC headquarters in Atlanta, and for their part, SNCC leaders in Atlanta complained that Sherrod treated the project as his "little baby." At first they decided to avoid confrontation and simply stay out of his way, but by the fall of 1963, an Atlanta office staffer complained that Sherrod's iron rule was "unhealthy psychologically." He noted that many of the black SNCC staffers in the Southwest Georgia Project had quit because they felt ignored by Sherrod. An Atlanta-based SNCC staffer pleaded for a pause in the project, to regroup and refocus and, if he had his way, to remove Charles Sherrod from the helm. He criticized Sherrod for behaving like a dictator, he alone deciding who would work where and when, exercising total control over finances, and essentially pursuing only those actions that he himself oversaw. When group strategy meetings were held, SNCC staff members felt "that the policy is already made before the meeting and the meeting lasts as long as it takes for Sherrod to persuade the others to think his way."[25]

One of the sticking points was Sherrod's insistence on an interracial staff. This angered some of the SNCC representatives, who worried that the Albany Movement had acquired "an image of failure," and blamed this partly on Sherrod's insistence on employing white volunteers.[26] By late 1963, SNCC staff in the Atlanta office were referring to the Southwest Georgia Project as a rogue program and refusing to send any new black volunteers to Albany for fear their talents would not be used, leaving behind locals and a few white SNCC volunteers, including John Perdew, who was arrested for his civil rights work in Americus in 1963 and charged with sedition.[27]

Sherrod maintained that the Atlanta officers disrespected his authority and discounted the contributions he and the people of Southwest Georgia had made to the civil rights movement. The SNCC leaders, he complained, showed an "apparent indifference" to Albany's needs. Sherrod angrily demanded to know if SNCC had forgotten what had happened there. "The city was one of the first in the South to erupt with really massive demonstrations," he wrote. "Techniques of protest we developed here spread across the nation. But now we are wondering. We are wondering if the pioneer role that the Albany people have played in the Struggle is still remembered."[28] Largely abandoned by SNCC leaders, Sherrod distanced himself from the organization, aligned himself with locals, and eventually went in search of other sponsors. Sherrod did not officially quit SNCC, but he did stop attending the national meetings, electing to stay in Albany.

Sherrod's and SNCC's disagreements came to a head in 1963 and early 1964. Preparing for the March on Washington for Jobs and Freedom in late August 1963, Sherrod petitioned the national office for funds to send several hundred Albany protest veterans to the capital by bus. The national office agreed to pay only half fares for one hundred of the three hundred people who had signed up for the Albany Freedom Train. Sherrod responded angrily that he feared that the sacrifices of the people of Albany had been forgotten and that they had given too much already and had "nothing left." The relationship worsened still in 1964, when SNCC permanently "borrowed" some of the Southwest Georgia staff for work in Selma, Alabama. At the end of that year, SNCC moved its own headquarters from Atlanta to Mississippi. Only a few SNCC volunteers and an assortment of young local recruits continued to work with Sherrod in the counties of Southwest Georgia. The Deep South frontier of the civil rights movement, the "buckle on the black belt," had been abandoned. But it was momentary only, and the future was far from bleak, promising the development of new partnerships and the resurrection of the movement's original spirit of the beloved community.

In the fall of 1964, Sherrod briefly retreated from Albany to New York City in order to pursue a master's degree in sacred theology at Union Theological Seminary. He was burned out by three years of near-constant struggle and took what he called "a movement sabbatical."[29] Roy Shields of Franconia College and later Isaac Simpkins of Miles College filled in as project director for the Southwest Georgia Project.[30]

In Sherrod, SIM saw an experienced civil rights veteran who still retained his commitment to the beloved community. He was also exceptionally magnetic and had the ability to inspire and ignite those whom he had just met. As one SIM volunteer recalled, "[He] started singing 'Oh Freedom' and for thirty minutes the auditorium really rocked. The charisma of Sherrod is incredible."[31] In the Southwest Georgia region, SIM saw a community in which economic disparities and lack of electoral power now outweighed concerns over access to segregated public facilities. It was also a place where SIM's traditional pastoral placement strategy had little chance of success. The established white churches in Albany and the surrounding counties had, for the most part, not actively engaged civil rights and were unreceptive to hosting SIM students. Most of the large black churches were unwilling to continue to support the movement after King's departure, especially after Mount Olive and two other churches that had been involved in the movement were burned to the ground.[32] In the counties, most black preachers were unwilling or unable to participate, having, according to SIM, "too narrow and limited conceptions of the role of the minister and mission."[33] These considerations called for new approaches to an activist ministry of reconciliation in Southwest Georgia.

In SIM, Sherrod also saw a group of eager, optimistic, intellectual, hard-working seminarians who still harbored a commitment to the ideals he espoused. By the time he left for New York, Sherrod was down to a few local volunteers and was in a constant search for new hands to help with the work. John Chappell, a former SIM participant and a strong supporter of Sherrod, suggested that part of Sherrod's motivation for attending Union Theological Seminary and for getting involved in SIM was to raise funds and recruit new volunteers for the Southwest Georgia Project.[34] Sherrod was indeed successful in gaining a constant stream of volunteers from the partnership, if not steady funding.

He formed a civil rights discussion group at Union and began to sow the seeds of interest for a group that would later travel south with him. A number of Union students recall Sherrod at that time as a stirring character full of intensity and stories from the trenches. Many of the students had participated on the fringes of the civil rights movement, but here was one of the legendary student leaders in the flesh! One recalled hearing Sherrod spontaneously break out into a freedom song in the seminary hallway and thinking that he wanted to learn what was behind such optimism. He got his chance when Sherrod, in early 1965, proposed to the Student Interracial Ministry that it oversee a special SIM summer project in Southwest Georgia.

Sherrod's proposal came just as SIM was evaluating its first five years and considering whether to continue its approach of placing white seminarians in black churches, and vice versa. Although it had already placed eighty-nine students from twenty-nine seminaries in ministries from coast to coast, students who were now entering seminaries had lived with the civil rights movement for four years, and many wanted to take a more active role than serving a church of another race.[35] The violent reception to Freedom Summer in 1964 also signaled a change in the national mood of the movement away from idealism and the beloved community and toward frustrated calls for immediate action and black independence. Just down the road from Union, Harlem erupted in flames in mid-July 1964, ushering in the first in a series of "long, hot summers."[36] By September, the civil rights movement and the nation had been changed significantly, and the seminarians wondered how effective their earlier strategies would prove in this new setting. At the same time, they were continuing to question the traditional roles of the professional ministry and, even more broadly, of the place of the church in society. They demanded "a more responsible and effective approach on the part of SIM and the Church to the larger social problems of the day."[37] Sherrod's experiences in Southwest Georgia and his conception of the role of the church in the movement seemed tailored to SIM. "I am a victim as well as a product of this church and this society," he wrote. "But the church is also a victim and, as an institution, as a group, as individuals, it too must be saved."[38] The students in SIM, who yearned to solve racial problems *and* change and renew the church, eagerly endorsed Sherrod's proposal to create a SIM project in Southwest Georgia. Charles Sherrod would serve as project director, and Reverend J. Oscar McCloud, who had left Raleigh by this time and was pastoring a church in Atlanta, would serve as project supervisor. According to long-time volunteer Edward Feaver, the project succeeded in its goal "to force seminarians out of their conventional manner of living and out of their intellectual, ivory-tower theological security" through engaging with local people on economic, political, and social issues "for the purpose of discovering how these relate to the church."[39]

As Sherrod's proposal was accepted and plans were being made to send SIM students to work with him in Southwest Georgia, another wave of troubling events unfolded. On February 21, 1965, Malcolm X was assassinated, and then on March 7, marchers with the SCLC's campaign in Selma were set upon by police in an event that came to be known as Bloody Sunday. Again, the violent repression of black rights in the South made front-page news across the country, and King and others used the Selma campaign and the events of Bloody Sunday and the then-resumed march to Montgomery as leverage in achieving a Voting Rights Act to support the Civil Rights Act of the previous year.

Five students accompanied Sherrod back to Albany and its surrounding counties at the end of May 1965. Twenty more seminarians joined the project in the summer of 1966, and twelve completed full intern years in 1966 and 1967. By 1967, the Southwest Georgia Project formally parted ways with SNCC and became partners with SIM, describing itself as "partially staffed and partially funded by the Student Interracial Ministry."[40] In 1967, there were twelve summer and five yearlong interns. In total, forty-four SIM volunteers served with the Southwest Georgia Project from 1965 to 1968, constituting the bulk of the project's staff during that time. Several SIM volunteers became temporary or permanent staff members, staying on in the area for periods ranging from one to ten years.

The program's initial call for volunteers promised that they would be "bound together by a common faith and concern . . . [to] constitute an involved Christian community, working directly with the existing civil rights groups in the area, and struggling together with the meaning of Christian faith in this situation." Seminarians would participate as laymen in local churches and, in addition, would be involved in whatever community activities were most pressing, including voter registration and working in Freedom Schools, community centers, and day cares. Students were offered a summer stipend of $300, urged to bring their own cars for transportation in the largely rural area, and required to have a bail contact capable of posting $500.[41]

Although the number of volunteers and their impact within local communities were both relatively large, Sherrod envisioned that the SIM organization would act in such humility and concert with both the local people and the handful of SNCC volunteers still working among them that SIM would leave few footprints in Southwest Georgia. The plan that first year was that the five SIM volunteers would partner with SNCC and local workers, forming a new and smoothly functioning team, and by design, a separate SIM identity never truly emerged. The name Student Interracial Ministry meant little to the locals "and less to fellow workers in other civil rights groups."[42] Those who have written previously about Southwest Georgia assumed that everyone with Sherrod was a SNCC worker and did not differentiate the seminarians, who had their own specific set of motivations for being there, from other volunteers.[43] Churches, too, assumed that the project was a SNCC project only, and some were wary of being aligned with the group through their support of SIM. The SIM leadership back in New York was also leery of bad press, with Oscar Lee at one point suggesting to the students that they run the Southwest Georgia project under the separate name "Ministry to the Movement," rather than as an identifiable part of the Student Interracial Ministry.[44]

In general, the project made good on its "below the radar" approach, and even today, there are few who know about the organization behind many of its influential volunteers. Indeed, this tactic was very much in the style of the entire SIM program, which may have made it more effective but has certainly rendered it nearly invisible within the history of the civil rights struggle. As Sherrod articulated from the outset, "In Albany we work with the Albany Movement, in Terrell with the Terrell County Movement, etc. If there is an operation requiring a joint effort from ten counties or twenty we just add to it. We are not to be called 'SIM' nor do we announce ourselves as preachers or even a group of seminarians. Rather, we are known only as 'some more students' who have come to live and work and suffer and share among the people of Southwest Georgia."[45]

Sherrod's choice of words carried in them the echo of an earlier Christian activist experiment in the region. Most of the SIM volunteers were aware of the history of Koinonia Farm and made numerous visits to the nearby Christian interracial community during their time in Georgia. One of Koinonia's first volunteers, Martin England, explained that the farm's goal was "to mak[e] a witness in the dirt as real farmers, not as professionals or as ministers going to tell people how to live on a farm in Georgia."[46] For these earlier missionaries, joining in the work and poverty of fellow farmers was an important symbolic part of their work and of the demonstration that they made for others that such work was not only for the poorest but for all. However, the truth of it was that the SIM volunteers, like the Koinonia volunteers, were more than simply additional workers; they had a different set of motivations.

Ed Feaver concluded that one had to actually experience the southern situation—the "racial injustice and irrational adherence to the status quo," the hatred toward blacks and white volunteers coming from even the most moderate of whites—in order to truly understand it and its importance to the current mission of the church. Feaver felt as though the experience had offered him the chance to see how both black and white churches, in their silence, had crippled black social and spiritual development. But he also saw how much good the church could do if and when it risked speaking out. Feaver reflected that experiencing the faith of poor southern blacks made his own beliefs and ability to forgive seem somewhat hollow by comparison, but it also made him see "life emerge out of death; hope out of despair." To a would-be minister like Feaver, the work in Southwest Georgia imparted a new appreciation of how to work with rather than lead a congregation. It also helped him understand the workings of poverty and the everyday realties of the poor—lessons that could be applied equally well in a northern urban congregation and in the farmlands of the South.[47]

The Southwest Georgia seminary students concluded that one need not have a church to have a ministry, nor need one be ordained to minister to the needs of the people. Asked to define the proper role of a minister in this context, Joe Pfister commented, "The answers to these questions cannot be found by remaining within the walls of church structures. They cannot be found in the roles of the white minister and his all white congregation or the black circuit preacher with his hit and run method. The ministry is the getting of the Message across to the people, . . . expressing it everywhere: in politics, in economics, in social life and even in the churches. This ministry cannot be contained by the structures of the churches, but it may be able to use them. This ministry may in fact undermine the church structures and break open a whole society in order to save the message it bears."[48]

Many in the project distinguished between the church as institution and the church as community, and some even likened their experiment to that of the early Christians just after the death of Jesus, an intentional community "of faith that binds us together."[49] The Koinonia Farm experiment had described itself in much the same way in the 1940s, although it was more consciously separate from society and disdained direct political engagement. Sherrod had an entirely different approach, and the use of white volunteers was crucial to his plans.

The first five volunteers, in 1965, were all white; the next year, nineteen out of twenty SIM participants in Southwest Georgia were white or Asian. The first five who served during the summer of 1965 were based in Albany but worked extensively in "Bad Baker" County. This was Sherrod's first foray into that fabled territory, where one of the worst of the backcountry southern sheriffs, L. Warren "the Gator" Johnson, ruled with fear and an oft-used pistol. And it was no coincidence that Sherrod chose white volunteers to go into Baker for voter registration work, often purposely putting them in harm's way. He had used this strategy since his first involvement in the Albany Movement, explaining in a 1963 report, "I knew that the Justice Department and the media and the country would not consciously let anything happen to them white kids."[50]

Even after the murders of white volunteers during Freedom Summer in Mississippi and of Jonathan Daniels, a white seminarian in Alabama, Sherrod continued to employ white SIM volunteers along the front lines.[51] Janet Vrchota, a white Union student, was shifted from relatively peaceful Albany to Baker County in June 1965, when black SNCC volunteers there, including Sherrod, reported threats and intimidation from the Gator and his deputies. Vrchota recalled that the project deployed her and other white volunteers into Baker County in the belief that if the whites were beaten or jailed, this would prove far more newsworthy than abuse of blacks, and such publicity would both help the cause in general and perhaps ease harassment.[52] The threat of personal violence was so great that Vrchota lived with one black family for only a week, moving nearly every night after that.[53]

Charles Sherrod's decision to bring in a large group of white volunteers in 1966 angered his half-dozen SNCC colleagues still working in Southwest Georgia. The black SNCC workers questioned Sherrod's insistence on continuing to work with white volunteers, and Sherrod tried to reassure them that the white seminary volunteers would "not sabotage the movement," since they would not hold leadership positions but would be immediately placed in black-led interracial teams.[54] But by the end of the summer, the remaining SNCC workers' enmity was reaching its peak; they had not been paid in a month, the rent was overdue, and the electricity and phone had been cut off in the office they shared with the SIM workers. The Student Interracial Ministry project hardly alleviated the tension when it stepped in to pay the bills, explaining that SNCC had lost crucial white financial support when it elevated Stokely Carmichael to its leadership position and especially after his articulation of the Black Power strategy in June 1966.[55]

As Shirley Sherrod, who had grown up locally before marrying Charles Sherrod, later described the situation, "Stokely felt that all whites needed to go and work in their own communities . . . [and] whites needed to leave SNCC. We did not agree with that here in Southwest Georgia. My husband . . . had recruited a large number of students from Union—we probably had 20 to 25 white people working with us during that time when Stokely was saying whites needed to leave—so we separated from SNCC at that point." The split had been coming for some time and reflected the Sherrods' belief in the beloved community ideal but also the practical help that white allies could provide. "We felt," Shirley Sherrod continued, that "in order to bring about change we needed the help of whites, whether they were from this area or not. And most of them were not; in fact, all of them were not. But we felt, too, that we needed each other in order to bring about the change that needed to happen here, and to mirror and set the example for other areas."[56]

The SIM and SNCC students spent countless hours meeting in SNCC's steamy Albany office at 229 ½ Jackson Street trying to find a way to work together. Mostly they agonized over what Black Power meant for their fieldwork and "what to do with the whites."[57] This problem seemed particularly acute in the case of a newly married SIM couple, Joe and Embry Howell. No provisions had been made for housing any of the SIM volunteers in the summer of 1966, and it turned out to be particularly difficult to find a black family able and willing to take in a married, white volunteer couple. So the Howells were shuttled from house to house, sleeping on floors for a night at a time, until they finally ended up bedding down in the SNCC office. It was hot and filthy, and another volunteer described sleeping on top of his desk to stay away from the rats. Joe Howell described the office as "eight rooms— quite dirty and disorganized. The walls of the main room are covered with various pictures and souvenirs of the movement. Two rooms serve for office work, three for sleeping, and two for a library. [It] has an atmosphere of intrigue about. One feels as if a revolution is under way."[58] But revolutions are by their nature tumultuous, and Howell recalled the SNCC workers expressing that "even having white people on the scene is patronizing. White people should be working in their own communities and changing the way white people treat black people. Don't come down here and lord over us in terms of 'helping' black people. Black people have to help themselves."[59] The Howells were left feeling that their presence was unwelcome and were thus unable to contribute as they wished.

Sherrod agreed that black people needed to help themselves, but he also defended his decision to bring the white volunteers. He did this in two ways, first by appealing to the power of the integrated beloved community, and second by arguing for the practical advantages of having white volunteers involved. White volunteers brought with them, Sherrod believed, the psychologically persuasive power of their skin color, and he was not above using that to his advantage. "We are using the system," he later recalled. "The system [says] white is right. I use this example: Who do they look at when you come to a door and you start talking about voter registration or about coming to a mass meeting? The white peoples. All right then. So you won't come to the meeting? Well, come because the white boy says so! I don't give a damn why you come to the meeting, just bring your black ass to the meeting! That's all I want, for you to be at the meeting." Sherrod was careful, however, to say that white volunteers needed to understand that "anytime they come down here, in the movement context, we blacks need to be in charge, we need to have the last word on what's going to reflect on us or what's going to move us or what's going to hurt us in some way or what's going to help us in some way. We need to have the last word on it."[60] Sherrod also dismissed the notion of the Beloved Community being simply an ideal and not a practical solution, and one that lacks great power because it is rooted in love. "It ain't so soft, it's got strength behind it, it had meaning in it. And there is love, there's love on top of it, there's love beside it, there's love on the bottom of the community. It's based on love. But while I love my child, I'll whip his tail."[61]

While the atmosphere could often be contentious, volunteers recall that SIM and SNCC workers did collaborate in the field with little actual difficulties. Even so, the presence of so many white volunteers likely contributed to the final disassociation of Sherrod from SNCC. Later that year, Sherrod effectively broke the relationship for good when he sought financial support from the SNCC central committee for even more white student volunteers. His request was unanimously rejected, and the remaining SNCC workers withdrew to Mississippi, Atlanta, and other locales.[62] Sherrod continued on without SNCC, further cementing the bond with SIM and seeking other sources of funding. The Howells were taken in by the Hope family in Baker County and put to work staffing a new Head Start day-care center.[63] Other volunteers lived throughout Albany and the surrounding counties, and worked closely with the SNCC workers before their departure. One such worker, Ramona Lockette, had grown up locally, and her mother's house became a central gathering place, with something always cooking on the stove. As Larry Mamiya, a Japanese American SIM student from Hawaii recalled, "From my experience, I always considered the local people to be the true heroes and heroines of the civil rights movement. They took us as strangers into their homes, fed us, and put their homes as collateral to bail us out of jail. Above all, after most of us left the area, they had to deal with the brutality and abuses that we had stirred up with our protests."[64]

Sherrod had his own take on Black Power, which to him essentially meant an equal share. His aim was not separatism but power sharing with whites, and he felt that integration as a goal unto itself was meaningless. In order to invest African Americans with power to the point of an equal share, the pat assurances of the church would have to be turned into concrete action.[65] Or, put in Sherrodian terms: "The white man is no longer going to get away with affirmations of Christian love toward his poor black brother. He is going to have to prove these affirmations by relinquishing some of his power and wealth."[66]

Set apart from the national apparatus of SNCC, Albany was once again a local struggle, and with Charles Sherrod as a sort of transplanted local, the movement there remained firmly rooted in both nonviolence and interracialism—and, undergirding both of these, a deep Christian ethos. Focusing on the Second and Third Congressional Districts, the Southwest Georgia Project conducted economic, cultural, or political projects in twenty of the twenty-three local counties. Sherrod delineated a strategic approach in which church reform and reinvention was an integral part. Sherrod's general plan included building political participation, community bonds, and economic opportunities while drawing on the influence of the church to accomplish racial reconciliation. He then supported these broad goals with a series of specific plans tailored to individual communities.

In the political arena, voter registration remained the primary activity of SIM volunteers throughout their involvement in the Southwest Georgia Project. Volunteers also worked on political campaigns, a strategy first put into action by SNCC for C. B. King's 1964 congressional campaign. Sherrod and his team developed a two-part strategy during that run—the first African American congressional campaign since Reconstruction—involving voter registration and candidate-specific campaigning. In early 1964, Don Harris, a white SNCC worker based in Americus, noted that there were 56,531 unregistered blacks of voting age in the Second Congressional District. He reasoned that the King candidacy could serve two goals—new black voters could be used to get King elected, and King's candidacy would be used to attract and enroll new voters.[67] The C. B. King campaign did help kick-start voter registration drives in the more distant counties, but only in a limited way.[68] It was more successful in Albany, where 500 blacks registered between King's announcement on April 4 and the close of registration; and in Tifton County, 350 new voters registered.[69]

Voting increased only gradually, due in part to the ever-present threat of violence against black citizens and both white and black volunteers. In "Terrible" Terrell County, where the project consisted of house-by-house canvassing, voter registration, and the running of a citizenship school, blacks attempting to register to vote were met with hostility and reprisals, and on December 8, 1963, the private home that housed the citizenship school was shot up, bombed, and partially burnt down.[70] Four years later, on August 19, 1967, the Southwest Georgia Project's headquarters in Albany was attacked and burned down by six white men.[71] Sherrod called the SIM headquarters a few days later and Carol Walters took down the phone message: "Sherrod called from Newtown, Georgia, to say the SIM office in Albany was burned by whites on Saturday. All papers, records, correspondence, and typewriters were destroyed. No one was hurt. It was a collect call which I accepted because he said it was an emergency."

SIM volunteers were arrested repeatedly on trumped-up charges, including suspicion of burglary and numerous traffic offenses, and were continuous targets of harassment, ranging from name-calling and bottle throwing to being run off the road by other vehicles.[72] Several of the interns later recalled homes they were staying in being shot at or stoned, and many had memories of dangerous, often high-speed pursuits by suspicious vehicles. (One intern, Maxim Rice, had already survived a terrible beating during an earlier volunteer posting with SCLC's Summer Community Organization and Political Education Project (SCOPE) in Laurens County, Georgia, in 1965. Attempting to integrate a white Baptist church along with the members of an NAACP youth group, Maxim was attacked and beaten by whites, requiring twenty-two stitches in his scalp.)[73] Although the interns joked in their newsletter about the automotive injuries they suffered or Joe Pfister being charged with burglary, the humor masked the serious danger into which all had put themselves.[74] But the seminarians insisted it would be a mistake to focus too much on their difficulties given the near-constant harassment and danger to which the general black population was subjected.

Volunteers also met with significant resistance from potential black voters largely due to fear of reprisals. Their jobs, homes, and credit were on the line, and they had spent lifetimes steeped in a culture of repression, from which breaking away proved very difficult. One organizer reflected, "You cannot come around and break a world in two. You cannot forget the force of two hundred years."[75] Working in Cairo, the county seat of Grady County, Willie Hall and SIM student Ed Feaver were frustrated to find that blacks regarded voting "as white folks' business," but they did understand that it was difficult to perceive the need to vote if the only candidates were white segregationists. In search of assistance, volunteers in Baker County applied for and, in December 1966, received Voter Education Program funds from the Southern Regional Council for a three-month program of voter registration and education, with the goal of registering four hundred new voters.[76]

Each county in Southwest Georgia had a locally appointed voting registrar, whose job it was to administer literacy tests and register new voters. Registrars in the region were all white, and particular registrars had established reputations for finding inventive ways to fail blacks taking the literacy exam or otherwise exclude would-be black voters. According to the law, the federal government could assign federal voting registrars to areas suspected of unfair registration practices, but the Southwest Georgia Project had been lobbying the government for federal voting registrars since 1962 without success. In 1964, Sherrod even drove a group of local residents, including three middle-aged Baker County women and a group of youths, to Washington, D.C., to petition the Department of Justice in person.[77] Throughout 1966, project staff and local people kept pressure on the Department of Justice, which continued to disavow that voting discrimination was an issue in Georgia.[78] In April 1967, after being requested for more than five years, federal registrars finally arrived in Lee and Terrell Counties, but they may as well not have made the journey. Rather than knock on doors in the counties in order to register any of the 89 percent of blacks who still remained unregistered, as the volunteers had done for years now, the registrars set themselves up in an office over the Leesburg farm bureau and announced that they were open for business. And because the few blacks who found the transportation and the bravery to come to the registration office were not met with any resistance, the registrars concluded that blacks were under no undue pressure, and therefore a federal presence wasn't warranted. Sherrod fumed that when his pleas for voting registrars were at last answered, the federal government sent "blockheaded, bumbling, insensitive fools." Having affirmation of the government's insincerity in pursuing fair voting, the project rededicated itself to handling voter registration and education work by itself.[79]

This was not the only incident in which a federal program failed to buck the pervasive climate of white supremacy. For example, the Baker County Community Action Panel, supported by a federal poverty-cessation program, not only refused to meet its obligation to have an interracial board but even included the notoriously corrupt and allegedly murderous sheriff Warren "the Gator" Johnson.[80] Joe Pfister concluded after one panel meeting that the federal antipoverty program was simply replicating the system of white supremacy that kept blacks and poor whites out of power.[81]

Black farmers were mobilizing, too, trying to elect some of their own to the county boards of the Agricultural Stabilization and Conservation Service (ASCS), which were charged with regulating crop allotments, setting prices, and administering cash loans and assistance for education and the purchase of fertilizer. The ASCS controlled services to farmers and had historically failed to represent the interests of black farmers. According to one SIM intern, the ASCS was powerful because it determined which farmers got to grow which crop, which meant it could either make or break an individual farmer. White farmers had traditionally been granted all the allotments for soybeans, the most valuable of local crops.[82] Each county in Georgia had a number of local community ASCS boards, which elected the three members of the county ASCS board. Up to that time, there had never been a black community board member, let alone a black county board member, in any of the 159 Georgia counties.

During the summer of 1966, black farmers got on the ballots in four counties—Worth, Clay, Baker, and Sumter—and used mass organization and block voting to elect L. B. Johnson in Worth County.[83] The Southwest Georgia Project continued to organize black farmers in advance of the ASCS elections the following year, and on September 22, 1967, nine black candidates were represented on ballots in famously repressive Baker County, although it would be a few more years before a black farmer was elected to the board.[84]

With the support of the Southwest Georgia Project, black candidates ran for other local offices as well, many for the first time in the region's history. Many of these early political campaigns, however, were hampered by fear of white backlash, lack of funds, and their own inefficiency. It would take much time and effort to wrest political control away from whites in parts of Southwest Georgia; however, there was no doubt that progress was being made, as black people were running for office and voting in unprecedented numbers.

While voter registration was a strong focus of the entire project, each county had its own issues, and a SIM volunteer would often work on a variety of them. In Cordele, in Crisp County, for example, blacks were struggling with open accommodations, which were still restricted even though they were now guaranteed under federal civil rights legislation. Within a week of their arrival in 1967, several of the SIM volunteers made national news when they helped stage a "swim-in" with black youths at a state park about eight miles from Cordele.[85] A white mob attacked the interracial group as they attempted to desegregate the park's swimming pool. The whites beat some of the black youngsters and threw bottles before overturning a SIM volunteer's car.[86] Some of the older children ran back to town and alerted the SNCC and SIM volunteers who had been attending the wedding of two of the SNCC workers. The SNCC workers armed themselves and set off for the state park to help the children. Police had been notified ahead of time of the potentially incendiary situation, but only five officers arrived, and none tried to stop the white mob. Instead, the police arrested the black organizer of the swim-in, a twenty-six year-old local barber and sanitation worker named Clemmie Gaston—who also hosted two of the SIM students—on a charge of causing malicious mischief and, when his truck grazed a sheriff's thumb, with assault with intent to murder.[87] According to SIM volunteer Larry Mamiya, Gaston was arrested by Sheriff Earlie Posey during a later trip to the park, but only after Posey knocked out several of Gaston's front teeth with a billy club.[88]

Later that evening, a large crowd of black folks, angered at the attacks and the arrest, gathered in downtown Cordele at an intersection at which two black-owned gas stations stood on two corners, facing two white-owned gas stations on the other side of the street. As the black crowd grew restless, a well-armed white mob began to arrive in pick-up trucks at the two white-owned gas stations that faced them. Georgia state troopers stood by but did not intervene. After a while, Charles Sherrod called a mass meeting in a nearby church just to clear the streets and try to release some of the tension. But the meeting could not last forever, and once the crowd had reassembled, a restless black teenager threw a bottle at a passing car. The car turned into one of the white gas stations, and a few minutes later, the whites opened fire. Mamiya recalls diving into the doorway of a black social club that was behind one of the black-owned gas stations. He could hear bullets hitting the wood above his head and remembers thinking, "Those aren't warning shots, they are trying to kill us." He sheltered in an apartment while the shooting went on for three nights and three days. Mamiya contends that the white mob's real goal was to destroy the black-owned gas stations in a hail of gunfire and so leave the white gas stations with a monopoly.[89] He also recalls being grateful that the SNCC volunteers with whom he worked were often armed. Less than a month later, a second attempt to desegregate the pool was met with a Ku Klux Klan rally at the state park.[90]

Achieving voting access and open public accommodations was just part of the plan, however; the Southwest Georgia Project, under Sherrod's leadership, recognized early on that equality for blacks would partly be achieved through black economic independence and power. In 1964, the project laid out a series of economic objectives, including developing black-owned businesses and using boycotts to pressure white-owned businesses to adopt fair pricing and hiring practices. Plans for each year were tailored to each of the counties and to the cities of Albany and Americus. Occasionally, the Southwest Georgia Project attempted a countywide approach, though it often took years of development at the county level before a successful regional program could be realized, and often the eventual program differed significantly from the original plans. For example, initial plans for a regional pecan farming and shelling cooperative, the Rural Areas Development project, were tabled by late 1963 over concerns about a lack of planning and technical expertise.[91] Instead, the project put forth more immediate political goals aimed toward improving the conditions of area farmers. Sherrod and his colleagues lobbied the counties to create positions for negro county agents, and focused their efforts on electing black members to the ASCS boards.[92]

SIM students within the Southwest Georgia Project also confronted the lack of affordable housing in the counties.[93] Summer student David Hawk worked with members of the Crisp County Movement in Cordele to organize tenants in the Sunset Homes housing project. They formed the Sunset Homes Improvement Association, with Clemmie Gaston—the same man who had been charged with assault at the swim-in—as chairman, to protest rent increases, charges for services like garbage collection, unlawful evictions, and abuse and intimidation of residents.[94] Hawk worried that little would be accomplished because "a trained sense of hopelessness is partner of the economically oppressive system."[95] It was clear to SIM workers that in order for blacks in Southwest Georgia to advance, they had to overcome not just material challenges but the psychological obstacles that were the inheritance of centuries of oppression.

Education lay at the root of the project's plan to help undo this damage, but school reform, like much of the progress in Southwest Georgia, moved in fits and starts. In Cordele in 1966, over five hundred junior and high school students boycotted classes in protest of poor school conditions, which consisted of such deprivations as lack of bathrooms, broken windows, and poor ventilation. Protests were met in April of that year by a Ku Klux Klan rally.[96] Baker County, for its part, earned the distinction in 1966 of being the first county in the southern United States to lose federal school funding for refusing to comply with its own desegregation plan.[97] In an attempt to regain federal funding, the school board transferred sixty black students to the formerly all-white school, but no black teachers were sent to the school, and no whites were sent to the black school. After the beating of a black student in October, the black students walked out of the school en masse.[98] In November, black students boycotted the formerly all-white school in Crisp County to protest their verbal and physical mistreatment; however, the students found little support from their parents, who feared economic reprisals.[99]

Change did come more quickly in the towns than in the rural counties. In 1966, the Albany school board voluntarily desegregated grades seven through nine, as well as the court-ordered lower grades, meaning that 587 blacks would be going to integrated schools.[100] In April 1967, hoping to stimulate progress in the rural areas as well, interns helped create a weekly Freedom School in Baker County, where approximately seventy locals learned about important people and events in black history, including Adam Clayton Powell and Black Reconstruction. Project workers also targeted educational reform at the youngest levels. Following the lead of SNCC in Mississippi, they built and staffed Head Start programs, one of the few ways in which local people could avail themselves of federal development monies. One such program was established in Baker County in 1966.[101] A facetious report from one of that program's six SIM volunteers, Don Steffa, demonstrates how a sense of humor could aid survival in a tense situation like that in Baker. Steffa reported on the activities of the children in Head Start but filled his report with civil rights movement language, describing the job of herding preschool children as "organizing independent black power." Steffa reported, "Leaders here have emphasized that the L.P.s (little people), must be organized. They must be organized to play games, eat lunch, and go to the bathroom. The L.P.s are powerful. They are independent. They neither listen to nor obey us." He went on to describe daily school sessions as "mass meetings," to refer to juice and cookies as a "Freedom Snack," and to lament the difficulties of convincing all the L.P.s of the wisdom of nonviolence. "There have been several cases of biting ... [and] there have been a few casualties: one large beetle, of drowning, and two goldfish, of unknown causes." Each day ended with a "Freedom Nap" and then a "Freedom Ride" home.[102]

Humor was one tactic that could be essential for surviving the grueling work in the Georgia heat with high stress and few rewards; one SIM volunteer recalled that Sherrod was particularly good at recognizing that movement workers could not labor incessantly, but needed some time off and relaxation to ease the pressure. He also insisted that votes and jobs alone would not sustain the black community and, to that end, planned a slate of drama, musical, and dance programs, as well as workshops in photography, painting, and writing, "to allow the black population to experience and enlarge their own culture."[103] One evening program in August 1966, organized by SIM's Joe Pfister, featured local storytellers, the Albany Freedom Singers, a SIM volunteer talking about African history, and local teenagers performing James Baldwin's *Blues for Mister Charlie*.[104] The following academic year, Sherrod and the Southwest Georgia Project proposed that SIM sponsor an Indigenous Theatre Project, not dissimilar to that of the Federal Theatre Project groups created by the New Deal–era Works Progress Administration.[105]

In addition to taking occasional breaks and engaging in local cultural activities, the seminary volunteers had to find other ways, often spiritual, to sustain themselves during work that could be repetitive, sometimes grueling, and usually without easily noticeable rewards. Joe Pfister reported that taking a long-range approach to social change was one way to avoid frustration and thus remain committed to the slow work of social change, but that the volunteers needed to find personal rewards as well. "I can't think of any other work to which society offers less social rewards," he wrote, "than in community organizing in the Movement. So the rewards must come from Movement groups themselves." Pfister and his colleagues attempted to keep each other committed and sane by playing music, studying, and working together.

The work of the SIM participants in the Southwest Georgia Project from 1965 through 1968 reflected Sherrod's growing understanding that it was time to "dig in for the long haul."[106] In his view, the days of marches and protests had passed, and immediate short-term goals had now to be replaced by a long-term struggle to build and consolidate community power. It was not a unique conclusion; other activists, including Bayard Rustin and Saul Alinsky, had come to a similar answer in different contexts. As Joe Pfister, who, all told, would spend ten years working with Sherrod and the Southwest Georgia Project, reflected, "The poor and disenfranchised people of this country will not be given their 'freedom' but will have to make themselves powerful enough to demand it. . . . The project has a great task of educating people to politics and economics in order to create a united group as a political force."[107]

As time would reveal, Sherrod and Pfister had a remarkably good understanding of both the deep roots of a vastly complex social situation and the difficulties that lay ahead in shifting the economic and social power structure. However, they may not have fully appreciated at the time just how long the struggle would last. Sherrod found few individuals willing to accompany him on the entire length of this journey. Pfister and a few other volunteers made long-term commitments, but even they left eventually, and the majority of movement activists moved on after spending a summer or a year in the Albany area. Charles Sherrod and his wife, Shirley Sherrod (a local girl), and others from Albany stayed on. Many of those born in the bottomlands found they had little choice but to stay and fight.

Joe Pfister suggested at the time that to survive the project would need a structure that encompassed both a long-range perspective on the movement and a generous understanding of what constituted progress. Project workers would also require some other way of drawing personal reward and meaning from the work, perhaps through the development of community ties or through communal study, or they would burn out and soon leave.[108] Finding such sustenance was difficult in the face of little perceivable progress and in light of daily reminders of white power, including Ku Klux Klan rallies, recalcitrant voting registrars, and murderous sheriffs. The "long haul" did not offer the same potential for excitement that the confrontations and promised paradigm shifts in race relations provoked in those first years. It also did not have as its basis the clear moral logic of those earlier years or of the other social movements that followed—the anti–Vietnam War movement chief among them—and which competed for followers. Joe Pfister put it well when he said that the time had now come to move from "the glory of the summer" into "the gloom of the winter."[109]

Set next to its sweeping goals of revolution and reconciliation, what was actually realized in Southwest Georgia was much more modest. Although some important electoral and economic advancements were begun under the auspices of the Southwest Georgia Project, SIM volunteers reckoned that from their point of view, the exposure to black people and Southern culture that resulted in the shattering of "middle-class myths" was both "the primary aim of the summer project" and its most successful result.[110] This exposure was not merely challenging but also threatening to many students' assumptions about social equality, their roles in society, and—especially—their roles within the church and white America. According to Ed Feaver, confronting the system was no longer theoretical, as it had become for all of them an unceasing demand.[111] But the volunteers also learned the depths of the system's roots and its hold on southern life. For many, it was quite a burden of discovery—to find out just how bad the system was and how urgently massive change was required, while seeing how nearly impossible creating that change was likely to be.

For many seminarians, their experience in Southwest Georgia was akin to a foreign cultural exchange, albeit at home in America and wrapped in a mission-like package. It provided a fascinating learning experience unto itself, regardless of the political or social implications of the work. Many students remarked in their summer reports that the experience had been "life changing" or "one of the best things that ever happened" to them.[112]

Locals, too, obviously gained from the sweat equity of these volunteers, and this mutual benefit is another way in which the Southwest Georgia Project differed from SIM's congregational placements. In the majority of congregational placements, in which white seminarians served black churches, the most noticeable benefit was the life experience and, in some cases, the racial awakening experienced by the white students. This had the potential to seed great change in the future, as those young ministers embarked on various careers in and out of the pulpit, but it had a less obvious immediate impact. The congregations of the black churches had been led and preached to by whites before, and they would host them again. In the few cases in which black ministerial students led white congregations and lived as equals in white communities, such as with James Forbes's ministry to Binkley Baptist Church in Chapel Hill, the change wrought within the white community was larger and more obvious. In Southwest Georgia, by approaching ministry outside the strict definition of preacher and congregation, the greater community stood to benefit more obviously and immediately. White students serving in the area could experience their cultural awakenings, while the black communities could benefit materially from the fieldwork of the students, whether they were registering voters, picking cotton or cucumbers, or running a printing press. One of the yearlong volunteers, Glen Pearcy, who served along with his wife Susan, made a short film about the Southwest Georgia Project titled *One More River to Cross*, while other volunteers produced a newspaper and newsletter, with Susan Pearcy sometimes contributing art work.[113] These outreach efforts were consciously devoted to promoting the mission of the project both locally and farther afield. The larger community might still experience changes in perception—could still move toward reconciliation—while concrete change outside the walls of the church was realized as well.

The Southwest Georgia project gave seminarians the chance to try out another definition of ministry, working outside the institutional church while still doing "church work." With the nation experiencing waves of social protest and reorder, theologians and some mainline Protestant church leaders were struggling to determine just what their work should be in order to remain relevant, or even to survive at all. The Southwest Georgia Project was an "experiment, at some considerable risk."[114] Not only did it test the traditional role of the clergy leader, but it did so in an explicitly interracial, and very public, way, and in the context of a particularly repressive stronghold of white supremacy in the Deep South.

Sherrod wrote at the time, "We acknowledge that the church is the means by which God chooses to save the world, but also acknowledge that the church has need of renewal and reconstruction in function, in our minds, in the world, and in the Scriptures."[115] The decision to work outside church structures was based on both logistical and theological concerns, although it was not always clear which came first or was stronger. Numerous ideologies, practical concerns, and crises seemed to be warring in the same space, putting a number of questions in play: Did work have to be done outside the church because there was no place within the church due to its inherent resistance? Or had the institutional church outlived its usefulness, calling for new definitions of ministry and new ways of defining the church itself? And were these, in fact, new ways, or a reconnection to the church's historical purpose?

One answer is that SIM clergy *had* to go outside the church walls, for there was no place for them within. Pushed outside the church, they would "stand as a witness to the responsible role which the Southern church must now assume if it is to become involved in the solution of the country's racial problems."[116] In contrast to this purely logistical answer was a more theological argument about the true nature of the church itself, and the need to recover its historical roots and mission. In this argument, the Church with a capital *C* was a mere institution, but *the church* was "the fellowship, both visible and invisible, of those committed 'in Christ,' to each other and to the world."[117] As Joe Pfister put it, the SIM students in Southwest Georgia were working toward "a common sense of purpose which extends beyond the immediate goals. It is a style of concern for all men and women. To my understanding it is the style of a group who would be obedient disciples of Jesus Christ."[118] At least some of the SIM volunteers in Southwest Georgia, then, understood their work as akin to that of the early Christian church. Even though much of their work was focused on "secular" concerns, like voting rights, the volunteers understood themselves to be the "church" gathered to do the work of God. They invoked such gathering not as a radical departure from church business as usual but as a return to the true path as practiced by Jesus and the prophets. "The prophets were the heretics of their day," Sherrod wrote in a local newspaper. "The Church, the real Church, has always been made up of people who refuse to accept things as they are."[119] Another writer agreed, exhorting readers to "turn to your New Testament. There is no word for 'congregation.' For three hundred years there were no buildings that they called churches. The early Christians were on the move, taking the Gospel to the poor, the needy, the enslaved, the captive, in all the highways and byways. This was the church: a fellowship of mission, changing as it became necessary, moving according to where the need was, preaching one to the other and *being* the church, not having church."[120]

For Sherrod, as for many of those who participated in SIM, *church* was the experience of brotherhood and of reconciliation, not the structures of buildings or even scripture. Sherrod was often eloquent on the subject, and quoting him in some length here affords a sense of both his goals and the language he employed to describe them:

Let me bear witness before you that I have seen the church, moving, surging and falling, struggling to breathe, eager to learn the truth; I have seen it in stinking jail cells packed with people, singing and sweating people, brought about before the Pilates of this day; I have seen the church under the stars praying and singing in the ashes of a burned down church building, in the winter shivering under a tent in the open country, in a home where people cried together without speech but with a common understanding; I have seen the church in a pool room. I have seen with my eyes whites protecting blacks with their bodies and blacks bleeding to shield whites from whites.

I have seen ministers lead their congregation from Sunday service to the City Hall to condemn the state. I have heard ministers with three grades of education put Ph.D.s to shame. I have seen men share their bread until the last was gone. I have seen a band of rugged brothers willing to risk death for each other if need be. I have seen the strength of fellowship among those who formally refuse the fellowship of the church. Somehow I think this life must be shared for it to be comprehended; we do have something to offer but there is probably much more to be received. This is an experiment in truth to find the truth.[121]

Calls to reform the church and the plans for how to approach the work on the ground in Southwest Georgia were often made using traditional Christian metaphors of death and rebirth. Noting that the goal of the project was to stimulate local self-sufficiency, entrepreneurialism, and leadership, Sherrod declared, "We as a staff are born to die."[122] Another time he wrote, "The task before SIM as it understands itself is as a participant in helping the churches die that the church might be reborn."[123] He hoped that his community organization program would be the shortest-lived program of its kind in history, for he wished the local people to take it over immediately from the outside professionals. He believed that only through the death of one way of organizing and thinking and sharing power would other methods be newly born. Pfister, too, predicted that the South itself would not change without the church, although most likely the church "will be one of the last things to change."[124]

The project certainly had a profound impact, however, back at Union Theological Seminary, the home campus for many of the SIM students. The Student Interracial Ministry program, and specifically its Southwest Georgia Project, was the catalyst for most of the subsequent social justice work at Union in the 1960s.[125] David Langston, a 1971 graduate of Union, wrote, "It is difficult to overstate the importance of the Southwest Georgia Project on student activism at Union Theological Seminary. Most of the student leadership and a few very influential faculty had been deeply influenced by its model of informed activism and readiness for personal sacrifice that often meant going to jail."[126] Faculty members reported that the students who had gone to Southwest Georgia beginning in 1965 returned to the seminary campus deeply affected by the experience, and they, too, began openly questioning both the form and the content of the seminary education system. The Southwest Georgia veterans formed "an important nucleus for change" on the campus.[127]

The Southwest Georgia Project may have been unique in deed; however, in substance it was but one of the numerous ways in which the church struggled to reinvent itself in the 1960s. Risto Lehtonen, general secretary of the World Student Christian Federation during the middle and late 1960s, described his generation's quest to challenge and change the church as "a storm" that would continue to wreak havoc in theological thought and institutional structure into the present day.[128] The fumbling attempts of SIM and the Southwest Georgia Project were but raindrops in this greater downpour.

The Student Interracial Ministry declared that it put seminarians into the world "at those places where decisions must be made and the tactics for revolution formulated."[129] Southwest Georgia was certainly one of those places. The call to *reconciliation*, for so long the goal fostered by SIM, was now joined, if not yet replaced, by a call to social and economic *revolution*. The Student Interracial Ministry project had entered a new phase.

CHAPTER FIVE

Seminarians in the Secular City

Embracing Urban Ministry, 1965–1968

> Not all laymen approve, but many tolerate the activism of their clergymen
> as long as they talk and act in the name of peace, reconciliation, and love. In
> growing numbers, however, clergymen have been turning to a kind of social
> action whose watchwords are conflict, power, and self-interest. As they have
> moved into this new area, they have found the ground less sure, the directions
> less well-marked, and predictably, the response less tolerant. The results thrill,
> confuse, distress, and anger, often all at the same time.
>
> —William C. Martin, *Christians in Conflict*

From the country soil of Southwest Georgia grew the change that carried
the Student Interracial Ministry further and further outside the walls of the
institutional church and into the now often-turbulent streets of America's
cities. When the SIM student leaders took stock of their progress after the
summer of 1965, they could see how they had moved from addressing racial
problems primarily within the structure of the church itself through interracial pulpit exchange, to using what it termed the "self-realizing church" as
a philosophical and physical base from which to reach out into the community.[1] The effects of this new direction—on both the churches and their
communities—were now more obvious, as SIM joined efforts to increase
electoral participation and provide new economic opportunities, and as it
witnessed an outmigration of churchgoers to the suburbs and a resulting
uncertainty of mission for those churches left "stranded" in the inner cities.
SIM's efforts, moreover, now took place within the context of new federal
civil rights legislation, rising calls within the civil rights movement for
greater black autonomy and power, the federal government's War on Poverty, and the increasing influence of the student and antiwar movements
both on and off university campuses. By the fall of 1965, SIM saw urban
America as the natural direction for the organization's next steps. In the
words of one former intern, "That's where it was happening."[2]

Now firmly in middle age, the Student Interracial Ministry had spent its
first six summers modeling integration and interracialism within the church.
It celebrated the small victories it achieved when "here and there a church

called a minister or accepted some members on an inclusive basis." At the same time, the seminarians acknowledged the limits of their and other religious efforts at the level of the individual church, noting that "many other congregations only shrank back in fear, threw up private property signs in front of their doors, and posted the police on the front steps during worship."[3] The student organizers concluded that their current approach could guarantee only limited returns, and they laid out a new plan for urban ministry in mid-1965 based on their belief that "SIM's philosophy had to change."[4]

They modeled the urban projects on their developing program in Southwest Georgia, which, although decidedly rural, shared many of the economic and social justice concerns found in the urban centers.[5] The Southwest Georgia Project's approach to ministry questioned traditional church and clergy boundaries and pastoral roles, and encouraged interracial cooperation not just within the church but also through political campaigns, voter registration, community activities, and business development. Under the leadership of Charles Sherrod, SIM's first summer with the project had combined the idealistic vision of the beloved community with pragmatic goals and strategies. The SIM students believed that applying a similar strategy in the urban context would serve to "humanize the social, political, and economic structures that deny and distort human dignity and freedom."[6] Many students also felt a spiritual call to serve in the urban setting, where 61 percent of the population now lived. They agreed with University of Chicago Divinity School professor Gibson Winter, who had recently argued that in fleeing urban centers for the suburbs, mainline churches expressed "an illusory hope for escape from the responsibility for shaping the metropolis."[7] Rather than fall for this illusion, SIM's students embraced the responsibility that they felt urban ministry demanded of them. It was a call to urban service commonly heard in the seminaries and progressive churches of the time and prompting theological discussions everywhere—from church boardrooms to campus classrooms to suburban living rooms.

One only needed to scan through the titles in the theology section of a local bookstore in the 1960s to see that something was brewing in the churches. *Race and the Renewal of the Church; The Church amid Revolution; God Is for Real, Man; No Ground Beneath Us: A Revolutionary Reader; Religion and Social Conflict; The Gathering Storm in the Churches*: these were but a few of the titles that appeared in that tumultuous decade.[8] Once a subject for discussion only in seminaries and Sunday schools, theology had spilled out into the streets. One book in particular transcended the boundaries of specialties and emerged on many an American bedside table: theologian

Harvey Cox's surprise 1965 best seller *The Secular City: Secularization and Urbanization in Theological Perspective*. Called "hands down, Protestantism's most discussed book" by the *Christian Century* magazine, the book sold nearly a million copies and stirred up much discussion in a nation eager to understand the implications of its racial and spiritual crises.[9]

Cox built upon the work of Dietrich Bonhoeffer to challenge the common portrayal of the modern industrial city as a soulless metropolis in which technology and modernity had replaced more traditional beliefs and value systems. In contrast to Arthur Schlesinger's argument that modern society would outgrow the need for religion, Bonheoffer had argued that as the world came "of age," it was not jettisoning religion but adapting it for its current purposes. By departing from strict biblical interpretation, modern Christians, he wrote, had been freed to practice the spirit of Christianity apart from outdated ritual. Cox agreed that modernity and changing religious practices did not spell the end of religion, but he argued for even greater theological and spiritual engagement with worldly concerns. "The secular," he claimed, "is not outside the realm of action or God's presence."[10] Christians need not lament secularization, he wrote, for it did not equate to secular*ism*, which itself served as a kind of substitute religion. Rather, secular*ization*, for Cox, represented an opportunity to authentically apply Christian thought, since it was the "liberation of man from religious and metaphysical tutelage, the turning of his attention away from other worlds and toward this one."[11] According to this view, Christians living fully in the secular world were freer than ever to practice the demands of their faith. In the urban context, this meant addressing the ills and needs of the city and its occupants.

The ideological turn to the cities and to economic concerns reflected what Cox termed a national shift in mood at mid-decade.[12] The first five years of the 1960s had seen major legislative advances for African American rights and pushed race issues to the fore of the nation's consciousness and conscience. Some parts of society joyously embraced these changes, others resisted or ignored them, and still others regarded the true work as having just begun. In the church, all of these reactions could be seen at once. Within the same denomination, some congregations fled to the suburbs while others recommitted to staying in the inner cities, where they tried to adapt to declining membership, connect to new populations, and respond to the community's need for social change. This latter group was a small minority in the overall church population, and yet it represented a continuity of engagement with urban mission on the part of the mainline churches, one that dated back to the Social Gospel Movement. The churches' move toward urban ministry in the late 1960s was therefore not a turn but a return, not a radical departure but a reembracing of a tradition of urban social service that had quietly persisted since the nineteenth century, and which a number of individual congregations had never abandoned.

The churches were spurred along by none other than SIM's Steve Rose, for the moment still living in Chicago and editing the journal *Renewal*. Since 1962, when he had helped establish the magazine, Rose had built it into an influential gathering place for progressive theologians and critics of the churches' often hesitant approaches to society's ills. He had been building toward a more vocal and organized call for major reform for some time—in 1964 a reader responded that Rose was "swinging a pretty heavy stick," and wanted to know if his targets were primarily the clergy or their congregants. "Depends on the issue," Rose replied. "Generally both and then some."[13] For roughly three years, Rose and *Renewal* had been discussing the perceived weaknesses in the Protestant churches, but in the January 1966 issue, Rose offered a rationale for moving from criticism to laying out a set of "practical proposals for renewal" that would be "so pragmatic that it hurts."[14] The following month, Rose put the full power of his years of thought on the subject and, with the help of some of his many influential friends on the Christian Left, came out swinging with a jeremiad for the times. He called it "The Grass Roots Church: Manifesto for a Renewal Movement," and accompanied it with a number of companion pieces by the likes of Malcolm Boyd and others on topics such as ecumenical movements and urban ministry. Rose styled the issue "the first volley in what we hope will turn into a grass roots movement for the restructuring of Protestantism."[15] Several months later, Rose published an expanded version in book form, with an introduction by Harvey Cox, with the slightly altered subtitle "A Manifesto for Protestant Renewal." He followed this in March 1966 with a collection of essays from *Renewal* published under the title *Who's Killing the Church?*, which he suggested could work as a study guide for those wanting to participate in the renewal discussion.[16] The manifesto captured the attention of the church and of the general public, with the *New York Times* likening Rose to Martin Luther and suggesting that the manifesto had the importance of a modern-day ninety-five theses, but nailed to the Protestant church door, and *Theology Today* devoting a portion of an issue to it, with responses from four critics.[17]

Rose's manifesto was rooted in five enumerated assertions: (1) "trained" Christians must participate in greater numbers in the international fight for social justice; (2) churches needed to not just engage with the world in new ways but also recover their traditional functions of teaching, preaching, and community nurturing; (3) the movement needed to be "radically" ecumenical and be willing to abandon denominational loyalties when they impeded holistic mission; (4) a new theology had to be formed for present times and made accessible by laypeople, not just seminarians and theologians; and (5) the renewal movement needed to prioritize ecumenicity at the local level so that church governmental structures would be elastic enough to allow for both decentralization and local control and a reimagining of how church membership itself might work.[18] In his editorial introduction to the January issue, Rose pointed out that *Renewal* was a good medium for his message, since 80 percent of its readers were members of the laity, and the laity would be at the core of his proposed renewal movement.[19] In an accompanying piece, Malcolm Boyd, the author of the best-selling book of contemporary poems *Are You Running with Me, Jesus?*, hammered home that the church needed to redefine the laity's role. "The church *is* people," he wrote, "yet the people have been strangely silent. The people must now seize the church. 'Laity' must really disappear as a practicing word, for the dichotomy between 'laity' and 'clergy' is destroying the common ministry." Boyd added, echoing Rose, that not only did the divisions between church roles need to come down, but so, too, did the divisions between denominations. He chose an analogy from the present racial and political struggle: "There needs NOW to be an ecumenical counterpart of the Mississippi Freedom Democratic Party. This grassroots body...the Ecumenical Freedom Body...can function as a community of people to destroy old idolatries and build up a new life of common ministry within the church."[20]

Rose and his colleagues also argued that the urban complex was at the center of the current social struggles and that a renewal movement would have to address and develop within its context. For example, Stanley Hallett, an urban planner and the director of research and planning for the Church Federation of Greater Chicago, suggested a structure of ecumenical partnerships aimed at concrete social change: one hundred local congregations could form into ten cooperative ministries, which would in turn spawn task forces each devoted to a particular urban issue. While the plan was hugely ambitious, Charles Harper of Boston's Cooperative Metropolitan Ministry saw it as highlighting the "adaptability and resulting relevance of the local congregation to life and death issues of the city."[21]

The voices in *Renewal*, tying the urban situation to the civil rights movement and to the crisis of identity within the mainline Protestant churches, were not alone. Ministry projects, many of them ecumenical, were springing up from Los Angeles to Chicago to Detroit to Boston. The Church's recommitment to urban ministry was in part a result of legislative gains in the civil rights arena. After the passage of civil rights legislation, racial inequities that fell outside strict legal control became more obvious, and the plight of economically disadvantaged blacks was thrown into greater relief.[22] White religious leaders ensconced in the urban North were suddenly more aware, or forced to address, the conditions of the inner cities. Religious activists saw the potential of the impersonal city to endanger human relationships, and countered with an urban offensive that would spread Christian values while providing substantive relief efforts.[23] Spurred on by the example of Saul Alinsky in Chicago, both Protestant and Catholic churches adopted community organizing as the most important single strategy for urban mission, and the SIM project embraced urban ministry with gusto in both the North and the South.[24]

For its part, SIM moved slowly into a more in-depth commitment to urban ministry. First modeled during the summer of 1965 by the successful team ministry pair of Carol Lucas and Keith Davis in Richmond, this turn to the cities was followed by three of the five interns who began full-year commitments that fall. James Lynwood "Lyn" Walker, a black student from Union, pioneered SIM's West Coast projects in Oakland; John Chappell, a white Union student, worked with a black church in Jamaica, New York; and Virginia Wadsley, another white Union student, worked with Zion Olivet Baptist Church in Charleston, South Carolina, to develop a community action program. Neither of the two remaining internships particularly adhered to SIM's traditional approach, either. Mark Lundeen, who had worked with the NCC's Delta Ministry project during the summer of 1965, stayed on as that project began a number of pioneering efforts in the delta.[25] And Jan Vrchota, a white Union student who had been with SIM in Southwest Georgia during the summer of 1965, interned on the Georgia sea islands near Charleston. Working under Reverend Esau Jenkins on John's Island, she supported his Citizen's Action Committee, another community action program. But unlike her classmate Virginia Wadsley, who was doing similar work in an urban environment a few miles away in Charleston, Vrchota found herself in tropical surroundings, working with a very rural community of mostly agricultural workers. Sharing an isolated old farmhouse with another young woman, she worked with two young men on the island in what they dubbed "Operation Lurch Forward"—a joking jab at the optimistic names of many of the government-sponsored advancement programs of the day—to foster community change efforts and to act as liaisons between islanders and social change groups in Charleston, as well as state and federal programs, including Office of Equal Opportunity (OEO) and Head Start.[26] They wrote grants, worked on voter registration, conducted civil rights workshops, and held a music festival. Vrchota's work ended up being very similar in many ways to what she and her colleagues had done in Southwest Georgia.

George Webber, a founder of the East Harlem Protestant Parish and one of the godfathers of the urban ministry movement, wrote in 1966 that he found SIM's move to the metropolis timely and laudable, although perhaps not surprising given SIM's earlier ventures: "The Student Interracial Ministry, time and again, has forced the churches to recognize the vital contribution which they can make in the social crisis of our time. They are now seeking to extend the pattern of interracial ministry [into] a far more significant emerging contribution."[27]

As the interns helped move the program toward community outreach and urban ministry, SIM's student administrators were also making major changes. During the fall of 1965, the organization expanded from its two committees of the previous year to a series of regional branches and committees, using its network of progressive seminaries. George Walters helped establish regional branches in the New York City (Northeast), Chicago (Midwest), San Francisco (West), and Atlanta (South). The regional committees were envisioned as independent branches of the SIM project, which, as they grew, would split off as separate entities. Walters wrote in late 1965 that he considered organizational structures to be "secondary to purposes"; thus, each of the regional committees was encouraged to develop its own program designed to meet specific regional needs.[28]

When all the committees met in a national meeting in early 1966, the growth of the SIM project was obvious. In addition to nearly three dozen students from Union, the national meeting was attended by student representatives from thirteen other seminaries and theological and divinity schools, including Harvard, Duke, Yale, Princeton, Southeastern Baptist, Southern Baptist, and the Interdenominational Theological Seminary. The expenses of SIM's programs grew along with its size, with a budget that year of $116,000. The new budget required constant, stressful fund-raising. By the end of April 1966, the students still needed to raise nearly $46,000 of its $116,000 budget. The larger budget reflected the involvement of three paid staff, ninety-two summer students, and twenty-four yearlong interns. Twenty-two denominational boards or religious agencies donated funds, as did three foundations, eighteen congregations, and twenty-one seminary organizations.[29] While SIM managed to meet its budgetary goals, the April shortfall heralded a series of anxious memos among the staff and marked the first of what would become an annual panic over money, harbingers of serious financial troubles on the near horizon.

In May 1966, George Walters decided to return to school to complete his BD, although he stayed on as chair of the National Committee. E. Maynard Moore—a Methodist minister, a graduate of Perkins School of Theology in Dallas, a veteran leader in both the Interseminary Movement and the Methodist Student Movement, and a graduate student in social ethics at the University of Chicago—was hired in late spring of 1966 to serve as SIM field secretary, charged with recruiting students and churches and checking on student assignments. He spent much of that summer in the field, and when Walters left for Chicago later in the summer, Moore took on the title of national program coordinator. Moore held the position for more than eighteen months, seeing SIM nearly to its final days. He spent the summer and fall of 1966 traveling the country by bus and hitched rides, visiting fifty-six seminaries and every student posting except that in San Francisco, and establishing new contacts at seminaries and church organizations. Moore had, like Charles Sherrod, been born and raised in Petersburg, Virginia, although race and economics had separated their childhoods, and it took SIM to bring them together.

The SIM committee structure grew yet again under Moore and Walters to include five regional or project committees—Northeast, West, Southeast, Southwest, and the Southwest Georgia Project—each with its own director. A publicity committee was also added and charged with developing a new SIM publication: the quarterly magazine *skandalon*. Again, funds were raised from individuals and congregations, though the significant majority of funding came from church denominational boards and from private foundations, including the Henry Luce Foundation, which signed on for a $5,000 donation.[30]

Although the interns of 1965–66 made some of the first steps toward a different kind of mission for SIM, it was the summer of 1966 that proved to be the definitive shift toward urban ministry and community organizing. Again the summer program grew in size and breadth, hosting fifty-five participants from a record twenty-five schools. For the first time, a few undergraduates were included. Of the thirty-eight male and seventeen female students, forty-six were white; eight were black, including two students from Haiti and one from Africa; and one was Japanese Hawaiian. Twenty-six were Union Theological Seminary students, while the remainder hailed from American Baptist (2), Bethany (2), Boston, Chicago (2), Columbia, Eden (2), Episcopal of the Caribbean (3), Harvard, ITC, Johnson C. Smith (2), Lutheran at Maywood, Lutheran at Rock Island (2), New York Theological, Presbyterian School of Christian Education (2), San Francisco, Scarritt, Southern Baptist, Southern University, Yale, and Tuskegee. The students served in Washington, D.C., and fifteen states: Virginia, Maryland, Georgia, North Carolina, South Carolina, Texas, Mississippi, Tennessee, Louisiana, Alabama, Wisconsin, Pennsylvania, Vermont, New York, and Illinois. At the end of the summer, a record twenty-four students took on yearlong internships for the 1966–67 school year.

However, expansion did not come without problems. At the conclusion of the summer of 1966, SIM coordinators received multiple negative reports from host pastors dissatisfied with their student interns, the first time in the history of the project that this had occurred. The increased size of the program, and the related increase in the number of individuals and amount of money to be managed, led to some breakdowns in the administration of the program and between its students in the field and their assigned churches. In one case, a pastor complained that a teenaged student was lacking the necessary maturity required for delicate racial relations. In another case, the student did not seem interested in any part of the "ordinary" work of the church, only in the most public and exciting demonstrations.[31] This latter sentiment was common in the reports of students who had been stirred by Freedom Summer and other tales and itched for action, but most kept their complaints to their journals or confidential reports back to SIM headquarters. This common complaint was almost certainly related to the second theme that was emerging that summer—that of a more radical outlook on both civil rights participation and church reform. The civil rights movement itself had by then taken a more radical turn, as attention turned from integration and voting rights to economic issues and power disparities—and, most starkly, with the June 1966 articulation of Black Power. This, as we shall see, profoundly affected SIM. Calls for reform morphed into calls for fundamental transformation of defunct systems.

The big shift in SIM could not be read in the numbers or geographical spread, however, but in the placements themselves. Only twelve of the forty-four students took on "traditional" SIM pastoral placements in a church of another color. Far more, twenty-seven in all, joined team ministries in seven cities on projects that, while sometimes still church rooted, were focused outward toward the surrounding communities. Two other students went to work on what were called "special appointments"—in one case, with a social agency, and in the other, directly inside a Freedom Movement organization. As the civil rights movement itself had progressed, so, too, had the desires and expectations of SIM students for direct participation and some sign of an immediate impact.

SIM's move toward direct urban ministry was also influenced by the philosophy of Chicago's Ecumenical Institute, with which both George Walters and Maynard Moore were affiliated and with which both would work following their time with SIM. The Ecumenical Institute (EI) was founded in 1956 as the result of a World Council of Churches' resolution to develop a lay training center in the United States. In 1962, Joe Matthews, the Austin-based campus minister who had profoundly influenced the students who would go on to create Students for a Democratic Society and write *The Port Huron Statement*, took over the direction of EI in Chicago. Under Matthews, it became an imaginative attempt to reinterpret the church's role in the metropolis by doing community organizing and creating community development out of the core of a neighborhood-based, family-oriented "community of worship."[32]

An EI cadre, as its study groups were known, was formed at Union Theological Seminary in 1965, but it was George Walters who really brought the group's approach to bear on SIM's developing strategies. The EI approach did not sit well with all SIM participants, however. Chris Gamwell, one of SIM's founders, recalled that Joe Matthews was a charismatic but polarizing figure. He was, Gamwell later recalled, "a very powerful person when he talked about the Christian faith and what it meant for how you lived your life," but it was also clear to him that the EI agenda was as clear "as it could possibly be: producing carbon copies of Joe Matthews."[33] Other SIM students objected to the EI approach when it was incorporated into the SIM orientation before the summer of 1966. An EI staff member had been brought in to lead some of the sessions and, on the second day, fomented a near riot. Joe Howell wrote in his diary that day, June 2, that he and a group of others, mostly those headed to Southwest Georgia, had walked out of the orientation after they had "listened to the most ludicrous distortion of theology (Hitler-like lectures!) by a doubtless well-meaning but blind and mechanical phony from the Ecumenical Institute." Howell wrote that several of the students "protested violently" but were told by the EI leader that they could only question the program after the conference was over, instigating a walkout. Howell, Ed Feaver, and a number of other students, thus determined that the remainder of the EI-led orientation was optional.[34]

The orientation must have been especially startling for those who were headed for what had by then become SIM's traditional approach through what they now began to term the "pastor assistantship program." For them, personal redemption through cultural understanding remained the goal. SIM leaders, however, once again rearticulated this mission, as they did often throughout the project's life, always searching for just the right words as the world around them shifted and changed. The program afforded a student the chance to "participate in the life of a single congregation, but also shar[e] the life and activities of the community as well." With student pastors expected to live in their host church communities, it was hoped that the student would also learn "at first hand the problems and potential of church-community relations."[35] But even for those students who chose pastoral placements, the program's goal of fostering personal change through facilitating unique interpersonal relationships across the boundaries of race—which had seemed both revolutionary and immensely challenging and satisfying to students in earlier years—was no longer always enough. Representative of these sentiments was Dwight Bozeman, a Union student who worked with Ralph Abernathy at West Hunter Street Baptist Church in Atlanta. Acknowledging that the major accomplishment of the summer was achieved through the personal relationships he developed, Bozeman nonetheless complained that "private change within individual persons is not change within the public structure of social life, and it is here I feel most acutely the shortcomings of the summer's work."[36] Students who had worked with Abernathy in previous years had been wowed by the experience of just working alongside the vice president of the SCLC and one of the movement's major voices, but Bozeman was harder to impress. He did eventually get to experience the streets himself when he accompanied Abernathy to the 1966 SCLC conventions in Jackson, Mississippi, and took part in demonstrations in nearby Grenada with Hosea Williams and others from the SCLC.[37]

For some students that summer, the experience of personal reconciliation was in itself a satisfying goal. Cynthia Nelson, a black undergraduate student from Southern University in New Orleans, worked in a white Lutheran parish in Philadelphia. Her host pastor reported that the summer occasioned personal growth for Cynthia, who was surprised and appalled by the size of the urban slum and the complexity of racial problems in this northern metropolis. He wrote that while she "acknowledged having some deep uncertainties and what she called 'prejudices' about whites and her abilities to work with them," she was able to engage with individuals in the congregation and the community in ways that "increased understanding and reconciliation for her."[38] For Nelson and most of the other pastoral assistants, their work was not confined to church services alone but embraced a number of activities and outreach similar to those taken on by Lucas and Davis in Richmond the previous year. Whereas one-on-one reconciliation and personal change may have seemed the most obvious rewards of their summers, churches don't exist in vacuums—much as some seemed to want them to—and the students inevitably worked on projects like girls clubs, preschools, and summer camps, which were occasions for community work and development, as well as racial interaction at a larger level.

The majority of the SIM summer students in 1966, however, ventured into the relatively new—for SIM—terrain of its urban ministry program, the stated aim of which was "to allow a more concentrated effort in the community than is possible in the pastor assistantship program ... [and] to 'break new ground'" through innovative community programs.[39] There were still great similarities between the two approaches, however. The pastoral assistants, like Nelson, inevitably worked in the community; and the students in the urban projects, although their primary orientation was decidedly outward facing from the church community, were for the most part rooted within congregations. In Buffalo, for instance, a group of three SIM students—two black and one white, two male and one female, from three different seminaries—joined an existing urban ministry project working in poverty-stricken inner-city parishes. The Cooperative Urban Ministry program was jointly overseen by the United Church of Christ and the United Presbyterian Task Force, and each student was assigned a home church in the inner city. Working with a group of seventeen college students, they ran day camps, organized neighborhoods around issues of local concern, and covered pastoral duties. Harold Nicol, a black seminarian from Union Theological Seminary, worked alongside Rev. Wayne Daugherty within a housing project known as the Commodore Perry homes to conduct services and bible studies. The Cooperative Urban Ministry, a congregation without a church building, ministered directly to the five thousand residents—55 percent white and 45 percent black—of the Perry homes. Nicol took on three main projects during his summer: working in an ecumenical vacation bible school, assisting the local Catholic parish to organize a softball league in the Perry projects, and doing house-to-house organizing under the auspices of a local affiliate of the War on Poverty.[40] In some ways, the work—running religious services or a vacation bible school or even a recreation league—was very much like that done in the pastor assistantship program, but the difference was in the outlook toward addressing community-wide problems, often through the assistance of federal programs.[41]

In addition to the Buffalo project, SIM placed four students in the Fells Point Methodist Parish in Baltimore, Maryland, under the supervision of Reverend Robert Fringo; six students back with the Reverend Robert Hare at First United Presbyterian Church and the newly developed Richmond Inner City Ministry in Richmond, Virginia; five students with the ecumenical Charlotte Urban Ministry in North Carolina; three students in Charleston, South Carolina, working with the Citizens' Committee of Charleston County and on other projects; two students in the area of Kingstree, South Carolina, to work on voter registration and community action group projects; and three students in Mississippi to work with the Delta Ministry.

Of the five students working in the Charlotte Urban Ministry project, two were from Union, two were from the historically black Johnson C. Smith University in Charlotte, and one was from Louisville's Southern Baptist Theological Seminary. Barbara Cox, one of the Union students, was actually a North Carolina native and had attended high school in Charlotte before attending Pfeiffer College and then Greensboro College, both also in North Carolina.[42] At Greensboro, a Methodist women's college from which she graduated in 1955, Cox and many of her classmates were being trained for careers in church education. While there, Cox participated in an interracial group of students from other area colleges, including North Carolina A&T, and also in the Methodist Student Movement through the local Student Christian Fellowship. She recalls attending interracial events in Charlotte organized through the student groups, including an interracial square dance held in 1953 or 1954, where she overheard a white observer comment, "'If that was my daughter, I'd take her out of here.' And I thought, well I'm not your daughter!" On another occasion, during a conference-wide Methodist retreat at Lake Junaluska, an interracial group desegregated the swimming pool together, resulting in it being temporarily closed.[43] Cox did her Christian education fieldwork with a Quaker meeting in Greensboro, Asheboro Street Friends, and when the community hosted Eleanor Roosevelt as a speaker, Barbara got to ride along with the former First Lady in her car.

Following graduation, Cox took a church education position at Wesley Methodist Church in Hartsville, South Carolina, pastored by a Dr. Griffith, whom Cox recalled as "a different kind of minister. He stood for integration when nobody else did, and he preached it from the pulpit. And I don't know how he was not in trouble all the time. But he had a way of putting things that made people laugh, and they would accept things from him that they

wouldn't from others." Cox served as the director of Christian education
there for several years before returning to take similar positions at churches
in Shelby and then back in Charlotte, North Carolina, where she worked
until she enrolled at Union Theological Seminary in 1965 at the age of
thirty-three, seeking a graduate degree in Christian education. She immediately encountered SIM, and the posting to Charlotte allowed her to return
home that summer to care for her father, who had suffered a stroke around
Christmas.[44]

Cox and the other four seminarians at the Charlotte Urban Ministry
project worked out of three host churches and created combined programs,
including a summer camp. Cox worked closely with Robert Shirley, an
African American minister who was fighting for equal educational opportunities for black youth in Charlotte. Cox found that such work through SIM
that summer helped her see the rhetoric of equality put into action. It put
"all those lofty concepts on legs," she recalled, and made them "real."[45]

Jerry Welch, a white student from Southern Baptist Theological Seminary, wrote that renewed inner-city ministries, like that of the Charlotte Urban Ministry, were a step in the right direction but that the churches also
"need to be led into a discussion of what part they have played in the exploitation of the Negro and other residents of the inner-city. If the church is
concerned with finding an answer to the problems of racial tensions, poverty, slums and other problems of the inner-city, it must not begin with a
program and easy answers, but rather, with a question: What part have we
played in the creation of this suffering and isolation?"[46] His question would
be repeated—and explosively answered—two years later in James Forman's
Black Manifesto and its demands that the white churches pay reparations
for the sins of slavery and segregation.

Although they attempted to take on inner-city ministry and outreach,
the students in Charlotte found themselves sometimes frustrated at the results. The group's main activity was running a summer camp that, although
centered in a poor inner-city environment, was nonetheless primarily ruled
by the concerns common to all summer camps. But the main problem, as
identified by the students, was that they were housed not in the poorer
community of Allen Street, where their daily work took place, but in a relatively more affluent area called Myers Park. Although the stated intent was
to provide a reconciliatory bridge between the two communities, at least
one student was left with the feeling of being "missionaries 'going in' to
the area to 'do something' " rather than becoming part of the community.
"We did not live in the community, we did not work with the people after

dark, and we did not have any contact with the older teenagers or men in the community." He urged SIM to find another solution for any future projects.[47]

The four SIM students in Baltimore—one American, one German, and two Haitians—formed an interracial, interdenominational, and international team that worked out of the Fells Point Methodist Parish, which offered church services along with youth groups, recreation, counseling services, and social services. Rev. Robert Fringo used this storefront on East Baltimore Street as a combination urban ministry training center, community gathering place, and social service center, offering services as diverse as a literacy program and a family planning clinic.[48] The students worked on a street cleanup campaign and voter registration, while maintaining affiliations with local churches.

MacDonald Jean, a Haitian student at the Episcopal Seminary of the Caribbean, was assigned as an assistant pastor at the all-white Rogers Memorial Methodist Church. In words that echo those of Robert Seymour in Chapel Hill when recalling James Forbes's ministry in 1962, Jean's supervisor, Rev. Carl Hickey, wrote of him in late 1966: "Perhaps the greatest ministry Mac performed was simply being present in the church and the community. His presence was a sign to the Negro community that this church is open. His presence was a sign to the white (and often bigoted) community that this church is Christian and not a social club." Hickey went on to write that Jean's presence forced his congregants to ask basic questions about the role of the church and openness to strangers regardless of background, questions that often "resulted in changed lives."[49] Therefore, while SIM may have shifted to more specifically target urban problems, it continued to foster racial reconciliation within communities and among individuals.

In Richmond, Virginia, Carol Lucas, who had stayed on for an intern for the year, was again joined by Keith Davis to continue their work with Robert Hare. This time they were accompanied by four other seminarians, and together this group continued the work of the Shepherd of the Streets community center and developed a number of summer recreation and theater programs as well as tutoring and Christian education programs. They also installed a new playground and began outreach work tailored to local gangs and drug users.

The team of Roger Sawtelle and Tom Leatherwood in Kingstree, South Carolina, experienced frustrations of a different sort. Originally recruited to work on voter registration efforts, the two white seminarians found themselves without a job when the local Voters League decided not to allow white volunteers to work on the primary drive, apparently fearing it would generate even more hostility from white voters. Although they eventually found campaign work, they experienced a second, if not anticipated, frustration when whites managed to register at 112 percent to handily elect their candidates in the primary. Leatherwood, a student at Union Theological Seminary, found the summer both frustrating and personally rewarding, discovering "a closeness to life in all its warmth and passions." But he predicted little long-term gain from the summer's work. Although he and others succeeded in building a movement among local youth aimed toward elevating understanding of the importance of voting and economic power, ultimately he felt that "the youngsters will probably not succeed in infusing the county with their enthusiasm, and they will eventually turn their eyes elsewhere. Like so many before them, they will turn to the North and to the cities, emigrating to 'the promised land.' They will leave in an attempt to escape the muffled and dulled humanity that comes from living under constant oppression and paucity of opportunity."[50] Leatherwood's words were pessimistic perhaps, but not inaccurate. The turn outward from the church to the real-life needs of people did not always make for happy, inspiring ministry; the injustice and cruelty and hopelessness hit some students like a two-by-four. Such reality was on ready display, both in the urban ferocity of a city like Chicago and in the painful scarcity of a rural landscape like the Mississippi Delta, as SIM students ventured into both frontiers in the summer of 1966.

The Windy City was no stranger to missions—churches and other religious organizations had been ministering to the special needs of its inner-city neighborhoods since the middle of the previous century. The Second Presbyterian Church began operating its Bethel Seaman's Mission in the early 1840s, and the YMCA erected its first American building, the three-thousand-seat Farwell Hall, in Chicago in 1867. These were soon joined by a great number of mission aid societies and, beginning in 1889, by new, non-church-based social reform efforts aligned with the Settlement House Movement. Chicago's Hull House, founded by Jane Addams and Ellen Gates Starr, grew to be the second largest settlement house in the country—and perhaps its best known.

Seminary students were important contributors to Chicago's early mission movement and, later, to social gospel ventures like Hull House, and they also created their own projects in the city. A seminarian from Chicago Theological Seminary founded the Newsboys and Bootblacks Mission in the 1860s, reaching out to the large population of boys working the city streets.[51] By the 1890s, Chicago, Garrett, Presbyterian, Baptist, and Mc-Cormick seminaries all had fieldwork programs in the city, which became known as one of liberal Protestantism's urban bases. In the 1920s and 1930s, the city was also the birthplace of a number of America's experiments with social work and community organizing, much of it originating from the University of Chicago. Saul Alinsky began his neighborhood organizing in the Back of the Yards area while a researcher at the university, and throughout his career, he worked primarily through the city's Catholic churches.

Experiments in urban mission increased in Chicago in 1960, most notably with the hiring of Donald Benedict as director of the Chicago City Missionary Society. Benedict was the Union alumnus who had cofounded the East Harlem Protestant Parish before leading similar efforts in Cleveland and Detroit during the 1950s. Benedict's arrival was followed by the establishment of the Westside Christian Parish; the Westside Organization; and, in 1964, the Urban Training Center for Christian Mission, based at the First Congregational Church and sponsored by the National Council of Churches. According to *Time* magazine in 1965, the training center's mission was "plucking the scales from churchly eyes," which it did with such success as to earn "a reputation as one of the liveliest and most provocative missionary experiments in the U.S."[52] Those who created the Urban Training Center believed that while God was at work in the world of the inner city, traditional church structures were ill suited to prepare clergy to embrace such work and required new strategies. At least some in the traditional liberal power structure agreed, and the Ford Foundation awarded the Urban Training Center a $600,000 grant in 1965 to expand its ministerial fellowship program.[53] Each clergy member who studied at the center began by taking "the plunge," which consisted of having to live for four days in the Chicago slums on a total of eight dollars. Afterwards, most clergy worked with one of the many local labor or civil rights organizations. Between 1965 and 1968, more than a dozen SIM students, including National Program Coordinator Maynard Moore, took the plunge before diving deeper into the murky waters of Chicago organizing for their summer and intern-year placements.

In 1965 and 1966, the SCLC and Martin Luther King Jr., at the invitation of local leaders, joined the ranks of those struggling for change in Chicago. King and his colleagues were eager to prove that the strategy of nonviolent protest would work beyond the South. Their arrival in Chicago had the effect of reinvigorating the many local efforts, some of them with deep historical roots and many of them interracial and ecumenical in nature.[54]

Reverend James Bevel led the advance troops in Chicago, preparing the ground for King and working closely with his friend and fellow SNCC founder and Nashville veteran Bernard Lafayette.[55] The two had also been students together at American Baptist Seminary, yet another indicator of the important role of religiously trained activists and of the connections between the seminaries and the movement.[56] The Chicago Freedom Movement was launched on July 10, 1966, with King declaring Chicago "now an open city" during a rally of almost sixty thousand people. The nation's eyes turned toward the Midwest that summer.[57]

Once again, the Student Interracial Ministry was in the middle of the action. Bruce Christie from the Chicago Theological Seminary worked with SCLC and the Chicago Freedom Movement. Christie described the SCLC and the Chicago churches as fighting a modern-day Battle of Jericho, "hoping to tumble the walls of the reservation: discrimination, exploitation and poverty in a major northern metropolis."[58]

Christie's major job was to act as participant-observer and journalist, reporting on the movement directly to the seminaries through a self-published newsletter founded immediately upon his arrival in the city. He described the many different projects based at the Warren Avenue Church, including efforts to form tenants' unions, Bernard Lafayette's "End the Slums" campaign for tenants' rights and open housing, and Operation Breadbasket, a selective buying campaign whose goal was increased hiring of minorities by businesses serving them. Masterminded by King protégé and seminary student Jesse Jackson, and staffed by a small group of fellow seminarians and ministers, Operation Breadbasket targeted businesses that had fewer than 20 percent black employees. The project was modeled on successful church-based boycotts led by the Reverend Leon Sullivan in Philadelphia in 1959. Both campaigns also harked back to a long history in the African American community of wielding economic power through selective buying campaigns.[59]

Writing as a seminarian experiencing the Chicago Freedom Movement from the inside, Christie remarked repeatedly on its religious nature, even its explicit theology as expressed by King and others in the SCLC. He also predicted, presciently, that race issues and the church's response to the civil rights movement would shape redefinitions of modern ministry and ministerial training.[60] James Bevel told him that *the* theological question for the movement was "Is the Negro a man or not," meaning that if all men were indeed brothers and worthy of equal respect, then there could be no excuse for unequal treatment based on race.[61] His gendered rhetoric and its assurance of black masculinity also prefigured that which later pervaded King's final campaign, the sanitation workers' strike in Memphis in 1968, which came to be represented by its commonly used placards declaring "I Am a Man." Christie also saw the civil rights movement and the attention to the black inner city as both the central animating force of ecumenical cooperation in Chicago and the engine that could possibly "save the city as a form of culture." He wrote, "The Christian who meets the viciousness of the city must be one of faith in the power of redemption NOW and not in the bye and bye!" The viciousness of the city was indeed readily apparent; after three days of violence and rioting in the West Side in July, King commented on the white response that fueled the fires, "I have never in my life seen such hate. Not in Mississippi or Alabama. This is a terrible thing."[62]

Christie worked primarily with one effort of the Chicago Freedom Movement that summer, the Union to End Slums, which brought approximately twenty-five community groups under the direction of the Warren Avenue Congregational Church and mobilized them against a particularly abusive landlord in late July and early August.[63] The organizers tried a range of approaches, from simple negotiation to threatening to picket; community pressure eventually led the landlord to negotiate and culminated in the nation's first collective-bargaining agreement between a tenants' rights union and a landlord.[64]

The Chicago Freedom Movement thought it had won another victory when Mayor Daley finally agreed to sit down at the negotiating table in August. Both sides still harbored misgivings when they signed the Open Housing Summit Agreement on August 26, 1966, but Chicago's organizers hoped that they had won open housing reforms at the cost of promising to end demonstrations.[65] This was the hopeful, cautiously victorious atmosphere in which Christie wrapped up his SIM work in Chicago in 1966. However, by the time the next set of SIM interns arrived in the fall of 1967, King and the SCLC had left town, and Daley, without their pressure, had not followed through on the promises of the summit agreement. Both movement insiders and outside media observers reported that King and the Chicago Freedom Movement had failed. However, just as Sherrod and the Southwest Georgia Project persisted in Albany after King's departure, the Chicago movement continued. Many more SIM students would join its effort in Chicago the following year, facilitated by National Program Coordinator Maynard Moore, who maintained residency on Chicago's South Side while continuing graduate study in the Divinity School at the University of Chicago. These students would report that the Chicago Freedom Movement had not failed, and although the work was indeed difficult and experienced setbacks, not only did it continue but it continued on a number of new fronts.

So, too, did the work in Mississippi, long after Freedom Summer focused the nation's attention on the delta. Three SIM students worked there with the Delta Ministry in the summer of 1966, including Mark Lundeen, who was continuing his internship from the previous year. He was joined by two white Union students, Bill Troy and Mac Hulslander. Troy and Hulslander spent the first half of the summer based at the organization's headquarters in Edwards, Mississippi, working with local community organizations and on the Delta Ministry's Poor People's Conference, before moving out to Swift-water, Mississippi, helping to build what was to become known as Freedom City. Troy participated in the Meredith March, also called the Mississippi Freedom March, that summer, and Hulslander joined it for the commemorative march portion that diverted to Philadelphia, Mississippi, to honor the memories of James Chaney, Andrew Goodman, and Mickey Schwerner, the three civil rights workers who had been murdered there during the summer of 1964. Hulslander admitted that he did not have the words to "justly describe the fear and anxiety that coursed through my body as I made the return visit to Philadelphia, the recent scene of racial violence and the dread landmark of the most notorious slaughter of civil rights workers."[66]

Freedom City was an effort to both dramatize and help solve the problems of impoverished agricultural workers. In January 1966, a group of Mississippi poor attempted an ultimately unsuccessful takeover of the Greenville Air Force Base for purposes of creating affordable housing. By the summer, with the help of an anonymous gift of $75,000 and the securing of four hundred acres of land, this had led to the development of Freedom City, conceived of as an intentional cooperative community created by and for poor agricultural workers fleeing the poverty of the plantation. As Hulslander saw it, the project was an attempt to head off further white exploitation while also stemming an increasing tide of northern migration that had been predicted by his SIM colleagues in South Carolina. Hulslander and Troy relocated to Freedom City, known among its residents by the more common name of "the Land," and set to work building platforms for the twenty-one planned houses, crafting outhouses and dining halls, and designing a school program for the Land's first six school-age children. Responsibility for the school fell completely on Hulslander and Troy, who fixed up a three-room shack into a serviceable school building complete with desks, blackboards, and shelves of books. Ultimately, Freedom City had ninety-four residents working for wages, but it failed to develop into the communal haven its founders envisioned. Nonetheless, it served as a beacon for some and as a symbol of the Delta Ministry's commitment to the idea that racial reconciliation would only be achieved "where mutual respect, justice, and comparable positions of power are present."[67] In many ways, this was an articulation of what was then becoming widely known as Black Power. Indeed, some of the first articulations of Black Power had come in the state of Mississippi earlier that summer, during the Mississippi Freedom March.

Begun on June 6, 1966, as the solo march of James Meredith from Memphis, Tennessee, to Jackson, Mississippi, to highlight the lack of change in Mississippi following the passage of federal civil rights legislation, the march changed drastically on its second day when Meredith was shot by a white gunman and hospitalized. Leaders of SNCC, the SCLC, and CORE vowed to pick up and continue Meredith's march in his absence. In addition to Bill Troy, several from SIM joined the march, including George Walters, the chairman of SIM's National Committee. They walked together with thousands of others, culminating in a crowd of fifteen thousand marching into Jackson. Along the route, they registered four thousand black voters.[68]

The march gained a significant amount of press coverage, often for the tension within the marchers' camps rather than for their goals. As George Walters—who was with the march for eight days from Belzoni to Jackson, Mississippi—recalled it several months later, "sometime before I became conscious of it, a division arose between those . . . who saw the march as carrying out the original intentions of Meredith of ridding himself and other Negroes of fear" and those who advocated "responding [in kind] to that violence as a sign that it would no longer be tolerated without reprisal."[69] The violence versus nonviolence debate was further exacerbated by the various organizational factions competing over march leadership, including King and the SCLC, which fostered nonviolence, and SNCC, which announced during the march its adoption of the guiding principle of Black Power.

The idea of black people seeking power—political, economic, cultural—was nothing new, and it undergirded approaches that ran the gamut of ideology, from the self-esteem and advancement championed by Booker T. Washington to complete black separatism. But SNCC's Stokely Carmichael and Willie Ricks gave the phrase, now with its capital letters, new gravitas and immediacy, as well as the power to cause fear among many whites and some blacks.[70] On June 16, the marchers arrived in Greenwood, Mississippi, and while setting up camp at a black elementary school, Carmichael, later

Kwame Ture, was arrested for trespassing. Released a few hours later, an angry Carmichael rejoined the marchers at a local park and took the speaker's stage. "This is the twenty-seventh time I have been arrested," he declared. "And I ain't going to jail no more! The only way we gonna stop them white men from whuppin' us is to take over. What we gonna start sayin' now is Black Power."[71] He defined Black Power as "a call for black people in this country to unite, to recognize their heritage, to build a sense of community . . . to define their own goals, to lead their own organizations." He also said that Black Power would help build "a movement that will smash everything Western civilization has created."[72]

George Walters had come to know the SNCC leaders fairly well during the march, and he stayed up late into the night in a little tent discussing Black Power with Stokely Carmichael, just as he spent many daylight hours marching beside and talking with Martin Luther King Jr. and Andy Young about nonviolence. As a white man well over six feet tall, he was made a parade marshal, assigned to walk along the outer edge of the demonstrators in order to keep the peace between them and the watching and jeering crowds. Walters recounted that Carmichael hated being misquoted and misinterpreted, so Walters listened carefully to Carmichael's public descriptions of Black Power and sought further clarification from him in private. Walters recalled,

> What he said to me in a conversation we had one night in a dark tent
> on a cornfield during the Mississippi march was that he was principally
> concerned with the organization of black communities and how that
> could lead to their participation in the electoral process to successfully
> elect people who represented their interest and the interest of the
> whole community. We'd been back and forth in many conversations
> during the march about Black Power equaling violent reaction versus
> non-violence. And in that conversation at least, I was satisfied that
> Stokely and his leadership of SNCC was not advocating violence as a
> strategy. He was advocating organization that led to power as a strategy.[73]

While Walters claimed that the internal conflicts of the march were actually "healthy dialogue seeking clarity on all sides," it seemed additionally clear that if this clarity were to be reached, it would mean overcoming prejudices on all sides. Bill Troy remembers a black organizer warning the crowd not to trust any whites with a southern accent. Troy, a native of Tennessee, was at that moment preparing to spend the night in the big communal tent the marchers shared. He recalled that he "just went over and crawled up in the corner of the tent, got in my sleeping bag, and never said a word the rest of the night."[74]

The moment may not have been a comfortable one for whites, but Walters remembers the march not as the time when a rift opened in the civil rights movement but rather as a special time when all the various parts of the movement maintained cohesion, however fragile and temporary. He says that he knew even then "that this event was going to be a memorable event. It was part of making the difference and building the sense of courage and camaraderie in a movement that was still struggling to put itself together. Its factions were there, but at that moment, its factions were all together."[75] But would they remain so?

That question, and the calls for Black Power, were very much on the minds of SIM leaders when they gathered in Chicago in September 1966 to assess the previous summer and to lay plans for the next year and for the summer of 1967. They outlined a new series of projects in which students would serve with both local churches and existing community organizations, some of them secular. They argued that "problems of poverty, segregation, and unequal opportunities have reached crisis proportions," and that the urban setting seemed the natural strategic "step in the growth process" of the Student Interracial Ministry.[76] Charles Sherrod, director of the Southwest Georgia Project and still a student at Union, led the way with a proposal that SIM's urban programs embrace nontraditional pastoral work, employing group ministries and direct community organizing, to create more opportunities for seminary students to engage with contemporary problems. Sherrod, in his typical and unique prose style, proposed a fourfold overall direction: "Toward Black Power; Toward the death of religion and the life of the church; Toward social change and change in personal values; Toward living."[77] Maynard Moore, SIM's field coordinator, translated Sherrod's vision into more concrete planning language, producing an agenda that called for the development of independent black economic projects, that reenvisioned seminary training to include long periods of urban ministry, and that attempted to put church people and their religious ethics to work in a way that directly benefited urban populations.

Ever the minister, Moore challenged the SIM "congregation" with a series of questions: Where does economic and political power reside, how does the system work, and how could wealth and power be redistributed? He also asked how the student–teacher relationship could be redefined, what new curriculum structures and teaching methods could be devised, and what the seminary's relationship to education in general could or should be.

How can an adequate doctrine of the church be recovered, and how can we redefine the relationship between the church and the laity? Moore returned to the project's founding concern, reconciliation in race relations, when considering the development of future projects. Of this goal he asked, What does reconciliation mean in relation to power and equality, what is the role of whites in the movement, and what is the church's new role in the freedom revolution?[78] Larry Blackman, who was at that time serving an internship with the Atlanta College Teaching Project, discussed in detail below, wrote, "Only the most incredibly naïve members of the erstwhile civil rights coalition could fail to see that the heyday of their 'movement' is at an end."[79] Moore's questions reflected where the project found itself at that moment: operating according to an older model that needed to be adapted in order to function in a new historical context, one moving from reconciliation to revolution.

In contrast to the project's founders' vision that the two races would find healing if they only understood each other, Moore's concerns reveal a greater understanding of the forces—among them economic and political power—that determine how a society functions and whether or not it will change. Moore's framing also implied a critique of the institutional church and challenged it to responsibly wield its own political, economic, and moral power. He and others in SIM argued that not only were the urban poor in dire straits, but so, too, were the urban churches—both "dying their slow and painful deaths."[80] Mainline churches at mid-decade reacted to the inner city in one of three ways, they argued: by fleeing from a decaying city center into the suburbs; by conducting the occasional mission foray from the suburbs back into "the bad-dark-dirty city" with a Christmas basket; or by remaining in the city, with their membership numbers deflated by suburban outmigration, and trying to survive in an environment where "problems of poverty, segregation, and unequal opportunities have reached crisis proportions."[81]

The Student Interracial Ministry, however, pointed to the genesis of a "fourth column" of urban ministry, proposing that all the congregations of a given urban *and* suburban area should be responsible for the totality of the area and its various concerns. They wrote that the church, by virtue of its independence and power as well as its central ethos of responsibility, should be *the* engine of urban social change. But how should the church go about doing this? The seminarians acknowledged that this question would not be answered easily, for it ran "deeply through the whole meaning of theological education, the Christian stance for life, the meaning of a congregation in mission, God's will, [and the] purpose and destiny for the city and for urbanites."[82]

SIM pursued congregation-based organizing and other strategies in urban ministry projects in seventeen American cities in its last few years up to 1968. Most of these were now described as "long range efforts at community reformulation."[83] Recruiters for the project called for seminarians to explore ministry in "the context of the revolutions of our time," stressing that the modern city was "where the action is."[84] The students drew both on social gospel ideas and their hard-won experience in traditional and urban ministry projects, but primarily that in Southwest Georgia, to argue that a church focused merely on sustaining itself missed its fundamental purpose—that of a mission of service and of potential renewal and reconciliation. They argued for a redefinition of the church as mission first, with the form of the church secondary. Religious reformers in SIM hoped that through experiments in urban ministry and the establishment of an "immediate missionary presence," some answers might be revealed. As the SIM leaders put it, "The dual encounter with Black Power and the tremendous problems of the urban world, north and south, has demanded that new directions be taken." Furthermore, they added, "There is no longer time to wait. The world does not stop for the church to get ready to serve it."[85]

The project did not regard urban as meaning the North, and it launched programs in Richmond, Oakland, and Los Angeles, California; Atlanta, Georgia; Chicago, Illinois; Indianapolis, Indiana; Baltimore, Maryland; Minneapolis, Minnesota; Jackson, Mississippi; Kansas City, Missouri; New York, Buffalo, and Richmond, New York; Charlotte, North Carolina; Charleston and Kingstree, South Carolina; and Washington, D.C.[86] By SIM's final year, 1967–68, of the eighty-five student participants—thirty-seven in the summer of 1967 and forty-eight for the 1967–68 year—only two were working in traditional pastoral assistantships, while eight were running the SIM program administration; the remaining seventy-five students were all working in SIM's urban ministry projects.

The Black Power movement especially influenced SIM in embracing its new urban direction. White students in SIM responded to the various articulations of Black Power with reactions that for the most part varied from intellectual support of the idea, to confusion as to the new proper role for white supporters to embrace as the next step in the freedom movement, to frustration at feeling unappreciated or underutilized. Black participants in the project, including Charles Sherrod, for the most part embraced Black Power as emblematic of the need for black political and economic strength but many times imbued the phrase with personal meanings and adapted it to fit a particular cultural space. Sherrod, for example, believed strongly in black electoral and economic independence but also espoused a commitment to interracialism when summarizing his own commitment to working with whites in Georgia: "Whatever the solution to the problem of race in our country," he said, "it's got to be a black and white one. And if it is going to be a black and white solution, at the end, then going toward the solution has also [to be integrated.]"[87]

Tim Kimrey worked with the Southwest Georgia Project in Cordele, Georgia, and wrote in 1966 that the goal of any good community organizer is to work him- or herself out of a job, and having done so within the civil rights movement, white activists should now step aside whether or not blacks wanted them to stay. "The fact is," Kimrey wrote, "that black revolutionaries do not *need* the white man in the role he has traditionally played. He is useless, at best, in the field. At worst, he is repressive and a real hindrance to the revolution."[88] Kimrey had come to believe that the civil rights movement had shifted into a new phase in which it required sole black leadership.

Not all activists were as ready to leave the interracial phase of the movement behind. Those who belonged to the religious tradition of interracial cooperation for social change, both whites and blacks, continued to call for cooperation. On July 31, 1966, "an informal group of Negro churchmen in America," who were affiliated with the NCC's Commission on Religion and Race, ran a full-page advertisement in the *New York Times* that affirmed the need for Black Power but also called for both black and white Americans to "work together at the task of rebuilding our cities."[89] The ministers consciously employed the religious language of reconciliation in support of Black Power *and* interracial cooperation in the urban setting. "Getting power necessarily involves reconciliation," they wrote. "We must first be reconciled to ourselves . . . as persons and to ourselves as an historical group. However, if power is sought merely as an end in itself, it tends to turn upon those who seek it. Negroes need power in order to participate more effectively at all levels of the life of our nation." But reconciliation "with our white brothers" must be based on "the firm ground that we and all other Americans *are* one. Our history and destiny are indissolubly linked. If the future is to belong to any of us, it must be prepared for all of us, whatever our racial or religious background. For in the final analysis, we are *persons* and the power of all groups must be wielded to make visible our common humanity."[90] The ministers' letter is but one example from that significant moment when some within the Black Power movement, the white churches, and the black churches saw they had the opportunity to stand on common ground.

One could argue, however, that common ground could be achieved through working separately toward the same goal, as George E. Riddick of the Church Federation of Greater Chicago, a partner in SIM's Chicago Urban Project, suggested in a 1966 paper titled "Black Power: A Christian Response." He wrote that the most urgent task for the church in responding to Black Power was first to reconceptualize its mission in the world. Philanthropy without mission had been discredited, he claimed, as had the possibility of employing anything other than an ecumenical and interfaith approach. Moreover, he wrote that the church should not expect or need the approval of the Black Power movement in pursuing an urban mission agenda.[91] In other words, Black Power was a response to the crisis of the inner cities, and the urban mission of the church was a parallel and complementary response.

Working for racial justice within racially distinct groups may indeed have been necessary for the advancement of a certain brand of black independence, but it carried a potential price. According to religious historian James Findlay, internal church struggles over Black Power, the formation of black caucuses within mainline denominations, the issuing of the Black Manifesto, and the National Committee of Black Churchmen forming within the NCC itself combined to cripple the efforts of liberals to reform the church in the 1960s.[92] Civil rights pioneer Bayard Rustin also warned in 1966 that organizing and politics based solely in the black community could only go so far. Citing the example of the eighty southern counties that held elections in 1966, he argued that even if blacks were to elect "eighty sheriffs, eighty tax assessors, and eighty school board members [it] might ease the tension for a while in their communities, but alone they could not create jobs and build low cost housing."[93] Looked at this way, Black Power could only influence advances up to a point, since communities did not exist within total racial isolation from one another, and a multiracial world demanded multiracial solutions.

The erosion of common ground was interpreted by some not as a loss for the civil rights movement or a gain for the Black Power movement but simply as the natural next step in their evolution. Thus, the more interracial phase of the civil rights movement and Black Power can be seen simply as different branches of the same tree.[94] Maynard Moore recalled that while interracialism had a strong place in the early years, it was black students who carried the movement forward. And so when "Black Power became the rallying cry, those black students didn't have much truck for having white colleagues. They were going to do their thing. And by that time, that was fine. They stepped up. Our position was, 'We'll respond, you call us if you want us. We'll come.' ... Black leaders had to call the shots. We had our thing to do in the white community."[95]

But it was not always so clear. Students in the SIM project struggled with the implications of the Black Power movement on very personal levels as they determined how it might inform future careers in or outside of traditional ministry. They produced pages and pages of statement papers, editorials, articles, and personal reflections, all wrestling with what Black Power meant to the civil rights struggle and to their own personal engagement. To read their writings is to glance inside the thought processes of deeply concerned whites trying to ascertain a path across a precarious fault line. White SIM students were for the most part understanding of the historical roots of and the need for Black Power, and in many cases they were willing to find a new role for themselves. As Tim Kimrey wrote in 1966, "Any way you cut it, Black Power says No to the traditional involvement of the white man in this struggle for social change. It is not so much that Black Power is an ideology which excludes the white man from the ranks of the revolution; there is simply no ideology to hold black and white together in any viable kind of cohesive grouping, as, for instance, non-violence did in the early 1960s."[96]

For those whites who did affirm Black Power, George Walters suggested they would go through their own period of transition. "For a time it is possible they must decide to be the least. The one who will be a man of faith may have to [be] willing to be used and abused—by choice to die for Black Power."[97] Steve Rose, who was now editor-at-large for *Renewal* magazine in Chicago while working for the World Council of Churches in Geneva, helped his magazine celebrate the rise of Black Power in a series of issues but also presented "the agonizing reappraisal and self-understanding of a white man involved in the Freedom Movement from the beginning."[98] In an issue of the magazine that included such articles as Preston Wilcox's "Is Integration Relevant?" and Malcolm Boyd's "Freedom Means Black Power," *Renewal* predicted that "this summer [of 1966] is only the beginning of the painful job of reorientation and readjustment in a society that has always successfully produced both open and subtle forms of resistance to change. Many of our pet images of the meaning of civil rights, freedom and 'what the Negro really wants' will have to go."[99]

Within SIM, George Walters elaborated that the interracial phase of the civil rights movement had graduated to a new period with two components: black people continuing to lead what had now become Black Power, and white people focusing on the concerns of their own race or heading toward new social justice pursuits. Both Moore and Walters in fact went from SIM to working with the Ecumenical Institute and Fifth City—an urban ministry, economic development, and intentional living project in Chicago. But Walters later recalled that at that point in 1966, the rifts or the strategies chosen going forward weren't what was most important about the discussions over Black Power and the future of the movement. Rather, what struck him as most meaningful was the determination and defiance of the group *to* go forward. As he recalled,

> 'Cause if you've said "no" to the way certain things are, even though you're unclear abut how you're going to get there, you do know what you want the end result to be. And if this community marching down the street here, of Christians and Jews and whites and blacks and atheists and militants and non-violent and everything else you could think of, could stand for one moment with one voice, then you actually have a vision of the future being manifest. Many times this movement has had that moment. It's those moments that have defined whether or not it's all worth it, what the real difference might be. [But] you have to move on from experience and event to the hard work. From the moment of sensing that we can all be one, as Martin [Luther King] so well characterized more than once in his magnificent speeches, to becoming one, that's where the blood, sweat, and tears set in, the hard work.[100]

Those like Walters and Moore and many others in SIM, who were steeped in modern theology, believed that the process of achieving redemption and reconciliation would take mankind through a series of steps and the adoption of various ideological lenses through which to view contemporary circumstance. Thus, interracialism might be appropriate in one circumstance and black separatism in another, as long as the work toward reconciliation and redemption continued.

The Student Interracial Ministry sought to understand how its members—most of whom were white, religiously faithful antiracists—would operate in the new world shaped by the Black Power movement. There seemed to be a number of potential paths forward. Walters and Moore suggested that white activists now focus on white communities. Several projects in fact formed to attempt just this, most notably SNCC's White

Folks Project, the Southern Student Organizing Committee, and the White Southern Students Project, all of which were meant to organize white communities on behalf of the movement.

Sherrod, as we have seen, called for the further involvement of whites, albeit in less obvious roles. This was acceptable to many of his white SIM colleagues, although not always easy. As Joe Pfister, who in total spent ten years with Sherrod in Southwest Georgia, recalled, "People like me [and] Joe [Howell], we had to learn that we were there not to be outspoken, to take a backseat. We were always paired with a black person, and we followed their lead. [That was not natural for me,] and it really influenced the way I [acted.] I was a ham. I've become much more pulled back, much less gregarious."[101] So, it seemed that for whites who wanted to remain active in the movement, they could adopt a less active role, although it meant sacrifices and sometimes retreat into positions of financial support alone, or turn toward the frustrations of white organizing. More commonly, however, as we shall see, white activists moved away from the civil rights struggle entirely and on to other issues, such as fighting against the Vietnam War. With the development of Black Power, the writing seemed on the wall for the "easy" interracialism that had informed SIM's pastoral exchange approach beginning in 1960. SIM responded by moving away from pastoral exchange and developing its summer 1966 team ministries into a varied program of urban ministry projects that, while still rooted within and connected to church networks, worked directly within communities to address economic, electoral, educational, and other needs.

Maynard Moore, it will be recalled, had taken on the position of SIM's national program coordinator in late summer 1966, and he spent the next sixteen months crisscrossing the country by bus and occasionally hitchhiking, visiting all the SIM students at their work placements, churches, and urban ministry projects while also recruiting additional students at seminaries and colleges. Twenty-four students were in the field as yearlong interns: two students in pastoral placements in Alabama and Maryland, four students working as instructors in historically black colleges as part of the Atlanta College Intern Project, eight students in Georgia with the Southwest Georgia Project, and ten students in New York with the Northern Urban Project. Only one black student, an exchange student from France, was among the twenty-four participants, of which nineteen were male. Seventeen of the interns hailed from Union Theological Seminary, with two from Bethany and one each from Perkins, Lutheran at Maywood, Yale, Princeton, and Chicago seminaries. Not only was the SIM project now shifting toward urban ministry projects, but it was also shifting toward full-year rather than summer-long opportunities.

The Atlanta College Teaching Project began in September 1966 as a "major experiment in seminary internships," with a three-fold goal of providing seminary students with an intensive interracial academic experience, making real-world training in teaching a ministerial vocation, and contributing to the educational mission of underfunded black colleges.[102] SIM recruited the interns, suggested assignments, and then turned the files over to the Atlanta colleges for the final selection of teachers. The colleges provided room and board and a contribution toward the intern's stipend. The way the program was described in SIM literature, the instructors seemed to be the primary learners in this educational scenario, as the white professors were to benefit from a kind of immersion program in the black college setting. What the colleges and African American students were to gain from this deal, other than a cheap teacher, was unclear, since the notion of a white teacher at a black institution was far from revolutionary. Historically dependent on whites for funding, black colleges in the 1960s frequently had a high percentage of white faculty members.[103] Indeed, with the emergence of Black Power consciousness, this arrangement was coming into question, as some scholars suggested that an opportunity was at hand to make the historically black institutions entirely black from the top down, to develop and judge their own pedagogy according to their "own yardsticks rather than the traditional white yardsticks," and questioned what white faculty had to offer in these situations other than to accept that their students had more to offer them than the other way around.[104] In fact, the SIM interns at Clark College discussed this very topic with students in the Freethinkers discussion group, some of whom questioned the motives and effectiveness of the white teachers and suggested that "the white man would do better in the matter of civil rights apologetics to the white community." Several of the white instructors, however, admitted that they feared that they would go unheard by bigoted whites.[105] SIM administrators responded by proposing that it send black teachers into white institutions, too, as it had done with the clergy pulpit exchanges, but this goal was never realized.

Applicants to the teaching program had to demonstrate professional teaching plans, emotional maturity, and an interest in participating in "an informal and quiet ministry" of racial reconciliation by witnessing through a "Christian presence" at the colleges.[106] *Christian presence*, a term in vogue at the time among student Christian groups internationally, meant providing the example of a Christian approach to everyday life without actually proselytizing. In keeping with the idea of Christian presence, the SIM interns in the black colleges did not identify themselves as part of a particular program nor even as ministers. In this way, the Atlanta project was very much informed by the Southwest Georgia Project, which had modeled this approach to missionary witness.

The four interns who taught in 1966 quickly found, however, that providing such presence in a meaningful way was a difficult task to accomplish. Submerging themselves in the routines of their schools, as if they were just any of a number of new white faculty members, did little to further social justice or race relations unless they consciously set out to do so through overt efforts. Therefore, they adopted a fourth goal for themselves: to increase their respective campuses' social activism, which they generally found to be lacking. Larry Blackman, who joined with the Spelman chaplain, Reverend Rate, to organize a weekly discussion forum, reported that "with a few real exceptions, I find the college generally apathetic and in dire need of a healthy dose of good old activism."[107] The other interns also tried to get students on their campuses more involved in politics: Tom Ross and Manfred Liebig joined Clark College's Freethinkers discussion group, and Charles Hinkle served as a campus adviser to the Young Democrats and also used a sermon at the Morehouse chapel to instigate a campus protest against recruiters from Dow Chemical. In some cases, the SIM students were more radical than their hosts; at Morehouse, Hinkle was prevented from assigning *The Autobiography of Malcolm X* to students in the Upward Bound program.[108]

Tom Ross became particularly involved in his internship and ended up spending two years teaching at Clark, although he was not officially a part of the intern project in his second year. He had become a favorite teacher during his first year there, bringing his interest in civil rights to the campus and his ideas about theology into the classroom. He taught the major religious survey course, supplementing the staid textbook with books such as Carl F. Burke's *God Is for Real, Man,* a collection of Bible stories told in urban street slang, and John A. T. Robinson's best-selling 1963 book *Honest to God,* in which Robinson reimagines God not as a holy being but as "Love with a capital L."[109] He encouraged his students to challenge the material and ask questions, something that many Clark professors still discouraged. Outside the classroom, he coached the debate team and promoted student involvement in politics and activism. Ross's campus apartment also became an unofficial headquarters for rap sessions and information about opposing the Vietnam War. Likewise, Charles Hinkle's Morehouse dorm room became a central hangout for many upperclassmen, who took advantage of his presence in the dorm by turning him into "a de facto counselor and confidant."[110]

In addition to the Atlanta College Teaching Project, the Southwest Georgia Project, and the regular pastorate-based internships, SIM assigned ten interns to its new Northern Urban Project. Closest to SIM's home base at Union Theological Seminary, the Northern Urban Project was also one of its first failures. In some ways, the project was not a new venture at all but rather an intersection of SIM's changing civil rights priorities with a longer-standing tradition of service at Union Theological Seminary. For many years the seminary had promoted mission in its immediate community, primarily through Riverside Church and the East Harlem Protestant Parish, which served as both training center and laboratory for generations of seminarians. For the Northern Urban Project, SIM planned to join forces with East Harlem Protestant Parish founder George Webber's new Metropolitan-Urban Service Training (MUST) program in New York City.[111] The SIM-MUST program was to include five white theological students working in black and Puerto Rican inner-city churches, and five black theological students working in congregations with a majority of white members. George Webber himself endorsed the project, judging it to have "very real significance for theological education" as well as being "a significant venture in giving expression to the unity of the church."[112] However, the joint effort never materialized, placements did not pan out, and the students rarely met; thus, by the end of the first semester, the project voted to voluntarily disband. Maynard Moore, SIM's national coordinator, reported in September 1967 that the only things that could be salvaged from the wreckage of the Northern Urban Project were lessons about "how *not* to operate an urban project."[113]

As the SIM interns were prospering in Atlanta and falling apart in New York, the news of the organization's move toward yearlong internships had clearly been heard. By January 1967, SIM had received 170 separate requests for full-year 1967–68 SIM interns from churches, urban development projects, and other potential hosts. The program laid out plans that called for 31 summer students and 110 yearlong interns under a total budget of just below $226,000. Summer students would receive stipends of between $300 and $500, and interns would receive between $1,500 and $2,500, specific amounts depending on marital status and the availability of additional incomes. The students predicted that they would successfully raise the full amount of their proposed quarter million dollar budget from denominations, foundations, seminaries, congregations, and individuals.[114] Their optimism, however, flew in the face of their negligible bank balance. That same month, Moore pitched the SIM project before the national conference of seminary field education directors. The project's new regional administrative structure was also put to use, with regional coordinators in the Northeast, Midwest, and Southwest doing additional recruiting.

As a result of the administration changes and aggressive recruiting, thirty-seven students went into the field that summer: twelve students in Southwest Georgia and the rest with urban projects in Chicago, Indianapolis, Los Angeles, Richmond (CA), Richmond (NY), and Washington D.C. There were thirty-two white and five black participants that summer, but the most notable statistic was that fifteen women joined the twenty-two men, the highest proportion of women ever in SIM and the closest the program got to gender parity. This represented the greater inclusion of undergraduates in the program, the higher number of women in seminaries, and the greater likelihood of couples to undertake summer ministries together, even when only one was a seminarian. There was also a grassroots movement afoot, which was small but rapidly gaining momentum, for greater roles for women in the church, both in the laity and in the ministry. In 1964, for example, Colin Williams, director of the NCC's Department of Evangelism, urged women to "start up a feminist movement in the churches to gain admission" to positions of authority, and by 1967, student ecumenical groups were also talking about the potential for "a new movement" of and for women.[115]

The summer of 1967 students represented the following seminaries and colleges: Boston, Chicago, Drew, Dubuque, Episcopal of the Caribbean (2), Episcopal of the Southwest, Hartford, Harvard, Immaculate Conception (2), Luther, Lutheran School of Theology, Payne, Perkins, Princeton, Union Theological Seminary (7), Yale, George Washington, Morris Brown, Spelman, Women's College of Georgia (2), and Wooster.

As the summer students set out for their urban ministry projects, they were mindful of the goals of SIM's National Committee: "that each SIM project should ... direct [its] attention at evolving new strategies for confronting the 'gut' social issues which the nation and the church faces," should demonstrate commitment to the "struggle to humanize those structures which deny and distort human dignity and freedom," and should do so "primarily outside the normal 'clergy' roles of residentially-based congregations."[116] This would especially be the case in Chicago.

Following up the lead of Bruce Christie's work in the summer of 1966, SIM developed its Chicago Urban Project, playing a small but significant role in the Chicago Freedom Movement by sponsoring fifteen seminarians working on a range of projects. The students made progress slowly; however, they also found their faith tested by encountering entrenched poverty and power imbalances that seemed to require more than racial cooperation and reconciliation could provide. They found that the first step in combating the problems of the inner city, including its spiritual ones, was understanding them.

More than forty years after taking the plunge sponsored by the Urban Training Center for Christian Mission, SIM alum Marv Dunn recalled it vividly and cited it as having a great impact on his life, giving him a "sensitivity to the plight of the homeless" and the urban poor.[117] As part of their orientation week in Chicago, Dunn and the other SIM students were given a few hours of information about life on the streets, provided with a set of old clothes and the requisite eight dollars, and sent out to spend the better part of a January week on the Chicago streets. Dunn was so youthful-looking he couldn't even shelter in bars. He ended up spending most of his time in bus stations and all-night movie theaters and was eventually able to cadge a few dollars from a Lutheran minister. One white priest who was on Dunn's plunge was beaten up by black gang members on the South Side and "was quite prophetic about the fact that he had begun to understand some of the pain that the black community goes through."[118]

Chicago was a center of "social and political ferment," and according to SIM's blueprint for its work in the city, "in the midst of this ferment, sometimes at the forefront of it, there has also been a restive searching for responsible religious forms—of belief, of action, of organization." Encountering resistance from some quarters within the church and from the Daly political machine had "not stopped this many-centered drive for a humanly acceptable city, and it has not killed the dream of a coherent, common humanity."[119] From SIM's point of view, Chicago's experiments in social change provided the perfect setting for students to explore "what it means for the church to be the church at the grassroots level in the twentieth century," which meant "humanizing all social structures."[120] By 1967, the SIM project had, in effect, adopted the strategy of social change known as "congregation-based community organizing," first developed in Chicago by Saul Alinsky in the 1950s. Congregation-based community organizing involved one-to-one conversations within church communities, leading first to a congregational commitment to improving social conditions and then to the creation of networks of urban congregations for the purposes of serving contemporary urban residents.[121]

SIM students in Chicago worked in a number of radical and experimental ventures, such as the School for Community Organization, created under the Center for Radical Research; the Garfield Organization, a black militant organization in the West Garfield neighborhood; and the Englewood neighborhood's School for Human Dignity, an alternative summer school for five- to twelve-year-olds, structured around a program of black pride and African and African American history and culture.[122] Though these projects shared a common heritage in Chicago's inner-city churches, their daily rhetoric and programs felt far divorced from traditional Christianity. Another student, John Fike, spent his year with the Chicago Urban Project working with one of the larger and more successful groups, the East Garfield Park Community Organization (EGPCO), which had helped lead the Union to End Slums the previous summer. But Fike described the work of 1966 as "novel, fascinating, and glamorous" when compared to that during 1967, by which time EGPCO was embroiled in the "hard, grinding, continuous work of incarnating the movement into organizational structures," work that "is neither glamorous nor novel."[123] In all, a dozen SIM interns worked with the Church Federation of Greater Chicago during the 1967–68 year, including five married couples and two singles, from five different seminaries. They were, according to intern Marv Dunn, in Chicago when the city "went up in smoke" following Martin Luther King Jr.'s assassination.[124] Dunn recalled that the most important thing he learned from his SIM semester in Chicago was that "individual salvation wasn't going to change the world"; the world's problems were too complex to be solved by reconciliation alone.[125]

While SIM's Northern Urban Project in New York City west bust after a few months, it developed a slightly more successful project nearby in Staten Island's Borough of Richmond. Two students were placed for the summer of 1967 and two more yearlong interns during the 1967–68 school year, although one summer student quickly dropped out of the project after finding its lack of structure frustrating. The other three seminarians persisted, offering a music program and other projects for a community association, helping to run a community development project called Youth Corps, and organizing within a housing project. Although their efforts were meaningful, they were a long way from the project plans, which called for a large group of SIM interns working in collaboration with an imagined group of eighteen local lay leaders and clergy futuristically dubbed "the Nucleus."[126] This wasn't to be. As in previous projects, the students interpreted their work as theological training, specifically as inner-city Christian witness, as well as a response to the biblical imperative to serve and their personal desires to push the church toward an effective role in society. As Ann Lin put it in one report: "Society has presented the challenge to the Church to broaden her horizons from her own interests and activities to include her surroundings as well. This needs to be done if the Church is going to become a part of the whole community. If the role of the Church does not function as salt and light in society, than She has not fulfilled her purpose as God expects." Roger Hughes more directly addressed the issue of some churches retreating to the suburbs, emphasizing that God wants not just the personal salvation that suburban churches tended to preach, but social transformation as well.[127]

In Indianapolis, the major concern was affordable housing, virtually none of which had been constructed since the World War II era. Working in collaboration with faculty at the Christian Theological Seminary, the SIM Indianapolis committee developed projects with churches, government agencies, and nonprofit housing organizations. One summer student, Shirley Wilburn Key—whose husband was serving in Vietnam—worked with Indianapolis's housing relocation office, while another, Ellie Charles from Episcopal Seminary of the Caribbean, pushed through the language barrier to work with the black congregation of Hillside Church in an economically depressed neighborhood.

The Indianapolis Project also laid plans for reinventing itself for the 1968–69 year as the Indianapolis Suburban Project, shifting its focus from the inner city to the primarily white western suburbs. The proposed project, which was never realized under SIM, was meant to "formalize a model of what white people who are working in white neighborhoods can do in order to bring about change in the 'racist' values and institutions of the white middle class that strangle the inner city neighborhoods." The planning for the project was heavily influenced by Joe Matthews's Ecumenical Institute in Chicago, with which SIM's George Walters and Maynard Moore were both affiliated.[128]

On the West Coast, two students ventured to Los Angeles in the summer of 1967 to join a project that promised to feature SIM's first venture into exploring the needs of Hispanic and Latino Americans, as well as African Americans. In a city that had exploded with the Watts Rebellion just two years earlier, the students worked primarily through a group known as COMMIT, the Center of Metropolitan Mission In-Service Training. While original plans called for four summer students and five yearlong interns during 1967–68, budget constraints and student interest determined the smaller project. As it was, Henry Florcak from Immaculate Conception

Seminary and Gesner Montes from Seminario Episcopal del Caribe spent their summer in Los Angeles working in churches and in community programs, including Head Start. Gesner Montes served with Ward African Methodist Episcopal Church in South Central Los Angeles, where he worked on a door-to-door survey of the church's neighborhood, admitting that he struggled against the urge to cover his nose with a handkerchief because of the level of dirt and smell in many of the houses but persevered because "if one really wants to help, one must put oneself on the same level with the ones one wants to help."[129]

In Richmond, California, SIM joined forces with the Richmond Inner-City Ministry (RIM), administered by the Greater Richmond Christian Parish. The two summer SIM students worked alongside about twenty students from the University of California on community development projects and on issues such as police violence. Imagined as an umbrella under which both church-based and locally and federally funded community agencies could work together, RIM was meant to be a forum through which "groups of indigenous community poor people could come together and organize themselves . . . to deal with the injustices and divisions under which they have been forced to live."[130]

Another effort, the Atlanta Urban Project, placed fifteen interns, including three spouses, for the summer of 1967 "in ministry to areas of racial brokenness in the Atlanta area."[131] They worked through churches, social agencies, federal government programs, and local seminaries in order to "renew the church; reform theological education; reshape the social order; and work towards reconciliation in race relations."[132] The first and last goals—church renewal and racial reconciliation—were consistent with SIM's long-standing approach, but it is notable that these were now joined by a desire to move backward into the seminaries to retool theological education for greater worldly relevance and by an even loftier and more radical call to reshape the social order itself.

The summer students' work included a great deal of youth outreach and community and welfare rights organizing, working within churches themselves and for the SCLC, and with one placement working in city government as part of the Community Relations Commission. One student worked in "a rather poor, vicious white area," another sign of SIM's shift toward efforts to organize white people. The students reported a certain amount of frustration working within established social work organizations in a city they found to harbor long established "modes and structures" that were difficult to penetrate and allowed them little access to the streets, which they seemed to romanticize highly as embodying a more authentic way of life than that perpetuated by the establishment. Other interns, working more independently, felt a greater sense of accomplishment. The students also attempted to form group cohesion and to ground their experience in their religious training by meeting for weekly theological discussion, sometimes hosting guest speakers. This effort revealed a number of fissures within the group, which reflect the changing nature of seminary students more broadly in the late 1960s. As one student wrote, "the more pagan amongst us felt that the theological context was superficially batted around and thus unnecessary," and suggested that SIM's purpose had evolved into a goal to "radicalize and secularize the ministry in order to inject it with more meaning and illustrate that God isn't really dead."[133] The seminarians increasingly saw a so-called secular ministry as a viable path, and pushed the seminaries themselves to consider such paths in their training programs. Seeking to involve the local seminaries, the students elected several prominent leaders from the Candler School of Theology at Emory University and from the Interdenominational Theological Center as advisers to the Atlanta SIM committee.[134]

While the students' project unfolded in the field, the National Committee convened four times during the 1966–67 year, focusing SIM's approach to urban ministry, revising and planning expansions of its urban offerings, evaluating SIM's relationship to the ever-changing "movement," and entertaining a number of suggestions for reforming the system of theological education in which they, as seminary students, had more than a small stake. Guided by Moore and Walters, they devised a four-prong program for their continued work: reforming theological education, creating a "revolutionary church," addressing problems of economic inequality, and bringing about reconciliation in race relations.[135] In many ways, these goals were the same as SIM had been exploring since 1960, although the urban program had replaced pastoral exchange as the tactic of choice.

The demand was obvious—170 requests for interns!—and yet the same communities and denominations calling for help were not able to provide funding for the program at the same level as their need. Thus, in September 1967, Moore reported that SIM had $5,000 in the bank while facing a program year that would require $5,000 *per month* to support. The SIM staff pared down the massive stack of requests to forty placements for the 1967–68 year.[136] The urban situation was certainly real, and SIM had clearly responded to the cities' zeitgeist, but would it be able to survive long enough to continue in its new urban mission—and did it even want to? By early

1967, the SIM folks were self-consciously referring to their "corporate goals."[137] Is that what they really wanted to be? Had the organization, with its decentralized regional structure and multiple placements and sometimes oscillating vision of its purpose, outgrown its usefulness?

When SIM's founding members based their project on the biblical idea of reconciliation, they laid out a clear mandate for the organization in terms that its seminary student members understood. Seven years later, amid calls for renewal and change and revolution, what was needed—indeed, what was expected—was much less clear. Students proposed revolution, but they did not really know what this would look like or mean. Even calls for Black Power could founder on their imprecision. For example, when Ivanhoe Donaldson was asked to define what Black Power meant and what its promoters wanted, he responded that they wanted no part of the white power system, "we want something entirely different."[138] George Walters of SIM added, "Black Power does not mean taking over white power, but replacing it with something far more just and humane."[139] For both Donaldson and Walters, however, what this new and different "something" would be was unclear.

In its urban projects, SIM attempted to define the actions of a revolutionary church as a combination of mission and movement. It often employed what seemed traditional tactics—urban mission, community organizing, and economic development—but while its tactics may have looked familiar, SIM leaders argued, the ideological and physical contexts in which they were applied made them revolutionary. SIM's leaders in 1966 and 1967 wrote that a revolutionary church that addressed the problems of the inner city and the concerns that resulted in expressions of Black Power was on the brink of being created out of the urban environment. The new church, one of them wrote, would not simply evince "a concern for slums or schools or hospitals, but [would lead] a grassroots ecumenical movement embodying regional strategies to attack with power the pervasive complex of interlocking metropolitan problems."[140] If the writer was a bit verbose, he or she nevertheless decently described the goals of the urban projects that SIM created in its last years. Thus, the Student Interracial Ministry was, by the late 1960s, attempting a reimagined form of the church itself.

Theologians at the time described two forms of the church: gathered and scattered. The gathered church, represented by denominations and congregations, was merely the form taken when members of the believing community came together for worship. But that larger believing community—the church scattered—was also a form of the church. Ed Feaver, who served several years with SIM in Southwest Georgia before returning to help manage the project in its final year, reasoned that "as a scattered community, the members are involved in all aspects of life—economic, political, social, cultural—for the purpose of creating a society in which all men treat each other with love and respect."[141] One could be a minister of this new church, revolutionary and scattered, through engaging social justice concerns but not necessarily through traditional church structures. The SIM students thus provided a prophetic reinterpretation of their own role and that which they projected for the church and ministry.

The race crisis that produced the Student Interracial Ministry at the start of the 1960s had turned some within the church inward, questioning their own institutions and beliefs. Now, as the decade wound toward a close, SIM students and their Christian progressive colleagues turned outward to face and embrace a world that seemed to grow ever more complex. As one student wrote in early 1967, "The clearness of the civil rights activities of 1962–64 exists no more, though the lines between brother and enemy become clearer." Would-be activists, he wrote, now experienced "daily indecision . . . not because there is no desire to decide and act, but because the elements of decision are now piled chaotically awaiting some force to rearrange them into imperatives for action."[142] As much of the world was to find out, the year 1968 would bring much of the chaos and unrest and built-up pressure pouring out into the streets. It would tear through the aisles of the churches and the hallways of the seminaries as well.

Hank Elkins, second from right, on the steps of Ebenezer Baptist Church with church secretary Mrs. Sarah Reed (left), Rev. Martin Luther King Jr. (second from left), and Mrs. Alberta Williams King, known as "Mother King" (right), 1962. Photo credit: Henry Elkins.

SIM volunteer Oscar Johnson (with child on his lap), visits with a family in North Carolina, 1966. Photo credit: "1966 Report: Student Interracial Ministry," SIM, UTS, 1C:2:f11.

Students gather around the table at the Student Interracial Ministry National Committee Meeting, New York City, 1965. George Walters is at near right. Photo credit: "1966 Report: Student Interracial Ministry," SIM, UTS, 1C:2:f11.

Charles Sherrod of the Southwest Georgia Project consults with the National Council of Churches' J. Oscar Lee during the National Committee Meeting, New York City, 1965. Photo credit: "1966 Report: Student Interracial Ministry," SIM, UTS, 1C:2:f11.

Keith Davis from the Chicago Lutheran Theological Seminary, Maywood, shooting pool with youth at the Shepherd of the Streets community center he helped create in Richmond, Virginia, summer 1965. Photo credit: "1966 Report: Student Interracial Ministry," SIM, UTS, 1C:2:f11.

Tom Boomershine, Union Theological Seminary, chats with kids on a street near Chambers Memorial Baptist Church, his placement in Harlem, New York, summer 1965. Photo credit: "1966 Report: Student Interracial Ministry," SIM, UTS, 1C:2:f11.

Staff meeting of Southwest Georgia Project. At the table are SIM interns Maxim Rice (near left, back to camera), Charles Sherrod (left, head down reading), Joe Pfister (to left of standing man), Susan Pearcy (right in striped tank top), and Southwest Georgia Project volunteers "Stick" (second from left), Shirley Sherrod (right, looking toward head of table), Ed Anderson (left of Sherrod), Joanne Christian Mants (in bandana), and Celestine Hill (near right). Albany, Georgia, 1967. Photo credit: Glen Pearcy Collection (AFC 2012/040), American Folklife Center, Library of Congress; afc2012040_204_ph18.

Joe Pfister (right), Union Theological Seminary, with children in Southwest Georgia. Worth County, Georgia, 1967. Photo credit: Glen Pearcy Collection (AFC 2012/040), American Folklife Center, Library of Congress; afc2012040_172_ph02.

SIM volunteer Susan Pearcy (left) with Rosie and Nelson Ernst, Southwest Georgia, 1967. Photo credit: Glen Pearcy Collection (AFC 2012/040), American Folklife Center, Library of Congress; afc2012040_180_ph24.

Southwest Georgia Project volunteers take a break in the office. Maxim Rice is at right. Albany, Georgia, 1967. Photo credit: Glen Pearcy Collection (AFC 2012/040), American Folklife Center, Library of Congress; afc2012040 210_ph01.

SIM volunteers Keith Davis (left) and Carol Lucas at the Shepherd of the Streets center, Richmond, Virginia, 1966. Photo credit: UTS1: Student Interracial Ministry Records, series 4, box 2, folder 6, The Burke Library at Union Theological Seminary, Columbia University in the City of New York.

SIM volunteers Bill Troy (left) and Mac Hulslander visit with residents at Freedom City, Mississippi, 1966. Photo credit: UTS1: Student Interracial Ministry Records, 4:2:f6, The Burke Library at Union Theological Seminary, Columbia University in the City of New York.

SIM volunteer Tim Kimrey with youth in Southwest Georgia, 1966. Photo credit: UTS1: Student Interracial Ministry Records, 4:2:f6, The Burke Library at Union Theological Seminary, Columbia University in the City of New York.

Unidentified SIM volunteer (with pipe), 1966. Photo credit: UTS1: Student Interracial Ministry Records, 4:2:f6, The Burke Library at Union Theological Seminary, Columbia University in the City of New York.

CHAPTER SIX

Seminaries in the Storm

Theological Education and the Collapse of SIM, 1967–1968

We live in a time of theological confusion and uncertainty which has accented rather than transformed the contemporary crisis of fear, apprehension, and pessimism about the future. The sustaining hope of early Christians is almost nowhere to be found.

—Rev. Charles Shelby Rooks, Fund for Theological Education, 1970

The Student Interracial Ministry began the 1967–68 school year having seemingly found its new niche in urban ministry and responding to the unprecedented demands from urban communities for seminary interns. Forty students, including eleven married couples, were serving yearlong internships in Atlanta, Southwest Georgia, St. Louis, Richmond (CA), Minneapolis, Chicago, and the New York City area, and many more requests for interns continued to come in to the office and to be farmed out to the five regional subcommittees. Additional projects in Los Angeles, Houston, Milwaukee, Toledo, and Daytona Beach, Florida, were under consideration. With a main administrative headquarters in New York City overseeing the project's finances, publications, and recruitment, and satellite programs and offices in a number of major cities, SIM seemed to have hit its stride. By May 1968, though, less than nine months later, SIM was no more, having shuttered its offices for good. How the program went from a position of growth, determined mission, and strength of service to total collapse is a story with three intertwined narratives: the crisis of meaning for both the churches and the seminaries as they struggled to maintain or reimagine relevance in the cataclysmically changing times of the late decade; the national climate of tumultuous social change as the civil rights movement segued into a series of interrelated movements and demands that, in 1968, would develop into a worldwide explosion of protest; and finally, the purely practical demands of an expensive and now decentralized ecumenical, interracial program managed by students who themselves were reeling from the chaos of the times, times in which both ecumenism and interracialism were suddenly out of favor.

Positioned with one foot in the university and one foot in the church, seminaries in the late 1960s found themselves buffeted by turbulent winds of change in both spheres. The dissatisfaction with the status quo that swept from the streets and through college and university campuses spawned a movement of social movements—Black Power, the antiwar and student movements, the women's and gay liberation movements, Latino and Native American rights, and a host of others—what one contemporary commentator correctly identified as a "proliferation of inter-related issues" that welled up within the seminaries as well.[1] As Christopher Queen, an education director at the National Council of Churches, wrote in 1970, "When students consider the problems of the future—the threat of glutted populations and a world of dirty skies and oily oceans, the continuation of insane political priorities, the military oppression of powerless peoples . . . and, always, the possibility of nuclear or biological warfare—they turn to the seminary as the most accessible institution to attack these issues."[2]

Students at Union Theological Seminary, from the early days of the sit-in movement, throughout the civil rights efforts of the 1960s, and on to other issues, were among the first to join each phase of action. As students of theology at the country's leading liberal seminary, they were predisposed toward cultural criticism and activism. Union's relationship with the progressive Riverside Church and its location in the New York metropolis also contributed to the seminary's tendency to attract "activist students from better colleges and universities."[3] These movements had spawned a number of creative responses at Union through the years; in addition to the Student Interracial Ministry, there was the Theological Students Vigil for Civil Rights at the Lincoln Memorial during 1964, a later vigil against the Vietnam War and in support of President Johnson's peace efforts, and the boycotting of banks related to South Africa's apartheid regime.[4]

Students were not the only activists on seminary campuses, and a campus like Union Theological Seminary could boast a long heritage of socially active professors and administrators. At Union, some of the younger professors participated in teach-ins and other events that supported student activism. Administrators were more reserved in public but were also often personally supportive. A few of the senior scholars actively participated in the civil rights movement, even while not committing the institution itself to the cause. SIM adviser Roger Shinn, a professor of social ethics, was arrested in an early Freedom Ride and was arrested again while protesting the arrest of a SIM student in Wilmington, North Carolina, in 1963. Robert McAfee Brown, it may be remembered, was also a Freedom Rider, and Union president John Bennett and professors Brown, William Sloane Coffin, and Rabbi Abraham Joshua Heschel all participated in the student-led

Lincoln Memorial civil rights vigil and other demonstrations. Bennett and his wife, Anne, even missed their own retirement party at the seminary when they were arrested and detained during an anti–Vietnam War protest in Washington D.C.[5]

Union students, in fact, helped spark an international justice movement in 1965 by devising a program of protests and bank withdrawals to highlight American financial complicity in South Africa's apartheid regime. Students quickly garnered support from faculty and administrators and generated coverage by the *New York Times*. Although Union's own board refused to divest, within a year the campaign had grown sufficiently to move off campus, and in 1969, the South African government announced it was no longer receiving support from the particular banking consortium that Union students had targeted.[6] Divestment as an antiapartheid strategy gained popularity, especially in American educational institutions, and proved slowly effective over the next twenty years.

The SIM program—specifically its Southwest Georgia Project—was the catalyst for most of the subsequent social justice work at Union in the 1960s, although these other concerns would eventually siphon away some of its potential participants.[7] Union Theological Seminary was electrified in 1965 when Charles Sherrod, who had married only twenty-four hours earlier and was accompanied by his new wife, Shirley, led a caravan from Georgia to New York City, arriving on campus with two carloads of SIM volunteers and local Georgia folk. The Southwest Georgia contingent piled out of the cars that they had dubbed "the Honeymoon Express" and ignited their fellow students to action with tales of the fight in the Deep South. The Sherrods, student volunteers, and a few Southwest Georgia natives told compelling stories and presented their field reports to SIM committees and the Union faculty and student body. It was the first time that those residing at the Union campus had a chance to hear in person from the Georgia workers, and they caught their infectious excitement for the program.

The presentations stimulated a number of conversations among faculty and students as to how fieldwork in combination with regular seminary work could be used to better train students to be "responsive to the needs of people in society."[8] The Southwest Georgia veterans' influence was felt as Union students became more engaged with the social problems of the time *and* pushed for reforming theological education to better prepare them for undertaking just such engagement.

Seminary students brought the battles of the time home to their own institutions in the form of social protest like the divestment program, but they also demanded radical change in the very manner in how they were being educated. Students parlayed their newly acquired knowledge of the art of protest into demands for greater contemporary relevance as well as more intellectual autonomy, insisting on institutional reform and questioning many of the assumptions of theological training. Already reeling from questions about secularization and new theological trends, like the Death of God movement and black theology; the popularization of liberation theology on the near horizon; and the need to train ministers for a world that at times seemed a moving target, the seminaries found themselves vulnerable to attack from within. By the end of the 1960s, talk of reform had grown into calls for revolution and finally into lamentations of a crisis at hand.

"The truth is," wrote Charles Shelby Rooks, an African American minister and the director of the program that administered the Rockefeller Grants to support would-be ministers, in 1970, "everywhere one goes in theological education today the word *crisis* is heard—from the lips of faculty, administrators, trustees, students, and alumni. In fact the word has become [a] conventional description of seminaries."[9] Indeed, as Rooks went on to detail, there was not one but a series of crises—pedagogical, theological, spiritual, financial, and organizational—affecting the seminaries as the 1960s grew toward the 1970s. The theological crisis was at the center of this maelstrom and was connected in some way to each of the others. In Rooks's opinion, so much theology was in doubt, and so many new approaches— not to mention new religions—were on offer, that an era of theological confusion now reigned, which "accented rather than transformed the contemporary crisis of fear, apprehension, and pessimism about the future."[10] As Harvey Cox had argued, the city and secularization were not oppositional to religion but actually potentially enmeshed. Lack of clear direction in and from the churches and synagogues, and a crumbling of faith in their traditions and theology, combined to magnify contemporary confusion rather than provide a path through it. The crises in the churches and in society fed each other.

Chief among the factors that had chipped away the solid footing of traditional Christian understanding and training for ministry was what Rooks called the "crisis of insensitivity" to others. Almost seventy years earlier, W. E. B. DuBois had written of the common insensitivity to the suffering of others: that "men knew so little of men."[11] Seminarians of the late 1960s and early 1970s "made the eradication of this insensitivity [their] passion."[12] This desire, and the related search for personal authenticity, underlay much of the turmoil on seminary and other educational campuses, and fueled support for the civil rights and Black Power movements, calls for curricular reform, demands for the responsible use of financial assets, protests against the war in Vietnam, and a host of other often related causes. Exacerbating the situation and perhaps guaranteeing an eventual conflagration was that at the same time, seemingly everything was being questioned, the seminaries were bursting at the seams. Seminary enrollment peaked nationally during 1967–68, and Union Theological Seminary enrolled an all-time high of 793 students.[13]

The nature of seminary students had changed as well during the decade. A sizable portion of the influx of new students saw the seminaries as a "safe haven," providing an educational deferment from compulsory service in Vietnam. According to Marv Dunn, who participated in SIM and attended Chicago Theological Seminary during 1967 and 1968, "Everyone there was hiding from the draft."[14] The small but influential group of students whom John Collins and others had dubbed "seekers" at the start of the decade had grown in size proportionate to the whole seminary population and now seemed to surpass that of those seeking ministerial careers. In addition to higher enrollments and fewer students bound for the pastorate, seminaries across the country saw the average age of incoming students steadily rise during the decade, as more of those people who had chosen the ministry did so as a second vocation. A substantial proportion of women entering the ministry were doing so later in life, after having raised families, and men were also switching to the ministry from other careers.[15] Proportions of minority and female seminarians also rose steadily during the 1960s, with women constituting 10 percent of all seminarians by 1972.[16] As one decade grew into the next, a larger, older, and more diverse student body had increasingly varied personal experiences to draw on when assessing their education and determining the future role of the ministry.

At the conclusion of its 1967 summer program, SIM gathered its interns for a debriefing. The students assessed their summer's work in relation to the civil rights movement, the church, and theological education by offering words and phrases about each, which were then compiled into lists. The list for the civil rights movement included "observer," "fuck it," "repugnant," "cog," "cooperation," and "temporary"; the list for the church included "alienation," "frustration," "peripheral," "great," "determined," "liaison," and "revolutionary"; and the list for theological education included "viable," "pastoral," "finished," and "ambiguous." Asked to describe the limits of SIM itself as a ministry, the students responded with "uncoordinated," "undisciplined," "uncommitted," and "provincial." Asked to describe SIM in the past, they offered a single word: "interracial." And finally, when asked for a description of SIM in the present, they responded with "theological revolution."[17]

The pace of political and social change on campus during the 1960s accelerated as the decade proceeded. According to a 1969 National Council of Churches' study on student-initiated change in theological schools, this was due to "the intensification of long-dormant feelings" and the advent of intersecting social change movements. The study found that at Union Theological Seminary, for example, more students became directly involved in social action or reform efforts in the final two years of the 1960s than had been involved in the previous eight years combined. Like secular campuses, seminaries during this period were home to student unrest and occasionally dramatic clashes. Seminarians occupied administration buildings at Andover Newtown, Chicago, McCormick, and Union in the latter years of the 1960s. The chapel of the Pacific School of Religion in Berkeley, California, was bombed in 1969, and seminarians at Boston Theological made national news when they used the school chapel to harbor a GI sought by authorities on charges of being AWOL from the U.S. military.[18]

Jon DeVries, who as a SIM student spent the summer of 1967 working with the Southwest Georgia Project, identified 1966 as the year that the national student mood shifted from dissent to resistance. DeVries saw the anti–Vietnam War movement and specifically the work of Students for a Democratic Society on college campuses as leading this wave of resistance toward "those civil authorities, campus officials, and corporations it consider[ed] oppressive." The war in Vietnam, he predicted, would force America to change: "If a military victory cannot be achieved on Washington's terms, the war will simply have to end at the point at which it causes unbearable stress on our society . . . [and] at that point American society itself will have to change in order to stop the war, and thus Vietnam becomes a symbol of the need to change."[19] And then, in the summer of 1967, when black demonstrators and police clashed bloodily more than seventy times, DeVries wrote, "Something happened to the thousands of students in the new left who had been involved in civil rights work over the past several years: something sobering in knowing that these were our brothers in the streets and this was the same government that we too were confronting."[20] The shift toward militancy was palpable at Union and other seminaries as clashes erupted over Vietnam and racial and economic inequities. But the spirit of resistance also gave the students voice as they called for changes to the seminary's curriculum that would reflect both more concern with the state of the world and more responsiveness to individual students' interests and learning styles.

These various crises were already nearing the boiling point when the Reverend Martin Luther King Jr. was assassinated on April 4, 1968, while in Memphis to lend his support to striking sanitation workers. At that point in his career, King had made some decisive shifts, including putting increasingly greater emphasis on economic justice as a cornerstone to civil rights and coming out against the Vietnam War. His death was met not with the nonviolence to which he had pledged himself but with cataclysmic protest and burning neighborhoods, as waves of social unrest tore through the country at a volume not seen since the Civil War.[21] Dozens of people were killed and thousands injured in outpourings of grief and violence that decimated cities from Washington, D.C., and Baltimore to Chicago and Louisville. The death of King shook the nation, including those SIM interns who were currently in the field. Maxim Rice, a student from Garrett Theological Seminary who was serving a SIM intern year with Charles Sherrod and the Southwest Georgia Project, recalled driving to a rural church one night in a van with about seven other volunteers, Sherrod at the wheel, when the news of King's death came over the radio. "The wailing and tears turned to singing, and when we arrived some went into the church for prayers, while others of us stayed outside in the dark in small groups comforting each other. The next day and night was full of tension and gunshots in Albany."[22]

For some of the SIM volunteers, Martin Luther King's death and the explosive reaction to it was just the latest in a series of explosions that had been building throughout the year. Roy Birchard, a white Berea College student who was working with SIM's College Teaching Program—the name having changed to represent the expansion from just Atlanta-area colleges—spent September 1967 through May 1968 at Pennsylvania's Lincoln University and had a unique view of the chaos to come, all of which he meticulously noted in his diary. He taught courses in religion and English, and served as the resident director of a 130-resident male dormitory at Lincoln, the first of the country's historically black colleges and universities. Founded in 1854, it had long had a reputation of training the black bourgeoisie, during its first hundred years producing a number of black doctors and lawyers. Birchard was afforded the rare chance, as a white outsider, to witness a black college in the throes of its own struggles over the social changes of the time, especially over the meaning of Black Power for an institution of higher education.

Lincoln was in revolt that year—among other campaigns was one to change the name to Frederick Douglass University—and Birchard experienced it as a place where "the Martin Luther King era in American race relations [was] over," and the ideology of Black Power was being honed by a group of educated students and instructors who were "the kind of people who could make *and master* a revolution."[23] Birchard described the campus as a powder keg just waiting for a spark to ignite it, and was told by a fellow white faculty member that when Stokely Carmichael had visited the campus the previous year, " 'if he'd told the students to cut all our throats, they'd have done it.' "[24] According to Birchard, race issues so dominated campus discussions that they were commonly referred to by the two-word moniker "the issue."

As winter moved toward spring at Lincoln, Birchard noted, "[The] fragmented, almost anarchic, student body seethes and heaves in many directions at once. Emotions run high and are unpredictable."[25] In March, the campus erupted over charges of racism in the maintenance program, and then someone attempted to burn down the campus library. Lincoln wasn't the only historically black college teetering on the brink during those final weeks of March 1968. Students at Howard University in Washington, D.C., occupied the administration building, and the college was shut down. Closer to Lincoln, Cheney State College in Cheney, Pennsylvania, was also closed down after a mob of students assaulted the school president. Delaware State, Morgan, Hampton, Bowie State, and Maryland State all shut down that week, and when students revolted at Tuskegee University and cut the power lines, the president and board of directors were trapped inside the administration building, which had only electrically powered locks.[26] And then came King's death on April 4, 1968. The Lincoln campus was almost immediately closed, and students were sent home the next day.

Birchard, too, left the campus for home, and on April 8, four days after the death of King, he wrote an open letter to his home congregation, Bridport-Shoreham Parish in Vermont. Responding to what he sensed was an attitude among whites that, following King's death and the subsequent unrest, there was nothing to be done and that a race war was inevitable, Birchard attempted to explain the situation from his perspective at a black college and to urge continued work toward reconciliation during a time when "the life of our nation, of our friends and even of the church hangs in the balance."[27] Birchard returned to Lincoln when it reopened on April 17, but the campus was now less one student, a committed nonviolent activist, who had been killed by a police officer in his hometown of Trenton, New Jersey, while walking home from a movie. The officer insisted the student had been looting from a nearby clothing store during a riot.[28]

Back at Union, the unrest of the spring of 1968 formed the context in which the seminary community would engage in intensive introspection and self-critique. It began to deal systematically with what the National Council of Churches study called "a crisis of faith in the seminary's integrity at many levels," including its relationships to its neighbors, its relationship "to the needs of the Church and to the Christian tradition," and its own policies and curricula.[29] Although self-analysis and concern with mission may have been nothing new for seminaries, the level of engagement—by both students and faculty—and the potential to radically restructure the institutions had never been seen before. For SIM's part, although it never gave up on its mission of changing the church, by its final year SIM students and many of their seminary colleagues had turned both outward to the cities and inward to their own theological institutions. Although SIM had expanded well beyond its origins at Union into a decentered national structure with a series of regional hubs, many of the leaders of the organization still came from Union, retained ties with the National Council of Churches, and operated out of New York City. And when student movements, theology, and social activism explosively intersected around the Columbia University protests in 1968, the campus of Union Theological Seminary was particularly vulnerable and volatile.

The Columbia protests and the student strike which rose of out of them evolved out of two separate issues, one related to the Vietnam War and the right to protest it freely, and the other to the rights and freedoms of the school's black neighbors. Students demanded the right to free speech after six student activists were placed on probation, without a hearing, for protesting Columbia's relationship with a military think tank. At approximately the same time, concerns developed regarding Columbia's construction of a gymnasium with facilities for university affiliates, but with separate facilities for their Harlem neighbors. Between seven hundred and one thousand students staged protests and occupied five buildings on the Columbia campus between April 23 and April 30, 1968.[30] Columbia's chapter of Students for a Democratic Society and the Student Afro-American Society led the Columbia strike, while Union Theological Seminary played a number of roles in the protests. In fact, the president of the Columbia University Student Council at the time, Daniel E. Pellegrom, was a seminarian enrolled in a joint degree program between Columbia and Union and had only recently been appointed to replace several other officers who had quit the student council in protest. As many as half of all Union students became involved in the strike—as protesters, as representatives of Union on the Columbia Strike Coordinating Committee, or as nonviolence "officers" invited by the Columbia Protestant Office to help model nonviolence during demonstrations. Some of the seminarian nonviolence officers wore clerical collars, many for the first time in their lives, in an effort to identify themselves as ministers and keepers of the peace. About one hundred Union students were there in the early morning hours of April 29, 1968, when New York City riot police stormed the occupied campus buildings and arrested 711 people.[31] Among the 147 injured was Daniel Pellegrom, who was struck in the head with a nightstick while attempting to block a police advance.[32]

Union students also reacted to the Columbia strike on their own campus, supporting the Columbia students but also demanding reforms in the seminary's own culture and curriculum. At the very beginning of the strike, they organized a sympathy march from the seminary rotunda to Low Memorial Plaza on the Columbia campus. And on May 1, Union students issued a statement in support of the Columbia strike and then called their own, to include a "cessation of classes for the duration of the class period or the duration of the strike, whichever comes first."[33] Bruce Tischler, president of the Union student government, read the statement to the students occupying Columbia's Fayerweather Hall.[34] With Union's normal slate of classes thus shut down, a group of students and professors began to offer new classes, a harbinger of the profound change in theological education that was soon to come to Union and other seminaries.

At the start of the decade, most seminaries were relatively quiet places of study and reflection. After mid-decade, however, these same institutions were filled with students who questioned not just literal interpretations of the bible, as Union students had done for most of the century, but now also the importance of many basic religious traditions. Seminary students resented being handed a package of learning in lectures and wanted to discover spiritual truth for themselves in relation to their own lives and the concerns of the day.[35] The National Council of Churches in 1969 gave examples of a number of specific seminary experiences that might convince a student that his or her seminary was ignoring potential practical applications of theology. One example was of a Christian ethics course that did not address the Vietnam War.[36]

On the other hand, so many theological fads had come and gone, Charles Rooks wrote in 1970, that much of the traditionally taught theology had been upended without replacement. Religious critics linked the spiritual crisis in the nation to the instability of the seminaries and their willingness to engage nontraditional pedagogy. With prayer and reflection being inadequately replaced by temporary experiments in liturgy and worship, Rooks said, the "meaning, purpose, and vitality" of Christian practice had drained out of the seminaries.[37] Charles L. Taylor, who retired in 1967 after a decade at the helm of the American Association of Theological Schools, worried that amid all the seeking and questioning, God himself may have gotten lost, and that without a basis of renewal, the search would become both frustrating and meaningless.[38] The result of these myriad crises, according to one observer, was "that our whole life as Christian educational institutions is being called into account today in dramatic and sometimes painful ways."[39] Seminaries, once simple training academies for the parish ministry, suddenly found themselves questioning their basic purpose and direction.

The Death of God movement, which gained brief national attention in 1966, came to symbolize for some how far off track Christianity and the seminaries had gone. Death of God theologians proposed that God either no longer existed or still existed but that the theologies and liturgies that had previously communicated God to the people were no longer effective. If there had been any doubt that the nation was unaware of its religious crisis, that was answered on April 6, 1966, when *Time* magazine ran an all-black cover with a bold red headline reading "Is God Dead?" It was the first time the magazine had failed to feature a picture on its front cover.[40] While Death of God theology had few followers after around 1968, it served as a symbol of the scope of the crisis in the seminaries and churches, in which even the presumption of faith had been destabilized. Philosopher Susanne Langer commented at the time that society and the churches were experiencing a transition out of an age dominated by Christian thought and into a new era that was as yet undefined: "We feel ourselves swept along in a violent passage from a world we cannot salvage to one we cannot see; and most people are afraid."[41]

The emergence of black liberation theology was also felt quite strongly at Union, which would soon hire its leading thinker. In many ways describing the religious application of Black Power, black liberation theology was defined by future Union professor James H. Cone not long after SNCC's articulations of Black Power in 1966. The legal advances of the civil rights movement, writes historian Jeffrey O. G. Ogbar, "dismantl[ed] the pervasive legal underpinnings of racial subjugation, but expressed no concern over the psychological consequences of being black (or white) in a virulently anti-black society."[42] Cone saw the Black Power movement as offering a corrective expression to this psychological damage, and determined that it was undergirded by a specific theology, black liberation theology, which emerged as a North American version of liberation theology, and which some saw as incorporating powerful components of the "confessing model" of prophetic theology. Liberation theology was an international theological movement in the late 1960s and early 1970s that focused on the promise of redemption for the poor and suffering of the world and the practical application of faith in order to remedy poverty and injustice. Liberation theology interprets the message of Jesus Christ not as providing a blueprint for social order but as a spark to disrupt the social order, encouraging unrest and righting social inequalities. Cone applied his black theology of liberation to the experience of black Americans under white oppression. He wrote in his seminal work *Black Theology and Black Power* that Black Power meant black people determining their own role in relationships with whites, and that not only was Black Power not antithetical to Christian doctrine, but by demanding that past injustices be righted by tipping the power balance toward eventual equilibrium, it was *the* central message of Christianity in twentieth-century America.[43] *Black Theology and Black Power* was published in 1969, the same year that Cone became an assistant professor of theology at Union Theological Seminary.

In addition to the newer theological approaches of the late decade, student Christian movements were also changing, often becoming more radical and, in some cases, splintering. The Student Interracial Ministry, although its genesis and purpose were particular to the civil rights movement, was very much of the mold of the ecumenical Protestant student groups that flourished and then foundered during the era. These included the National Student Christian Federation and its successor, the University Christian Movement (UCM), as well as groups under its fold, such as the Methodist Student Movement. By the end of the decade, most of the groups had seen profound changes, if not total collapse, and a new set of experimental and underground student Christian groups were taking the baton, painting it in psychedelic swirls, and forging forward.

The National Student Christian Federation (NSCF), the American member of the World Student Christian Federation, was a related organization of the NCC and was formed in 1959 with the merger of three earlier groups—the Interseminary Movement, the Student Volunteer Movement, and the United States Christian Council—each of which had been within separate departments of the NCC. Other organizations came into the federation as members, including the Methodist Student Movement. In some ways the merger of the original three groups was not a merger at all, since each kept its individual identity, staff, and budget under the federation. So when, for example, the Interseminary Movement sponsored SIM, it did so in its own name. The YMCA and YWCA were originally members but later changed their status to "related organizations" to maintain their independence and nondenominational philosophy. The NSCF's mission was to "create an ecumenical community in which college students could participate in Christian fellowship, join in the mission of the church, and witness to the world."[44]

Most NSCF programming was mission or theology oriented until 1964, when a shift in programming refocused the federation on social and political concerns, among them the civil rights movement, South African apartheid, and the peace movement. This same year, a group of students led by Rebecca Own argued for greater attention to be paid to the student lay community.[45] By this time, the Interseminary Movement was already in major transition; in 1963, finding itself stretched too thin, it had closed its national office and maintained only its eight regional groups. By 1965, trying to respond to student demands, the NSCF had reduced its administrative costs and funneled the savings into programming, and was even considering disbanding entirely. Instead, arguing that it needed to become a student movement directed by students themselves at the grassroots level rather than a top-down federation, the NSCF dissolved by vote at the annual meeting in September 1966 and reorganized as the University Christian Movement. However, it would not last long in this form, either.[46]

As the successor organization, the University Christian Movement devoted itself to supporting social action and expanded to include not just Protestant organizations but Catholic, Orthodox, and secular groups, including SDS. Among its most notable contributions to the ecumenical student scene was a national convocation called Process '67. The Student Volunteer Movement, both before it joined the NSCF and after, had held quadrennial conferences, and the Process '67 weeklong gathering—held in Cleveland the day after Christmas 1967 through January 1 of 1968—was for all purposes a quadrennial, but a decidedly radical one. Coincidentally, as we shall see later, this was one week before the Student Interracial Ministry would hold its own meeting of the National Committee, the last time it would meet as an organization.[47]

Back in 1955, it will be recalled, more than three thousand religious students gathered for the "Revolution and Reconciliation" conference sponsored in Cleveland by the Student Volunteer Movement. Now, twelve years later and closer to revolution than ever, another, very different set of three thousand students attended Cleveland Week, characterized by one set of chroniclers as "the most visible expression of the UCM to date."[48] At the center of Process '67 was the so-called Depth Education Groups, small groups that gathered to discuss a single issue and to design strategies for addressing it, meant to embody "a style of education which is dialogical, non-authoritarian, issue- or problem-center[ed], and future-oriented."[49] Issues included "White Power and the Exploitation of the Ghetto," "Abortion: Moral and Legal Dilemmas," "The Racist Society: Coping with White Oppression and Developing a New Lifestyle in White America," "Women: Liberated or Oppressed—Potential for a New Movement," "Theology of a Revolution," "The Church's Role in Social Change," and "Curriculum Reform as a Means for Social Change."[50] After the conference, one participant judged that the Depth Education Groups had been successful but only in that they "enable[d] people in face to face discussions to express themselves . . . [but did not] get to the heart of basic issues."[51] Others were more enthusiastic; one participant, in language reminiscent of a number of SIM writings that heralded a new day for the church, declared Process '67 as signaling "a new style of life!"[52]

In some ways, the Process '67 conference was the beginning of the end for the UCM, as the Depth Education Groups signaled and may even have supported the establishment of special interest groups that would soon organize as caucuses. The Radical Caucus, the Black Caucus, the Women's Caucus, and others focused on such specific demands that the organization itself could not reach consensus on issues or policies. At a meeting of the UCM General Committee in Washington, D.C., in February and March 1969, the University Christian Movement dissolved.[53]

It is unclear whether any students from SIM attended Process '67, but Cleveland Week materials in the SIM records attest to the fact that SIM folks were at least aware of it. The Interseminary Movement did endorse the gathering and sent a delegation to Cleveland "to reflect about what it means for seminary education."[54] But the Cleveland gathering was only the latest in a series of events and discussions that were taking place as seminarians across the country came to understand the pivotal role of their education in relation to the crisis of faith, the new developments in theology, and the future of ministry. In addition to what was represented by Process '67, seminarians proposed and auditioned a number of reforms for religious education. The result was a period of experimentation that, although it produced little lasting change, continued to stretch the definitions of church and ministry. Most prescriptions for change in the seminaries addressed at least one of three key components: the structure of the educational system, the theological context in which ideas were presented and debated, and the theological content of this material—especially how it related to the contemporary world. Reflecting on the many proposed seminary reforms, religious studies scholar Martin E. Marty said that the institutions were "in a buying mood concerning what to do where they are."[55]

The Student Interracial Ministry, as early as 1966, firmly inserted itself in the discussions about theological education, while also redefining its own role in the civil rights movement. SIM students complained that seminaries traditionally trained pastors for churches that were becoming increasingly conservative and inward looking at the same time that society demanded the opposite. Students in programs like SIM, they argued, had received "rather intensive exposure" to the real world, which left them both unfit for traditional ministry and demanding of a "full commitment of lives to a 'revolutionary' stance in the form of the Christ-style of life which will do what is necessary to forge a new world."[56] SIM, they hoped, would pressure and enable the seminaries to restructure their programs to facilitate training for such lives. Initially, SIM offered itself as an example of a new model of seminary training—extended exposure to the racial situation and social conditions and needs through a yearlong interracial internship, not necessarily linked to a traditional congregation. In the spring of 1966, George Walters and SIM students Douglas Renick, James Crawford, John F. Chappell, and Wayne Marshall Jones sketched out some ideas for what would be required to have "a revolutionary impact upon theological education." These included desegregating the seminaries; including much broader theological perspective in training; reorienting the seminaries "toward mission oriented goals," such as the peace movement and the civil rights movement; involving multiple seminaries; involving laymen; and placing seminarians in secular jobs.[57] Building on these early ideas, the students developed what they grandly titled "A Proposal for a Transition Model One Year Seminary Aimed at Having a Revolutionary Impact upon the Seminaries for Their Restructuring and for the Redefinition of the Nature and Purpose of Theological Education." They brought this draft to the SIM Strategy Conference in August 1966, producing a new document with the much shorter title of "The Transition Model Seminary." They conceived of their plan as a working paper to be distributed throughout SIM as well as among seminaries nationally.[58]

"The Transition Model Seminary" plan began with a statement on SIM itself, declaring that as an organization, it had "emerged this year with a new self-understanding which has called [us] to assume responsibility for being both a radical activity and voice to the church and all the institutional structures of the church," including the seminaries. Their goal for the seminaries, they went on, "is their restructuring . . . for the purpose of causing them to become an enabling force to bring the people of God into the stance of a revolutionary presence in mission to the world."[59] They proposed a one-year "transitional model" between current seminary education and what would eventually be developed as a complete reimagining of theological study.[60] Maynard Moore and George Walters approached the Church Federation in Chicago about trying out the model beginning in the fall of 1967, although this did not come to pass.[61] Moore and Walters also participated in a meeting at Notre Dame in early December 1966 to discuss the possibility of a "national ecumenical congress for seminary renewal" to be held under the auspices of the Interseminary Council.[62] Again, this event did not come to pass, indicative of the difficulty of organizing and creating consensus during a time when everyone seemed to be heading in a different direction.

In order to engage other seminaries nationwide in the discussion on theological education, as well as on such topics as the urban church and the current state of the movement, SIM introduced a new magazine around this time in 1966. Tentatively titled *Church in Revolution*, the magazine was eventually named *skandalon*, taken from a word used in the New Testament to mean a snare, a stumbling block, or something that arouses prejudice, although it is often used in a positive light to refer to something that is a "good hindrance" that causes the wicked to stumble. SIM published four issues of *skandalon* in 1966 and 1967, each preceded by working papers on a topic meant to spark discussion by bringing the lessons learned by SIM volunteers over seven years in the field to a larger audience of socially concerned seminarians. The project also distributed reading lists of suggested books along with its working papers. These included works by Liston Pope, C. Vann Woodward, and Martin Luther King Jr., as well as a large number of recent books—over eighty in all—about the crises in the church and the seminaries.[63]

The first two issues of *skandalon* and the white papers concerned Black Power and urban ministry, and the editors proposed that these first topics would help to illuminate the third: the crisis in theological education and the necessity for its reform.[64] The three working papers were prefaced, in true seminary style, with a "Prolegomenon," the Greek term for a formal essay that introduces a larger interpretive work. The authors considered the working papers themselves to be just the introduction to a conversation to be played out on seminary campuses, and to this end, SIM provided a list of suggested questions for discussion. "The Transition Model Seminary" document was repackaged into Working Paper III during the spring of 1966 and distributed to faculty at Union and Princeton seminaries, to the National Council of Churches, at the Ecumenical Institute in Chicago, and within leadership boards of various denominations in preparation for the third issue of *skandalon*.[65] Steve Rose, who had moved to Geneva, Switzerland, in May 1966 to work for the World Council of Churches, was asked to contribute an article based on an excerpt from his recent manifesto for church renewal, *The Grassroots Church*.[66]

In the working paper on theological education, Walters and his colleagues declared that serious questions were being raised regarding the future of seminary training in relation to mission and "the movement." Among these questions were the very definition of a theological education, curriculum content and goals, practical relationships to other academic disciplines, and the "nature and duration" of student work outside the seminary walls.[67] The relationships of clergy and laity and of other forms of graduate education to the seminaries were also considered for discussion.[68] Walters predicted that change would not come easily but would require courage on the part of those who would abandon the existing structures "to experiment boldly and radically" without being assured of what would replace them. The world needed another new breed of preachers, Walters and his colleagues contended, "trained revolutionaries who will lead and train others in alleviating the present crisis and in creating the necessary new structures." Walters wrote that most of the clergy members who would take such roles had already been driven from their congregations. He hoped the seminaries could be changed before they, too, eradicated these necessary radicals.[69]

The Student Interracial Ministry's major contribution to discussions about seminary education, however, was the composition of its own program, a model for an intensive fieldwork experience that might stretch outside the boundaries of the traditional congregation. A few years after SIM first began discussing reforms to theological training, its new leaders, while imagining fresh roles for the organization in what now seemed to be the post–civil rights era, still trumpeted its expertise in both meaningful action in the world and the transformation of the seminaries. The Student Interracial Ministry, they wrote, did not want to be seen as "another competing civil rights organization which operates under its own name, but prefers to be a catalyst and supply line ... [and] an agent for involvement in the world ... [and] a force for change in theological education."[70] Across the country, an increasing number of seminaries accepted and adopted extended fieldwork as part of theological training, until by the early 1970s, it had become a routine and expected part of the seminary experience.

The Student Interracial Ministry's proposals on theological education were far from alone, however, as a number of ideas for seminary education reforms were on offer during the last years of the 1960s, united by a common desire to make ministry and the church better connected to contemporary social and economic concerns. Many of the proposals reflected a desire to reduce the authoritarian role of the pastor and create a more democratic lay leadership. Six seminarians from Yale University published one such plan in the journal *Theological Education* in 1968. One of the six, George Rupp, would go on to a distinguished career in higher education, including serving as president of Columbia University from 1993 to 2002. Accusing traditional seminaries of perpetuating a professional caste "with an ostrich view" of the world around it, the Yale students claimed that ministry should be the responsibility of the whole parish. Education for ministry, then, should be adapted to serve not only a professional clergy but also a "priesthood of all believers." Boundaries between clergy and laity would be broken down, and each member of the church would treat his or her chosen vocation—be it law, medicine, teaching, or city planning—as a priestly mission, enacting "how to be the Church in the world."[71] The role of the laity and the continued authority of the clergy were central points of discussion in the church renewal movement of the late decade, and debated not just among seminarians but within the churches as well.[72]

The Yale seminarians also offered two suggestions for new courses of study: a fourteen-month Core Program and a one-year training program in the problems of urban life. The Core Program was to be further separated into twelve months of biblical and theological study, augmented by one month of study with lay and secular cultural leaders, and one month of study of non-Christian religions. Like several of the other proposals, the Core Program dispensed with both lectures and grades, preferring group learning, discussion, and self-guided study. Following their fourteen months in the Core Program, students would be sent in groups of ten or twelve for one year of work in an urban training program in a large American city. Students would undertake volunteer or secular employment, become active lay members of a local church, and join one another in intensive weekly seminar discussions. The end result of the Core and urban programs, the students hoped, would be to depose the clergy class from its throne and engage a wider variety of people in both faith and the world, thereby increasing numbers and renewing both the church and society. The proposed Core Program and its urban training program bore a startling resemblance to the Student Interracial Ministry's urban projects, indicative not of plagiarism but of the common direction pursued by progressive seminarians at the end of the decade.[73]

From his vantage point as national coordinator of SIM and president of the Interseminary Movement, Maynard Moore urged that educators embrace the time of change—"between the times," he called it—and experiment with transitional models "as temporary phases through which theological education for the future and new forms of ministry can be molded."[74] Moore proposed approaching theological training as mission in an article, "Theological Education for a Revolutional Church," published in the same issue of *Theological Education* as the Yale students' piece. Moore, too, called for seminaries to be reconceived, arguing that they should not simply be places for the training of parish ministers, nor should they be solely—as H. Richard Niebuhr suggested in his 1956 study *The Purpose of the Church and Its Ministry*—the "intellectual center of the church's life," where theological problems were studied and critiqued but not acted on. Like the Yale students, Moore wanted to see seminary training move beyond this theoretical–practical dichotomy. Instead, he encouraged seminaries to embrace new patterns of mission and ministry in which they would serve as training centers not just for professional pastors but for "the entire church."[75] To accomplish this, he advised that both the church and the seminary needed to be fundamentally restructured. Focusing on the curricular content would be useless unless the basic reasons for being a minister, and for training one, were reconceived. As long as seminaries continued to see their goal as training parish ministers—for a church and world that Moore claimed no longer existed—curriculum revision would have little effect. Instead, he wrote, "*the entire seminary, conceptually and physically, must be overhauled from inside out*, in much the same way as the church must be renewed only from the bottom up."[76]

In 1968, at the time Moore wrote, there were approximately 160 separate Protestant theological schools—too many, Moore argued, to reasonably maintain. Indeed, seminary bankruptcies and closures were increasingly common in the late 1960s. Moore suggested collaborating with rather than competing with urban training centers and university departments of religion by "downsizing" the current number of seminaries and relocating scholarly resources to about twenty major ecumenical university centers. Moore argued for a reevaluation of the role of the laity and of the relationship between clergy and laity. The seminaries, he wrote, had for too long propped up and promoted "the illusion of the minister as a holy man with a special status apart from the laymen."[77] Repositioning the nonprofessional minister would be one aspect of what the SIM project called a "functional ministry."[78]

Although Moore argued that focusing on curricular content was useless without fundamental restructuring of form and mission, others focused on exactly that. John C. Bennett, president of Union Theological Seminary, preferred only moderate change, arguing in 1966 that the traditional disciplines of church history, Bible studies, and systematic theology could certainly be taught differently and more effectively, but they should still form the basis of both theological education and participation in social struggles. Bennett argued that each generation does not get to reinvent Christian faith; rather, it interprets and applies traditions to the realities of its time. He noted that in revolutionary times, the Bible and belief in God are seen in revolutionary terms, but they still remain relatively fixed; thus, they should continue to be at the core of seminary training.[79] Bennett's approach, however, was as optimistic with regard to the power of traditional religion as it was blind to the stringent demands of seminary students for radical change.

Bennett had been the president of Union Theological Seminary since 1964. He supported the civil rights movement, participated in marches, and was pleased by Union's contributions to it. At his inauguration ceremony, held at Riverside Church on April 10, 1964, he had even proclaimed that the "American form of the world-wide social revolution is very close to Union Seminary," and he committed himself to doing all he could "to help our students prepare to participate in it wherever they are."[80] Bennett encouraged students to be, as he said, "alive and sensitive, with a capacity for moral outrage, with a sense of the importance of political action, with a willingness to stand up and be counted, even if they go too far for my own circumspect self."[81] A few years later, after having been buffeted by the winds of change at Union, especially in regard to reforming the curriculum, Bennett was not as enthusiastic about a revolution within his seminary. By 1967, Bennett was strongly urging the preservation of current seminary curricula and warning students not to become "too self-righteous" or "oversimplify complex issues" as they attempted to adapt the church and seminary to their perceptions of the world's needs.[82] Although he acknowledged that scripture would always be interpreted based on the context of the times, he insisted that seminary training continue to be based on bible study, church history, and systematic theology. However, even while arguing strongly against radical curricular reform, Bennett recognized that the curriculum was vitally linked to an agenda of social concerns. In this respect, he was not very different from many other college and university administrators of his day.

Despite Bennett's objections, Union did experiment with curricular change beginning midway through the 1966–67 academic year. Responding to complaints from both students and faculty, Bennett created a special committee of representatives from both groups to study the curriculum. Although there was some disagreement as to Bennett's intentions, the notion of according student members of a committee equal standing with faculty was itself an unprecedented step. While some reformers saw him as truly concerned about the curriculum, others understood the committee to be Bennett's attempt to distract and isolate some of the younger and more outspoken members of the faculty. In any case, two concrete results emerged from the collaboration: the establishment of an Educational Policy Commission, with both student and faculty members; and the adoption, after serious amendments, of a syllabus unit, which would replace courses in theology with self-guided study and a series of three competency exams, as an optional way to satisfy the BD coursework requirements. Since the syllabus unit was passed after much opposition and then only as an option rather than as true structural change, many on campus regarded it as a failure.[83]

Others nearby Union were attempting to influence theological education as well. John E. Biersdorf, a UCC minister and the director of the NCC's Department of Ministry, turned his attention to theological education in November 1966. Young people entering seminary now, he wrote, did so in an age of rapid social change that put seminaries in the position of not only making theological education "always be seen as 'relevant,' . . . [but] sometimes it should raise . . . concerns that have not yet occurred to the minds of students." It can be difficult, he wrote, to connect to students who are "primarily concerned with 'being where the action is' in contemporary social change, and cannot see the connection between this and theological disciplines," like homiletics or church history.[84] Be relevant by making connections, Biersdorf urged, rather than throwing the baby out with the bathwater in a quest to reinvent to suit the demands of the times.

Suggested change in theological education varied from Bennett's rather conservative approach to more radical reinventions posed by theologians Richard Shaull and Harvey Cox. Contemporary times were so different from those that had produced our traditions and institutions, argued Shaull and others, that the current generation was convinced of the need to completely overhaul the structure of society and saw little in theological and cultural traditions that they wished to retain. Simply arguing that universal truths would hold fast because they were universal truths was not enough, Shaull argued, and educators would need to enter this revolutionary world "and deal with the crucial issues *as they arise there.*"[85] In other words, biblical and theological traditions were not in themselves enough, but needed to be put in conversation with the contemporary situation—a subject to which Harvey Cox devoted much attention. Cox claimed that a church–world dialogue was beside the point, since the church is itself a part of the world, not apart from the world—or, put another way, "Church and world are *not* static categories [and] the people of God are part of both church and world. This ongoing dialogue in, not with, the world provides the only viable context for theologizing and for theological education." As to content, Cox called for the embrace of a multiplicity of viewpoints and sources of education, "a riotous variety of theological styles and positions," but offered little in the way of concrete proposals.[86]

At Union Theological Seminary, concrete proposals were not only offered but also pushed into existence by the turmoil of the strike at Columbia University in the spring of 1968, and the related sympathy strike at Union. President Bennett had correctly predicted three years earlier that the war in Vietnam would eventually precipitate major campus unrest and "serious crises at Union and at other seminaries, as well as in colleges and universities."[87] This was certainly the case, but Bennett failed to predict exactly how the zeitgeist of the streets would lead to substantial change in how seminaries trained seminarians.

At a seminary-wide meeting on May 1, 1968, as the strike burned on at Columbia, a majority of the students voted to cancel the rest of that week's classes and to use the remaining time to discuss reform efforts.[88] These discussions soon led to the creation of a temporary educational experiment that would fill out the academic year. A joint-degree student at Union and Columbia, Ted Kachel, and visiting Dutch Jesuit student Ton Veerkamp, who had been a student at the Free University of Berlin, became the major leaders of what was to be called the "Free University," a reform experiment that lasted a scant two weeks but which eventually led to more substantial curricular changes. On May 2, students elected Kachel to chair the Free University, and he selected a small volunteer committee to begin planning. The next day, they announced plans for three task forces that would study educational policies, decision making, and public relations.[89] While the latter had to do with Union's politics and its neighbors, the first task force was devoted to the curriculum and pedagogical structure. SIM's Ed Feaver, recently returned from the Southwest Georgia Project, contributed key ideas to the Kachel committee. The first slate of "liberation classes," which bore a striking resemblance to the core educational groups at Process '67 the previous year, included courses on white power, women's liberation, and the New Left, as well as a liberation theater workshop.[90] By May 3, a group became dissatisfied with "endless unproductive meetings" challenging their momentum and formed what they called the Radical Caucus, arguing against mild reforms of the current seminary and calling for "question[ing] radically the purpose, operations, and structure of this institution." The Radical Caucus, which included four former SIM participants among the twenty-seven signers of its "Statement of Identity," described its mission as providing criticism of the "more or less liberal self-consciousness" of Union and proposing new political and educational models.[91]

According to a later survey of faculty and students, most students saw and understood the Free University at Union and the Columbia strike as "dealing with similar issues." For some faculty and the administration, on the other hand, "there was little readiness to see Union's problems in the same light" as Columbia's. This latter viewpoint became more entrenched the closer the interviewers got to the president's inner circle. President Bennett himself admitted that he did not know how the transition between the Columbia protests and the Free University occurred because "we did not have great grievances here. I think the rhetoric at that time rather exceeded the grievances."[92]

The two weeks of the Free University system were defined by a seemingly endless series of exhaustive and exhausting meetings that continued until what would ordinarily have been the last day of the spring semester, May 15. At the final meeting, the task force on decision making proposed the creation of a thirty-six-member Union Commission, composed equally of members of the student body, the faculty, and the board of directors. In fact, some of the first steps in curriculum revision from 1966, including the syllabus unit, helped to inform the development and work of the Union Commission, which eventually secured more successful changes to the curriculum.[93]

The Free University period, which student activists called "unquestionably one of the significant events in Union's educational history," culminated with the creation of the Core Experimental Education Groups, a radical approach to theological study.[94] The Free University had spawned several task forces, among them one to study the "reorganization of educational process."

This task force's members suggested that seminarians should begin developing a theological perspective by working toward "an integration of social concerns, the Christian tradition, and personal faith." Seminarians could best realize this, they wrote, through small-group learning, student-driven goals and procedures, and a conversation between experiences both within the seminary and outside it. Stating their desire to completely reformulate Union's educational programs, the task force members conceded that they could not come up with a workable plan by the coming fall, but they suggested that while further study was made, a small group of volunteer students and faculty should try out an experimental vision of seminary learning for one year.[95] The Union Commission agreed and approved the creation of the Core Experimental Education Groups.

Although developed independently of the core group idea of the Yale students, they were similar in concept, and both drew on a common lexicon and ideas then in circulation about pedagogical change. The Core project began in the fall of 1968 and consisted of one full-time group of ten upperclassmen, and two part-time groups, which met together with faculty advisers to create their own course of study for one year. According to the original charge for the Core, it was to be "an integration of the Christian tradition and our historical situation" and "the point of synthesis in the total process of theological education."[96] The first Core students were asked to consider a list of objectives: increased awareness of the theological aspects of contemporary problems and of the relevance and/or limitations of theology in human affairs, the development of a personal synthesis of theological ideas, increased knowledge about a variety of aspects of theology, and clarification about intended career goals. Additional possible objectives included modeling the idea of Christian community within the Core group, developing self-understanding, developing potential styles of group ministry, and developing a Christian identity that informs one's actions.[97] The language concerning Christian community and group ministry, especially, bore more than a passing resemblance to the rhetoric SIM had been batting around for years.

The first full-time Core group met for the year 1968–69 and was advised by a charismatic British instructor of theology, Jeffrey W. Rowthorn, who had himself graduated from Union in 1961 and who supervised the Core groups for two years before moving up in the seminary, first to chaplain and later to dean.[98] As he set out with the students on their new experiment in the fall of 1968, he played with the word "core," wondering if the Core experiment would find itself soon thrown away or "end up surviving the Fall unlike Adam and Eve and all the rest of the apple of traditional theological education?"[99]

Before the Core group could even begin its studies, members had to agree collectively what those studies would be and to what ends. Frustrated at their inability to reach consensus, they took a twenty-four-hour hiatus to a New Jersey YMCA camp and came back ready to delve into their studies. They started by considering the present condition of humankind in a technological age, then went on to look at the nature of humankind as discussed by a wide variety of philosophers and theologians. Students read on their own but met in group discussions as well as in one-on-one tutorials with Rowthorn. Writing after the first eight weeks of the program, Rowthorn reported that he was perceiving from the group "a concern to replace theology required as a tool by theology understood as a way of life." The greatest appeal of the program, he concluded, was that it "turns students on to the study of theology whilst enabling them to remain planted fairly and squarely in the real world which matters so intensely to them."[100] The Core groups continued for a total of three years, but once Rowthorn moved to his new position, they were advised by lecturers who lacked the kind of leadership he had provided and which students felt was necessary for keeping a self-guided program on track.[101] Unfortunately, Rowthorn's discarded apple core metaphor wasn't far from the mark, and the school year 1970–71 would be the Core program's third and final year.

The interest of many of the original participants in the first Core group, however, not only did not wane but continues to the present time. Some dozen Union alumni, including David Langston, still gather every summer for what they call their "Core reunions." Forty years on, they are still debating educational reform. At least one of them has devoted much of his more than thirty-year academic career to developing new pedagogical strategies, and as mentioned previously, George Rupp, who as a Yale seminarian called for radical structural and curricular change, went on to the presidency of Columbia University.

But in the fall of 1968, as the Core program was just beginning, there was plenty of radical momentum to go around. The first-year divinity students at Union, who had not even been around for the events of late spring at Columbia and at the seminary but a number of whom had been involved in demonstrations on their undergraduate campuses, now joined the calls for wholesale reenvisioning of their theological training.[102] Several of the first-year cohort, claiming to represent their entire class, issued a statement that fall addressed to "all in this community who take themselves seriously as actors in history." The students went on to proclaim that they were at Union to "form a new community amidst the decaying city in a divided nation and a world in the throes of revolution." Employing rhetoric that drew together the secular city debates with a desire for experimentation in theology, ministry, and seminary training, they went on: "sensitive moral people in our midst have taught us that education can no longer be . . . an exercise in the manipulation of abstract ideas. Learning in our community must be for keeps. The ideas with which we struggle here must transform and shape our lives. . . . The world is with us too much. We cannot explore our faith apart from the world our faith calls us to serve."[103] The students questioned required courses and even grades, and called for others to join them in designing their own classes, much as the Core group was doing.

All of this change at Union Theological Seminary did not come without a price. Public perception of the seminary after 1968 was that of a place in turmoil. Enrollment, which had recently peaked, now began to drop off, and continued to fall precipitously year after year through the 1970s.[104] As Union historian Robert Handy puts it, "Union had long been highly regarded as a leader in church life and theological education in such areas as critical scholarship, preparation through field experience for urban ministry, ecumenical leadership, and civil rights. Now it was involved in the crises of the liberal causes for which it had long stood."[105] John Bennett retired as president at the end of May 1969, but he didn't escape one final crisis, one redolent with the themes—by now long familiar to SIM returnees—of Black Power, church responsibility, and reconciliation-cum-revolution.

James Forman, onetime leader of SNCC, interrupted a Sunday communion service on May 4 at the Riverside Church to read the Black Manifesto. Forman had been the executive secretary of SNCC from 1961 to 1965, and was currently serving as its international director. He had become increasingly frustrated with the slow pace of change produced by the civil rights movement. Forman, on behalf of a group called the Black Economic Development Conference (BEDC), demanded that American churches and synagogues pay $500 million as reparations to black people, based on a computation of "15 dollars per nigger." The Manifesto, first unveiled in Detroit a week earlier, on April 26, included plans for the establishment of a southern land bank from which to create black cooperative farms, black publishing houses and television networks, a $30 million research institute, a center for training community organizers, a project for sponsoring international black businesses, and a $130 million black Southern university.[106]

Having occupied the pulpit at Riverside Church, Forman called for "sustained guerilla warfare" in America's streets and noted that the money would be collected "by any means necessary."[107] He then visited the New York City headquarters of the Lutheran Church in America and tacked a copy of the Manifesto to the front door, together with a "bill" for $50 million, apparently its portion of the total $500 million tab. Forman next visited the New York Archdiocese to demand that Roman Catholics pony up their $200 million portion of the receipt.[108] Forman returned to Riverside Church for its next Sunday service, despite the fact that the church had gotten an injunction against further disruptions. Instead of attempting to read the Manifesto again, he arrived clad in a bright blue African robe and stood silently in front of his pew for the full length of that morning's sermon.[109] Albert Cleage, formerly a pastor in integrated churches and later the founder of both the Black Christian National Movement and the Shrine of the Black Madonna, called Forman's reading of the Black Manifesto from the symbolic home of liberal Protestantism "one of the truly beautiful moments in the Black man's dismal captivity in America."[110] In a different take on the Manifesto, sociologist Charles V. Willie commented, "The prophetic comes to us sometimes in preposterous wrappings. It presented us with the uncomfortable task of sorting out the meaningful from the foolish."[111] Despite dismissing Forman's theatricality, Willie still acknowledged the truth at the core of his demands, which included that Riverside Church immediately donate 60 percent of its investment income to the BEDC.

Around the corner from Riverside Church, the student body at Union Theological Seminary had just recently voted overwhelmingly to approve a new governance structure and significant curricular changes, the result of a year of review following the Columbia strike and the advent of the Free University. The pioneering changes were still awaiting approval by the faculty, staff, board, and alumni council when some seventy-five to eighty Union students, in sympathy with Forman's demands, occupied the administration building for four days. Other students, including SIM's Joe Pfister, dramatized their demands that the Manifesto be taken seriously by occupying the offices of the Presbyterian Church (USA) in the Interchurch Center building on Riverside Drive.

The Union students demanded that the seminary's board of directors allocate more than $1.5 million for black projects, including $25,000 to go directly to the BEDC.[112] The protest may have had specific demands related to black economic and educational improvement, but it was also the culmination of concerns over a host of issues that one student activist appraised as having grown "directly out of a fundamental difference in philosophy that divided the students from Union's faculty and administration."[113] The students' demands were partially successful. While they "repudiate[d] the coercive and divisive tactics used by a minority of the student body," the faculty did pass a resolution committing to raise $100,000 in the coming year "to aid black development." The seminary's board of directors, for its part, further committed to trying to raise at least $1 million as special funds to finance "the involvement of the whole seminary community in projects directly related to the life of the people in the surrounding area, under policies to be determined by the black community of the seminary."[114] Such commitments further pointed Union in the direction of embracing a diversity of theological, racial, and gender views going forward; in other words, the seminary continued to endorse the traditional goal of racial reconciliation but also reconciled to, and in some ways embraced, the new revolutionary tactics and spirit.

For his part, outgoing seminary president John C. Bennett acknowledged the demands of the Black Manifesto and its student supporters with grace. Speaking at the seminary's graduation ceremony on May 20, 1969, Bennett commented that he would not soon forget the events that had just passed, but he reflected that the "black revolution" had come home to Union, and that when "history [catches] up with us, . . . this seldom takes place in ways that one would choose." But he hastened to add that those at Union should be grateful to live in a time when the oppressed could speak rather than being "inert, silent, intimidated, and hopeless." As an administrator, he said, he opposed events meant to shock and intimidate, but as a person he could appreciate their message and even their necessity. He concluded with a benediction: "May all of you in these turbulent times be blessed in your lives and ministries and may you find your own ways of combining commitment to the goals that claim you with a sense of God's judgment upon them and with the hope that he will use you and them for his loving purpose."[115]

In all, church congregations donated about $300,000 directly to the BEDC in the first year after the demand, and an estimated $100 million was allocated by religious organizations toward other social justice programs and efforts at providing "reparations."[116] Many donors, however, chose to sponsor efforts other than Forman's and the BEDC. The Manifesto prompted intense conversations within the national board of the Episcopal Church, for example, and the board eventually donated $200,000, but chose to give it to the mainstream National Committee of Black Churchmen. The General Board of the NCC pledged $500,000 toward black economic development, with "tens of millions of dollars" to follow. The Presbyterian Church responded to the Manifesto with a pledge to raise $50 million "for general works against poverty." The Catholic National Association of Laymen called on the Catholic Church for a yearly $400 million donation to black-controlled organizations. The World Council of Churches created a $200,000 reserve fund for "oppressed people" and requested more than $300,000 from members.[117] The churches, thus, did not cede to Forman's demands as such, but in supporting mainstream, trusted black institutions, they nevertheless acknowledged the spirit of the Manifesto while sidestepping some of its more radical demands.

For its part, Riverside Church refused to donate directly to Forman's organization, but Pastor Ernest Campbell took the issue seriously, delivering a response sermon, "The Case for Reparations," on July 13, 1969.[118] In this sermon, Campbell affirmed the existence of systematic racial discrimination and outlined the scriptural justifications for reparations. Under Campbell's leadership, the church created the Riverside Fund for Social Justice, a three-year, $450,000 grant for "work among the poor" in New York City as "restitution" and "penance" for the church's complicity in slavery and racism.[119]

The Black Manifesto also had quite an effect on SIM's Steve Rose, who had already been thinking of a similar idea before Forman's proposal and would go on to create, in response to it, one of the great "happenings" in the liberal religious history of that decade. Writing in the pages of his old magazine, *Renewal*, in June 1969, Rose endorsed the plan and commented that, "morally speaking, the case for reparations is clear."[120] In fact, while a delegate to the Consultation on Church Union—an event that might have fulfilled some of Rose's ecumenical vision if it had gone differently—in Atlanta a few weeks earlier, he had organized a kind of rap session with SIM's Oscar McCloud and others, at which he himself had proposed a similar plan. (In *The Grass Roots Church*, he had suggested that churches funnel their endowments into social causes; now he suggested that they do the same but put the money specifically toward black economic development.) Rose recalled that after he made his case for reparations, a black minister at the rap session stood up and announced, "This is not the time for a white person to be putting forth an agenda for black people."[121] Rose demurred that day, but when Forman issued his own Manifesto, Rose threw his support behind it. He was then living in Stockbridge, Massachusetts, doing

some writing and thinking about what role he could play in a church renewal movement that seemed to have gone off in far different directions
than he had intended. He came up with Jonathan's Wake.

Naming his new group for the New England churchman Jonathan Edwards, Rose called for volunteers to join him at the National Council of
Churches General Assembly on December 4, 1969. Their agenda would
be twofold: to call again for radical ecumenism and for reparations, with
churches asked to transfer the entirety of the funds from their endowments
to Forman's Black Economic Development Conference for immediate use
in poverty-stricken black areas. Rose's intentions were entirely on the level,
and he had some serious allies with him, including Will Campbell and Malcolm Boyd, but most of those who joined Jonathan's Wake at the assembly
had more in common with Ken Kesey's Merry Pranksters than with church
reformers like Campbell and Boyd. The group that stormed the assembly
included a large denomination from Berkeley Free Church and other adher-
ents to the far-out submarine church movement; together they turned Jonathan's Wake into a goofy happening, interrupting the meeting, carrying in a
coffin to signify the death of the institutional church, and pouring "blood"
on the rostrum. For Rose, whose serious attempt at revolutionary change
for the church seemed to have been usurped by more radical and whimsical
forces and shunted into the realm of the farcical, it was the end of his hope
that a true church reform movement could be created. As the other Wake
delegates delighted in their tomfoolery, Rose, by his own admission, "went
berserk," running through the hall crying "crucify me now."[122] His reform
efforts had gotten caught up in the wild spirit and tactics of the times, and
the message had been lost in the medium.

Back at Union, J. Brooke Mosley replaced John Bennett as the seminary's
president, hailed by *Time* for his bravery in taking on the job, in which, as
the magazine correctly predicted, he would face the great challenge of creating cohesion on a campus that was then sharply divided between conserva-
tives and radical reformers.[123] Mosley wouldn't survive more than four
years, his tenure marked not by new cohesion but by retrenchment and an
ever-widening chasm between campus factions. Union Theological Seminary had been the largest and most distinguished interdenominational divinity school in North America for most of the twentieth century, but when
it opened its doors for the new school year in 1972, it was now only the sixth
largest. Mosley had lost students and wracked up a budget deficit of several
hundred thousand dollars. He admitted to a journalist in 1972 that for several years the seminary had "lacked a clear focus."[124] One of the few victo-

ries that Mosley could point to resulted directly from the campus turmoil of the late 1960s—especially from the concerns highlighted by the demands of the Black Manifesto, but also from the activist efforts of the Student Interracial Ministry. From that period onward, the level of student participation in campus affairs and in social concerns off campus remained high. Fieldwork, modeled on the SIM approach, was instituted as a requirement and helped take many students outside the seminary walls and into the community.[125] And particularly in the first half of the 1970s, Union led the way nationally among seminaries in creating a racially and sexually diverse learning environment.

The Student Interracial Ministry did not last long enough to see those advances in the 1970s. It came to an end during the dramatic 1967–68 school year, and wouldn't even make it as far as the Columbia strike or see the Free University at Union. For even as it began its ambitious slate of urban projects in 1967, it was already in serious financial straits, its economic difficulties partially related to the turmoil in the streets and within the seminaries. Some traditional funders of liberal causes, like the Sealantic and Field Foundations, had pulled back their philanthropy as the optimism of the early civil rights movement was gradually lost, so that by July 1967, Maynard Moore was reporting that SIM had "not received a penny from a foundation this year" and that the denominations, too, had contributed far less than had been requested of them.[126] That month, Moore and Walters, declining any reimbursements for their own expenses, were finally able to get long overdue stipends to students in the field, explaining that they "had to wait until sufficient funds came in to cover the checks" and begging the students to make any connections they could that might lead to financial support.[127] SIM had been a victim of its own success—having grown so large so quickly in the previous years that it found itself in the fall of 1967 unable to support itself going forward—as well as a victim of timing, as the Vietnam War and a host of other issues drew students away from civil rights work, however innovative.

As efforts at reconciliation gave way to a gathering revolution, SIM continued to pursue its ever more ambitious and multifaceted goals—to reform theological education, revolutionize the idea of what being a church meant by experimenting with clergy and lay roles, reshape social structures through political involvement, *and* achieve reconciliation in race relations. The major difference between SIM's approach in 1967 and its earlier programs was that by the late 1960s it had turned toward urban ministry and, in so doing, had both decentralized and taken on many more students and a greater financial burden. It now saw itself as a network that would work with and coordinate the efforts of "existing ecumenical and interracial action ministries across the country in a common thrust of purpose."[128] However, SIM still had the financial resources of a small student organization, not a national network, and it did not survive under the weight of its new responsibilities.

SIM did manage to bring in $43,000 in support during the first nine months of 1967, funding the program through the summer.[129] But by September 1, 1967, SIM had received and spent nearly all of the money it had raised to cover project expenses through May 1968. Facing expenses of $5,000 per month going forward, it expected only an additional $5,000 in total incoming revenue.[130] In addition, J. Oscar Lee, who had been SIM's chief adviser at the National Council of Churches since the project's inception, announced he would be leaving the council at the end of September to take a new position with the National Conference of Christians and Jews. And with George Walters in full-time residence at the Ecumenical Institute in Chicago and Maynard Moore returning to the University of Chicago Divinity School to complete his graduate program, the leadership that had kept SIM together through its years of growth was all leaving at the same time.

By October, Maynard Moore had stepped away from the position of National Coordinator, and Ed Ruen, who had been running the New York office, assumed the title and the helm of a now sinking ship. On October 20, Moore referred to a fund-raising letter he had written as "the latest (and last?) effort on behalf of the old cause (is it lost?)."[131] While Ruen and the SIM officers tried to find a solution to their money woes and assurances that they would not be put out of their National Council–owned offices in the Interchurch Center, word of their perilous position gradually became clear to their students scattered around the country. John Stumme, who was working in Chicago's West Garfield neighborhood that year, noted in his diary in September that the SIM Chicago project was having trouble getting off the ground because it had no money. By late October, SIM was appealing directly to its students past and present for help paying its current interns' stipends, a figure amounting to some $45,000. Ed Feaver, the finance director, admitted, "We do not have this money."[132]

Ruen called a National Committee meeting for the first week of January 1968. The agenda called for discussions not of SIM's perilous financial condition, however, but of SIM's mission and its continued relevancy. Without mentioning SIM's empty bank accounts, Ruen laid out an agenda for organizational change that would effectively end its functioning as a large—and expensive—program. Ruen instead asked what "the movement" now was and what the proper role should be for the white student in the black liberation movement. He answered his own questions: the movement was no longer civil rights but was now antiwar, and the black liberation movement did not require the involvement of whites. These two conditions meant that SIM, Ruen wrote, which had a tradition of being "on the cutting edge . . . where the need for change is the greatest . . . should join the student movement of resistance to end the war in Vietnam, committing herself to a renewal of the political life of America." White students' place, he went on, was to put their bodies on the line to resist the war, while black students "should be in the ghettos organizing blacks for liberation."[133] SIM would cease placing and paying interns, he announced, but would honor its financial commitments to interns currently in the field; would transfer the supervision of the College Teaching Program to Union's auspices; and would henceforth serve as a clearinghouse, directing white students "to jobs of a radical nature in white areas and in the resistance to end the war in Vietnam" and black students "to jobs of a radical nature in the black ghetto."[134] Other than the commitment to paying its current fieldworkers, nowhere was there any mention of SIM's bank balance. Taken at face value, the decision to shut down SIM seemed as much ideological as it was financial.

But when Maynard Moore, who was now back in Chicago, received his invitation to the national meeting in January, scrawled along the bottom of the first page was a handwritten note from Bill Thompson, the coordinator for the Northeast region. "Maynard, we need you at the meeting," Thompson pleaded, before adding, "but we have no money to pay travel expenses." He urged that Maynard, George Walters, and two other SIM students in the Midwest find a car and get themselves to New York "because some crucial decisions have to be made about SIM. The financial situation is very bad. If at all possible try to be here even if you have to hitchhike."[135] The financial situation for SIM was in fact worse than bad. Stumme and the other interns in Chicago, as well as those in the rest of the country, remained unpaid for most of the school year. Eventually Ruen and the others managed to get enough money in the door to pay most of the money owed their students in the field. On June 16, 1968, Stumme returned to his journal to note that he had been paid only $1,000 of a promised payment of $1,750, but that "they have promised to pay me $600 more [and] this will be satisfactory to me."[136] The Student Interracial Ministry had limped to its end.

In a very real way, however, the spirit of SIM lived on in the programs it had fostered, in the experiments it had encouraged, and in the people who had created and nurtured this unique venture that was equal parts civil rights organization and religious change movement. Maynard Moore returned to Chicago to finish a graduate degree, and George Walters was supposed to be running the Chicago Urban Project but was instead becoming increasingly more involved in Joe Matthews's Ecumenical Institute project. In fact, by mid-September, Moore indicated that he and George, Steve Rose, and a few others were already looking beyond the Student Interracial Ministry. Moore wrote of this "post-SIM project" that "George, typically, calls it 'Global Urban Resource Development Project,' but I prefer something less auspicious like Social Action Ministries," and that they had been gathering a circle of "floating SIM alums and other young radical types." He noted that he had discovered in 1966 that SIM "was not adequate . . . as a vehicle" for such a project, which he described as "a kind of coordinating, funding, resource center type thing with long range components."[137]

Others went in different directions, expected and unexpected. Ed Feaver became increasingly involved in draft resistance in the short run, and eventually wound up directing the Department of Health and Human Services in Florida. John Collins was a minister in the Methodist Church for forty years and is currently retired in New York State. Jane Stembridge finished a theological degree and continued to write. George and Carol Walters spent their careers working in international economic development, including long stays in India. Steve Rose moved to Sturbridge, Massachusetts, in the late 1960s to become a journalist and has continued to publish numerous works of theology, although his ideas continue to change. J. Oscar McCloud moved on from his Raleigh church in 1964 to work as part of an interracial team ministry, Ministries in Areas of Racial Tension, sponsored by the Board of Christian Education of the United Presbyterian Church. In 1969, he moved from Atlanta to New York to head the United Presbyterian Church's Commission on Religion and Race, and later became associate general secretary for the Latin America and Africa sections of the church's Commission on Ecumenical Mission and Relations. Maynard Moore also worked within his denomination as a clergy member of the Baltimore-Washington Conference of the United Methodist Church, rising to a leadership position in the 1980s as a staff member of the Conference Program Council addressing racial issues, and he has also been a consultant in financial resource development and management for nonprofit organizations for more than twenty-five years. Maxim Rice, after his intern year in Southwest

Georgia, returned to Garrett Theological Seminary in 1968 and helped start Seminarians Organized for Racial Justice, which until 1974 worked on issues ranging from the Vietnam War to low-income housing and picketed the Catholic Church in order to bring about racial change. Maxim and his wife Nancy worked on low-income housing again in the San Francisco Bay area, before establishing Dorea Peace Community, a Christian commune in rural Wisconsin. They later moved to Jubilee Partners, a similar community in Georgia, and focused on refugee issues. Longtime war tax resistors, Maxim eventually served time in jail for this "offence." Ruth Brandon, who was Ruth Minter when she spent several tours with SIM, worked in Africa for many years before returning to the United States to serve as an association minister working with eighty-nine churches in rural Ohio. Bob Hare, who hosted SIM urban ministry interns in his church in Richmond, Virginia, was arrested in 1969 in Ohio for referring women for illegal abortions; the case was eventually thrown out after the Roe v. Wade decision, and he currently directs a ministry training program for inmates in Sing Sing Correctional Facility. Glen and Susan Pearcy have remained married since their time in Southwest Georgia in 1967. Susan is an artist, and Glen went on to become a filmmaker, including making Fighting for Our Lives, an Oscar-nominated documentary about the United Farm Workers. Joe Pfister ran the Southwest Georgia Project's print shop for about ten years, then moved to North Carolina, where he lived on a farm and practiced acupuncture until his death not long ago. Larry Mamiya, who served in Southwest Georgia, went on to a career as a professor of religion and religious history. Ralph Luker, who served in the summer of 1962 and whose 1991 book, *The Social Gospel in Black and White*, is further proof of the influence of the social gospel in the seminaries in the 1960s, also became a history professor.[138] Bob Carey, too, went into academia, enrolling in the history program at Columbia University before beginning a lifelong career as a teacher and administrator at Empire State College in New York, where in the early 1970s he helped start a program of study called God and the City and where he is now dean of graduate education; his wife, Pat, is assistant chancellor and an associate dean at NYU's Steinhardt School of Education. Barbara Cox worked as a Christian educator in Charlotte churches through 1976, took time off to care for her mother, then returned to church work, retiring from the Methodist Conference Office in 1992.

At the end of the 1960s, Union Theological Seminary, like many institutions of higher learning, was reeling from the multiple storms then raging in society—civil rights concerns, moral questions relating to the Vietnam War, a burgeoning women's movement, American economic support of a repressive regime in South Africa, the imbalance of wealth in American society, and the demands of the Black Power movement for electoral and economic self-control. Of paramount concern at Union was the church's role in response to these fundamental social issues. Participation in the civil rights movement, educational reform efforts, and protests against the Vietnam War shared a common theme: students insisted that institutions be held responsible for their policies and practices. Students demanded that their universities and seminaries take responsibility for their contributions to the war, to institutionalized racism, and to the economic deprivation of large segments of society. When Forman delivered the Black Manifesto, for example, students responded that it represented an opportunity for institutions to step up to their responsibilities.

It has been argued that the Vietnam War displaced civil rights as the major social issue for Protestant clergy and that the Black Power movement hastened this shift.[139] But from the point of view of a seminarian at Union or Yale or the Pacific School of Religion in 1969, the war and Black Power were just links in a chain of concerns that were central to a changing American culture. At Union, the students did indeed tend to focus on one issue at a time, but they also saw civil rights, economic empowerment, curriculum reform, students' rights, the war in Vietnam, financial investments in South Africa, and other issues as all linked. As Maynard Moore wrote from Chicago on September 30, 1967, "The demands placed upon those committed to social change become all the more urgent as the opposition consolidates its position, and those who are aware of the issues camouflaged by the daily headlines must rededicate themselves to the deepening struggle. Those of us who have been involved in the Student Interracial Ministry should be awake and alive to the new imperatives, for we have participated, if only in a small way, in a much larger effort to involve the church in the battle for human dignity."[140]

Afterword

Joe Pfister grew up in Northern California in the 1940s and 1950s. He attended the University of California, Berkeley; joined the Student Christian
Movement; and studied psychology. Thinking he would eventually pursue
a career in counseling, perhaps with a spiritual component to it, he enrolled
at Union Theological Seminary in 1964. Once there, he found he was less
interested in psychology than in the urban ministry work that was taking
place in nearby Harlem.

He recalled:

> I did my field work in East Harlem at the East Harlem Protestant Parish
> [with] Bill Webber. Well, it was a big eye-opening thing for me, [being]
> middle-class, well-fed. I worked with a junior high school class, and they
> were all kind of street kids, [including a] fourteen-year-old girl with a
> baby. They were good kids and the two of us working with them, we
> just sort of decided, "Okay, what we're going to do is to get them some
> exposure to other things in the City of New York." Because they had this
> little narrow, two- or three-block area, that was their block, that's where
> they hung, they knew this. Of course, [it was] laced with drugs and
> whatnot. So we took them on the subway to go to the Cloisters or went
> downtown to let them see, "Okay, this is also New York. You might
> relate to this at some point." That was probably our major accomplish-
> ment. We taught Sunday school and stuff, but that wasn't nearly as
> interesting as the trips we took.[1]

At Union Theological Seminary that same fall, as he was getting his
first experience of urban ministry and the problems of the inner city, he met
Charles Sherrod, who recruited him to come down and work in Southwest
Georgia. "Charles was doing an STM, a Master's in Sacred Theology. He
was taking a break. He had been a field coordinator for SNCC and all kinds
of crazy stuff had happened, so he was taking a little time off and studying
and came to Union. And while he was there, he was recruiting students to
come down and volunteer. A bunch of us thought it would be great." Pfister
was eager to do civil rights work and had already dabbled in a small way. He
had participated in the activist YWCA at Berkeley, and had worked on a

voter registration drive his senior year and supported a fair housing amend-ment to the California constitution. When he got to Union Theological Seminary, he befriended several students who had just returned from Free-dom Summer in Mississippi, and he drove down to Jackson, Mississippi, in a Volkswagen Beetle with them in October 1964 to help support the Missis-sippi Freedom Democratic Party. That was the first time that the native Californian had ventured into the American South. It wouldn't be the last.

Pfister and several others convinced the Union administration to let them do their intern-year fieldwork with the Southwest Georgia Project. Pfister recalled that "there was some resistance at first, sort of rooted in the seminary and the more traditional way of doing it, and the concepts of com-munity organizing were only starting to get recognized." Pfister and five others spent the academic year 1966–67 as interns working with Sherrod in Albany and its surrounding counties. Pfister and another intern, Jim Rom-berg, both of whom would do a second intern year in 1967–68, lived with a sixty-five-year-old one-armed black farmer named Terrell Ford in Worth County. Ford had fourteen children, all of whom had gone to college, but was divorced and living alone at the time; he enjoyed having the two interns for company. "He was a dynamo," Pfister recalls. "He'd get you up at dawn, work you to death." The interns tried to help Ford pick cotton and butter-beans on the farm, "but of course us with our two hands were about half the speed of him going up and down the rows." When they weren't on the farm, the interns spent their days that first fall working with the Worth County Improvement Association, whose major focus at the time was making sure that elderly black citizens received the welfare benefits to which they were entitled. They also registered voters and supported black youth in their un-successful attempts to integrate the local school system.

Pfister received his ordination in a Presbyterian church in Albany. "I wasn't interested in being a church pastor, but I managed to get ordained under the category of 'evangelist,' which is a little bit weird, because I wasn't doing anything which you'd actually call evangelism. [After I was ordained, I was] able to say, "Reverend So-and-so is supporting this," and that [gave] us the weight of the church. I don't know how much effect that actually had, [but] that was the thinking, it would be helpful. That was as close to any traditional ministry that I did there. Occasionally someone would want me to do a prayer, you know, or say something. Our job was to pretty much stay in the background, so I tried to avoid as much of that as possible, but every-one now and then, they want you to do it so you just do it."

As Christmas 1966 approached, the SIM interns were sitting in Ford's farmhouse one day making vacation plans. Pfister, Romberg, and a third white SIM intern, Ed Feaver, decided they would take the car Feaver's parents had loaned him—an old Cadillac they nicknamed the Great White Whale—and drive cross-country. They would drop off Ed in Oklahoma, then drive on to Seattle where Jim had a girlfriend. Pfister would finish off the trip solo to his parents' house in Berkeley. As soon as he heard the plan, however, Mr. Ford "jumped up and said, I want to go too! Here's a man who had never been north of Greenville, South Carolina, never been south of Jacksonville, Florida, and never been west of Birmingham, Alabama. That was his entire parameter. But his oldest son lived in Berkeley, and he wanted to go out. He of course hadn't seen him for many years. And I said, Should we call him up and make sure it's okay? No, [Mr. Ford said,] I want to surprise him."

They drove across the country together, the three white seminarians in their twenties and old Mr. Ford, the one-armed farmer. They took the southern route because the Great White Whale's heater did not work, dropped off Ed Feaver in Oklahoma, and then went on through New Mexico before deciding to take a side trip into Arizona to see the Grand Canyon. More than forty years later, Pfister still easily recalled Mr. Ford's reaction when they got out next to the snow-covered lip of the Canyon: "Old Mr. Ford, he looks at this thing, the man who had never been west of [Birmingham,] he looks at this thing, and he just looks out over the canyon, and he just shakes his head. And he says, 'I know Jesus must be in this somewhere,' he says. Then we get back in the car and drive across on to L.A." A week or so later, after successfully uniting Mr. Ford with his son Buford, they drove back across the country again to Worth County, Georgia.

At the end of that year, Sherrod asked if one of the interns would stay over for continuity. Pfister recalls thinking at the time, "God, I'm going to be staying here much longer than I [planned]! I'll do it." Pfister stayed a second year, went back to Union to finish his degree, then returned to Southwest Georgia, where he stayed for another seven years. For Pfister, the experience, even over all that time, was a form of ministry in action: "This was my ministry, to be among the people and help them with what they needed help with. I considered it my ministry."[2] He left Georgia for North Carolina, where he lived on a farm until his passing on July 6, 2013. Over the years, he ran printing presses, served as a hospital chaplain, and practiced acupuncture.

The Student Interracial Ministry project set out to create social change and promote racial healing through interpersonal connections, while forcing the institutional church to be more racially inclusive. The students worked throughout the civil rights movement as well as inside the church and the academy. By the end of the 1960s, however, a project that had started out based in churches was trying to reinvent the meaning of church itself, embracing instead of congregations and denominations an idea of a "revolutional church" that adhered to the individual. For them, "the church is those people who see themselves as mission, doing whatever is necessary, deciding to die to shatter present barriers to the possibilities of the future."[3] For others in the project, as for many others in their generation, institutional church attendance was just one part of their quest for authenticity, an ingredient in the larger group of influences on their personal choices and paths.

Many of the individual participants in SIM felt personally changed by the process of having served with it; former participants interviewed forty years later spoke repeatedly of the transformative effect of their brief time in the project on the future course of their life and work. For many, that work took place outside the church, and it led them to lives outside the church as well. Perhaps 25 percent of the seminarians who worked with SIM went on to careers in the ministry. The rest, for the most part, took one of three paths: pursuing academic careers, going into government or nonprofit social justice work, or doing something seemingly unrelated to their religious training. While nearly all the veterans of the project seem to have retained some level of belief or faith—a pursuit of the authentic—the majority have moved away from the institutional church.

Religious historian Charles C. West has argued that the late-1960s student rebellions, such as those that took place at Columbia University and at Union Theological Seminary, undid the Student Christian Movement's traditional commitment to the church's evangelical mission. Their faith shaken in institutions, including the government, the church, and the academy, students withdrew from the ecumenical movement and from lives in the ministry, diminishing the ranks of the latter and depriving the former of the next generation of leaders.[4] SIM's George Walters, writing from within this community in 1967, saw the situation similarly but from a different angle; seminarians like himself should not be blamed for rebelling against a defunct system, he argued; rather, the churches were at fault for not recognizing and encouraging the efforts of their young ministers to save them. Would-be reformers, Walters wrote, "are at best ill-supported by the church that sent them out there and at worst lambasted for abandoning the institution which begat them, accused of hating the church rather than encouraged in their efforts to be the church."[5]

Joe Pfister and old Mr. Ford, in their unusual companionship and their willingness to walk in each other's shoes, demonstrated one way of being the church. They also demonstrated that the "church" and the civil rights movement could be one and the same. As Pfister remarked, "The workers in the Movement need to have a common sense of purpose which extends beyond the immediate goals of gathering the community together and the long range goals of gaining power for the powerless. This sense of purpose includes these goals, but it also includes the building of a style of sharing, of serving one another as brothers and friends."[6]

As the 1960s unfolded into the 1970s, carrying this particular Christian progressive vision forward would prove to be a challenge, although not an insurmountable one. The twin urgencies of revolution and reconciliation could perhaps exist side by side; although fulfilling either might be in doubt, the goals behind them were noble and worth pursuing. John Bennett, former president of Union Theological Seminary, wrote in 1970, "Christians, even when they are called to be revolutionaries—and I am sure there are situations when they are so called—can never renounce their faith that those on the other side are human, that those on the other side, wrong as they may be, still belong to the circle within which forgiveness and reconciliation should be sought in spite of all external difficulties. Reconciliation may take time and changes in circumstance, but it remains the goal."[7]

The mainline churches continued to persist, although shaken and shedding members, but religion remained central to American life thanks to two forces that gathered strength at the fringes—the continuing quest of those searching for the authentic and the evangelical revival of the 1970s—and gradually shifted toward the center. The result is that religion is playing a greater role in American life than it ever has. The question remains, as it did at the founding of the church and as it did for Martin Luther King Jr. in the 1960s, not "whether we will be extremists but what kind of extremists we will be."[8]

Acknowledgments

I incurred many debts of gratitude while working on this gratifying project, but none more than to those who served in various capacities with SIM and who shared their memories, their papers, and sometimes their homes with me. Among them, I need to particularly thank John Collins, Maynard Moore, George and Carol Walters, Bob Seymour, Joe Pfister, Glen and Susan Pearcy, and Steve Rose. John, Maynard, George, and Steve additionally gave generously of their time in reviewing sections of the manuscript and answering endless questions. David Langston, an alumnus of Union Theological Seminary's turbulent years in the late 1960s and early 1970s, although not of the SIM program, has similarly given me many, many hours of his time, for which I am extremely grateful.

My colleagues in the History Department at Virginia Tech were terrifically supportive as I worked on this project, especially Peter Wallenstein, who was always ready for a quick hallway pep talk or to magically produce just the right book from within a teetering stack. I also am lucky to have a generous and understanding family, a fantastic partner-in-all-things in Laura McGuire, and two charming little girls, Genevieve and Clara, who think I'm cool for "making a book." My father, Dr. Martin Cline, read many early drafts of various forms of the manuscript and added greatly to the development of any writing style I can now claim to have.

I would also like to thank the extraordinary archivists who helped along the way, including at the Yale Divinity School Library, but most especially Laura Hart and her colleagues at Wilson Special Collections Library at UNC, and Ruth Tonkiss Cameron and Elizabeth Call at the Burke Library, Union Theological Seminary. Finally, thank you to Brandon Proia and Mark Simpson-Vos at UNC Press for believing in this project and guiding it forward.

Notes

Preface

1. Sara M. Evans, *Journeys That Opened Up the World: Women, Student Christian Movements, and Social Justice, 1955–1975* (New Brunswick, NJ: Rutgers University Press, 2003), 4–5.

2. The Student Volunteer Movement for Foreign Missions later changed its name to the Student Volunteer Movement for Christian Missions.

3. World Student Christian Federation founder John R. Mott had laid out his vision for a global evangelical movement in the 1897 book *Strategic Points in the World's Conquest*, and this strain persisted, making the Student Christian Movement into a global phenomenon with far-reaching theological and political consequences. Mott focused on universities, and through them the movement and his organization quickly spread across the world, both English and non-English speaking.

4. Risto Lehtonen, *Story of a Storm: The Ecumenical Student Movement in the Turmoil of Revolution, 1968 to 1973* (Grand Rapids, MI: Eerdmans, 1998), xiv.

5. Evans, *Journeys That Opened Up the World*, 4–5.

6. Ibid., 4–6.

7. Clayborne Carson, *In Struggle: SNCC and the Black Awakening of the 1960s* (Cambridge, MA: Harvard University Press, 1995), 20.

8. "An Attempt at Understanding," *Grain of Salt* (Union Theological Seminary student newspaper), May 1960, 3. The Burke Library Archives at Union Theological Seminary, New York. (Hereafter known as SIM UTS.)

9. "Delegates to the Youth Leadership Conference, Shaw University, Raleigh, N.C., April 15–17, 1960." List provided to author by the SNCC Legacy Project, August 10, 2015.

10. Charles C. West, foreword to Lehtonen, *Story of a Storm*, xv.

11. First coined within the context of the Fellowship of Reconciliation at the beginning of the twentieth century, the term was rejuvenated by Lawson and later by Martin Luther King Jr. Lawson introduced the term early in his Nashville workshops on nonviolence. As used by Lawson, the term meant "nothing less than the Christian concept of the kingdom of God on earth." Wesley C. Hogan, *Many Minds, One Heart: SNCC's Dream for a New America* (Chapel Hill: University of North Carolina Press, 2007), 22.

12. Taylor Branch, *Parting the Waters: America in the King Years, 1954–63* (New York: Simon & Schuster, 1989), 292.

13. James Lawson, "Speech at Shaw University, Raleigh, North Carolina, April 15, 1960," in Davis Houck and David Dixon, eds., *Rhetoric, Religion, and the Civil Rights Movement, 1954–1965* (Waco, TX: Baylor University Press, 2006), 357.

14. Ibid., 360–361; John Webster, "The Conference at Shaw," *Grain of Salt*, April 27, 1960, 6.

15. Jane Stembridge, "A Wind Is Rising," *Grain of Salt*, April 27, 1960, 4–5. Shuttlesworth's words proved uncannily prescient. He himself would survive four beatings and assassination attempts during his movement work, but his friend and co-pastor Charles Billups, who also spoke with the Union students at the Raleigh conference, was killed in 1968, not long after the assassination of Martin Luther King Jr. The Billups murder remains one of the unsolved civil rights figure killings.

16. Ibid.

17. Hogan, *Many Minds, One Heart*, 35.

18. Webster, "The Conference at Shaw," 6.

19. Webster, "The Conference at Shaw," and Stembridge, "A Wind Is Rising."

20. Richard F. Moore, "Which Way to the Revolution?" *Renewal*, March 3, 1964, 7.

21. Stembridge, "A Wind Is Rising."

22. Hogan, *Many Minds, One Heart*, 35.

23. Martin Luther King Jr. "Letter from a Birmingham Jail," April 16, 1963, Martin Luther King, Jr. Papers Project, Martin Luther King, Jr. Research and Education Institute, Stanford University, https://kinginstitute.stanford.edu/king-papers /documents/letter-birmingham-jail, accessed March 20, 2016.

24. Ed Feaver, "1966 Report: Student Interracial Ministry," 45–67. UTS1: Student Interracial Ministry Papers, 1960–1968, 1C:2:f11.

25. Martin Luther King Jr. "A Witness to the Truth" (Eulogy for the Reverend James Reeb), as published on https://www.ptsem.edu/Publications/inspire2/6.2 /pdf/feature4.pdf, accessed March 20, 2016. In April 1965, James Reeb, a white minister from Boston, was killed by a white mob on a street corner in Selma, Alabama. He was there at the behest of Martin Luther King Jr., who had invited all clergy to join him for the second Selma-to-Montgomery march.

26. Quoted in Charles Marsh, *The Beloved Community: How Faith Shapes Social Justice, from the Civil Rights Movement to Today* (New York: Basic Books, 2005), 207.

27. 1 Chron. 14:15.

Chapter One

1. "Summary of [Civil Rights Movement] Events," *Grain of Salt*, March 31, 1960, 2.

2. John Collins, "Statement on the Student Interracial Ministry, 1960," SIM, UTS, H1:1:f7.

3. John Collins diary, entry for May 31, 1960. Possession of John Collins; copy loaned to author.

4. Statistics from a March 16, 1960, report of the National Student Christian Federation, as reported in *Grain of Salt*, March 31, 1960, 2.

5. *Grain of Salt*, March 24, 1960, 1.

6. Ibid., 2.

7. "An Attempt at Understanding," *Grain of Salt*, May 4, 1960, 3.

8. Statement from Vanderbilt Divinity School faculty as quoted by the *Nashville Tennessean* and reprinted in *Grain of Salt*, March 10, 1960, 4.

9. *Grain of Salt*, March 31, 1960, 5.

10. Taylor Branch, *Parting the Waters: America in the King Years, 1954–63* (New York: Simon & Schuster, 1989), 259–63.

11. Letter to Board of Trustees, Vanderbilt University, March 8, 1960, as printed in *Grain of Salt*, March 10, 1960.

12. Central Committee, National Student Christian Federation, "Letter to Christian Students and Campus Christian Student Groups in the U.S.A.," quoted in *Grain of Salt*, March 31, 1960, 3.

13. "Letter to Christian Students," March 6, 1960, printed in full in "The Basis of Concern," *Grain of Salt*, March 21, 1960, 3.

14. "How Can We Respond?" *Grain of Salt*, March 21, 1960, 4.

15. Jane Stembridge, oral history with Pete Daniel, December 5, 1996, for the Southern Oral History Program, R-0553, Southern Historical Collection, University of North Carolina at Chapel Hill, 7, 9–10.

16. *Grain of Salt*, April 27, 1960, 6b.

17. Ibid.

18. "The Story of the Student Interracial Ministry: An Experiment That Worked," August 1966, 2, SIM, UTS, 4A:1:f9; *Grain of Salt*, March 31, 1960.

19. "The Story of the Student Interracial Ministry: An Experiment That Worked," August 1966, 1, SIM, UTS, 4A:1:f9.

20. Jane Stembridge, "A Statement on the Interracial Student Ministry," SIM, UTS, 1F:1:f7.

21. Stembridge, oral history, December 5, 1996, 10.

22. Ibid., 6.

23. Jane Stembridge, "The Trouble Is the Fear," *Grain of Salt*, Fall 1960, 7.

24. "Text of Resolution to Be Submitted to an Open Meeting of the Student Body, April 28, 1960," *Grain of Salt*, April 27, 1960, 6b.

25. Stembridge, oral history, December 5, 1996, 6.

26. Constance Curry described Stembridge as a "pixie and poet" in Curry et al., *Deep in Our Hearts: Nine White Women in the Freedom Movement* (Athens: University of Georgia Press, 2000), 16.

27. John Collins, oral history interview with author, December 5, 2006.

28. Jonathan Strom, *A Half-Century of Strengthening Christian Ministry: The Fund for Theological Education* (Atlanta: Fund for Theological Education, 2002), 6.

29. Charles Helms, oral history interview with author, October 30, 2009.

30. Stembridge, "The Trouble Is the Fear," 7.

31. Stembridge, oral history, December 5, 1996, 10.

32. Jane Stembridge, oral history with Pete Daniel, September 17, 1997, for the Southern Oral History Program, R-0552, Southern Historical Collection, University of North Carolina at Chapel Hill, 2.

33. Curry et al., *Deep in Our Hearts*, 16.

34. Pete Daniel, *Lost Revolutions: The South in the 1950s* (Chapel Hill: University of North Carolina Press, 2000), 292.

35. Curry et al., *Deep in Our Hearts*, 16.

36. Clayborne Carson, *In Struggle: SNCC and the Black Awakening of the 1960s* (Cambridge, MA: Harvard University Press, 1995), 25–26.

37. Jared E. Leighton, "Freedom Indivisible: Gays and Lesbians in the African American Civil Rights Movement" (PhD diss., Department of History, University of Nebraska-Lincoln, May 1, 2013), 179.

38. Southeastern Baptist Theological Seminary Bulletin, 1976–1977 Catalog, https://archive.org/stream/southeasternbapto5sout/southeasternbapto5sout_djvu .txt, accessed November 4, 2015.

39. Jane Stembridge, "Statement on the Student Interracial Ministry," January 1961, SIM, UTS, 1H:1:f7.

40. John Collins diary, entry for June 3, 1960. Possession of John Collins.

41. Ibid.

42. Ibid.

43. Collins, oral history, December 5, 2006.

44. John Collins, correspondence with author, January 14, 2016.

45. Collins, oral history, December 5, 2006; Collins, correspondence, January 14, 2016.

46. Franklin "Chris" Gamwell, oral history interview with author, December 4, 2009.

47. Ibid.

48. Chris Gamwell, "A Statement on the Interracial Student Ministry," 1960, SIM, UTS, 1H:1:f7. Also published as "A Bulldog Goes to Bethel," *Grain of Salt*, Fall 1960, 5.

49. Ibid.

50. Chris Gamwell, oral history interview with author, December 4, 2009.

51. Ibid.

52. Helms, oral history, November 30, 2009.

53. Ibid.

54. Ibid.

55. Barney Blakeney, "Remembering the Rev. Willis T. Goodwin: A Friend to the Poor," *Charleston City Paper*, December 26, 2007; http://www.charlestoncitypaper .com/charleston/remembering-the-rev-willis-t-goodwin/Content?oid=1112600, accessed April 19, 2016.

56. Helms, oral history, November 30, 2009.

57. Charles G. Helms, "Statement on the Interracial Student Ministry," 1960, SIM, UTS, 1H:1:f7; Charles Helms, oral history interview with author, November 30, 2009.

58. William E. Crewes, "A Statement on the Student Interracial Ministry," 1960, SIM, UTS, 1C:2:f8.

59. Report, "1963: Student Interracial Ministry," 1, SIM, UTS, 1C:2:f11.

60. Stephen C. Rose, "Student Interracial Ministry: A Break in the Wall," *Christian Century*, February 1962.

61. Helms, oral history, November 30, 2009.

62. "Statement of Purpose of the Student Interracial Ministry, August 24, 1960," SIM, UTS, 1H:1:f7.

63. Report, "1963: Student Interracial Ministry," 1, 2, SIM, UTS, 1C:2:11.

64. "Statement of Purpose," SIM, UTS, 1H:1:f7.

65. Rev. Roger L. Shinn, "A Statement on the Interracial Summer Ministry," January 1961, SIM, UTS, 1H:1:f7.

66. Roger Shinn, oral history video with Eileen Crowley-Horak, 1999, Roger L. Shinn Papers, The Burke Library at Union Theological Seminary, Columbia University in the City of New York.

67. Martin Luther King Jr. to the Student Interracial Ministry Committee, March 29, 1961, SIM, UTS, 1A:2:f1.

68. Interseminary Movement, *A Brief History of the Interseminary Movement*, pamphlet published in 1967. E. Maynard Moore collection, possession of E. Maynard Moore, loaned to the author.

69. Crewes, "A Statement on the Interracial Student Ministry," SIM, UTS, 1C:2:f8.

70. Emily Langer, "Will D. Campbell, Preacher and Civil Rights Activist, Dies at 88," *Washington Post*, June 8, 2013, http://www.washingtonpost.com/national/will-d-campbell-preacher-and-civil-rights-activist-dies-at-88/2013/06/08/70b67d0a-cee4-11e2-9f1a-1a7cdee20287_story.html.

71. Merrill M. Hawkins Jr., *Will Campbell: Radical Prophet of the South* (Macon, GA: Mercer University Press, 1997), 30–40.

72. Ibid., 40–42.

73. Will D. Campbell, "A Statement on the Interracial Student Ministry," SIM, UTS, 1H:1:f7.

74. Ibid.

75. Ibid.

76. "Final Report of John Collins—1960–61," Student Interracial Ministry, SIM, UTS, 1F:1:f6.

77. Robert McAfee Brown, "Freedom Rides in Retrospect," *Grain of Salt*, October 23, 1961, 1; Robert McAfee Brown, "The Freedom Riders: A Clergyman's View," reprinted from the *Amherst College Alumni News*, published by CORE, 1962.

78. Brown, "Freedom Rides in Retrospect," 13.

Chapter Two

1. Walter T. Davis, "Student Interracial Ministry Report—1960–61," SIM, UTS, 1C:2:f8.

2. Wyatt Tee Walker, Letter to the Student Interracial Ministry, February 17, 1961; Wyatt Tee Walker, Letter to the Student Interracial Ministry, May 8, 1961; Constance Curry, Letter to the Student Interracial Ministry, April 27, 1961; SIM, UTS, 1F:1:f1.

3. Schedule, Student Interracial Ministry Orientation Conference, June 13–15, 1961, Fellowship Center, Swannanoa, North Carolina, SIM, UTS, 1F:1:f1.

4. "Student Interracial Ministry: 1961 Mid-Summer Reports," 3, SIM, UTS, 1F:1:f1.

5. Martin Luther King Jr. Letter to the Student Interracial Ministry, May 19, 1961, SIM, UTS, 1F:1:f1.

6. See Gurdon Brewster, *No Turning Back: My Summer with Daddy King* (Maryknoll, NY: Orbis Books, 2007).

7. Rinaldo "Bud" Walker, Union Theological Seminary, interned with Ralph Abernathy for the summer of 1963.

8. Gurdon Brewster, "1961 Mid-Summer Report, Student Interracial Ministry: A Ministry of Reconciliation," 7, SIM, UTS, 1F:1:f6; Gurdon Brewster, "No Turning Back: Living with Daddy King, Working at Ebenezer, 1961," draft in possession of author, 14. This work has since been published as *No Turning Back: My Summer with Daddy King.*

9. Stephen C. Rose, oral history interview with author, September 21, 2009.

10. Ibid.

11. Ibid.

12. Ibid.

13. Operationcrossroadsafrica.org.

14. Rose, oral history, September 21, 2009.

15. Ibid.

16. Steve Rose, "Union: Where We Are Today," *Grain of Salt*, Fall 1960.

17. Rose, oral history, September 21, 2009.

18. Rose, "Union: Where We Are Today," 4.

19. Roger Shinn, *The Tower*, Fall 1963, 3.

20. Rose, oral history, September 21, 2009.

21. David Stricklin, *A Genealogy of Dissent: Southern Baptist Protest in the 20th Century* (Frankfort: University Press of Kentucky, 2000). In fact, as further proof on a northern genealogy of dissent, J. Oscar McCloud, who served as both SIM student and host pastor, would end up forty years later supervising seminary field education work at the very same Brick Church.

22. Stephen C. Rose, *The Day the Country Mouse Expired* (New York: National Student Christian Federation, 1964); Stephen C. Rose, ed. *Who's Killing the Church?* (Chicago: Chicago City Missionary Society, 1966).

23. Stephen C. Rose, "Student Interracial Ministry: A Break in the Wall," *Christian Century*, March 14, 1962, 327.

24. Ibid.

25. Rose, "Student Interracial Ministry," 327.

26. Glenn T. Miller, *Piety and Profession: American Protestant Theological Education, 1870–1970* (Grand Rapids, MI: Eerdmans, 2007), 726–27.

27. Harvey Cox, "The 'New Breed' in American Churches: Sources of Social Activism in American Religion," *Daedalus* 96, no. 1 (Winter 1967): 135.

28. As quoted in ibid.

29. Doug Rossinow, *The Politics of Authenticity: Liberalism, Christianity, and the New Left in America* (New York: Columbia University Press, 1998), 55; Sara M. Evans, *Journeys That Opened Up the World: Women, Students Christian Movements, and Social Justice, 1955–1975* (New Brunswick, NJ: Rutgers University Press, 2003), 4–5; Dietrich Bonhoeffer, *Prisoner for God: Letters and Papers from Prison*, ed. Eberhard Bethge, rev. ed. (1953; repr., New York: Macmillan, 1967), 172.

30. Rossinow, *Politics of Authenticity*, 55. Tillich and Bultmann both referred to themselves under the Christian existentialist label. Tillich and Bonhoeffer were also, along with Reinhold Niebuhr, considered neo-orthodox.

31. James Miller, *Democracy Is in the Streets: From Port Huron to the Siege of Chicago* (Cambridge, MA: Harvard University Press, 1987), 204–5.

32. Trilling, quoted in Robert Cohen and Reginald E. Zelnick, eds., *The Free Speech Movement: Reflections on Berkeley in the 1960s* (Berkeley: University of California Press, 2002), 544.

33. See Evans, *Journeys That Opened Up the World*.

34. "Student Interracial Ministry: 1961 Mid-Summer Reports," 3, SIM, UTS, 1F:1:f1.

35. Will D. Campbell and Iva May Foster, "Report of the Evaluation Conference of the Student Interracial Ministry Held August 29–30, 1961," October 11, 1961, 1, SIM, UTS, 1F:1:f6.

36. Ibid., 3–4.

37. Charles M. Payne, *I've Got the Light of Freedom: The Organizing Tradition and the Mississippi Freedom Struggle*, 2nd ed. (Berkeley: University of California Press, 2007), and John Dittmer, *Local People: The Struggle for Civil Rights in Mississippi* (Chicago: University of Illinois Press, 2005), both speak to the conservatism of many southern black ministers.

38. Campbell and Foster, "Report of the Evaluation Conference"; "Student Interracial Ministry: 1961 Mid-Summer Reports," 3, SIM, UTS, 1F:1:f1.

39. Ibid., 2; Franklin I. Gamwell, "Report: Student Interracial Ministry Evaluation Conference, Nashville, Tennessee, August 29 and 30, 1961," 4, SIM, UTS, 1F:1:f6.

40. Douglas Renick, "SIM: A Student's Evaluation," *Interseminarian* 1, no. 4 (December 1962): 27, SIM, UTS, 2A:1:f5.

41. "Description of the Student Interracial Ministry Project," August 24, 1960, SIM, UTS, 1H:1:f7.

42. Roger L. Shinn, "A Statement on the Student Interracial Ministry," New York City, January 5, 1961, SIM, UTS, 1H:1:f7.

43. Campbell and Foster, "Report of the Evaluation Conference."

44. Gamwell, "Report: Student Interracial Ministry Evaluation Conference, Nashville, Tennessee, August 29 and 30, 1961," 5–6, SIM, UTS, 1F:1:f6.

45. "Final Report of John Collins—1960–61," Student Interracial Ministry, SIM, UTS, 1F:1:f6.

46. Rose, "Union: Where We Are Today," 1.

47. "Student Interracial Ministry Committee, Income and Statement of Balance, January, 1962—September, 1962," 1–2, SIM, UTS, 1D:1:f3.

48. Ralph Luker, oral history interview with author, November 5, 2006.

49. Ralph E. Luker, *The Social Gospel in Black and White: American Racial Reform, 1885–1912*, 2nd ed. (Chapel Hill, University of North Carolina Press, 1998), xii.

50. Hank Elkins, oral history interview with author, November 10, 2015.

51. *Jet*, August 23, 1962, 19.

52. Hank Elkins, oral history interview with author, November 10, 2015.

53. Ibid.

54. Ibid.

55. *Jet*, August 23, 1962, 8, 9.

56. Douglas Renick, "A Southern Student Evaluates," *Student Interracial Ministry: 1962*, 11, SIM, UTS, 1C:2:f11.

57. J. Oscar McCloud, "Words from a Negro Pastor," *Student Interracial Ministry: 1962*, 7, SIM, UTS, 1C:2:f11.

58. "Student Interracial Ministry: J. Oscar McCloud Report," SIM, UTS, 1C:2:f11.

59. Stephen B. Oates. *Let the Trumpet Sound: A Life of Martin Luther King, Jr.* (New York: HarperCollins, 1994), 21.

60. "A Church That Pioneered," *Southern Patriot*, Winter 1963, 3.

61. John Collins, "Student Interracial Ministry: A Venture in Reconciliation," *Interracial News Service* 33, no. 4 (September–October, 1962): 2, SIM, UTS, 2A:1:f4.

62. Roger Shinn, "The Student Interracial Ministry: A Venture of Faith," *Student Interracial Ministry: 1962*, 5, SIM, UTS, 1C:2:f11.

63. J. Oscar McCloud, oral history interview with author, December 9, 2006.

64. Ibid.; Oscar McCloud, "Report from a Local Church," *Interseminarian*, December 1962, 30, SIM, UTS, 2A:1:f6.

65. Collins Kilburn, "A White Minister Reports," *Student Interracial Ministry: 1962*, 10, SIM, UTS, 1C:2:f11.

66. See Stricklin, *A Genealogy of Dissent*.

67. Carlyle Marney, in fact, was close friends with Henry Stembridge, the minister father of Jane Stembridge, who had worked with SNCC and Ella Baker during SIM's pilot summer. The two ministers became close when they both pastored Baptist churches in Paducah, Kentucky. Jane Stembridge later said of Carlyle Marney, "He was always my mentor." Stembridge, oral history with Pete Daniel, December 5, 1996, 16.

68. Seymour, *Whites Only*, 21; conversation between Robert Seymour and author, April 10, 2004.

69. Seymour, *Whites Only*, 39.

70. Robert Seymour, oral history with Bruce Kalk, May 21, 1985, for the Southern Oral History Program, C-20, Southern Historical Collection, University of North Carolina at Chapel Hill, 5.

71. *Warren Record*, July 31, 1953.

72. Robert Seymour, sermon, in possession of Robert Seymour.

73. Seymour, *Whites Only*, 77–79.

74. Ibid., 77–79; letter in possession of Robert Seymour.

75. Seymour, *Whites Only*, 95; "Statement of Convictions," *Chapel Hill Weekly*, March 24, 1960. Copy of original signed petition in possession of Robert Seymour.

76. Seymour, Robert. "Interracial Ministry in North Carolina: What It Was Like for a Southern White Church to Have a Negro Assistant on Its Staff One Summer," *Christian Century*, January 23, 1963, 109.

77. Robert Seymour, oral history with Bruce Kalk, May 21, 1985, for the Southern Oral History Program. C-20, Southern Historical Collection, University of North Carolina at Chapel Hill, 6.

78. Jean Bradley Anderson, *Durham County* (Durham: Duke University Press, 1990), 437.

79. "From the Pulpit, a Struggle for Justice," *New York Times*, October 12, 2004; "James Forbes, Jr.: Speaking to Power," *NOW with Bill Moyers*, December 26, 2003.

80. James Forbes, oral history interview with author, February 15, 2008.

81. Ibid.

82. James Forbes, "Mid-Summer Report for the Student Interracial Ministry," August 1962, SIM, UTS, 1C:2:f11.

83. Ibid.

84. Seymour, "Interracial Ministry in North Carolina," 110.

85. Seymour, *Whites Only*, 92, 93.

86. "A Church That Pioneered," 1.

87. Forbes, oral history, February 15, 2008.

88. Elkins, oral history, November 10, 2015.

89. Reverend Martin Luther King Jr., Western Michigan University, December 18, 1963.

90. James Forbes biography on Riverside Church website, http://www.theriver sidechurchny.org/about/?minister-emeritus, accessed November 30, 2015.

91. Forbes, oral history, February 15, 2008

92. Letters in possession of Robert Seymour.

93. Seymour, oral history, May 21, 1985, 7.

94. Art Chansky, *Dean's Domain: The Inside Story of Dean Smith and His College Basketball Empire* (Marietta, GA: Longstreet Press, 1999), 63; Robert Seymour, oral history with author, February 22, 2005.

95. *Sports Illustrated*, November 29, 1982.

96. Chansky, *Dean's Domain*, 63.

97. "Howard Lee: Still Going Strong," *Chapel Hill Herald*, February 7, 2005. Lee failed in bids for Congress and lieutenant governor in 1972 and 1976, but was elected to the state senate twice, and was later named as the first black chairman of the State Board of Education, per http://ncpedia.org/biography/lee-howard, accessed May 4, 2006.

98. "Dean Smith Had a Coach of His Own," *Independent Weekly*, November 24, 2004.

99. S. Collins Kilburn, "Risking a Christian Ministry," *Interseminarian* 1, no. 4 (December 1962): 29.

Chapter Three

1. Ed Feaver, "1966 Report: The Student Interracial Ministry," 79; also quoted in "The Story of the Student Interracial Ministry: An Experiment That Worked," 10, SIM, UTS, 1C:2:f11.

2. "Minutes, the Student Interracial Ministry Committee, September 28, 1962," 1–4, SIM, UTS, 1B:1:f11.

3. "Student Interracial Ministry, 1963," 10, SIM, UTS, 1C:2:f11.

4. Stephen C. Rose, "Religious Conference," *Christianity and Crisis*, March 1963, 158–59.

5. Merrill M. Hawkins, *Will Campbell: Radical Prophet of the South*, 45–46. For more on both Will Campbell and the National Conference on Religion and Race, see also James Findlay, *Church People in the Struggle: The National Council of Churches and the Black Freedom Movement, 1950–1970* (New York: Oxford University Press, 1993), 22–34.

6. Stanley Pieza, "Rev. King Urges Boycott by Churches to Fight Bias," *Chicago's American*, January 16, 1963.

7. "'Segregation Forever': A Fiery Pledge Forgiven, but Not Forgotten," Radio Diaries, *All Things Considered*, NPR, January 10, 2013, http://www.npr.org/2013/01/14 /169080969/segregation-forever-a-fiery-pledge-forgiven-but-not-forgotten.

8. Martin Luther King Jr., "Letter from Birmingham Jail," April 16, 1963, The King Center, Atlanta, Georgia, http://coursesa.matrix.msu.edu/~hst306/documents /letter.html, accessed April 19, 2016. For more on Birmingham, see Diane McWhorter, *Carry Me Home: Birmingham, Alabama; The Climactic Battle of the Civil Rights Revolution* (New York: Simon & Schuster, 2001), and Taylor Branch, *Parting the Waters*.

9. Val Frakes and Lefty Schultz, "A Response to Birmingham," 1963, SIM, UTS, 1H:1:f7.

10. "Birmingham Comes Up at Baptist Meet," *Kansas City Star*, Wednesday, May 8, 1963. From Box 5, Scrapbook File No. 1 in the Robert E. Seymour papers #4554, Southern Historical Collection, The Wilson Library, University of North Carolina at Chapel Hill.

11. *Christian Century*, May 22, 1963. From Box 5, Scrapbook File No. 1 in the Robert E. Seymour papers #4554, Southern Historical Collection, The Wilson Library, University of North Carolina at Chapel Hill.

12. Findlay, *Church People in the Struggle*, 33.

13. "Synopsis of the Student Interracial Ministry, Raleigh, North Carolina, Orientation Conference, 1.

14. Report of George McClain in "Student Interracial Ministry Mid-Summer Reports, July 1963," 13, SIM, UTS, 1C:1:f3.

15. George McClain, oral history interview with author, July 10, 2007.

16. Robert Carey, oral history interview with author, November 6, 2015.

17. Robert Carey, Final Report, September 1963, SIM, UTS, 1C:2:f11.

18. Carey, oral history, November 6, 2015.

19. Ibid.

20. Ibid.

21. Ibid.

22. Interview with Pat and Bob Carey, http://www.longmarriedcouples.com/p-b_intw.html, accessed July 27, 2015.

23. Report of Robert Sullivan in "Student Interracial Ministry Mid-Summer Reports, July 1963," SIM, UTS, 1C:1:f3.

24. Carey, oral history, November 6, 2015.

25. Ibid.

26. Kirk A. Moll, "Theological Education in Action: Adult Learning about Race in the Student Interracial Ministry of Union Theological Seminary, 1960–68," D.Ed diss., Pennsylvania State University, 2011, 180.

27. Ibid.

28. Ibid., 183.

29. Report of Rinaldo "Bud" Walker in "Student Interracial Ministry Mid-Summer Reports, July 1963," 22, SIM, UTS, 1C:1:f3.

30. Moll, "Theological Education in Action," 183. Moll writes that Walker took this pledge at the time of the Birmingham bombing but before his summer with Abernathy. The bombing, however, occurred in September 1963—after that summer, not before it.

31. Chana Kai Lee, *For Freedom's Sake: The Life of Fannie Lou Hamer* (Champaign: University of Illinois Press, 2000), 47–49.

32. Jonathan Rieder, "The Day President Kennedy Embraced Civil Rights—and the Story Behind It," *Atlantic*, June 11, 2013, http://www.theatlantic.com/national/archive/2013/06/the-day-president-kennedy-embraced-civil-rights-and-the-story-behind-it/276749/.

33. Report of Donald Black in "Student Interracial Ministry Mid-Summer Reports, July 1963," 2, SIM, UTS, 1C:1:f3.

34. Report of Charles Boyer in "Student Interracial Ministry Mid-Summer Reports, July 1963," 4, SIM, UTS, 1C:1:f3.

35. Report of Douglas Parks in "Student Interracial Ministry Mid-Summer Reports, July 1963," 16, SIM, UTS, 1C:1:f3.

36. Report of Thomas Hoyt in "Student Interracial Ministry Mid-Summer Reports, July 1963," 8, SIM, UTS, 1C:1:f3. Interdenominational had formerly been Gammon, the home institution of three of the seven participants in SIM's first year.

37. Report, "1963, Student Interracial Ministry."

38. Report of Daniel A. Klement in "Student Interracial Ministry Mid-Summer Reports, July 1963," 11, SIM, UTS, 1C:1:f3.

39. Final Report of Ronald Young, November 12, 1963, SIM, UTS, 2:3:f1.

40. Ronald J. Young, "Report to the SIM Committee," March 1963, SIM, UTS, 2:3:f1.

41. See, for example, Gibson Winter, *The Suburban Captivity of the Churches: An Analysis of Protestant Responsibility in the Expanding Metropolis* (New York: Macmillan, 1962).

42. Report of Robert Lynn in "Student Interracial Ministry Mid-Summer Reports, July 1963," 12, SIM, UTS, 1C:1:f3.

43. Report of Warren Moore in "Student Interracial Ministry Mid-Summer Reports, July 1963," 15, SIM, UTS, 1C:1:f3.

44. Final Report of Warren Moore, Kansas City, Missouri, date-stamped September 16, 1963, SIM, UTS, 1C:1:f1.

45. The Wilmington Race Riot of 1898 saw the death of at least twenty-two African Americans at the hands of white supremacists rebelling against Reconstruction. See, for example, David S. Cecelski and Timothy B. Tyson, eds. *Democracy Betrayed: The Wilmington Race Riot and Its Legacy* (Chapel Hill: University of North Carolina Press, 1998).

46. David Jones, Mid-Summer Report, July 1963, 9–10, SIM, UTS, 1C:1:f3.

47. Ibid.

48. "After Wilmington Court Lecture, 96 Demonstrators Freed; Seminarian Gets Jail Term," *Raleigh News and Observer*, July 11, 1963, 1.

49. "Adults, Kids Sing and Pray for Jailed White Minister," *Wilmington Journal*, July 20, 1963, 10; "After Wilmington Court Lecture," *Raleigh News and Observer*, 1.

50. "Adults, Kids Sing and Pray," *Wilmington Journal*, 10.

51. David Jones, "An Evaluation of a Summer in the Student Interracial Ministry," *Interseminarian of the Midwest Region* 1, no. 1 (January 1964): 2, 4, SIM, UTS, 1C:1:f1.

52. Ibid., 3.

53. "Adults, Kids Sing and Pray," *Wilmington Journal*, 10.

54. Jones, "An Evaluation"; letters to National Council of Churches, SIM, UTS, 1A:1:f3.

55. Letter dated September 13, 1963, to the National Council of Churches from Harley M. Williams, Minister, Central Methodist Church, Monroe, North Carolina, SIM, UTS, 1A:1:f3.

56. For details of the NCC's gradual involvement, see Findlay, *Church People in the Struggle*, and Mark Newman, *Divine Agitators*.

57. Memo from Fletcher Coates to Oscar Lee, September 6, 1963, SIM, UTS, 1A:1:f3.

58. Undated memo, SIM, UTS, 1A:1:f3.

59. The commission was funded with $175,000 for the last half of 1963, and $275,000 for 1964. In a significant reversal of policy toward demonstrations, a sum of $25,000, donated from member denominations, was earmarked expressly for the purpose of funding bail for those who might be arrested during council-sponsored activities. Oscar Lee continued to direct the Department of Racial and Cultural Relations and was named to serve on the new commission, but he was passed over for all

the leadership positions, a clear statement that the NCC was distancing itself from its past efforts and entering into a new and very public phase of wrestling with the racial crisis.

60. Findlay, *Church People in the Struggle*, 3.

61. Letter to Harley M. Williams, September 18, 1963, SIM, UTS, 1A:1:f3.

62. Findlay, *Church People in the Struggle*, 48.

63. Ibid., 49–50.

64. Robert Hare, oral history interview with author, November 19, 2009.

65. Moll, "Theological Education in Action," 184.

66. Ibid., 184, 275.

67. Ibid., 155.

68. "The March in Washington," *Time*, August 30, 1963, http://www.time.com /time/magazine/article/0,9171,940697,00.html#ixzz0czbhiT3u.

69. As quoted in Findlay, *Church People in the Struggle*, 50.

70. Eugene Carson Blake, "Late We Come," in *Rhetoric, Religion, and the Civil Rights Movement, 1954–1965*, ed. Houck and Dixon (Waco, TX: Baylor University Press, 2006), 581–83.

71. David Hein, *Noble Powell and the Episcopal Establishment in the Twentieth Century* (Eugene, OR: Wipf and Stock, 2001), 90.

72. Bill Troy, oral history interview with author, October 5, 2009.

73. "Statement of Purpose of the Student Interracial Ministry, August 24, 1960," SIM, UTS, 1H:1:f7.

74. "1963: Student Interracial Ministry," report, 2, SIM, UTS, 1C:2:f3.

75. *Renewal*, III/9, December 1963.

76. "The Way Ahead," *Renewal*, III/9, December 1963, 2.

77. "Another Kind of Civil Rights 'Filibuster,' " *Evening Independent*, April 29, 1964, 8A; David Langston and William McKeown, "The Student Movement at Union Theological Seminary, 1963–1969" (New York: Department of Ministry, National Council of Churches), 1–2; Burke Library, Union Theological Seminary.

78. "Students Stage Vigil for Rights," *New York Times*, May 2, 1964.

79. Virginia Wadsley, letter to author, August 4, 2006. Possession of author.

80. William V. Shannon, "The Voice of the Churches," *Commonweal*, May 15, 1964, 227–28.

81. In late June, the students in the vigil learned that three civil rights workers, James Cheney, Andrew Goodman, and Michael Schwerner, had gone missing in Mississippi while participating in Freedom Summer. The bodies of Cheney, Goodman, and Schwerner were discovered on August 4 in an earthen dam south of the town of Philadelphia, Mississippi.

82. Mary McGrory, "Students Behind the Civil Rights Vigil," *America*, May 16, 1964, 666.

83. Wadsley, letter to author, August 4, 2006.

84. Letter from Tom Boomershine in New York City to Russ Richey in Rocky Mount, North Carolina, August 7, 1964, SIM, UTS, 1A:1:f4.

85. Wadsley, letter to author, August 4, 2006.

86. The New Stage of S.I.M.'s Development," report, SIM, UTS, 1G:1:f1.

87. Jane Stembridge, "Open Letter to America," King Papers, State Historical Society of Wisconsin, Madison.

88. Wesley Hogan, *Many Minds, One Heart: SNCC's Dream for a New America* (Chapel Hill: University of North Carolina Press, 2007), 164.

89. Maryka Matthews, "SIM Summer Report," SIM, UTS, 2:3:f2.

90. Greg Michel, *Struggle for a Better South: The Southern Student Organizing Committee, 1964–1969* (New York: Palgrave Macmillan, 2004), 253, n13.

91. "Student Interracial Ministry: Mid-Summer Reports, July 1964," 16, SIM, UTS, 2:3:f2.

92. Ruth Brandon, "SIM Midsummer Report," SIM, UTS, 2:3:f2.

93. Russell E. Richey, "Student Interracial Ministry: Midsummer Report," 2, SIM, UTS, 2:3:f2.

94. Ken Rupp Letter, SIM, UTS, 2:3:f2.

95. Robert B. Blair, "Mid-Summer Report," SIM, UTS, 2:3:f2.

96. William C. White, "Student Interracial Ministry Final Report, SIM, UTS, 2:3:f2.

97. Michel, *Struggle for a Better South*, 33–34.

98. Russell E. Richey, "Student Interracial Ministry: Midsummer Report," 1, SIM, UTS, 2:3:f2.

99. M. George Walters, "Report on Activities and Observations: SIM at Davie Street Presbyterian Church," 1–2.

100. "Impressions from the Field," *Grain of Salt*, September 29, 1964, 7, 8.

101. Letter from Tom Boomershine in New York to Russ Richey in Rocky Mount, North Carolina, dated July 15, 1964, SIM, UTS, 1A:1:f4.

102. Letter from Russ Richey, SIM student coordinator, to C. J. Malloy Jr. at Virginia Union University, dated November 23, 1964, SIM, UTS, 1A:1:f4.

103. Letter of July 23, 1964, from Russell Richey to "the Ministers of Rocky Mount," SIM, UTS, 1A:1:f4.

104. Memorandum regarding Evaluation Conference, Internships and Publicity, written by Tom Boomershine to SIM participants, August 6, 1964, SIM, UTS, 1F:1:f7.

105. Memorandum, August 6, 1964.

106. Michel, *Struggle for a Better South*.

107. "1965 Report, Student Interracial Ministry," 3, 5, 6, SIM, UTS, 1C:2:f11.

108. Ibid., 6.

109. Robert Hare, oral history with author, November 23, 2009.

110. Ibid.

111. "Student Interracial Ministry Press Release," SIM UTS, 2A:2:f5.

112. "1965 Report: Student Interracial Ministry," 7–8.

113. Edgar R. Trexler, "He's Safe on These Streets," *Lutheran*, September 28, 1966, 6.

114. "Student Interracial Ministry—1966," 7–8, SIM, UTS, 1C:2:f11.

115. "1965 Report: Student Interracial Ministry," 7–8, SIM, UTS, 1C:2:f11.

116. Ibid.

117. Ibid.

118. Ibid.; Trexler, "He's Safe on These Streets," 9.

119. "Student Interracial Ministry Press Release," SIM, UTS, 2A:2:f5; Trexler, "He's Safe on These Streets."

120. "1965 Report: Student Interracial Ministry," 7–8.

121. Trexler, "He's Safe on These Streets," 7.

122. "1966 Report: Student Interracial Ministry," 55.

123. W. M. Jones, "SIM Evaluation," SIM, UTS, 1A:2:f6.

Chapter Four

1. W. E. B. DuBois, *The Souls of Black Folk*, rev. ed. (1903; New York: Barnes and Noble, 2003), 83.

2. Stephen G. N. Tuck, *Beyond Atlanta: The Struggle for Racial Equality in Georgia, 1940–1980* (Athens: University of Georgia Press, 2001), 159.

3. SNCC worker John Perdew in 1965, quoted in Tuck, 159.

4. Dr. Larry Mamiya, "SNCC, SIM, and the Southwest Georgia Project," August 2011, http://www.crmvet.org/nars/mamiya.htm.

5. Tuck, *Beyond Atlanta*, 159.

6. Chandler Davidson and Bernard Grofman, *Quiet Revolution in the South: The Impact of the Voting Rights Act, 1965–1990* (Princeton, NJ: Princeton University Press, 1994), 71–72.

7. Ibid.

8. For information on the internal debate within SNCC about going to Southwest Georgia, see Aldon Morris, *The Origins of the Civil Rights Movement: Black Communities Organizing for Change.* (New York: Free Press, 1984), 239.

9. Taylor Branch, *At Canaan's Edge: America in the King Years, 1965–1968* (New York: Simon & Schuster, 2006), 465.

10. Barbara Ransby, *Ella Baker and the Black Freedom Movement: A Radical Democratic Vision* (Chapel Hill: University of North Carolina Press, 2003), 309. See also Taylor Branch, *Pillar of Fire: America in the King Years: 1964–66* (New York: Simon & Schuster, 1998), and *At Canaan's Edge.*

11. Charles Sherrod, 1986, C-5047/59, in the Taylor Branch Papers #5047, Southern Historical Collection, The Wilson Library, University of North Carolina at Chapel Hill.

12. Tuck, *Beyond Atlanta*, 161.

13. The NAACP dragged its feet, but others in Albany were "willing and ready to go" into battle to achieve civil rights. (Cordell Reagon, "Voices Old and Young, Albany Georgia," Guy and Candie Carawan Collection, SHC, 20008, FT-3692, side one.) C. B. King, the only black attorney in town, had in 1960 filed an unsuccessful petition for relief from segregated voting lists and voting facilities. Also that year, Albany's black ministers wrote a joint letter of complaint to the Albany Herald

protesting what they regarded as only negative coverage of blacks. In response to the letter, local whites vandalized some of the ministers' homes, breaking the windows. One resident recalled that attack as "the first overt act which sparked the diehard attitude of the present movement. It seemed like, if you had to die, you might as well die fighting." ("Voices Old and Young," Albany Georgia, speaker unknown, Guy and Candie Carawan Collection, SHC, 20008, FT-3692, side one.) Morris, 241. In addition to SNCC, its members represented the Ministerial Alliance, the NAACP, the NAACP Youth Council, the Federation of Women's Clubs, the Negro Voters' League, and the Criterion Council, a fraternal organization. The NAACP joined despite avowing that it would not cooperate with the SNCC students.

14. From untitled pamphlet, undated but likely from the summer of 1967. E. Maynard Moore collection, possession of E. Maynard Moore, loaned to the author.

15. Charles Sherrod, 1986, C-5047/59, in the Taylor Branch Papers #5047, Southern Historical Collection, The Wilson Library, University of North Carolina at Chapel Hill.

16. Quoted in Marsh, *Beloved Community*, 3.

17. Bernice Johnson Reagon, "In Our Hands: Thoughts on Black Music," *Sing Out!* 24 (January–February 1976): 1. Quoted in Howard Zinn, "SNCC and the Albany Movement," *Journal of Southwest Georgia History* 2 (Fall 1984): 23. Reagon was a local Albany student who was among those first organized by SNCC in 1961. Bernice Johnson, Cordell Reagon, Charles Neblett, and Rutha Harris formed the Freedom Singers in 1962. She married Cordell Reagon in 1963. She was a professor of history at American University in Washington, D.C., and also worked as a guest curator for the Smithsonian Institution. She continued singing and recording albums, most notably as a founding member of the vocal ensemble Sweet Honey in the Rock.

18. Morris, *Origins of the Civil Rights Movement*, 241. See also Josh Dunson, *Freedom in the Air: Song Movements of the Sixties* (New York: International, 1965); Guy and Candie Carawan, *Sing for Freedom: The Story of the Civil Rights Movement through Its Songs* (Montgomery: NewSouth Books, 2008), and *Songs of the Southern Freedom Movement: We Shall Overcome!* (New York: Oak, 1963).

19. Charles Sherrod recorded by Alan Lomax, from "Freedom in the Air," side B, FT-9649, in the Guy and Candie Carawan Collection #20008, Southern Folklife Collection, Wilson Library, University of North Carolina at Chapel Hill.

20. Pat Watters, *Down to Now: Reflections on the Southern Civil Rights Movement* (New York, 1971), 158. Quoted in Howard Zinn, "SNCC and the Albany Movement," *Journal of Southwest Georgia History* 2 (Fall 1984), 23.

21. Looking back three years later, King regretted that he had chosen "to protest against segregation generally rather than against a single and distinct facet of it. Our protest was so vague that we got nothing, and the people were left very depressed and in despair." But, he did not regard Albany as a failure because "the Negro people there straightened up their bent backs: You can't ride a man's back unless it's bent. And what we learned from our mistakes in Albany helped our later campaigns in other cities to be more effective." Martin Luther King Jr., "The Playboy Interview," *Playboy*, January 1965.

22. Carson, *In Struggle*, 61–62.

23. "Charles Sherrod," in Hampton and Fayer, *Voices of Freedom*, 114; "Moving Forward by Recalling the Past," *Albany Herald*, November 15, 1998; "Charles Sherrod" in Hampton and Fayer, *Voices of Freedom*, 114.

24. Howard Zinn, *You Can't be Neutral on a Moving Train* (Boston: Beacon Press, 1994), 54; Julian Bond, quoted in Carson, *In Struggle*, 62.

25. "Southwest Georgia," undated report from fall 1963, author unknown, SNCC papers, microfilm, reel A-IV, frames 1010.

26. Branch, *Pillar of Fire*, 194.

27. "Southwest Georgia," undated report from fall 1963, author unknown, SNCC papers, microfilm, reel A-IV, frame 1009. John Perdew was one of the "Americus Four" charged with sedition and threatened with execution in 1963. For more, see http://www.civilrights.uga.edu/bibliographies/americus/ (accessed February 19, 2010).

28. SNCC papers, microfilm, reel XV, frame 32.

29. Charles Sherrod, oral history interview with author, June 8, 2009.

30. Untitled pamphlet. E. Maynard Moore collection, possession of E. Maynard Moore, loaned to the author, 2. They were directors in name only. In fact, Sherrod recalled that even though Simpkins was supposed to be in charge, he had no actual authority there. When Sherrod returned to the area with five SIM seminarians in tow in the summer of 1965, he continued to run the show "as if nothing had happened." Sherrod interview with Taylor Branch, 1986.

31. Joseph Howell, "Civil Rights Diary," Summer 1966, copy in possession of author.

32. Tuck, *Beyond Atlanta*, 166.

33. "The Story of the Student Interracial Ministry: An Experiment That Worked," August 1966, 10, SIM, UTS, 4A:1:f9.

34. John Chappell, oral history interview with author, April 15, 2006.

35. "The Story of the Student Interracial Ministry," 6–7, SIM, UTS, 1F:1:f9.

36. Among many other references, see "All the Long Hot Summers," *Time*, June 2, 1980.

37. "The Story of the Student Interracial Ministry," 8, SIM, UTS, 1F:1:f9.

38. Charles Sherrod, "For the Student Interracial Ministry—a Proposal," SIM, UTS, 4A:4:f4.

39. Edward A. Feaver, "Taking All the Money and Giving All the Jesus," *skandalon* I (Fall 1966): 3, SIM, UTS, 2A:1:f8.

40. Charles Sherrod, Jack Quigley, and David Hawk, "A Proposal for the Maximum Ministry of the Gillespie Seldon Institute," unknown day in 1967, 6, UTS: 4A:4:f3.

41. "S.I.M. in Southwest Georgia," program advertisement, undated. SIM, UTS, 4A:3:F7.

42. *Southwest Georgia Project Newsletter*, August 2, 1966, no. 5, 1, SIM, UTS, 2B:1:f3. The Southwest Georgia newsletters are not contained in the SNCC records, only in the SIM records at Union Theological Seminary, where there is a nearly complete

run from June 15, 1966, through July 3, 1967. Some additional information can be found in the SNCC newsletters "News of the Field," located in the SNCC papers at the King Center in Atlanta, which contain blurbs on all the regional projects and only brief updates on Southwest Georgia.

43. *Southwest Georgia Project Newsletter*, August 2, 1966, no. 5, 1, SIM, UTS, 2B:1:f3; "1965 Report, Student Interracial Ministry," 19, SIM, UTS, 1C:2:f9.

44. "Comment on SNCC, SIM, and MUST" and "SIM Internships," *Methodist Woman*, November 1966, SIM, UTS, 2A:1:f13; Letter from Russ [Richey] to Bill [Minter], SIM, UTS, 4A:3:f3.

45. "1966 Report, Student Interracial Ministry," 78, SIM, UTS, 1C:1:f10.

46. Quoted in Harvey, *Freedom's Coming*, 80. For the definitive analysis of Koinonia Farm as a location of prophetic Christianity, see Tracy Elaine K'Meyer, *Interracialism and Christian Community in the Postwar South: The Story of Koinonia Farm* (Charlottesville: University of Virginia Press), 2000.

47. Ed Feaver, *Grain of Salt*, October 12, 1965, 1.

48. Joe Pfister, "The Meaning of Ministry," *Southwest Georgia Project Newsletter*, January 20, 1967, 3, SIM, UTS, 2B:1:f7.

49. Joe Pfister, "The State of the Project," *Southwest Georgia Project Newsletter*, April 15, 1968, 8. Collection of Joe Pfister.

50. Tuck, *Beyond Atlanta*, 165, citing SNCC papers, microfilm, Reel 2, frame 19.

51. For more on Daniels, see Charles W. Eagles, *Jon Daniels and the Civil Rights Movement in Alabama* (Huntsville: University of Alabama Press, 2000).

52. Jan Vrchota final report, SIM, UTS, 1C:1:f4.

53. 1965 Report, 11–12; Menzel report, 3, SIM, UTS, 1C:1:f4.

54. Charles Sherrod, "For the Student Interracial Ministry—a Proposal," 3, UTS: 4A:4:f4.

55. "Southwest Georgia Newsletter," August 2, 1966, no. 5, 2, SIM, UTS, 2B:1:f3.

56. "Shirley Sherrod," Mary Reynolds Babcock Foundation, Southern Voices: MRBF Video Archive.

57. Joe Pfister, oral history interview with author, November 29, 2006.

58. Joseph Howell, *Civil Rights Journey* (Bloomington: AuthorHouse, 2011), 93.

59. Joe Howell, oral history interview with author, November 27, 2006.

60. Charles Sherrod, oral history interview with author, June 11, 2009.

61. Ibid.

62. Tuck, *Beyond Atlanta*, 190.

63. Howell, oral history, November 27, 2006.

64. Mamiya, "SNCC, SIM, and the Southwest Georgia Project."

65. Edward A. Feaver, "Taking All the Money and Giving All the Jesus," *skandalon* 1 (Fall 1966): 5–6, SIM, UTS, 2A:1:f8.

66. Feaver, "Taking All the Money," 7.

67. Don Harris report, undated, SNCC papers, microfilm, Reel 10, frame 1.

68. C. B. King attempted a second run for Congress in 1966. SWGA workers obtained a total of 7,400 signatures, 1,600 more than necessary, on petitions to place

King on the ballot. Sherrod, along with SIM interns Jim Romberg and Ed Feaver, delivered the petitions to the secretary of state in Atlanta on the final day they were due, but the secretary of state refused to accept the petitions on the grounds that they had to be turned in by the candidate himself. King was thus not included on the ballot. The volunteers wrote in the *Southwest Georgia Project Newsletter* (nos. 6 and 8) that their work was not in vain, however, as the canvassing brought them into new areas, giving them a chance to enroll new voters and spread the word about political involvement. Many black voters even wrote in former governor Ellis Arnall, a progressive, in the gubernatorial race rather than vote for either of the segregationist candidates running. The write-in campaign muddied the election results and resulted in a court battle, making a point about the potential of black voting power in the state.

69. Peter de Lissovoy, "Gambler's Choice in Georgia," *Nation*, June 22, 1964.

70. "Southwest Georgia Project: Report and Proposals," December 27, 1963, 17, SNCC papers, microfilm Reel A-IV, frame 360.

71. "Help the Southwest Georgia Project," undated memo. E. Maynard Moore collection, possession of E. Maynard Moore, loaned to the author; phone memo, SIM, UTS. Joe Pfister, "Building: Long Range Style," *skandalon* 4 (Summer 1967): 12, SIM, UTS, 2A:1:f10; phone message from Carole Walters to Maynard Moore, August 23, 1967, SIM, UTS, 4A: 3:f5.

72. See, for example, Pfister "burglary" arrest in *Southwest Georgia Project Newsletter*, no. 6, October 9, 1966, 3–4; Charles Wallace traffic arrest in *Southwest Georgia Project Newsletter*, no. 3, June 29, 1966, 1–2; Ed Feaver traffic arrest in *Southwest Georgia Project Newsletter*, no. 4, July 15, 1966, 1. SIM, UTS, 2B:1:f3.

73. "Maxim K. Rice," Civil Rights Movement Veterans biography, http://www.crmvet.org/vet/ricem.htm.

74. *Southwest Georgia Project Newsletter*, no. 4, July 15, 1966, 1, SIM, UTS, 2B:1:f3.

75. Francesca Polletta, *Freedom Is an Endless Meeting: Democracy in American Social Movements* (Chicago: University of Chicago Press, 2002), 60. Quoting SNCC papers, microfilm, Reel 178.

76. *Southwest Georgia Project Newsletter*, no. 9, December 13, 1966, 3, SIM, UTS, 2B:1:f3. It was estimated at the time that Baker had a black population of about 65 percent, but only 20 percent of blacks were registered voters. The Voter Education Program was funded by the Taconic, Field, New World, and Stern Brothers foundations at the private urging of the Kennedy brothers. Robert Kennedy especially hoped to turn the tide of the civil rights movement away from demonstrations and toward "quieter" voter registration work. The program ran between 1962 and 1968.

77. Janet M. Vrchota, "Final Report, Summer 1965: SIM in Southwest Georgia," SIM, UTS, 1C:1:f4.

78. *News of the Field*, no. 5, March 23, 1966, 1. SNCC papers, microfilm.

79. *Southwest Georgia Project Newsletter*, no. 12, April 15, 1967, 3. SIM, UTS, 2B:1:f9.

80. *Southwest Georgia Project Newsletter*, no. 13, July 3 1967, 3. SIM, UTS, 2B:1:f9.

81. Ibid.

82. Howell, oral history, November 27, 2006.

83. *Southwest Georgia Project Newsletter*, no. 6, October 9, 1966, 2–3. SIM, UTS, 2B:1:f3.

84. "A.S.C.S. Elections and You," *The Other Side: Southwest Georgia News* 1, no. 1 (July 1967): 1. SIM, UTS, 2B:1:f10.

85. *Southwest Georgia Project Newsletter*, no. 1, June 15, 1966; *Southwest Georgia Project Newsletter*, no. 2, June 22, 1966, 2. SIM, UTS, 2B:1:f3.

86. *Southwest Georgia Project Newsletter*, no. 3, June 29, 1966, 1. SIM, UTS, 2B:1:f3

87. Ibid.

88. Mamiya, "SNCC, SIM, and the Southwest Georgia Project."

89. Larry Mamiya, oral history interview with author, June 6, 2009, Albany, Georgia.

90. *Southwest Georgia Project Newsletter*, no. 4, July 15, 1966, 1. SIM, UTS, 2B:1:f3.

91. The Rural Areas Development project and other unsuccessful efforts can be seen as the forerunners of the ambitious New Communities, Inc., cooperative farm project created by Charles and Shirley Sherrod and others in 1969. New Communities, Inc., was a cooperatively owned community land trust, modeled on the *kibbutzim* and *moshavim* of Israel. It comprised 5,700 acres of cropland jointly occupied and farmed by eight hundred rural families, the vast majority of them black. New Communities was the largest black-owned farm in the United States and lasted for seventeen years before collapsing under the weight of its mortgage. TaRessa Stovall, "Charles Sherrod: Passing on the Blood and Pulse of the Civil Rights Movement," *Aspire*, Summer/Fall 2007, 13; unpublished autobiography of Bob Swann, chaps. 19 and 20, collection of the E.F. Schumacher Society, http://www.centerforneweconomics.org/schumacher; Ed Feaver, oral history, August 3, 2008; Joe Pfister, oral history, November 29, 2006.

92. SNCC papers, microfilm, REEL A-IV, frames 366–67.

93. Two of the interns would later go on to careers in the public housing sector—Ed Feaver as director of the Department of Health and Social Services in Florida, and Joe Howell as a developer of affordable housing communities in Washington, D.C., and Maryland.

94. "The Southwest Georgia Project: A Prospectus," 1967, 11, SIM, UTS, 4A:4:f5.

95. "The Southwest Georgia Project: A Prospectus," 12, SIM, UTS, 4A:4:f5.

96. *News of the Field*, no. 6, March 30, 1966, 2, SNCC papers.

97. Ibid., No. 7, April 6, 1966, 2–3, SNCC papers.

98. *Southwest Georgia Project Newsletter*, no. 7, November 7, 1966, 1; no. 8, November 28, 1966, 1–2, SIM, UTS, 2b:1:f5.

99. *Southwest Georgia Project Newsletter*, no. 8, November 28, 1966, 2–3, SIM, UTS, 2b:1:f5.

100. *News of the Field*, no. 11, April 27, 1966, 3–4, SNCC papers.

101. *Southwest Georgia Project Newsletter*, no. 9, December 13, 1966, 4, SIM, UTS, 2b:1:f6.

102. *Southwest Georgia Project Newsletter*, no. 3, June 29, 1966, 2, SIM, UTS, 2b:1:f3.

103. "1965 Report: Student Interracial Ministry," 13, SIM, UTS, 1C:2:f11.

104. "Southwest Georgia Project Newsletter," no. 5, August 2, 1966, 1, SIM, UTS, 2b:1:f5.

105. "Proposal for an Indigenous Theatre Project in Southwest Georgia sponsored by the Student Interracial Ministry," undated. E. Maynard Moore collection, possession of E. Maynard Moore, loaned to the author.

106. Joe Pfister, "Notes from Southwest Georgia: Building Long Range Style," *skandalon* 4 (Summer 1967): 11, SIM, UTS, 2A:1:f10.

107. *skandalon* 4 (Summer 1967): 11–12, SIM, UTS, 2A:1:f10.

108. *skandalon* 4 (Summer 1967): 12, SIM, UTS, 2A:1:f10.

109. Feaver, "Taking All the Money," 7. After the SIM project ended in the spring of 1968, Sherrod reorganized the project as the Southwest Georgia Project for Community Education. The organization has been overseen by an all-black board of directors since 1974. Today, the Southwest Georgia Project for Community Education celebrates itself as an all-black project devoted to addressing social, economic, health, and education concerns in black communities; it publicly gives no acknowledgment to its beginnings as an explicitly interracial, religious-based effort to reform not just the lives of blacks in Southwest Georgia but the very nature of the church and society itself. See http://www.swgaproject.com/about-us.html. Joe Pfister returned to Union to finish his degree but then came back and stayed another seven years in Albany. But he no longer went out into the field to do community organizing or voter registration, saying he no longer felt it was his place to do so. He later supported the local activists by operating a printing business that published movement publications. Sherrod continued to organize in the counties of Southwest Georgia, though he spent much of his time in the 1970s and 1980s working on the New Communities project. He also got involved in local politics, getting elected to the Albany City Council in 1976 and serving until 1990. See "This Far by Faith," http://www.pbs.org/thisfarbyfaith/witnesses/charles_sherrod.html, accessed January 25, 2009. New Communities made the news again in the first two decades of the twenty-first century in relation to legal action on behalf of black farmers as well as new developments on behalf of the project itself. For more, see http://www.ruraldevelopment.org/shirleydirector.html; http://www.wkkf.org/what-we-do/featured-work/the-arc-of-justice-bends-toward-cypress-pond; and http://www.albanyherald.com/news/2014/jun/14/new-communities-group-in-albany-opens-resora/.

110. "1965 Report: Student Interracial Ministry," 13; Feaver, "Taking All the Money," 6.

111. Ed Feaver, "1966 Report: The Student Interracial Ministry," 79, SIM, UTS, 1C:2:f11.

112. See, for example, Joe Pfister report in "1966 Report: Student Interracial Ministry," 84.

113. *One More River to Cross*, Glen Pearcy Productions, 1969/2012.

114. See, for example, "The Story of the Student Interracial Ministry: An Experiment That Worked," August 1966, 9–10, SIM, UTS, 4A:1:f9.

115. "The Story of the Student Interracial Ministry: An Experiment That Worked," August 1966, 1, SIM, UTS, 4A:1:f9.

116. Ed Feaver, "1966 Report: The Student Interracial Ministry," 79, SIM, UTS, 1C:2:f11.

117. Ibid.; also quoted in "The Story of the Student Interracial Ministry: An Experiment That Worked," 10.

118. Joe Pfister, "Notes from Southwest Georgia: Building Long Range Style," *skandalon 4 (Summer 1967):* 12. SIM, UTS, 2A:1:f10.

119. Charles Sherrod, "The Revolutionaries and the Church," *The Other Side: Southwest Georgia News* 1, no. 2 (August 1967): 4.

120. "What Is the Church?" *The Other Side: Southwest Georgia News* 1, no. 1 (July 1967): 4.

121. "The Story of the Student Interracial Ministry: An Experiment That Worked," 4.

122. "The Southwest Georgia Project: A Prospectus," 6.

123. "SIM in the Urban Situation," 1, SIM, UTS, 1C:2:f13.

124. "1966 Report: Student Interracial Ministry," 86.

125. Langston and McKeown, *The Student Movement at Union Theological Seminary*, 3–6.

126. David Langston e-mail to author, June 15, 2008, in possession of author.

127. Langston and McKeown, *The Student Movement at Union Theological Seminary*, 1.

128. Risto Lehtonen, *Story of a Storm: The Ecumenical Student Movement in the Turmoil of Revolution, 1968 to 1973* (Grand Rapids, MI: Eerdmans, 1998), 5.

129. "The Story of the Student Interracial Ministry: An Experiment That Worked," 10.

Chapter Five

1. Martin, *Christians in Conflict*, 1.

2. John Stumme, oral history telephone interview with author, December 9, 2008.

3. "SIM in the Urban Situation," 1, SIM, UTS, 1C:2:f13.

4. Ibid., 1.

5. Ibid., 1.

6. Ibid., 2.

7. Gibson Winter, *The Suburban Captivity of the Churches: An Analysis of Protestant Responsibility in the Expanding Metropolis* (New York: Macmillan, 1962).

8. Will D. Campbell, *Race and the Renewal of the Church* (Philadelphia: Westminster Press, 1962); Harvey Cox, *The Church amid Revolution* (New York: Association Press, 1967); Carl F. Burke, *God Is for Real, Man* (New York: Association Press, 1966); Martin E. Marty, *No Ground Beneath Us: A Revolutionary Reader* (New York: National Methodist Student Movement, 1964); James Sellers, *The South and Christian Ethics* (New York: Association Press, 1962); Robert Lee and Martin E. Marty, *Reli-*

gion and Social Conflict (New York: Oxford University Press, 1964); Jeffrey K. Hadden, *The Gathering Storm in the Churches* (New York: Doubleday, 1969).

9. Harvey Cox, *The Secular City: Secularization and Urbanization in Theological Perspective* (New York: Macmillan, 1965); Walter E. Ziegenhals's *Urban Churches in Transition* (1978) includes a bibliography of forty-four publications about urban ministry, and many more have been written since. See Ziegenhals, *Urban Churches in Transition* (New York: Pilgrim Press, 1978), 195–201.

10. Rodney L. Petersen, "Training Prophets," *Religion in the Secular City: Essays in Honor of Harvey Cox* (San Antonio, TX: Trinity University Press, 2001), 30.

11. Cox, *Secular City*, 15.

12. "SIM in the Urban Situation," 1, SIM, UTS, 1C:2:f13.

13. Letter to the editor from Ernest Rosenfeld with response, *Renewal* 4, no. 2 (February 1964): 31.

14. *Renewal*, January 1966.

15. *Renewal*, February 1966.

16. Stephen C. Rose, *The Grass Roots Church: A Manifesto for Protestant Renewal* (Nashville: Abingdon Press, 1966); Stephen C. Rose, *Who's Killing the Church?* (New York: Holt, Rhinehart, and Winston, 1966).

17. Paraphrased in *Theology Today* 24, no. 1 (April 1967).

18. Rose, *The Grass Roots Church*, 4–6.

19. *Renewal*, February 1966, 2.

20. Malcolm Boyd, "The Ecumenical Freedom Body: A Call to the People," *Renewal*, February 1966, 6–7.

21. *Renewal*, December 1965; Charles Harper, "Responsible Urban Strategy: A Case Study, *Renewal*, February 1966, 7.

22. Daniel Callahan, ed. *The Secular City Debate* (New York: Macmillan, 1966), 1–2.

23. Ibid.

24. Robert V. Kemper and Julie Atkins, "The World As It Should Be: Faith-Based Community Development in America," in *Community Building in the Twenty-First Century*, ed. Stanley Hyland (Santa Fe: School of American Research Press, 2005), 71–100.

25. See Mark Newman, *Divine Agitators: The Delta Ministry and Civil Rights in Mississippi* (Athens: University of Georgia Press, 2004).

26. "1966 Report: Student Interracial Ministry," 90, 8–10, SIM, UTS, 1C:2:f11.

27. Letter from G.W. Webber, March 9, 1966, SIM, UTS.

28. SIM Budget Report, April 28, 1966, SIM, UTS, 1D:1:f2.

29. "1966 Report: Student Interracial Ministry," 90, 98–99, SIM, UTS, 1C:2:f11.

30. SIM Budget Report, April 28, 1966, SIM, UTS, 1D:1:f2.

31. "1966 Report: Student Interracial Ministry," 26, SIM, UTS, 1C:2:f12.

32. Moll, 224.

33. Franklin "Chris" Gamwell, oral history interview with author, December 4, 2009.

34. Joe Howell, "Civil Rights Diary," 6–10.

35. "1966 Report: Student Interracial Ministry," 26.

36. Ibid., 29–30.

37. Ibid.

38. Ibid., 38.

39. Ibid., 50.

40. Ibid., 50–52.

41. Ibid., 50–51.

42. Kirk A. Moll, "Theological Education in Action: Adult Learning about Race in the Student Interracial Ministry of Union Theological Seminary, 1960–68," D.Ed diss., Pennsylvania State University, 2011, 226–27.

43. Barbara Cox, oral history interview with author, November 24, 2009.

44. Ibid.

45. Moll, "Theological Education in Action," 229.

46. "1966 Report: Student Interracial Ministry," 57–58.

47. Ibid., 56–58.

48. For more on mainline church involvement in birth control and abortion resources, see David Cline, *Creating Choice: A Community Responds to the Need for Abortion and Birth Control, 1961–1973* (New York: Palgrave Macmillan, 2006).

49. "1966 Report: Student Interracial Ministry," 53.

50. Ibid., 62–63.

51. Clinton E. Stockwell, "A Sketch of the Church's Urban Ministry, 1620–1990, with Particular Reference to Chicago," 1991, 7.

52. "School for a New Creation," *Time*, Friday, November 19, 1965.

53. Ibid.

54. Several such organizations, including the United Packinghouse Workers, Saul Alinsky's Woodlawn Organization, and the Westside Organization, united under the banner of the Coordinating Council of Community Organizations, or CCCO. The CCCO, directed by Al Raby, had first emerged out of the local fight against school and housing segregation, a struggle that had led in 1961 to the NAACP suing the Chicago School Board over racially discriminatory policies and, over the next year, to a number of public demonstrations related to the suit. The Chicago Urban League, the NAACP, the Parent-Teacher Associations, and other groups involved in the fight pooled their resources and formed the CCCO, which led to a series of school boycotts and public protests throughout 1963 and 1964. For more, see Gordon K. Mantler, "Black, Brown, and Poor: Martin Luther King Jr., the Poor People's Campaign and Its Legacies," PhD diss., Duke University, Department of History, 2008, 72–74. Raby invited King to Chicago in 1965 in the hopes that his presence would provide an additional spark to a movement that despite numerous rallies and public demonstrations had accomplished little in terms of actual change. Ewell J. Reagin, "Footnotes," *Chicago SIM Newsletter*, no. 1, July 18, 1966, 2, SIM, UTS, 2B:1:f1. Reagin was a graduate student at the University of Chicago Divinity School and an early volunteer in the Chicago Freedom Movement.

55. Bevel had been a part of the Nashville sit-in movement and an early SNCC stalwart before shifting to the SCLC in 1961 and playing a key role in organizing the voting rights movement in Selma. Bevel served as project director of the Westside Christian Parish, an inner-city ecumenical church project based on the East Harlem Protestant Parish, and used the congregation as a launching pad for the Chicago Freedom Movement.

56. See profiles of James Bevel and Bernard Lafayette Jr. on the Chicago Freedom Movement's "Fulfilling the Dream" website, http://sites.middlebury.edu/chicago-freedommovement/. Lafayette became the director of the Poor People's Campaign in 1968.

57. Reagin, "Footnotes."

58. Bruce D. Christie, "Early Reflections on the Chicago Movement," *Chicago SIM Newsletter*, no. 1, July 18, 1966, 4, SIM, UTS, 2B:1:f1.

59. Mantler, "Black, Brown, and Poor," 79.

60. *Chicago SIM Newsletter*, no. 2, August 8, 1966, 5; *Chicago SIM Newsletter*, no. 4, September 1, 1966, 3, SIM, UTS, 2B:1:f1.

61. Reagin, "Footnotes."

62. Branch, *At Cannan's Edge*, 511, quoting *Jet*, August 25, 1966.

63. Bruce D. Christie, "Early Reflections on the Chicago Movement," in *Chicago SIM Newsletter*, no. 1, July 18, 1966, 5, SIM, UTS, 2B:1:f1. Modeled on an early 1930s-era trade union, the union organized each slum building, with each building represented by a union steward, each block by a chief steward, and each ten blocks organized into a local union. The seminarians wrote that the slum union structure served two purposes—to provide a ready channel through which tenants could file grievances and band together, and to provide "a ready army for mass movement."

64. John Fike, "EGPCO: Where Is It and Where Is It Headed?" *Chicago Urban Project Newsletter*, no. 1, July 13, 1967, 3, SIM,UTS, 2B:1:f1.

65. Branch, *At Canaan's Edge*, 521–22.

66. "1966 Report: Student Interracial Ministry," 65.

67. Ibid.

68. Aram Goudsouzian, *Down to the Crossroads: Civil Rights, Black Power and the Meredith March Against Fear* (New York: MacMillan, 2014), 246–47.

69. George Walters, "The Mississippi Freedom March and Issues Raised for the Movement," 8, copy in possession of George Walters.

70. James H. Cone, *Black Theology and Black Power*, 8th ed. (Maryknoll, NY: Orbis Books, 2006), 5; Peniel E. Joseph, ed., *The Black Power Movement: Rethinking the Civil Rights–Black Power Era* (New York: Routledge, 2006), 1.

71. Stokely Carmichael with Ekwueme Michael Thelwell, *Ready for Revolution: The Life and Struggles of Stokely Carmichael (Kwame Ture)* (New York: Scribner, 2003), 507.

72. Stokely Carmichael obituary, *New York Times*, November 16, 1998, http://www.nytimes.com/1998/11/16/us/stokely-carmichael-rights-leader-who-coined-black-power-dies-at-57.html?pagewanted=all.

73. George Walters, oral history interview with author, June 2006.

74. Bill Troy, oral history interview with author, October 5, 2009.

75. M. George Walters, oral history interview with author, October 23, 2006.

76. "SIM in the Urban Situation," 2, SIM, UTS, 1C:2:f13.

77. "National Committee, Student Interracial Ministry: Summary of Discussion on Aims and Purposes," March 10–11, 1967, New York, 1, SIM, UTS, 1B:1:f10.

78. "Summary of Discussion on Aims and Purposes," March 10–11, 1967.

79. "1966 Report: Student Interracial Ministry," 76; Larry Blackman, "Black Power Reconsidered," i–26.

80. "SIM in the Urban Situation," 2, SIM, UTS, 1C:2:f13.

81. Ibid., 2.

82. Ibid., 3.

83. "Sim Launches 1967–1968 Program," 2.

84. "Advertisement," *skandalon* 1 (Fall 1966): 17.

85. "Accent on Responsibility: Student Interracial Ministry Prospectus," 2, SIM, UTS, 1G:1:f3.

86. "1966 Report: Student Interracial Ministry," 45–67.

87. Charles Sherrod, oral history interview with author, June 8, 2009.

88. Kimrey, "Black Revolution and White Revolutionaries," 4. A year after writing that, however, Kimrey had rejected his own advice and was back to working on an interracial project, this time with SIM's new urban project in Richmond, California.

89. "'Black Power:' Statement by National Committee of Negro Churchmen," *New York Times*, July 31, 1966, E5.

90. Ibid.

91. George E. Riddick, "Black Power: A Christian Response," 1966, SIM, UTS.

92. Findlay, *Church People in the Struggle*, 4, 202.

93. Bayard Rustin, "'Black Power' and Coalition Politics," *Commentary* 2 (September 1966).

94. Joseph, *The Black Power Movement*, 4.

95. Maynard Moore, oral history with author, December 20, 2006.

96. Tim Kimrey, "Black Revolution and White Revolutionaries," in Union Theological Seminary Field Education Interns' writing packet, 1966, 3. Possession of Mac Hulslander.

97. M. George Walters, "Black Power and the Church," *skandalon* 1 (1966), SIM, UTS, 2A:1:f9.

98. *Renewal*, August 1966, 2.

99. Editorial Comment, *Renewal*, August 1966, 2.

100. George Walters, oral history interview with author, October 23, 2006.

101. Pfister, oral history, November 29, 2006.

102. "Accent on Possibility: Student Interracial Ministry Prospectus 1967," 8–9.

103. Robert Bruce Slater, "White Professors at Black Colleges," *Journal of Blacks in Higher Education* 1 (Autumn 1993): 67.

104. Monro, John U. "Black Studies, White Teachers, and Black Colleges." *Teaching Forum* 3, no. 3 (April 1970), http://files.eric.ed.gov/fulltext/ED097812.pdf.

105. C. Tom Ross, "My Year as an Atlanta College Intern: Success and Failure (Final Report)," 6–7.

106. "Atlanta College Intern Project," *1966 Report: Student Interracial Ministry*, 75.

107. "1966 Report: Student Interracial Ministry," 76; Larry Blackman, "Black Power Reconsidered," i–26.

108. Charles F. Hinkle, "Atlanta College Intern Project" Report, July 17, 1967, UTS papers, 4A.1.13.

109. Carl F. Burke. *God Is for Real, Man* (New York: Association Press, 1966); John A. T. Robinson, *Honest to God* (New York: Westminster Press, 1963).

110. C. Tom Ross, "My Year as an Atlanta College Intern: Success and Failure (Final Report)," 1–8; Charles F. Hinkle, "Atlanta College Intern Project" Report, July 17, 1967, UTS papers, 4A.1.13.

111. "1965 Report: Student Interracial Ministry," 21, SIM, UTS, 1C:2:f11.

112. Letter for G.W. Webber, March 9, 1966 SIM, UTS, 1C:2:f11.

113. E. Maynard Moore, "Report to the SIM National Committee," September 1, 1967, 2, SIM, UTS, 1A:2:f6.

114. "Student Interracial Ministry: Executive Committee Minutes," January 23, 1967, 3; February 14, 1967, 1, SIM, UTS, 2:1:f1.

115. Frances S. Smith, "Women and Renewal: A Survey," *Renewal* 4, no. 7 (October 1964): 13; "Just Thinking Doesn't Count," Depth Education Group listing in Process '67 registration materials, University Christian Movement Archives, RG 235, Series IV Conferences, 30:386.

116. "National Committee Summary of Discussion on Aims and Purposes," March 10–11, 1967, 2, SIM, UTS, 2:1:f1.

117. Marvin Dunn, oral history telephone interview with author, November 29, 2008.

118. Dunn, oral history interview, November 29, 2008.

119. "Chicago Metropolitan Project of the Student Interracial Ministry," SIM, UTS, 4B.1, 1.

120. "Chicago Metropolitan Project," 2.

121. Benjamin Ross, "Congregation-Based Organizing," *Tikkun* 22, no. 1 (January/ February 2007): 55.

122. Peter Kamuyu, "The School for Human Dignity," *Chicago Urban Project Newsletter*, no. 1, July 13, 1967, 2–3; George Hahn, "More on Woodlawn's School," *Chicago Urban Project Newsletter*, no. 1, July 13, 1967, 5–6.

123. Fike, "EGPCO," 3, SIM, UTS, 2B:1:f1.

124. This individual had been arrested with Stumme, Dunn, and other Garfield members earlier that year, thus gaining entrée to the group.

125. Dunn, oral history interview, November 29, 2008. Dunn's focus shifted away from the ministry and toward more general sociological interests. Prior to pursuing a PhD in sociology, he spent nine months of 1968 and 1969 in a Volkswagen van with a group of a dozen Methodist seminarians, traveling to Bolivia and Brazil to study the church and social change, the first stirrings of the liberation theology movement.

126. "Accent on Possibility," 12.

127. "Report on SIM Project, Borough of Richmond," 7.

128. "Commitment to Change," E. Maynard Moore collection, possession of E. Maynard Moore, loaned to the author.

129. "Report of Gesner Montes, June–August 1967," SIM, UTS, 6:8:5.

130. "Commitment to Change."

131. "Atlanta Urban Project Report," August 22, 1967, 1.

132. "Commitment to Change."

133. "Atlanta Urban Project Report," August 22, 1967, 2, 4.

134. "Accent on Possibility," 52.

135. Moore, "Report to the SIM National Committee."

136. Ibid.; Moore, "The Story of the Student Interracial Ministry: An Experiment That Worked."

137. E. Maynard Moore, "Report to the SIM National Committee," September 1, 1967, 2, SIM, UTS, 1G:1:f2.

138. "Conversations on Revolution," *National Catholic Reporter*, February 28, 1968, 5.

139. M. George Walters, "Black Power and the Church," *skandalon* 1 (Fall 1966), SIM, UTS, 2A:1:f9.

140. W. Marshall Jones, "The Revolutional Church," *skandalon* 7 (Winter 1967): 2, SIM, UTS, 2A:1:f9.

141. Edward A. Feaver, "The Death of Religion and the Rebirth of the Church: An Introduction," *skandalon* 2 (Winter 1967): 3, SIM, UTS, 2A:1:f9.

142. Jim Romberg, "A Question of Virginity," *skandalon* 4 (Summer 1967): 9, Mac Hulslander papers, copy in possession of author.

Chapter Six

1. Van Gosse, "A Movement of Movements: The Definition and Periodization of the New Left," in *A Companion to Post-1945 America*, ed. Jean-Christophe Agnew and Roy Rosenzweig (Malden, MA: Blackwell, 2002).

2. Christopher Queen, "Student Initiated Change in Theological Schools," in *Ministry in the Seventies*, ed. John Biersdorf, (New York: IDOC, 1971), 17.

3. David Langston and William McKeown, *The Student Movement at Union Theological Seminary, 1963–1969* (New York: National Council of Churches, Department of Ministry, 1971), 23.

4. Union Theological Seminary Timeline, 1960–1979, http://www.utsnyc.edu /NETCOMMUNITY/Page.aspx?&pid=760, accessed on June 16, 2008.

5. Langston and McKeown, *The Student Movement*, 1–2; Leon Howell, "Ethical Engagement—Theologian John Coleman Bennett" (obituary), *Christian Century*, May 24, 1995.

6. Langston and McKeown, *The Student Movement*, 3–6.

7. Ibid.

8. *Southwest Georgia Project Newsletter*, October 9, 1966, no. 6, 3, 1–2, SIM, UTS, 2B:1:f4.

9. Rooks, "Crisis in Theological Education," 16.

10. Ibid., 17.

11. W. E. B. DuBois, *The Souls of Black Folk* (1903; repr., New York: Barnes and Noble, 2003), 165, as quoted in Rooks, "Crisis in Theological Education," 18.

12. Rooks, "Crisis in Theological Education," 18.

13. Robert T. Handy, *A History of Union Theological Seminary in New York* (New York: Columbia University Press, 1987), 265.

14. Marvin Dunn, oral history interview with author, November 11, 2008.

15. Jesse H. Ziegler, *ATS [the Association of Theological Schools] through Two Decades: Reflections on Theological Education, 1960–1980* (Vandalia, OH: self-published, 1984), 17.

16. Ziegler, *ATS through Two Decades*, 18.

17. Untitled 1967–68 planning document, SIM, UTS, 2:1:f5.

18. Queen, "Student Initiated Change in Theological Schools," 48, 17.

19. Jon DeVries, "Bound," *skandalon* 4 (Summer 1967): 4–5.

20. Ibid.

21. Peter V. Levy, "The Dream Deferred: The Assassination of Martin Luther King, Jr., and the Holy Week Uprisings of 1968," in *Baltimore '68: Riots and Rebirth in an American City*, ed. Jessica L. Effenbein, Thomas L. Hollowak, and Elizabeth M. Nix (Philadelphia: Temple University Press, 2011).

22. Maxim K. Rice, correspondence with author, April 14, 2016.

23. Roy Birchard, "Journal of Roy Birchard, Lincoln University, September 22, 1967–May 31, 1968," 21, Special Collections, Langston Hughes Memorial Library, Lincoln University, Lincoln University, Pennsylvania.

24. Ibid., 4.

25. Ibid., 195.

26. F. Eric Brooks and Glenn L. Starks, *Historically Black Colleges and Universities: An Encyclopedia* (Santa Barbara: Greenwood, 2011), 175.

27. Birchard, "Journal of Roy Birchard," 195.

28. Ibid., 190.

29. Queen, "Student Initiated Change in Theological Schools," 48–49.

30. Handy, *A History of Union Theological Seminary*, 274.

31. Ibid.

32. Ibid.; Langston, email to author. Pellegrom is the long-time director of Pathfinder International, a not-for-profit reproductive health organization.

33. "Statement Adopted Mar 1, 1968 to Support the Columbia Strike," Appendix, 5.

34. Per David Langston, December 6, 2016.

35. Lee Bailey, "Editorial," *The Tower: Union Theological Seminary Alumni Magazine*, Fall 1968, 2.

36. Queen, Biersdorf, ed. *Ministry in the Seventies* (New York: IDOC, 1971), 17.

37. Rooks, "Crisis in Theological Education," 17.

38. Charles L. Taylor, "Sources of Renewal," *Theological Education*, Winter 1967, 319–20.

39. Rooks, "Crisis in Theological Education," 19.

40. "Is God Dead?" *Time*, April 8, 1966. The movement's foremost practitioner, Thomas J. J. Altizer, a professor of religion at Emory University, claimed that God had died during our own historical period—for how could a living God tolerate the condition of the world. According to him, this did not undermine the fundamental truths inherent in Christianity.

41. Susanne Langer, *Philosophical Sketches* (New York: Mentor Books, 1964), 141.

42. Jeffrey O. G. Ogbar, *Black Power: Radical Politics and African American Identity* (Baltimore: Johns Hopkins University Press, 2004), 2.

43. James H. Cone, *Black Theology and Black Power*, 8th ed. (Maryknoll, NY: Orbis Books, 2006), 1.

44. Historical Note, Guide to the Student Christian Federation Archives, RG 247, Yale Divinity Library, Yale University, New Haven, CT.

45. Historical Note, Student Christian Federation, Yale.

46. Ibid.; Historical Note, Guide to the University Christian Movement Archives, RG 235, Yale Divinity Library, Yale University, New Haven, CT.

47. Historical Note, UCM. Yale.

48. Lincoln Richardson, "3,000 Students at Cleveland: The Process Is the Purpose?" *Presbyterian Life*, February 1, 1968, 23; "An Official Non-Report on the Cleveland Week of Process '67," 4, UCM, Yale.

49. "Process '67: The Cleveland Week" pamphlet, UCM, Yale.

50. "Just Thinking Doesn't Count," Depth Education Group listing in Process '67 registration materials, UCM, Yale.

51. Isaac H. Bivens, "Cleveland and Urbana—UCM and IVCF," January 1968, UCM, Yale.

52. Charles M. Savage, "Reflections on Cleveland in the Style of Process '67," UCM, Yale.

53. "An Ecumenical Community of Students: Archival Documentation of Worldwide Student Christian Movements," Yale University Libraries exhibit, June–October 2014; Historical Note, UCM, Yale.

54. "Minutes of National InterSeminary Council," April 21–22, 1967, E. Maynard Moore collection, possession of E. Maynard Moore, loaned to the author.

55. Martin E. Marty, "Response to Professor Cox—II," *Theological Education*, Winter 1967, 281.

56. "The Transition Model Seminary: A Project Proposal for SIM," SIM, UTS, 1G:1:f7, f8.

57. Transitional Model Seminary planning document, untitled, undated, SIM, UTS, 1G:1:f7, f8.

58. "A Proposal for a Transition Model One Year Seminary Aimed at Having a Revolutionary Impact upon the Seminaries for Their Restructuring and for the Redefinition of the Nature and Purpose of Theological Education"; "The Transition Model Seminary: A Project Proposal for SIM," SIM, UTS, 1G:1:f7, f8.

59. "The Transition Model Seminary: A Project Proposal for SIM," SIM, UTS, 1G:1:f7, f8.

60. Ibid.; "Working Papers on Theological Education," 2, SIM, UTS, 1G:1:f7, f8.

61. Letter of July 12, 1966, from Maynard Moore to Bruce Birch, E. Maynard Moore collection, possession of E. Maynard Moore, loaned to the author.

62. Correspondence regarding consultation at Notre Dame, E. Maynard Moore collection, possession of E. Maynard Moore, loaned to the author.

63. "Working Papers on Theological Education," 2, SIM, UTS, 1G:1:f7, f8.

64. Ibid.

65. Walters drew on the ideas in this working paper for an article in *skandalon*, and Maynard Moore would package many of the working paper ideas in his journal article, "Theological Education for a Revolutional Church"; "The Transition Model Seminary," 1G:1:f8, 1C.2.F6.

66. Letter from Maynard Moore to Steve Rose, February 26, 1967.

67. "Working Papers on Theological Education," 4.

68. The working paper itself does not seem to have survived but what has is the *skandalon* article, a series of press releases supporting the working paper and the magazine issue's publication, reading lists for further study, and several drafts of a proposal, apparently based on the working document and ensuing discussions, for "A Transition Model One Year Seminary Aimed at Having a Revolutionary Impact upon the Seminaries for Their Restructuring and for the Redefinition of the Nature and Purposes of Theological Education." (In the later draft, this title was shortened to "The Transition Model Seminary: A Project Proposal for SIM.") George Walters, Douglas Renick, James Crawford, John F. Chappell, and Wayne Marshall Jones, "A Transition Model One Year Seminary Aimed at Having a Revolutionary Impact upon the Seminaries for Their Restructuring and for the Redefinition of the Nature and Purposes of Theological Education," SIM, UTS, 4B.1:f2.

69. M. George Walters, "Theological Education: Crisis and Task," *skandalon* 3 (Spring 1967): 8. SIM, UTS, 2A:1:f10.

70. Untitled 1967–68 planning document, SIM, UTS, 2:1:f5.

71. "A Prescription for Seminaries," *Theological Education*, Winter 1968, 629–31.

72. The recognition of the pastoral role of the laity and the demystification of the ultimate authority of the pastor were fodder for numerous sermons, speeches, journal articles, and books during the latter years of the 1960s and into the 1970s. Reuel L. Howe's 1967 *Partners in Preaching* is representative of the genre, but it is only one of many. Reuel L. Howe, *Partners in Preaching: Clergy and Laity in Dialogue* (New York: Seabury Press, 1967). See also Glenn Richard Bucher and Patricia Ruth Hill, eds., *Confusion and Hope: Clergy, Laity and the Church in Transition* (Philadelphia: Fortress Press, 1974). Howe was the director of the Institute of Advanced Pastoral Studies, and the book is based on his Princeton Seminary Alumni Lectures, delivered in 1965. Howe maintains that the church need not go out into the world because it is already in the world, encourages the translation of word into action, decries the "monological" nature of the typical sermon, and recommends its replacement by "dialogical preaching" that involves both the professional clergyperson and the laity. According to Howe, one cannot discuss the church's mission in the world or call

for its reform without recognizing and also reforming the role of laity, for the laity are "the true ministers of the church because they live in the world where the church's mission is." The professional, parish-based minister's job is to train the laity and direct them as they disperse this ministry. Howe added that the means by which the laity would be "trained" to minister in the world needed to be created, but that the development of such a strategy should come from within the church because "we can longer afford to leave this part of the church's ministry to chance" (Howe, 109, 103).

73. "A Prescription for Seminaries," 631–32.

74. E. Maynard Moore, "Theological Education for a Revolutional Church," *Theological Education* 4, no. 2 (Winter 1968): 609.

75. Ibid., 605, 608.

76. Ibid., 605–7. Emphasis in original.

77. E. Maynard Moore, "Student Interracial Ministry Evidences Concern for Reform in Theological Education," 1. E. Maynard Moore collection, possession of E. Maynard Moore, loaned to the author.

78. Ibid., 2.

79. John C. Bennett, "Theological Education and Social Revolution," *Theological Education* 3, no. 2 (Winter 1967): 286–87.

80. Handy, *A History of Union Theological Seminary*, 260–62. Quotations from *Union Seminary Quarterly Review* 19, no. 4, pt. 2 (May 1964): 406–7.

81. John C. Bennet, "Theological Education and Social Revolution," 289.

82. Ibid., 286, 289.

83. Handy, *A History of Union Theological Seminary*, 260–62.

84. John E. Biersdorf, "Issues in Theological Education, November 1966, 1, SIM, UTS, 8:2:f9.

85. Richard Shaull, "Response to President Bennett—I," *Theological Education*, Winter 1967, 291, 293; Harvey Cox, "The Significance of the Church-World Dialogue for Theological Education," *Theological Education*, Winter 1967, 272.

86. Cox, "The Significance of the Church-World Dialogue," 272.

87. Handy, *A History of Union Theological Seminary*, 273.

88. Ibid., 274.

89. Langston and McKeown, *The Student Movement at Union*, 274.

90. "Notice of Free University Classes," Langston and McKeowen, *The Student Movement at Union*, Appendix, item 7.

91. "Radical Caucus Statement," May 6, 1968, Langston and McKeowen, *The Student Movement at Union*, Appendix, item 8.

92. Langston and McKeowen, *The Student Movement at Union*, 13–14.

93. Ibid., 7–8.

94. Ibid., 13.

95. "Document from the Free University Task Force on the Reorganization of Educational Process, Task Force II: a Theology of Theological Education," Langston and McKeowen, *The Student Movement at Union*, Appendix, Item 9.

96. Jeffrey Rowthorn, "The CORE Experiment: Independent Synthesis for BDs," *Tower*, Fall 1968, 9.

97. "Memorandum from Student-Faculty Committee on Core Experimental Program," July 26, 1968, 1–3. Possession of David Langston, copy provided to author.

98. Handy, *A History of Union Theological Seminary*, 276.

99. Rowthorn, "The CORE Experiment," 9.

100. Ibid., 10.

101. Langston, e-mail to author.

102. Handy, *A History of Union Theological Seminary*, 276.

103. Langston and McKeowen, *The Student Movement at Union*, Appendix, Item 10.

104. Handy, *A History of Union Theological Seminary*, 291.

105. Ibid., 292.

106. Black National Economic Conference, "Black Manifesto," *New York Review of Books*, July 10, 1969.

107. Thomas J. Sugrue, *Sweet Land of Liberty: The Forgotten Struggle for Civil Rights in the North* (New York: Random House, 2008), 437; Lawrence H. Williams, "Christianity and Reparations: Revisiting James Forman's 'Black Manifesto,' 1969," *Currents in Theology and Mission*, February 2005.

108. "A Black Manifesto," *Time*, May 16, 1969.

109. Sugrue, *Sweet Land of Liberty*, 436.

110. Quoted in Sugrue, *Sweet Land of Liberty*, 436.

111. Charles Eric Lincoln, *Race, Religion, and the Continuing American Dilemma* (New York: Hill and Wang, 1984), 112.

112. Stephen C. Rose, "Putting It to the Churches: Reparations for Blacks?" *New Republic*, June 21, 1969, 19–20.

113. Per e-mail correspondence between author and David Langston, November 26, 2008.

114. Handy, *A History of Union Theological Seminary*, 281–82.

115. John C. Bennett, "Union Theological Seminary Commencement Address," May 20, 1969; Langston and McKeowen, *The Student Movement at Union*, Appendix, Item 16.

116. Amy Kedron, in "Freedom, Reparations and the Black Manifesto," citing the *National Catholic Reporter* estimate that churches contributed about $127 million.

117. The donated amounts are per Jerry K. Frye, "The 'Black Manifesto' and the Tactic of Objectification," *Journal of Black Studies* 5, no. 1 (September 1974): 68–69, quoting sources including *Christian Century, Commonweal, Christianity Today, Time*, and R. S. Lecky and H. E. Wright, eds. *Black Manifesto: Religion, Racism, and Reparations* (New York: Sheed & Ward, 1969).

118. The Riverside Church Congregational Profile, http://www.theriversidechurchny.org/about/?minister-emeritus, accessed on April 19, 2016.

119. Ibid.; Amy Kedron, "Freedom, Reparations and the Black Manifesto," http://www.reparationsthecure.org/Articles/Kedron/BlackManifesto, accessed November 18, 2008; Sugrue, *Sweet Land of Liberty*, 436.

120. Stephen C. Rose, "Reparation Now!," *Renewal* 9, no. 6 (June 1969): 14.

121. Rose, oral history, September 28, 2009.

122. Ibid.; Steve Rose, "Jonathan's Wake—a Personal Reflection," *Triadic Philosophy* (blog), accessed September 9, 2009, http://shortformcontent.blogspot.com/2012/05/jonathans-wake-personal-reflection.html.

123. "Union Finds a President," *Time*, April 13, 1970.

124. "The State of Union," *Time*, October 9, 1972.

125. Handy, *A History of Union Theological Seminary*, 269, 291–92.

126. Financial Report from Maynard Moore to SIM Project Directors, July 3, 1967, SIM, UTS, 1B:1:f10.

127. Letter to SIM students from Maynard Moore and George Walters, June 30, 1967, SIM, UTS, 1B:1:f10.

128. "Summary of SIM Procedures," 1967, SIM, UTS, 1A:2:f6.

129. E. Maynard Moore, "Report to the National Committee," September 1, 1967, SIM, UTS, 1B:1:f10.

130. Ibid.

131. Letter from Maynard Moore to Marshall Jones, October 20, 1967, E. Maynard Moore collection, possession of E. Maynard Moore, loaned to the author.

132. Ed Feaver, letter to SIM alumni dated October 21, 1967, SIM, UTS, 1A:2:f12.

133. Letter from Ed Ruen to project directors and the National Committee of SIM, undated, E. Maynard Moore collection, possession of E. Maynard Moore, loaned to the author.

134. Ibid.

135. Ibid.

136. John Stumme, "log" entries for September 28, 1967, and June 6, 1968. Possession of John Stumme, Chicago, IL.

137. Letter from Maynard Moore to Frank Wright, September 18, 1967; Letter from Maynard Moore to Marshall Jones, October 20, 1967, E. Maynard Moore collection, possession of E. Maynard Moore, loaned to the author.

138. Ralph E. Luker, *The Social Gospel in Black and White: American Racial Reform, 1885–1912*, 2nd ed. (Chapel Hill: University of North Carolina Press, 1998).

139. Michael Brooks Friedland, *Lift Up Your Voice Like a Trumpet: White Clergy and the Civil Rights and Antiwar Movements, 1954–1973* (Chapel Hill: University of North Carolina Press, 1998). In *God's Long Summer: Stories of Faith and Civil Rights* (Princeton, NJ: Princeton University Press, 1999), 8, Charles Marsh argues that Black Power "killed" the beloved community ideal.

140. E. Maynard Moore, letter announcing formation of SIM Alumni Committee, September 30, 1967, SIM, UTS, 1A:2:f6.

Afterword

1. Pfister, oral history, November 15, 2006.

2. Ibid.

3. Walters, "Theological Education: Crisis and Task," *skandalon* 3 (Spring 1967): 7. SIM, UTS, 2A:1:f10.

4. Charles C. West, "Introduction," in Lehtonen, *Story of a Storm*, xvi.

5. Walters, "Theological Education: Crisis and Task," *skandalon* 3 (Winter 1967): 7.

6. Joe Pfister, "Building: Long Range Style," *skandalon* 4 (Fall 1967): 12. SIM, UTS, 2A:1:f10.

7. John C. Bennett, "The Great Controversy in the Churches: A Sermon Preached at New York's Riverside Church on April 12," *The Christian Century* 87, no. 21 (May 27, 1970) 662.

8. King, "The Letter from Birmingham Jail."

Bibliography

Manuscript Collections

King Papers, State Historical Society of Wisconsin, Madison, Wisconsin.
Lincoln University Archives of PA, Langston Hughes Memorial Library, Lincoln University, Pennsylvania.
Martin Luther King Jr. Paper Project, Stanford University, Palo Alto, California.
SNCC Legacy Project, Duke University Libraries, Duke University, Durham, North Carolina.
Southern Folklife Collection, Wilson Library, University of North Carolina at Chapel Hill.
Southern Historical Collection (SHC), Wilson Library, University of North Carolina at Chapel Hill.
Southern Oral History Program (SOHP), Southern Historical Collection, Wilson Library, University of North Carolina at Chapel Hill.
Student Interracial Ministry papers (SIM, UTS), 1960–1968, The Burke Library Archives at Union Theological Seminary, New York, New York.
Student Non-Violent Coordinating Committee (SNCC) Papers, 1959–1972. Microfilm. University of North Carolina at Chapel Hill.
University Christian Movement, Record Group No. 235, Yale University Library, Divinity Library Special Collections, New Haven, Connecticut.
World Student Christian Federation, Record Group No. 46/4, Yale University Library, Divinity Library Special Collections, New Haven, Connecticut.

Newspapers and Magazines

Albany Herald (Albany, Georgia)
Aspire (Albany State University, Albany, Georgia)
Atlantic
Chapel Hill Herald
Chapel Hill Weekly
Chicago's American
Christian Century
Christian Science Monitor
Christianity and Crisis
Chronicle of Higher Education
Church History
Commentary
Commonweal
Currents in Theology and Mission
Durham Morning Herald
Esquire
Evening Independent (St. Petersburg, Florida)
Grain of Salt (Union Theological Seminary)
Independent Weekly (Durham, North Carolina)
Interracial News Service

Interseminarian
Jet
Kansas City Star
Lutheran
Methodist Woman
Nashville Tennessean
Nation
National Catholic Reporter
National Review
New York Review of Books
New York Times
Other Side: Southwest Georgia News
 (Albany, Georgia)
Philadelphia Inquirer
Playboy
Presbyterian Life
Raleigh News and Observer

Renewal
skandalon (Student Interracial Ministry,
 Union Theological Seminary)
Social Policy
Southern Patriot
Sports Illustrated
Theological Education
Theology Today
Tikkun
Time
The Tower: Union Theological Seminary
 Alumni Magazine
U.S. News & World Report
Wall Street Journal
Warren Record (Warrenton, North
 Carolina)
Wilmington Journal

Oral Histories by Author

Dave Campbell, June 7, 2009, Albany, Georgia.
Robert Carey, November 6, 2015, by telephone.
John Chappell, December 15, 2008, Carthage, North Carolina.
John Collins. December 5, 2006, Long Island, New York.
Barbara Cox, November 24, 2009, by telephone.
Jon DeVries, June 6, 2009, Albany, Georgia.
Marvin Dunn, November 29, 2008, by telephone.
Hank Elkins, November 9, 2015, by telephone.
Ed Feaver, August 3, 2008, by telephone.
Otis Flournoy, August 27, 2007, by telephone.
James Forbes, February 15, 2008, by telephone.
Franklin "Chris" Gamwell, December 4, 2009, by telephone.
Robert Hare, November 19, 2009, by telephone; November 23, 2009, by telephone.
Charles Helms, November 30, 2009, by telephone.
Joe Howell, November 27, 2006, Washington, D.C.
Mac Hulslander, July 1, 2008, Raleigh, North Carolina.
Vann Joines, December 10, 2009, Chapel Hill, North Carolina.
Collins Kilburn, October 13, 2009, Chapel Hill, North Carolina.
Ralph Luker, November 4, 2005, Atlanta, Georgia.
Larry Mamiya, June 6, 2009, Albany, Georgia.
George McClain, July 10, 2007, by telephone.
Oscar McCloud, December 9, 2006, by telephone.

E. Maynard Moore, December 20, 2005, Rockville, Maryland; July 1, 2008, Rockville, Maryland; November 29, 2008, Rockville, Maryland.

Joe Pfister, November 15, 2006; November 29, 2006, Butner, North Carolina.

Stephen C. Rose, August 20, 2007, New York, New York; September 21, 2009, by telephone; September 28, 2009, by telephone.

Robert Seymour, February 22, 2005, Chapel Hill, North Carolina.

Charles Sherrod, June 8, 2009, Albany, Georgia.

John Stumme, December 9, 2008, by telephone.

Bill Troy, October 5, 2009, by telephone; November 2, 2009, by telephone.

M. George Walters, October 23, 2006, Tampa, Florida; October 24, 2006, Tampa, Florida.

Other Oral Histories

Will D. Campbell, oral history with Kieran W. Taylor, November 17, 1996. SOHP.

Robert Carey and Patricia Carey with Robert Fass, undated. longmarriedcouples .com.

William Minter, oral history with Kieran W. Taylor, November 17, 1996. SOHP.

Robert Seymour, oral history with Bruce Kalk, May 21, 1985. SOHP.

Charles Sherrod, oral history with Taylor Branch, October 7, 1985. SHC.

Roger Shinn, oral history with Eileen Crowly-Horak, 1999. Union Seminary Archive.

Jane Stembridge, oral history with Pete Daniel, December 5, 1996; September 17, 1997. SOHP.

Websites

The American Presidency Project, http://www.presidency.ucsb.edu.

Martin Luther King, Jr. Papers Project, Stanford University, *www.stanford.edu/group /King/frequentdocs.*

Perspectives: An Online Publication of the Office of the General Assembly of the Presbyterian Church, U.S.A., http://www.pcusa.org/oga/perspectives/.

Books and Articles

Adams, Frank T. *James A. Dombrowski: An American Heretic, 1897–1983.* Knoxville: University of Tennessee Press, 1992.

Agnew, Jean-Christophe, and Roy Rosenzweig, eds. *A Companion to Post-1945 America.* Malden, MA: Blackwell, 2002.

Albanese, Catherine L. *America: Religions and Religion.* 4th ed. Belmont, CA: Thomson/Wadsworth, 2007.

Allport, Gordon. *The Nature of Prejudice.* Cambridge, MA: Addison-Wesley, 1954.

Alpert, Rebecca T. *Voices of the Religious Left: A Contemporary Sourcebook*. Philadelphia: Temple University Press, 2000.

Altizer, Thomas J. J. "Is God Dead?" *Time*, April 8, 1966.

Anderson, Jean Bradley. *Durham County: A History of Durham County, North Carolina*. Durham: Duke University Press, 1990.

Ashmore, Harry S. *The Other Side of Jordan*. New York: Norton, 1960.

Baldwin, James. *Blues for Mister Charlie*. New York: Dell, 1964.

————. *The Fire Next Time*. New York: Dell, 1963.

Bardoph, Richard. *The Negro Vanguard*. Westport: Negro Universities Press, 1959.

Bass, Dorothy C., Benton Johnson, and Wade Clark Roof. *Mainstream Protestantism in the Twentieth Century: Its Problems and Prospects*. Philadelphia: Presbyterian Church (USA), 1986.

Bell, Inge Powell. *CORE and the Strategy of Non-violence*. New York: Random House, 1968.

Benedict, Ruth. *Race: Science and Politics*. New York: Viking Press, 1959.

Bennet, David H. *The Party of Fear: From Nativist Movements to the New Right in American History*. Chapel Hill: University of North Carolina Press, 1988.

Bennett, John C. "The Great Controversy in the Churches: A Sermon Preached at New York's Riverside Church on April 12." *Christian Century*, May 1970.

————. "Theological Education and Social Revolution." *Theological Education* 3, no. 2 (Winter 1967).

Berryman, Phillip. *Liberation Theology: Essential Facts about the Revolutionary Religious Movement in Latin America and Beyond*. New York: Pantheon Books, 1987.

Biersdorf, John, ed. *Ministry in the Seventies*. New York: IDOC, 1971.

Billingsly, K. L. *From Mainline to Sideline: The Social Witness of the National Council of Churches*. Lanham, MD: University Press of America, 1990.

Biondi, Martha. *To Stand and Fight: The Struggle for Civil Rights in Postwar New York City*. Cambridge, MA: Harvard University Press, 2003.

Bivins, Jason. *The Fracture of Good Order: Christian Anti-Liberalism and the Challenge to American Politics*. Chapel Hill: University of North Carolina Press, 2003.

Blakeney, Barney. "Remember the Rev. Willis T. Goodwin: Friend to the Poor." *Charleston City Paper*, December 26, 2007.

Bonhoeffer, Dietrich. *Prisoner for God: Letters and Papers from Prison*. Edited by Eberhard Bethge. 1953. Rev. ed., New York: Macmillan, 1967.

Booty, John E. *Mission and Ministry: A History of Virginia Theological Seminary*. Harrisburg, PA: Morehouse, 1995.

Botson, Michael R., Jr. *Labor, Civil Rights, and the Hughes Tool Company*. College Station: Texas A&M University Press, 2005.

Boyd, Malcolm. *Are You Running with Me, Jesus?* New York: Avon Books, 1965.

————. "The Ecumenical Freedom Body: A Call to the People." *Renewal*, February 1966.

————. *Free to Live, Free to Die*. New York: Signet, 1967.

Branch, Taylor. *At Canaan's Edge: America in the King Years: 1965–68*. New York: Simon & Schuster, 2006.

———. *Parting the Waters: America in the King Years: 1954–63*. New York: Simon & Schuster, 1989.

———. *Pillar of Fire: America in the King Years: 1964–66*. New York: Simon & Schuster, 1998.

Brewster, Gurdon. *No Turning Back: My Summer with Daddy King*. Maryknoll, NY: Orbis Books, 2007.

Brinkley, Alan. "The Problem of American Conservatism." *American Historical Review* 99 (April 94).

Brooks, F. Eric, and Glenn L. Starks. *Historically Black Colleges and Universities: An Encyclopedia*. Santa Barbara: Greenwood, 2011.

Brouwer, Steve, Paul Gifford, and Susan D. Rose. *Exporting the American Gospel: Global Christian Fundamentalism*. New York: Routledge, 1996.

Brown, Cynthia Stokes. *Refusing Racism: White Allies and the Struggle for Civil Rights*. New York: Teacher's College Press, 2002.

Brown, Robert McAfee. "The Freedom Riders: A Clergyman's View." *Amherst College Alumni News*. Reprinted by CORE. 1962.

Brundage, W. Fitzhugh. *The Southern Past: A Clash of Race and Memory*. Cambridge, MA: Belknap Press of Harvard University, 2008.

Bryan, G. McLeod. *These Few Also Paid a Price: Southern Whites Who Fought for Civil Rights*. Macon: Mercer University Press, 2001.

Bucher, Glenn Richard, and Patricia Ruth Hill, eds. *Confusion and Hope: Clergy, Laity and the Church in Transition*. Philadelphia: Fortress Press, 1974.

Burke, Carl F. *God Is for Real, Man*. New York: Association Press, 1966.

Burkhart, Roy A. "Action from the Pulpit." *Annals of the American Academy of Political and Social Science* 250 (March 1947).

Butler, Jon. "Jack-in-the-Box-Faith: The Religion Problem in Modern American History." *Journal of American History* (March 2004).

Callahan, Daniel, ed. *The Secular City Debate*. New York: Macmillan, 1966.

Campbell, Ernest Q. and Thomas F. Pettigrew. *Christians in Racial Crisis*. Washington, DC: Public Affairs Press, 1959.

Campbell, Will. *Brother to a Dragon Fly*. New York: Seabury Press, 1977.

———. *Race and Renewal of the Church: Christian Perspectives on Social Problems*. New York: Westminster Press, 1962.

Carawan, Guy, and Candie. *Sing for Freedom: The Story of the Civil Rights Movement through Its Songs*. Montgomery: NewSouth Books, 2008.

———. *Songs of the Southern Freedom Movement: We Shall Overcome!* New York: Oak, 1963.

Carmichael, Stokely, with Ekwueme Michael Thelwell. *Ready for Revolution: The Life and Struggles of Stokely Carmichael (Kwame Ture)*. New York: Scribner, 2003.

Carroll, Jackson, and Wade Clark Roof. *Beyond Establishment: Protestant Identity in a Post-Protestant Age*. Louisville, KY: Westminster John Knox Press, 1993.

Carson, Clayborne. *In Struggle: SNCC and the Black Awakening of the 1960s.* Cambridge, MA: Harvard University Press, 1995.

———. "King Scholarship and Iconoclastic Myths." *Reviews in American History* 16, no. 1 (March 1998).

Carter, Dan T. *The Politics of Rage: George Wallace, the Origins of the New Conservatism, and the Transformation of American Politics.* Baton Rouge: LSU Press, 1995.

Carter, Paul A. *The Decline and Revival of the Social Gospel: Social and Political Liberalism in American Protestant Churches, 1920–1940.* Ithaca: Cornell University Press, 1954.

Cash, W. James. *The Mind of the South.* New York: Knopff, 1941.

Cauthon, Kenneth. *The Impact of American Religious Liberalism.* New York: Harper & Row, 1962.

Cavert, Samuel M. *The American Churches in the Ecumenical Movement.* New York: Association Press, 1968.

Cecelski, David S. and Timothy B. Tyson, eds. *Democracy Betrayed: The Wilmington Race Riot and Its Legacy.* Chapel Hill: University of North Carolina Press, 1998.

Chafe, William Henry. *Civilities and Civil Rights: Greensboro, North Carolina, and the Black Struggle for Freedom.* New York: Oxford University Press, 1980.

Chansky, Art. *Dean's Domain: The Inside Story of Dean Smith and His College Basketball Empire.* Marietta, GA: Longstreet Press, 1999.

Chappell, David L. *Inside Agitators: White Southerners in the Civil Rights Movement.* Baltimore: Johns Hopkins, 1994.

———. *A Stone of Hope: Prophetic Religion and the Death of Jim Crow.* Chapel Hill: University of North Carolina Press, 2004.

Clarkson, Frederick. *Dispatches from the Religious Left.* New York: Ig, 2009.

Cline, David. *Creating Choice: A Community Responds to the Need for Abortion and Birth Control, 1961–1973.* New York: Palgrave Macmillan, 2006.

Cobb, Charles E., Jr. *This Nonviolent Stuff'll Get You Killed: How Guns Made the Civil Rights Movement Possible.* New York: Basic Books, 2014.

Coffin, Henry Sloane. *A Half Century of Union Theological Seminary, 1896–1945: An Informal History.* New York: Union Theological Seminary, 1954.

Cohen, Robert. *When the Old Left Was Young: Student Radicals and America's First Mass Student Movement, 1929–1941.* New York: Oxford University Press, 1993.

Cohen, Robert, and Reginald E. Zelnick, eds. *The Free Speech Movement: Reflections on Berkeley in the 1960s.* Berkeley: University of California Press, 2002.

Collins, Donald E. *When the Church Bell Rang Racist: The Methodist Church and the Civil Rights Movement in Alabama.* Macon, GA: Mercer University Press, 1998.

Cone, James H. *Black Theology and Black Power.* 8th ed. Maryknoll, NY: Orbis Books, 2006.

———. *Risks of Faith: The Emergence of a Black Theology of Liberation, 1968–1998.* Boston: Beacon, 2000.

Cowan, Wayne H. *Witness to a Generation: Significant Writings from Christianity and Crisis (1941–1966).* Indianapolis: Bobbs-Merrill, 1966.

Cox, Harvey. *The Church amid Revolution.* New York: Abingdon Press, 1967.

———. "The 'New Breed' in American Churches: Sources of Social Activism in American Religion." *Daedalus* 96, no. 1 (Winter 1967).

———. *The Secular City: Secularization and Urbanization in Theological Perspective.* New York: Macmillan, 1966.

———. "The Significance of the Church-World Dialogue for Theological Education." *Theological Education,* Winter 1967.

Craig, Robert H. *Religion and Radical Politics: An Alternative Christian Tradition in the United States.* Philadelphia: Temple University Press, 1992.

Crook, Roger, H. *No North or South.* St. Louis: Bethany Press: 1959.

Curry, Constance, Joan C. Browning, Dorothy Dawson Burlage, Penny Patch, Theresa Del Pozzo, Sue Thrasher, Elaine DeLott Baker, Emmie Schrader Adams, and Casey Hayden. *Deep in Our Hearts: Nine White Women in the Freedom Movement.* Athens: University of Georgia Press, 2000.

Dabbs, James McBride. *The Southern Heritage.* New York: Knopf, 1958.

Dailey, Jane. "The Theology of Massive Resistance: Sex, Segregation, and the Sacred after *Brown.*" In *Massive Resistance: Southern Opposition to the Second Reconstruction,* edited by Clive Webb, 151–80. New York: Oxford University Press, 2005.

Daniel, Pete. *Lost Revolutions: The South in the 1950s.* Chapel Hill: University of North Carolina Press, 2000.

Davidson, Chandler, and Bernard Grofman. *Quiet Revolution in the South: The Impact of the Voting Rights Act, 1965–1990.* Princeton, NJ: Princeton University Press, 1994.

Davies, J. G. *Christian Politics and Violent Revolution.* Maryknoll, NY: Orbis, 1976.

Davis, Tom. *Sacred Work: Planned Parenthood and Its Clergy Alliances.* New Brunswick, NJ: Rutgers University Press, 2006.

Dawson, Michael C. *Black Visions: The Roots of Contemporary African-American Political Ideologies.* Chicago: University of Chicago Press, 2001.

D'Emilio, John. *Lost Prophet: The Life and Times of Bayard Rustin.* New York: Free Press, 2003.

Denney, James. *The Christian Doctrine of Reconciliation.* New York: George H. Doran, 1918.

Dittmer, John. *The Good Doctors: The Medical Committee for Human Rights and the Struggle for Social Justice in Health Care.* New York: Bloomsbury Press, 2009.

———. *Local People: The Struggle for Civil Rights in Mississippi.* Urbana: University of Illinois Press, 1994.

Djupe, Paul A., and Christopher P. Gilbert. *The Prophetic Pulpit: Clergy, Churches, and Communities in American Politics.* Lanham, MD: Rowman and Littlefield, 2003.

Dollard, John. *Caste and Class in a Southern Town.* Madison: University of Wisconsin Press, 1949.

Dorien, Gary. *The Making of American Liberal Theology: Idealism, Realism, and Modernity, 1900–1950.* Louisville, KY: Westminster John Knox Press, 2003.

DuBois, W. E. B. *Black Reconstruction.* New York: Russel and Russel, 1935.

———. *The Souls of Black Folk.* New York: Barnes and Noble, 2003. First published 1903 by A. C. McClurg.

Dunbar, Anthony. *Against the Grain: Southern Radicals and Prophets, 1929–1959.* Charlotte: University Press of Virginia, 1981.

Dunbar, Leslie. *The Shame of Southern Politics: Essays and Speeches.* Lexington: University Press of Kentucky, 2002.

Dunson, Josh. *Freedom in the Air: Song Movements of the Sixties.* New York: International, 1965.

Eagles, Charles. *Jon Daniels and the Civil Rights Movement in Alabama.* Huntsville: University of Alabama Press, 2000.

———. "Toward New Histories of the Civil Rights Era." *Journal of Southern History* 66 (November 2000).

Effenbein, Jessica L., Thomas L. Hollowack, and Elizabeth M. Nix, eds. *Baltimore '68: Riots and Rebirth in an American City.* Philadelphia: Temple University Press, 2011.

Egerton, John. *Speak Now Against the Day: The Generation Before the Civil Rights Movement in the South.* Chapel Hill: University of North Carolina Press, 1994.

Ellis, Richard. *The Dark Side of the Left: Illiberal Egalitarianism in America.* Lawrence: University Press of Kansas, 1998.

Ellison, Ralph. *The Invisible Man.* New York: Random House, 1952.

Emerson, Michael O., and Christian Smith. *Evangelical Religion and the Problem of Race in America.* New York: Oxford University Press, 2000.

Eskew, Glenn. *But for Birmingham: The Local and National Movements in the Civil Rights Struggle.* Chapel Hill: University of North Carolina Press, 1997.

Essien-Udom, E. U. *Black Nationalism: A Search for an Identity in America.* Chicago: University of Chicago Press, 1962.

Evans, G. Russell. *Apathy, Apostasy and Apostles: A Study of the History and Activities of the National Council of Churches of Christ in the U.S.A. with Sidelights on Its Ally, the World Council of Churches.* New York: Vantage Press, 1973.

Evans, Sara M. *Journeys That Opened Up the World: Women, Student Christian Movements, and Social Justice, 1955–1975.* New Brunswick, NJ: Rutgers University Press, 2003.

Evans, Sara M., and Harry C. Boyte. *Free Spaces: The Sources of Democratic Change in America.* Chicago: University of Chicago Press, 1986.

Fairclough, Adam. "The Preachers and the People: The Origins and Early Years of the Southern Christian Leadership Conference, 1955–1959." *Journal of Southern History,* August 1986.

———. *Race and Democracy: The Civil Rights Struggle in Louisiana, 1915–1972.* 1995. Reprint, Athens: University of Georgia Press, 1999.

———. *To Redeem the Soul of America: The Southern Christian Leadership Conference and Martin Luther King, Jr.* Athens: University of Georgia Press, 1987.

Farnsley, Arthur E. "Can Churches Save the City? A Look at Resources." *Christian Century,* December 9, 1998.

Findlay, James. *Church People in the Struggle: The National Council of Churches and the Black Freedom Movement, 1950–1970.* New York: Oxford University Press, 1993.

Finger, Bill. "Preaching the Gospel, South of God: An Interview with Carlyle Marney." *Christian Century,* October 4, 1978.

Flurer, James Albert. *Towers in the Light: Rebuilding the Liberal Christian Vision and the Mainline Church.* Lima, OH: Fairway Press, 1994.

Forman, James. *The Making of Black Revolutionaries.* Seattle: University of Washington Press, 1997.

Forrester, Duncan B. *Theology and Politics.* Oxford: Basil Blackwell, 1988.

Fox, Richard Wightman. *Reinhold Niebuhr: A Biography.* New York: Pantheon, 1985.

Franklin, John Hope. *From Slavery to Freedom: A History of American Negroes.* New York: Knopf, 1956.

Frazier, E. Franklin. *Black Bourgeousie.* Glencoe, IL: Free Press, 1957.

Friedland, Michael Brooks. *Lift Up Your Voice Like a Trumpet: White Clergy and the Civil Rights and Antiwar Movements, 1954–1973.* Chapel Hill: University of North Carolina Press, 1998.

———. " 'To Proclaim the Acceptable Year of the Lord': Social Activism and Ecumenical Cooperation among White Clergy in the Civil Rights and Antiwar Movements of the 1950's and 1960's." PhD diss., Boston College, 1993.

Frye, Jerry K. "The 'Black Manifesto' and the Tactic of Objectification." *Journal of Black Studies,* September 1974.

Geyer, Alan. *Piety and Politics: Protestantism in the World Arena.* Richmond: John Knox Press, 1963.

Glock, Charles, Y., Benjamin B. Ringer, and Earl R. Barbie. *To Comfort and to Challenge: A Dilemma of the Contemporary Church.* Berkeley: University of California Press, 1967.

Goldfield, David R. *Black, White, and Southern: Race Relations and Southern Culture, 1940 to the Present.* Baton Rouge: Louisiana University Press, 1990.

Goldstein, Warren. "A Liberal Dose of Religious Fervor." *Chronicle of Higher Education,* July 8, 2005.

Gosse, Van. "A Movement of Movements: The Definition and Periodization of the New Left." In *A Companion to Post-1945 America,* edited by Jean-Christophe Agnew and Roy Rosenzweig, 277–302. Malden, MA: Blackwell, 2002.

———. *Rethinking the New Left: An Interpretive History.* New York: Palgrave Macmillan, 2005.

Gosse, Van, and Richard R. Moser. *The World the Sixties Made: Politics and Culture in Recent America.* Philadelphia: Temple University Press, 2003.

Goudsouzian, Aram. *Down to the Crossroads: Civil Rights, Black Power, and the Meredith March Against Fear.* New York: MacMillan, 2014.

Green, Clifford J. "History in the Service of the Future: Studying Urban Ministry." In *Churches, Cities, and Human Community: Urban Ministry in the United States, 1945–1985,* edited by Clifford J. Green, 1–22. Grand Rapids, MI: William B. Eerdmans, 1996.

Greenberg, Jack. *Race Relations and American Law*. New York: Columbia University Press, 1959.

Griffin, John Howard. *Black Like Me*. New York: Houghton Mifflin, 1961.

Guth, James L., John C. Green, Corwin E. Smidt, Lyman A. Kellstedt, and Margaret M. Poloma. *The Bully Pulpit: The Politics of Protestant Clergy*. Lawrence: University Press of Kansas, 1998.

Hadden, Jeffrey. *The Gathering Storm in the Churches*. Garden City: Doubleday, 1969.

Haines, Herbert. *Black Radicals and the Civil Rights Mainstream: 1954–1970*. Knoxville: University of Tennessee Press, 1988.

Hall, Jacquelyn Dowd. "The Long Civil Rights Movement and the Political Uses of the Past." *Journal of American History* 91, no. 4 (March 2005).

———. *Revolt against Chivalry: Jessie Daniel Ames and the Women's Campaign against Lynching*. New York: Columbia University Press, 1993. First published 1979.

Hampton, Henry, and Steve Fayer. *Voices of Freedom: An Oral History of the Civil Rights Movement from the 1950s through the 1980s*. New York: Bantam Books, 1990.

Handlin, Oscar. *Race and Nationality in American Life*. Boston: Little, Brown, 1957.

Handy, Robert T. *A Christian America: Protestant Hopes and Historical Realities*. New York: Oxford University Press, 1984.

———. *A History of Union Theological Seminary in New York*. New York: Columbia University Press, 1987.

Harper, Charles. "Responsible Urban Strategy: A Case Study." *Renewal*, February 1966.

Harvey, Paul. *Freedom's Coming: Religious Culture and the Shaping of the South from the Civil War through the Civil Rights Era*. Chapel Hill: University of North Carolina Press, 2005.

Haselden, Kyle. *The Racial Problem in Christian Perspective*. New York: Harper and Bros., 1959.

Hawkins, Merrill M., Jr. *Will Campbell: Radical Prophet of the South*. Macon: Mercer University Press, 1997.

Hein, David. *Noble Powell and the Episcopal Establishment in the Twentieth Century*. Eugene, OR: Wipf and Stock, 2001.

Hentoff, Nat. *The New Equality*. New York: Viking, 1964.

Herberg, Will. *Protestant, Catholic, Jew: An Essay in American Sociology*. New York: Doubleday, 1955.

Highland, Stanley, ed. *Community Building in the Twenty-First Century*. Santa Fe: School of American Research Press, 2005.

Hill, Lance. *The Deacons for Defense: Armed Resistance and the Civil Rights Movement*. Chapel Hill: University of North Carolina Press, 2004.

Hobson, Fred. *But Now I See: The White Southern Racial Conversion Narrative*. Baton Rouge: Louisiana State University Press, 1999.

Hogan, Wesley C. *Many Minds, One Heart: SNCC's Dream for a New America*. Chapel Hill: University of North Carolina Press, 2007.

Holsaert, Faith S., Martha Prescod Norman Noonan, Judy Richardson, Betty Garman Robinson, Jean Smith Young, and Dorothy M. Zellner. *Hands on the Freedom Plow: Personal Accounts by Women in SNCC.* Urbana: University of Illinois Press, 2010.

Honey, Michael K. *Southern Labor and Black Civil Rights: Organizing Memphis Workers.* Chicago: University of Illinois Press, 1993.

Houck, Davis W., and David E. Dixon, eds. *Rhetoric, Religion and the Civil Rights Movement, 1954–1965.* Waco, TX: Baylor University Press, 2006.

Howe, Reuel L. *Partners in Preaching: Clergy and Laity in Dialogue.* New York: Seabury Press, 1967.

Howell, Joseph T. *Civil Rights Journey: The Story of a White Southerner Coming of Age during the Civil Rights Revolution.* Bloomington, IN: Author House, 2011.

———. *Hard Living on Clay Street: Portraits of Blue Collar Families.* Long Grove, IL: Waveland Press, 1972.

Hulsether, Mark. *Building a Protestant Left: Christianity and Crisis Magazine, 1941–1993.* Knoxville: University of Tennessee Press, 1999.

Hunter, James Davison. *Culture Wars: The Struggle to Define America.* New York: Basic Books, 1991.

Hutchison, William R., ed. *Between the Times: The Travail of the Protestant Establishment in America, 1900–1960.* New York: Cambridge University Press, 1990.

Interseminary Movement. *A Brief History of the Interseminary Movement* (pamphlet). N.p., 1967.

Jones, William R. *Is God a White Racist? A Preamble to Black Theology.* Garden City, New York: Anchor Books, 1973.

Joseph, Peniel E., ed. *The Black Power Movement: Rethinking the Civil Rights–Black Power Era.* New York: Routledge, 2006.

Kemper, Robert V., and Julie Atkins. "The World as It Should Be: Faith-Based Community Development in America." In *Community Building in the Twenty-First Century,* edited by Stanley Hyland, 71–100. Santa Fe: School of American Research Press, 2005.

Kenrick, Bruce. *Come Out of the Wilderness: The Story of the East Harlem Protestant Parish.* New York: Harper & Brothers, 1962.

Kerr, Hugh T. "Reactions to a Manifesto." *Theology Today,* April 1967.

King, Martin Luther, Jr. "Letter from a Birmingham Jail." April 16, 1963. Martin Luther King, Jr. Research and Education Institute, Stanford University, https://kinginstitute.stanford.edu/king-papers/documents/letter-birmingham-jail.

———. *Stride Toward Freedom: The Montgomery Story.* New York: Harper, 1958.

K'Meyer, Tracy Elaine. *Interracialism and Christian Community in the Postwar South: The Story of Koinonia Farm.* Charlottesville: University Press of Virginia, 1997.

Korstad, Robert L. *Civil Rights Unionism: Tobacco Workers and the Struggle for Democracy in the Mid-Twentieth Century South.* Chapel Hill: University of North Carolina Press, 2003.

Korstad, Robert L., and Nelson Lichtenstein. "Opportunities Found and Lost: Labor, Radicals, and the Early Civil Rights Movement." *Journal of American History* 75, no. 3 (1988).

Kuklick, Bruce, and D. G. Hart, eds. *Religious Advocacy and American History*. Grand Rapids, MI: William B. Eerdmans, 1997.

Laarman, Rev. Peter, ed. *Getting on Message: Challenging the Christian Right from the Heart of the Gospel*. Boston: Beacon Press, 2006.

La Farge, John. *The Catholic Viewpoint on Race Relations*. Garden City, NY: Hanover House, 1956.

Langer, Susanne. *Philosophical Sketches*. New York: Mentor Books, 1964.

Langford, Michael. *A Liberal Theology for the Twenty-First Century*. Burlington: Ashgate, 2001.

Langston, David, and William McKeown. *The Student Movement at Union Theological Seminary, 1963–1969*. New York: National Council of Churches, Department of Ministry, 1971.

Latta, Maurice C. "The Background for the Social Gospel in American Protestantism." *Church History* 5, no. 3 (September 1936).

Lawson, Stephen F. "Freedom Then, Freedom Now: The Historiography of the Civil Rights Movement." *American Historical Review* 96 (April 1991).

Lecky, R. S., and H. E. Wright, eds. *Black Manifesto: Religion, Racism, and Reparations*. New York: Sheed & Ward, 1969.

Lee, Chana Kai. *For Freedom's Sake: The Life of Fannie Lou Hamer*. Chicago: University of Illinois Press, 1999.

Lee, Michael, and Louis J. Putz, eds. *Seminary Education in a Time of Change*. Notre Dame, IN: Fides, 1965.

Lee, Robert. *Cities and Churches*. Philadelphia: Westminster Press, 1962.

Lee, Robert, and Martin E. Marty. *Religion and Social Conflict*. New York: Oxford University Press, 1964.

Lehtonen, Risto. *Story of a Storm: The Ecumenical Student Movement in the Turmoil of Revolution, 1968 to 1973*. Grand Rapids, MI: Eerdmans, 1998.

Leighton, Jared E. "Freedom Invisible: Gays and Lesbians in the African American Civil Rights Movement." PhD diss., Department of History, University of Nebraska-Lincoln, 2013.

Leith, John H. *Crisis in the Church: The Plight of Theological Education*. Louisville, KY: Westminster John Knox Press, 1997.

Lerner, Michael. *The Left Hand of God: Taking Back Our Country from the Religious Right*. San Francisco: Harper San Francisco, 2006.

Lewis, John. *Walking with the Wind: A Memoir of the Movement*. New York: Harcourt Brace, 1998.

Lichterman, Paul. *The Search for Political Community: American Activists Reinventing Commitment*. New York: Cambridge University Press, 1996.

Lincoln, Charles Eric. *The Black Muslims in America*. Boston: Beacon Press, 1961.

———. *Race, Religion, and the Continuing American Dilemma.* New York: Hill and Wang, 1984.

Ling, Peter J., and Sharon Monteith, eds. *Gender in the Civil Rights Movement.* New York: Routledge, 1999.

Link, William A. *The Paradox of Southern Progressivism, 1880–1930.* Chapel Hill: University of North Carolina Press, 1992.

Linn, Jan G. *Big Christianity: What's Right with the Religious Left.* Louisville, KY: Westminster John Knox Press, 2006.

Livezey, Lowell W. "Church as Parish: Union Theological Seminary's East Harlem Protestant Parish." *Christian Century,* December 9, 1998.

Loevery, Robert D., ed. *The Civil Rights Act of 1964: The Passage of the Law That Ended Racial Segregation.* Albany: State University of New York Press, 1997.

Lomax, Louis E. *The Negro Revolt.* New York: Harper, 1962.

Luker, Ralph E. *The Social Gospel in Black and White: American Racial Reform, 1885–1912.* 2nd ed. Chapel Hill: University of North Carolina Press, 1998.

Lynn, Susan. *Progressive Women in Conservative Times: Racial Justice, Peace, and Feminism, 1945 to the 1960s.* New Brunswick, NJ: Rutgers University Press, 1992.

Maffly-Kipp, Laurie, Leigh E. Schmidt, and Mark Valeri, eds. *Practicing Protestants: Histories of Christian Life in America, 1630–1965.* Baltimore: Johns Hopkins University Press, 2006.

Manis, Andrew Michael. *Southern Civil Religions in Conflict: Black and White Baptists and Civil Rights, 1947–1957.* Athens: University of Georgia Press, 1987.

———. *Southern Civil Religions in Conflict: Civil Rights and the Culture Wars.* Macon: Mercer University Press, 2002.

Mantler, Gordon K. "Black, Brown, and Poor: Martin Luther King Jr., the Poor People's Campaign and Its Legacies." PhD diss., Duke University, 2008.

———. *Power to the Poor: Black-Brown Coalition and the Fight for Economic Justice, 1960–1974.* Chapel Hill: University of North Carolina Press, 2013.

Marable, Manning. *Race, Reform and Rebellion: The Second Reconstruction in Black America, 1945–1982.* Jackson: University Press of Mississippi, 1984.

Marsh, Charles. *The Beloved Community: How Faith Shapes Social Justice, from the Civil Rights Movement to Today.* New York: Basic Books, 2005.

———. *God's Long Summer: Stories of Faith and Civil Rights.* Princeton, NJ: Princeton University Press, 1999.

Martin, Robert F. *Howard Kester and the Struggle for Social Justice in the South, 1904–1977.* Charlottesville: University Press of Virginia, 1991.

Martin, William C. *Christians in Conflict.* Chicago: Center for the Scientific Study of Religion, 1972.

Marty, Martin E. *A Nation of Believers.* Chicago: University of Chicago Press, 1976.

———. *No Ground Beneath Us: A Revolutionary Reader.* New York: National Methodist Student Movement, 1964.

———. "Response to Professor Cox—II." *Theological Education,* Winter 1967.

Maston, T. B. *Segregation and Desegregation*. New York: Macmillan, 1959.

Mays, Benjamin E. *Seeking to Be Christian in Race Relations*. New York: Friendship Press, 1957.

McAdam, Doug. *Political Process and the Development of Black Insurgency, 1930–1970*. Chicago: University of Chicago Press, 1982.

McCarraher, Eugene. *Christian Critics: Religion and the Impasse in Modern American Social Thought*. Ithaca, NY: Cornell University Press, 2000.

McClain, George D. *Claiming All Things for God: Prayer, Discernment, and Ritual for Social Change*. Nashville: Abingdon Press, 1998.

McKanan, Dan. *Prophetic Encounters: Religion and the American Radical Tradition*. Boston: Beacon Press, 2011.

McLaughlin, Connie. *Spiritual Politics: Changing the World from the Inside Out*. New York: Ballantine Books, 1994.

McWhorter, Diane. *Carry Me Home: Birmingham, Alabama; The Climactic Battle of the Civil Rights Revolution*. New York: Simon & Schuster, 2001.

Meier, August, and Elliott Rudwick. *CORE: A Study in the Civil Rights Movement, 1942–1968*. New York: Oxford University Press, 1973.

Merton, Thomas. *Faith and Violence*. South Bend, IN: University of Notre Dame Press, 1968.

Meyer, Donald B. *The Protestant Search for Political Realism, 1919–1941*. Berkeley: University of California Press, 1960.

Michaelson, Robert S., and Roof, Wade Clark, eds. *Liberal Protestantism: Realities and Possibilities*. New York: Pilgrim Press, 1986.

Michel, Gregg L. *Struggle for a Better South: The Southern Student Organizing Committee, 1964–1969*. New York: Palgrave Macmillan, 2004.

Miller, Glenn T. *Piety and Profession: American Protestant Theological Education, 1870–1970*. Grand Rapids, MI: Eerdmans, 2007.

Miller, James. *Democracy Is in the Streets: From Port Huron to the Siege of Chicago*. Cambridge, MA: Harvard University Press, 1987.

Miller, Keith D. *Voice of Deliverance: The Language of Dr. Martin Luther King and Its Sources*. Athens: University of Georgia Press, 1998.

Miller, Mike. "The 60s Student Movement and Saul Alinsky: An Alliance That Never Happened." *Social Policy*, Winter 2003/Spring 2004.

Miller, Robert M. *American Protestantism and Social Issues, 1919–1939*. Chapel Hill: University of North Carolina Press, 1958.

Moll, Kirk A. "Theological Education in Action: Adult Learning about Race in the Student Interracial Ministry of Union Theological Seminary, 1960–68." D.Ed diss., Pennsylvania State University, 2011.

Mollin, Marian. *Radical Pacifism in Modern America: Egalitarianism and Protest*. Philadelphia: University of Pennsylvania Press, 2006.

Monro, John U. "Black Studies, White Teachers, and Black Colleges." *Teaching Forum* 3, no. 3 (April 1970).

Moody, Anne. *Coming of Age in Mississippi*. New York: Dell, 1968.

Moore, E. Maynard. "Theological Education for a Revolutionary Church." *Theological Education*, Winter 1968.

Morris, Aldon. *The Origins of the Civil Rights Movement: Black Communities Organizing for Change*. New York: Free Press, 1984.

Morton, Nelle. *The Journey Is Home*. Boston: Beacon Press, 1985.

Myrdal, Gunar. *An American Dilemma*. New York: Harper, 1944.

Newman, Mark. *Divine Agitators: The Delta Ministry and the Civil Rights in Mississippi*. Athens: University of Georgia, 2004.

———. "Getting Right with God: Southern Baptists and Race Relations." PhD diss., University of Mississippi, 1993.

Niebuhr, H. Richard, and Niebuhr, Reinhold. *War as Crucifixion: Essays on Peace, Violence, and "Just War" from the "Christian Century."* Chicago: Christian Century Press, 2002.

Norrell, Robert. *Reaping the Whirlwind: Civil Rights in Tuskeegee*. Chapel Hill: University of North Carolina Press, 1998.

Oates, Stephen B. *Let the Trumpet Sound: A Life of Martin Luther King, Jr.* New York: HarperCollins, 1994.

Ogbar, Jeffrey O. G. *Black Power: Radical Politics and African American Identity*. Baltimore: Johns Hopkins University Press, 2004.

Okholm, Dennis, ed. *The Gospel in Black and White: Theological Resources for Racial Reconciliation*. Downers Grove, IL: InterVarsity Press, 1997.

Payne, Charles M. *I've Got the Light of Freedom: The Organizing Tradition and the Mississippi Freedom Struggle*. 2nd ed. Berkeley: University of California Press, 2007.

Payne, Charles M., and Adam Green, eds. *Time Longer Than Rope: A Century of African American Activism, 1850–1950*. New York: New York University Press, 2003.

Petersen, Rodney L. "Training Prophets." *Religion in the Secular City: Essays in Honor of Harvey Cox*. San Antonio, TX: Trinity University Press, 2001.

Pieza, Stanley. "Rev. King Urges Boycott by Churches to Fight Bias." *Chicago's American*, January 16, 1963.

Polletta, Francesca. *Freedom Is an Endless Meeting: Democracy in American Social Movements*. Chicago: University of Chicago Press, 2002.

Pope, Liston. *Kingdom beyond Caste*. New York: Friendship Press, 1957.

Powell, Inge. *CORE and the Strategy of Non-violence*. New York: Random House, 1968.

Proudfoot, Merrill. *Diary of a Sit-In*. Urbana: University of Illinois Press, 1990.

Pryor, Mark. *Faith, Grace, and Heresy: The Biography of Rev. Charles M. Jones*. San Jose: Writer's Showcase, 2002.

Quinley, Harold E. *The Prophetic Clergy: Social Activism among Protestant Ministers*. New York: John Wiley & Sons, 1974.

Ramsey, Paul. *Christian Ethics and the Sit-in*. New York: Association Press, 1961.

Ransby, Barbara. *Ella Baker and the Black Freedom Movement: A Radical Vision*. Chapel Hill: University of North Carolina Press, 2003.

Reagon, Bernice Johnson. "In Our Hands: Thoughts on Black Music." *Sing Out!* 24 (January–February 1976).

Reed, Linda. *Simple Decency and Common Sense: The Southern Conference Movement, 1938–1963*. Bloomington: Indiana University Press, 1991.

Reeves, Marjorie, ed. *Christian Thinking and Social Order: Conviction Politics from the 1930s to the Present Day*. London: Cassell, 1999.

Reeves, Thomas. *The Empty Church: The Suicide of Liberal Christianity*. New York: Free Press, 1996.

Rich, Marvin. "The Congress of Racial Equality and Its Strategy." *Annals of the American Academy of Political and Social Science*, January 1965.

Richardson, Lincoln. "3,000 Students at Cleveland: The Process Is the Purpose?" *Presbyterian Life*, February 1968.

Rieder, Jonathan. "The Day President Kennedy Embraced Civil Rights—and the Story Behind It." *Atlantic*, June 2013.

Riga, Peter J. *The Church and Revolution: Some Reflections on the Relationship of the Church to the Modern World*. Milwaukee: Bruce, 1967.

Robinson, John A. T. *Honest to God*. New York: Westminster Press, 1963.

Roof, Wade Clark, and William McKinney. *American Mainline Religion: Its Changing Shape and Future*. New Brunswick, NJ: Rutgers University Press, 1987.

Rooks, Charles Shelby. "Crisis in Theological Education." *Theological Education* 7, no. 1 (Autumn 1970).

Rose, Arnold. *The Negro in Postwar America*. New York: Anti-Defamation League of B'nai Brith, 1950.

Rose, Stephen C. *The Day the Country Mouse Expired*. New York: National Student Christian Federation, 1964.

———. *The Grass Roots Church: A Manifesto for Protestant Renewal*. New York: Abingdon Press, 1966.

———. "Putting It to the Churches: Reparations for Blacks?" *New Republic*, June 21, 1969.

———. "Religious Conference." *Christianity and Crisis*, March 1963.

———. *Sermons Not Preached in the White House*. New York: Cambria Press Books, 1970.

———. "Student Interracial Ministry: A Break in the Wall." *Christian Century*, March 14, 1962.

———. *Who's Killing the Church?* Chicago: Chicago City Missionary Society, 1966.

Ross, Benjamin. "Congregation-Based Organizing." *Tikkun*, January/February 2007.

Rossinow, Doug. *The Politics of Authenticity: Liberalism, Christianity, and the New Left in America*. New York: Columbia University Press, 1998.

Rouner, Leroy S., ed. *Civil Religion and Political Theology*. Notre Dame: University of Notre Dame Press, 1986.

Rowthorn, Jeffrey. "The CORE Experiment: Independent Synthesis for BDs." *Tower*, Fall 1968.

Rustin, Bayard. "'Black Power' and Coalition Politics." *Commentary*, September 1966.

Salmand, John A. *Southern Struggles: The Southern Labor Movement and the Civil Rights Struggle*. Gainesville: University Press of Florida.

Schlesinger, Arthur M., Jr. "Reinhold Niebuhr's Role in American Politics, Thought and Life." *The Politics of Hope*. Boston: Houghton Mifflin, 1963.

Schner, George. *Education for Ministry: Reform and Renewal in Theological Education*. Kansas City: Shee & Ward, 1993.

Schulman, Bruce J. *The Seventies: The Great Shift in American Culture, Society, and Politics*. New York: Da Capo Press, 2001.

"'Segregation Forever': A Fiery Pledge Forgiven, but Not Forgotten." Radio Diaries. *All Things Considered*. NPR, January 10, 2013, http://www.npr.org/2013/01/14 /169080969/segregation-forever-a-fiery-pledge-forgiven-but-not-forgotten.

Sellers, James. *The South and Christian Ethics*. New York: Association Press, 1962.

Seymour, Robert. "Interracial Ministry in North Carolina: What It Was Like for a Southern White Church to Have a Negro Assistant on Its Staff One Summer." *Christian Century*, January 23, 1963.

———. *Whites Only: A Pastor's Retrospective on Signs of the New South*. Valley Forge, NY: Judson Press, 1991.

Shannon, William V. "The Voice of the Churches." *Commonweal*, May 15, 1964.

Shaull, Richard. "Response to President Bennett—I." *Theological Education*, Winter 1967.

Silberman, Charles. *Crisis in Black and White*. New York: Random House, 1964.

Silk, Mark. *Spiritual Politics: Religion and America since World War II*. New York: Simon and Schuster, 1988.

Slater, Robert Bruce. "White Professors at Black Colleges." *Journal of Blacks in Higher Education* 1 (Autumn 1993).

Smith, Frances S. "Women and Renewal: A Survey." *Renewal*, October 1964.

Smith, Gary Scott, ed. *God and Politics: Four Views on the Reformation of Civil Government*. Phillipsburg, NJ: Presbyterian and Reformed, 1989.

Smith, Lillian. *Killers of a Dream*. New York: Anchor, 1961.

———. *Strange Fruit*. New York: Reynal & Hitchcock, 1944.

Spike, Robert W. *The Freedom Revolution and the Churches*. New York: National Board of Young Men's Christian Associations, 1965.

Stembridge, Jane. *I Play Flute and Other Poems*. New York: Seabury Press, 1968.

Stovall, TaRessa. "Charles Sherrod: Passing on the Blood and Pulse of the Civil Rights Movement." *Aspire*, Summer/Fall 2007.

Stricklin, David. *A Genealogy of Dissent: Southern Baptist Protest in the Twentieth Century*. Lexington: University Press of Kentucky, 1999.

Strom, Jonathan. *A Half-Century of Strengthening Christian Ministry: The Fund for Theological Education*. Atlanta: Fund for Theological Education, 2002.

Sugrue, Thomas J. *Sweet Land of Liberty: The Forgotten Struggle for Civil Rights in the North*. New York: Random House, 2008.

Sullivan, Patricia. *Days of Hope: Race and Democracy in the New Deal Era*. Chapel Hill: University of North Carolina Press, 1996.

Tabb, William K., ed. *Churches in Struggle: Liberation Theologies and Social Change in North America*. New York: Monthly Review Press, 1986.

Taylor, Charles L. "Sources of Renewal." *Theological Education*, Winter 1967.

Theoharris, Jeanne, and Komozi Woodward, eds. *Freedom North: Black Freedom Struggles Outside the South, 1940–1980*. New York: Palgrave Macmillan, 2003.

Tilson, Everett. *Segregation and the Bible*. New York: Abingdon Press, 1958.

Tipton, Steven M. *Public Pulpits: Methodists and Mainline Churches in the Moral Argument in Public Life*. Chicago: University of Chicago Press, 2007.

Tlapa, Richard J. *The New Apostles: The Mission to the Inner City*. Chicago: Franciscan Herald Press, 1977.

Tomasi, John. *Liberalism beyond Justice: Citizens, Society, and the Boundaries of Political Theory*. Princeton, NJ: Princeton University Press, 2001.

Tracy, James. *Direct Action: Radical Pacifism from the Union Eight to the Chicago Seven*. Chicago: University of Chicago Press, 1996.

Trexler, Edgar R. "He's Safe on These Streets." *Lutheran*, September 28, 1966.

Tuck, Stephen G. N. *Beyond Atlanta: The Struggle for Racial Equality in Georgia, 1940–1980*. Athens: University of Georgia Press, 2001.

Turner, James. *Without God, without Creed: The Origins of Unbelief in America*. Baltimore: Johns Hopkins University Press, 1985.

Tyson, Timothy. *Blood Done Sign My Name*. New York: Crown, 2004.

———. *Radio Free Dixie: Robert F. Williams and the Roots of Black Power*. Chapel Hill: University of North Carolina Press, 1999.

———. "Robert F. Williams, 'Black Power,' and the Roots of the African American Freedom Struggle." *Journal of American History* 85, no. 2 (September 1998).

Van Deburg, William. *New Day in Babylon: The Black Power Movement and American Culture, 1965–1975*. Chicago: University of Chicago Press, 1992.

Wallenstein, Peter. *Higher Education and the Civil Rights Movement: White Supremacy, Black Southerners, and College Campuses*. Gainesville: University Press of Florida, 2009.

Wallerstein, Immanuel. *After Liberalism*. New York: New Press, 1995.

Wallis, Jim. *God's Politics: Why the Right Gets It Wrong and the Left Doesn't Get It*. San Francisco: Harper San Francisco, 2005.

Walzer, Michael. *Interpretation and Social Criticism*. Cambridge, MA: Harvard University Press, 1987.

———. *Politics and Passion: Toward a More Egalitarian Liberalism*. New Haven, CT: Yale University Press, 2004.

Watson, Bruce. *Freedom Summer: The Savage Summer of 1964 That Made Mississippi Burn and Made America a Democracy*. New York: Penguin Books, 2010.

Watters, Pat. *Down to Now: Reflections on the Southern Civil Rights Movement*. New York: Pantheon Books, 1971.

Weaver, Mary Jo, David Brakke, and Jason Bivins, eds. 3rd ed. *Introduction to Christianity*. Belmont, CA: Wadsworth, 1998.

Weisbrot, Robert. *Freedom Bound: A History of America's Civil Rights Movement*. New York: Norton, 1990.

White, Ronald C., Jr. *Liberty and Justice for All: Racial Reform and the Social Gospel, 1877–1925*. Louisville: Westminster John Knox Press, 1990.

Williams, Lawrence H. "Christianity and Reparations: Revisiting James Forman's 'Black Manifesto,' 1969." *Currents in Theology and Mission* 32, no. 1 (February 2005).

Williams, Rhys H. "Political Theology on the Right and Left." *Christian Century*, July 29, 1998.

Winter, Gibson. *The Suburban Captivity of the Churches: An Analysis of Protestant Responsibility in the Expanding Metropolis*. New York: Macmillan, 1962.

Woodward, C. Vann. *The Strange Career of Jim Crow*. New York: Oxford University Press, 1966.

Wright, Richard. *White Man, Listen!* New York: Doubleday, 1957.

Ziegenhals, Walter E. *Urban Churches in Transition*. New York: Pilgrim Press, 1978.

Ziegler, Jesse H. *ATS [the Association of Theological Schools] through Two Decades: Reflections on Theological Education, 1960–1980*. Vandalia, OH: self-published, 1984.

Zinn, Howard. "SNCC and the Albany Movement." *Journal of Southwest Georgia History* 2 (Fall 1984).

———. *SNCC: The New Abolitionists*. Cambridge, MA: South End Press, 1964.

———. *You Can't Be Neutral on a Moving Train*. Boston: Beacon Press, 1994.

Unpublished Sources

Birchard, Roy. Diary of Roy Birchard, 1967–1968. Special Collections, Langston Hughes Memorial Library, Lincoln University.

Collins, John. Diary of John Collins, in the possession of John Collins.

Howell, Joe. "Civil Rights Diary," in the possession of Joe Howell.

Seymour, Robert. Sermons, in the possession of Robert Seymour.

Stockwell, Clinton E. "A Sketch of the Church's Urban Ministry, 1620–1990, with Particular Reference to Chicago." 1991. In the possession of Clinton Stockwell and shared with author.

Stumme, John. Diary of John Stumme, in the possession of John Stumme.

Index